The Private Franklin
The Man and His Family

Franklin's birthplace on Milk Street in Boston. On a visit to Boston in 1820, William Wood Thackara made this drawing from an almost obliterated pencil sketch done shortly before the house burned down in 1810. Mrs. Robert D. Crompton.

THE PRIVATE FRANKLIN

FRANKLIN

The Man and His Family

BY

CLAUDE-ANNE LOPEZ

AND EUGENIA W. HERBERT

W • W • Norton & Company • Inc •
New York

To Etienne

⚜

To Tim, Rosie, and Cathy

Contents

List of Illustrations

Frontispiece: William Wood Thackara, Franklin's birthplace on Milk Street, Boston, 1820

Illustrations following page 128

Benjamin Wilson, *Mrs. Deborah Franklin*, ca. 1759
Mather Brown, *William Franklin*, ca. 1790
John Hoppner, *Sarah Bache*, 1791
Artist unknown, *Mary Stevenson Hewson*
John Trumbull, *William Temple Franklin*, 1790
Franklin's magic square of squares
Franklin's glass armonica
François Nicolas Martinet, *Benjamin Franklin*, 1773
Letter from Benjamin Franklin to Polly Stevenson in phonetic alphabet, dated July 20, 1768
Letter from Margaret Stevenson to Benjamin Franklin, ca. 1763
Deborah Franklin's last letter to her husband, dated October 29, 1773

Illustrations following page 224

Advertisement for Jane Mecom's millinery business, May 30, 1768
Benjamin Franklin, sketch of dinner with the king of Denmark in 1768
Benjamin Franklin Bache, doodle portrait of Franklin, 1790
Franklin's marginalia to *Good Humor*, 1769
Charles Willson Peale, presumed sketch of Franklin and a lady friend, 1767
Artist unknown, *The March of the Paxton Men*, 1764
Ch. de Lorimier, balloon ascension, September 21, 1783
Artist unknown, *Le Magnétisme dévoilé*, 1784–85

An Objective Preface

"HISTORY is not the province of the ladies," declared John Adams, stung by some unflattering but astute comments of Mercy Otis Warren, historian of the American Revolution. As long as history was the record of great men and events, battles and political upheavals, his view had some merit, for how could women understand a world they had no part of?

The concept of history has changed, however. Historians are casting their nets more widely, studying groups and individuals earlier ignored, and asking different questions even of the heroic figures. The family has at last become a legitimate historical topic, part of this "new history." Nevertheless it is a subject that often stymies the researcher who attempts to go beyond mere demographic data because the details of home life are so thoroughly taken for granted by the parties concerned that they are rarely reported. The case of Benjamin Franklin is exceptional: There is a rare richness of material, especially letters, that invites one to essay a reconstruction of his family relationships.

He was a nest builder par excellence, at home and abroad. He needed a family every bit as much as he needed "ingenious acquaintance." A great deal has been made of his alleged sexual promiscuity; far more evidence exists for a kind of emotional promiscuity in creating familial surroundings wherever he happened to be. After twenty-seven years of unprotesting domesticity with his Deborah in Philadelphia, he stepped into a tailor-made second ménage in London consisting of Mrs. Margaret Stevenson and her daughter Polly. Later in Paris he grafted himself onto the household of his landlord Leray de Chaumont and had legions of ladies of all ages vying for the honor of calling him *papa*.

Franklin's own family, numbering only two living children, was more like the nuclear unit of the present day than the teeming hearths of his contemporaries, but he compensated by taking on quite willingly the responsibilities of a virtual "extended family"—brothers, sisters, nephews, nieces, cousins—as the obligation of wealth and prominence. Theoreticians may argue about the character of the Puritan and post-

Puritan family; Franklin simply assumed his role of lineage head as part of the nature of things.

Michael Kammen has observed that "Franklin, unlike Jefferson, did not compartmentalize his life. The public personality and the private man were of a piece." A study of his family relationships therefore serves a purpose beyond mere gossip or simply "humanizing" a founding father. Such relationships are perhaps the most subtle that exist and the most difficult for an observer to fathom, especially at a distance of two centuries. We have preferred not to follow the bolder of the current psychohistorians, for we believe that psychoanalysis of living persons is difficult enough, that of those long-dead a futile exercise. The evidence is insufficient even for a man as well documented as Franklin. Furthermore, anyone who reads deeply in eighteenth-century sources must be acutely aware that words have altered their meanings, that the formulae and phrases which were then the warp and woof of communication no longer have the same connotations.

This book has been written primarily from original sources, published and unpublished, and in particular from the surviving letters that passed between Franklin and his family and friends—only a fraction, alas, of the total written—and including a good many not likely to be printed anywhere else (for even the monumental edition of the Franklin Papers at Yale has to be limited to letters *by* or *to* Franklin in person). It is not intended as a general biography of Franklin: We have filled in the background of his life only to the extent that it seemed necessary to our theme, and we have tried to see his many activities first and foremost from the vantage point of his family. At the same time we have endeavored to keep the cast of characters down, excluding many worthy relatives, friends, and enemies, out of consideration for the nonspecialist reader, preferring to offer a sample rather than a multitude.

A word about quotations: Not all letters exist in the original manuscript, some survive only in edited versions. Hence there is considerable variation in capitalization, spelling, and punctuation. We have followed the best text available, making only such changes as are necessary for easy comprehension. In the cases of Franklin's wife and sister we have given samples of their spelling but modernized all the longer passages.

E.H.

A Subjective Preface

E.H. aims at objectivity. She is a historian by training, holds a Yale Ph.D., and is knowledgeable about trends in historiography. I, C.L., trained in literature, see myself basically as a biographer. My fascination is with people. With this man in particular, this Benjamin Franklin, who still perplexes me after more than fifteen years of deciphering and transcribing his correspondence. When I am tempted to conclude that those who call him cool and detached are in the right, I stumble upon a paragraph of his, fairly shaking with fury. When I feel that "mellow" is the right word for him, at least in his later years, I fall upon some incredibly harsh remark to his daughter, or I am reminded of his inexorable break with his son. About to decide that he was hard, after all, I remember his infinite patience and tenderness toward his sister Jane. Neither demigod nor unfeeling egotist, this is the Franklin I have been groping to understand and that we have tried to present: some warts, some laurels, some sins, some virtues.

Every morning on my way to work at Yale's Sterling Library, I walk by his bust standing guard near the entrance. I look at that very English face, eyes serene, skin flabby, thin and determined mouth, ironic smile. And I wonder what it was like to be his wife, ardently desired in the lust of the early years, warmly appreciated during their two decades in business, coolly left to age and die alone when history swept him on. What about Sally, the daughter, so protected and so shackled, yet unaware of being shackled because it was the common lot of girls?

And William, the once-cherished son? When our own boys proclaim that it is difficult to be a professor's child—doctors surely hear the same complaint, and lawyers, and clergymen, and farmers, and the recent immigrants and the old settlers—I think of William and *his* problems. To be the son of such a genius. Such a charismatic man. And to be illegitimate besides, the perfect target for anyone's hostility, the perfect foil for invidious comparison. This in a society where the only feelings a son was allowed to express were devotion and respect.

Did it make life easier for any of them, the grandchildren and the nephews, to be related to this great and famous man? Were they made to pay the price for his glory? Were they overwhelmed by their unearned spot in the limelight, as relatives of illustrious people are apt to be?

So many questions to which a patient reading of the letters, hours of brooding over the ways of families, and many years of living may provide some answers.

C.L.

Acknowledgments

WE ARE OFTEN asked how a joint authorship works. It works the way a marriage does, quite differently from the original plan. We had decided at first that C.L. would draw from the primary sources while E.H. would do the outside reading and provide the historical context. As it turned out, everybody did everything amid a collective juggling of two husbands, two daughters, three sons, one dog, two cats, and two goats, all of whom are thanked here for their patience, cooperation, and for the insights they provided into family life.

Most of the research was carried out at Yale and we express our gratitude to the entire staff of the Franklin Collection. William Willcox, editor of *The Papers of Benjamin Franklin*, read portions of the manuscript and allowed us to roam and rummage. G. B. Warden, assistant editor of the Papers, went over the pre-Revolutionary chapters and shared with us his special knowledge of Boston and Massachusetts. Dorothy Bridgwater and Mary L. Hart, who between them can locate almost any piece of information, were generous with their time and skills.

At the American Philosophical Society, Whitfield J. Bell was as always a helpful and encouraging friend. We also wish to acknowledge the assistance of the Franklin Institute in Philadelphia.

C.L. is grateful to the John Simon Guggenheim Memorial Foundation for a fellowship grant to work on this book. At an earlier date, as a guest of the Rockefeller Foundation, she spent one month in the stimulating atmosphere of Villa Serbelloni in Bellagio. E.H. expresses her thanks to Susan Achenbach and Alice Miskimin for support of a very different kind, and C.L. to Naomi Gordon, Dorothee Finkelstein, Mary Kleiner, and Florence Stankiewicz.

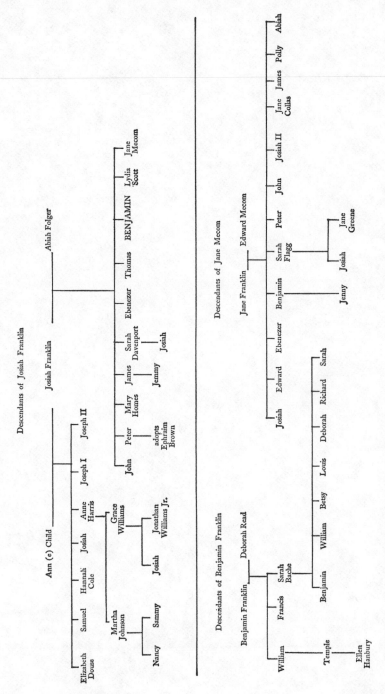

Descendants of Josiah Franklin

Josiah Franklin — Abiah Folger

Ann (e) Child

Elizabeth Douse | Samuel | Hannah Cole | Josiah | Anne Harris | Joseph I | Joseph II
Grace Williams

Martha Johnson
Nancy | Sammy

Jonathan Williams Jr.
Josiah

John | Peter | Mary Homes | James — Sarah Davenport | Ebenezer | Thomas | BENJAMIN | Lydia Scott | Jane Mecom

adopts Ephraim Brown

Jemmy | Josiah

Descendants of Jane Mecom

Jane Franklin — Edward Mecom

Josiah | Edward | Ebenezer | Benjamin | Sarah Flagg | Peter | John | Josiah II | Jane Collas | James | Polly | Abiah

Jenny | Josiah

Jane Greene

Descendants of Benjamin Franklin

Benjamin Franklin — Deborah Read

William | Francis | Sarah Bache

Temple

Ellen Hanbury

Benjamin | William | Betsy | Louis | Deborah | Richard | Sarah

NOTE: This chart has been simplified to include only those mentioned in the text.

Prologue: The Sweet Air of Twyford

EVERY EVENING, tradition has it, the five daughters of the bishop of St. Asaph, five lively girls ranging in age from eleven to twenty-three, gathered with their parents to listen to the pages the family guest had written during the day. The setting was the tiny village of Twyford in the English countryside near Southampton. The time was August 1771. The girls' father was Jonathan Shipley, a liberal, a supporter of the cause of those restless colonies across the ocean, their mother a wealthy aristocrat, former maid of honor to the queen. The guest was a portly gentleman of sixty-five, a grandfatherly type somewhat given to gout, the American Doctor Franklin. The scientific pursuits that had brought him world renown along with his honorary degrees had been relegated to the wings for many years, and politics now held center stage in his life. No longer a universally beloved and respected figure, he was deeply embroiled in controversy, and after seven years away from home, the mission that had brought him to London seemed further from completion than ever.

At Twyford, however, during those enchanted summer weeks, politics was forgotten. The smoky, sooty air of London was left behind. So were the shrillness of pamphlets, the humiliating hours of waiting in antechambers, the snubbings of arrogant peers, the pressures from the dissatisfied provinces back home. What the guest was writing in a room that would be revered as "Doctor Franklin's room" had nothing to do with electricity or taxation. He was writing the story of the poor, lean, tough boy he had once been. A crafty, resourceful, and immensely determined boy who had made many mistakes on his way to the top, but repaired them more or less as he went and above all managed to learn from them. He had had to fight for every advantage, ruthlessly at times, but had never deviated from the central credo at the core of his being: Nobody was going to push him or his countrymen around.

Thus, in that serene interlude, was begun Franklin's most influential work, his fairest title to literary fame, the *Autobiography*.

Why does a man write the story of his life?

Out of vanity, of course. Franklin made no bones about that: "Most People dislike Vanity in others whatever Share they have of it them-

selves, but I give it fair Quarter wherever I meet with it, being persuaded that it is often productive of Good."[1] It would not be absurd, he
added, for a man to thank God for his vanity as one of the comforts of
life. Indeed, he regretted that the natural boastfulness of children was
early discouraged by their elders; repression simply led to backbiting
and malicious gossip as a roundabout means of self-advertisement.

Writing about himself and his life was made more pleasurable still
by the conviction that it was a worthy self and, all in all, an edifying
life. Franklin's age, the optimistic age of the Enlightenment, had a
profound—and, to modern eyes, touchingly naïve—belief in the efficacy
of preaching to the young. Fathers wrote letters of advice to their children, and the children of that polite era were obliging enough to respond that they would heed the advice and benefit from their parents'
experience. Virtue was in the air, and so was the confident assumption
that it could be taught.

A moralist rather than a philosopher, Franklin presents himself in
the *Autobiography* as what would be called today a role model, someone who has achieved success and is now willing to share the recipe.
And that recipe, his famous early American blend of hard work, thrift,
self-reliance, and the pooling of resources, was meant for his own children as well as for posterity. In fact, the first part of the story is in the
form of a letter to his son William. William was in his forties at the
time, Franklin's daughter Sarah a married woman with children of her
own. Both, however, were still helped financially by their father, and as
Franklin considered their lives, across the ocean and over the years, he
may well have felt that, compared to him, they were soft. Hence the
often repeated message of independence, of "doing without."

To William, more than a message, the *Autobiography* was an appeal,
an attempt to recapture the closeness that had once been theirs.
Franklin and his son were beginning to drift apart in 1771. So long
his father's understudy, inseparable companion, political lieutenant,
William was now in his eighth year as governor of New Jersey and fast
becoming more sympathetic to the claims of the British crown than to
the protests of the American colonies voiced by his father. For the sake
of this elegant and snobbish William, whom he loved but did not admire, who had dreams of grandeur but was incapable of supporting
himself in the style he thought fit, Franklin painted a family album of
hard-working craftsmen, proud, down-to-earth, frugal, resourceful—the
people from whom William had sprung.

The family album was strictly limited to the past, however, to those
who had influenced Benjamin's early life and helped him become the
remarkable person he was. His present family is practically nonexistent

in the *Autobiography*: his daughter not mentioned a single time, his son alluded to quite casually, his wife brought into the picture mainly in the days when they were not yet married—and then not as a personality but as the illustration of a wrong set to right. The focus is exclusively on himself, or rather on a portion of himself. No soul-searching here à la St. Augustine, no searing confession à la Jean-Jacques Rousseau, but a do-it-yourself manual on how to go up in the world in an acceptable way.

If hundreds of sources project light and shadow on Franklin the man, his *Autobiography*, for all its deliberate gaps and bias, remains the only beam on those crucial years during which Benjamin the child was molded by his parents, his siblings, and the Boston of his day into the Franklin of history.

I

Son and Sibling

Aversion to arbitrary Power . . . has stuck to me thro' my whole Life.
—*Autobiography*

JOSIAH FRANKLIN, Benjamin's father, had come to America in 1683 in search of religious freedom. A convert to nonconformism, he had left his native village of Ecton in Northamptonshire rather than submit to the beliefs and practices of the Church of England. Still in his twenties when he landed in Boston, Josiah quickly found that Massachusetts had little use for his skills as a silk dyer and turned to making candles and soap, for which there was considerably more demand. If he did not exactly prosper, at least he managed. His family grew fast, too fast. Three children had come over from England; two more were born soon after the arrival in America. Nowhere is the mother's name mentioned, nowhere except on her tombstone modestly tucked away to the side of that of her more durable successor. There lies "Ann Franclin, aged about 34 years," buried with her sixth child, a little Joseph who died at the age of five days, and with her seventh child, another little Joseph born fifteen months later, who died at fifteen days, one week after his mother.*

Five months after losing his wife, Josiah married again, this time a strong native girl hailing from Nantucket, Abiah Folger. She raised Ann's five surviving children, gave her husband ten more, and lived well into her eighties, never sick a day until her final illness. Of her own brood, four girls and six boys, the youngest son was Benjamin, born January 6, 1706 (to become January 17 after the calendar reform in mid-century).

Boston was seventy-six years old, Harvard College was seventy. The

---

* Harsh as it sounds, her fate was not quite as dismal as that of the first women who landed in Massachusetts Bay in 1628. Of those eighteen, only four survived the first winter. Men frequently outlived two or three of their wives. As an English visitor ungallantly remarked, "the women here, like early fruit, are soon ripe and soon rotten."[1]

epic era of settling and struggling, of casting out the heretic, of hating and killing for the survival of soul and body, was over. No serious war had been fought with the Indians for the last thirty years. The witches' trials in Salem were receding into the past. A new century (which he would span almost in its entirety), the first stirrings of a more tolerant spirit, the first newspaper on the continent, those were the gifts around the cradle of Josiah Franklin's fifteenth child.

In a society where the privileges of seniority were firmly rooted, being the youngest son, the one who had to defer to the others, to obey, to pick whatever trade had not already been pre-empted, must have been galling to an eager and self-assertive boy. Luckily, he was not absolutely at the tail end of the family. Two brothers who immediately preceded him had died in infancy: one at three, the other—Ebenezer, drowned in a tub of suds—at the age of sixteen months, or rather sixteen and a half months as his tombstone carefully indicates, for in the parents' eyes every day of the little life had counted. Thus Benjamin was in effect the oldest child of the last cluster of three, made up of himself and two younger sisters who looked up to him and contributed to the self-confidence that was to be one of his prime assets.

The earliest stories he tells about himself are stories of proficiency. He was the one to whom his fellows turned in moments of crisis when they were out in their boats. He also was the one who led the others into scrapes, the one who organized the neighborhood boys into building a wharf out of stolen stones, with the result that most of them got soundly "corrected." The immediate moral of this anecdote, of course, is that one should not steal, as Josiah pointed out, not even for a useful purpose; but what Franklin is also saying is that at the age of ten he was already a leader of men.

He was a proud child, determined never to be made fun of twice for the same mistake. One day, he was given a little money to buy whatever he wished. On his way to the shop he met an older boy blowing a whistle. Charmed by this marvel, he bought it for all the coins in his pocket. When he got home and exasperated everybody with his shrill whistling, he was teased by one and all for having paid such an exorbitant price for a silly object, a lesson he never forgot. Spending your money unwisely not only makes you look foolish but it is wrong. The goods of this world, said the Puritan catechism, are a divine trust, to be administered to best advantage by human stewards. It was a dictate of Protestant virtue to "get one's goods honestly, to keep them safely, and to spend them thriftily."[2]

Even though several of the older siblings had already married and left home by the time Benjamin was growing up, the Franklin house on Union Street, at the sign of the Blue Ball, was crowded. Thirteen members of the family sat around the table in celebration when brother Josiah, a seaman, returned from the East Indies after an absence of nine years, only to go off again and disappear forever. The children were never allowed to take notice of what was served: Franklin professed to have found this culinary indifference a great asset in later life, but the number of recipes in his own hand found among his papers and the evident delight he took in French food belie that Spartan self-image. In order to have the young people benefit from intelligent conversation, his father would often invite some well-educated acquaintance to share their supper. As a man of recognized good sense, he in turn was frequently consulted by leading people on affairs of church and town.

Everybody still rubbed shoulders with everybody else in the Boston of those days, a society small enough to be fluid and almost devoid of class distinctions. Along the town's narrow streets one thousand houses, roughly, huddled together against the winter gales, outfitted with as few windows as possible but painted in bright colors to offset the gloom of rain and fog. Candles and glass panes were expensive and so interiors stayed dark. When the harbor froze over, firewood became scarce. Fresh water was hard to come by. Open sewers ran down the middle of the streets. Epidemics raged periodically, and one out of four newborn babies died within a few days, an appalling percentage, yet not as bad as that prevailing in many European cities of the same period. Of this stern life, however, the Puritans endeavored to make the best. They dressed as elegantly as their budgets allowed, in spite of their pastors' objections, and drank heartily: homemade cider for the poor, rum for the better off, imported wine for the rich. There was no lack of houses of prostitution flourishing on the Boston waterfront. Just around the corner from Franklin's Old South Church, the most notorious establishment of all was kept by a woman known as "the Little Prude of Pleasure"[3] and said to be patronized by the leading citizens of the town.

A new wave of English immigration combined with natural increase to stimulate the rapid growth of Boston, from six thousand inhabitants in 1700 to twelve thousand some twenty years later. To many, the town's harsh living conditions seemed better than life in London with its inflationary prices and low wages, its cramped housing, its air full of soot, its chaotic traffic, its want of social mobility. Old Bostonians resented the recent settlers, fearing that new-fangled ideas might dilute and corrupt their own strict Puritanism. For all its sinfulness, they still considered Boston the closest thing to the New Jerusalem, the "city on the hill." Although churches of various denominations competed for the direction of souls, Congregationalism kept its hold on the civil as well as the religious life of the town.

The Franklin children were raised "piously in the Dissenting Way,"[4] according to the very simple practices of the Congregational Church. An austere and egalitarian creed, without hierarchy, vestments, pomp, or ritual, Puritan Congregationalism recognized only two kinds of people: the "visible saints," who had received signs of their sanctity, thus earning admission into church membership—and everybody else. Even the "saints" could not be positively sure of salvation, but the others had a fairly certain prospect of damnation. Benjamin's father and mother became full-fledged members of the Old South Church soon after his birth, thereby joining the religious élite. They often opened up their house to prayer meetings, and Josiah's library was made up exclusively of works dealing with theology. These books would have been useful to Benjamin if his father had carried out his original intention of devoting his tenth son to the church as the tithe of his male offspring.

Franklin hardly mentions his mother in his childhood recollections, and the few surviving letters between them belong to his married years. He was proud of her lineage, however, the Folgers who had been among the earliest settlers of Nantucket, and remembered with obvious satisfaction the words spoken by his Quaker grandfather, Peter Folger, with "decent plainness and manly freedom"[5] in favor of liberty of conscience. But of his mother he conveys only that she must have met perfectly the demands of her day: pious, prolific, robust, she suckled all ten of her children. The epithets he chose for her tombstone, "discreet and virtuous," are equally unrevealing. Were one to depend only on the *Autobiography*, one would know next to nothing about Abiah Franklin's personality. This need not denote hostility on her son's part, only the common masculine reluctance to speak publicly of the women in their families.

The most memorable event of Benjamin's childhood was the arrival from England of his Uncle Benjamin, who had lost his wife and decided to end his days in the New World. Josiah and Uncle Benjamin had been each other's favorite brother and had corresponded for over thirty years with little hope of meeting again. But when they were reunited and lived under the same roof, they found it hard to get along. By the time Uncle Benjamin arrived in 1715, he was too old to switch from silk dyeing to a new craft; he just hung around the house, spending his time in ways that were exasperating to his brother, delightful to his nephew. He had invented a shorthand system for taking down sermons, a pastime he much enjoyed, now justified by the necessity of storing up a large collection against the day when his namesake would become a minister. He told the younger Benjamin many family stories, especially the one about their ancestor who in the days of religious persecution had concealed a Protestant Bible by taping it under a stool, to be quickly turned over in cases of emergency. Pleasant as it was to have an old uncle around with so much time on his hands, Benjamin was to remember for the rest of his life his father's growing irritation. Josiah's impatience with "visits to Relations in distant Places which could not well be short enough for them to part good Friends"[6] would make its way into the many versions of Poor Richard's admonition that fish and guests stink after three days.*

Annoyance with his brother's idleness may have provoked an anti-intellectual reaction in Josiah. Benjamin at eight had risen to the head of the class, yet his father withdrew him from grammar school after one year, declaring that in view of his large family a college education was more than he could afford for his son; many educated people never earned more than a "mean living" anyway. All thoughts of an ecclesiastical future were abandoned, and he was switched to a more down-to-earth type of school. He studied there for one year more, doing very well in writing, quite poorly in arithmetic. Those two years of formal education were the only ones he was ever to receive. At ten he was put to work in his father's shop, cutting wicks, dipping molds, running errands. He hated it. He wanted to go to sea, but his father would not hear of it.

A lucky man, Josiah. He played what looks like a dampening role in his son's life, saying no to just about everything, yet he has been portrayed for posterity in glowing colors. When Benjamin was doing well in school, his father took him out. When the boy, his distaste for candlemaking now obvious to all, was apprenticed to a cutler, his father called him home again rather than pay the fee. When Benjamin at thirteen composed verse and hawked his ballads on the streets with some success—another echo of his woolgathering Uncle Benjamin?—his father told him bluntly that his poetry was awful. When Benjamin, at eighteen, tried to borrow some parental money to set himself up in business under the sponsorship of the governor of Pennsylvania, his father flatly refused to lend him a farthing.

* By a curious coincidence, a dealer in rare books paid a visit to Franklin's London residence in the early summer of 1771 and offered him an extensive collection of political pamphlets going back to the preceding century. Franklin thought he recognized in the margins the handwriting of Uncle Benjamin and bought the collection. This incident may have stimulated him to begin his memoirs a few weeks later.

Nonpermissive, nonsupportive as he appears to modern eyes, this father shone in his son's memory as a wise and wonderful person. Was it because the son, in turn, was writing for his own son and wanted to establish that father knows best? Did he feel that his father had intended to toughen him for life? Franklin seems to look back on Josiah as a preview of himself—a stifled preview, to be sure, bogged down by near poverty and a huge family, but endowed with many of the qualities that would, in his own case, be allowed to soar. Well set and strong (so was Benjamin), ingenious (so was Benjamin), Josiah "could draw prettily, was skill'd a little in Music and had a clear and pleasing Voice, so that when he play'd Psalm Tunes on his Violin and sung withal as he sometimes did in an Evening after the Business of the Day was over, it was extremely agreeable to hear." In Benjamin's life, too, music would play its part. Josiah, furthermore, "had a mechanical Genius"[7] and was very handy in the use of other tradesmen's tools, another proud bond between the generations. "Be encouraged to Diligence in thy Calling" reads the inscription composed for Josiah's tombstone. "Diligence in thy Calling"[8] are the very words of Solomon that his father so often quoted: "Seest thou a Man diligent in his Calling, he shall stand before Kings, he shall not stand before mean Men" (*Proverbs* 22:29). Benjamin turned this into prophecy: In the course of his life he would stand before four kings—George II and George III of England, Louis XV and Louis XVI of France—and sit down to dinner with a fifth, Christian VII of Denmark.

Having cast his father as a hero, Franklin quite unfairly cast his brother James as a villain. Nine years his senior, James had been away in England learning the printer's trade while Benjamin was growing up. He returned to Boston just when the family did not know what to do with Benjamin: The boy was not attracted to any of the trades proposed, not that of joiner, or bricklayer, or turner, or brazier. Josiah would have preferred each of his sons to embrace a different profession, but he finally yielded to this one's bookish inclinations and apprenticed him to James at the age of twelve.

The contract to which Benjamin reluctantly put his signature—he was still dreaming of the sea—was stringent but standard for the times. What, one wonders, was an apprentice allowed to do besides work and worship? He pledged to obey his master, keep his master's secrets, refrain from fornication or matrimony, stay away from cards and dice, never haunt alehouses, taverns, or playhouses, never absent himself day or night without leave. For all this, he was dressed and boarded, and received one good suit at the expiration of the contract.

James has gone down in history as the bully who beat his little

brother out of jealousy over his greater gifts. He is depicted as the vindictive master who prevented his unhappy apprentice from finding any
other employer in town, thus forcing him to flee his native city at seventeen. And when Benjamin, as "saucy and provoking" as only a
younger sibling can be, reappeared in Boston after a seven-month absence, his pockets lined with silver, flaunting a new watch and "genteel
new Suit from Head to Foot,"[9] grandly buying his former fellow
workers a drink, James is shown as sullen and resentful, silently staring
at him, and then turning back to his work and telling their mother he
would never forgive this last offense.

Later, much later, Benjamin would admit that his behavior toward
James had been his first great error. Eventually they were reconciled,
and when James, still in his thirties, felt that his end was near, he
asked Benjamin to raise his little son Jemmy and "bring him up to the
printer's business."[10]*

In truth, James was the powerful liberating force in his brother's life.
It was he who opened up to Benjamin the world of words, of books, of
ideas: not their father's books on divinity nor his ideas circumscribed
by prudence, but London's ideas, those of the *Spectator* and the *Tatler*,
witty and satirical, systematically in the opposition. James's tutelage
brought Benjamin his first heady taste of challenging authority. The
rebel in him which would one day defy the rule of the Penns, the sovereignty of the king, and the terror of lightning, had taken his initial
steps in the brother's printing shop, not amid the father's candles.

The printing shop was the meeting place of a lively group of young
men seething with joyfully irreverent views. With their help James
launched the *New-England Courant* (1721), the fourth newspaper to
be printed in America. More than a means of disseminating the news,
he meant it to be a mouthpiece for those who presumed, without benefit
of pulpit, to comment on the state of the commonweal and the foibles of
their fellow citizens. The two Boston newspapers already publishing
were anything but glad to see the advent of the *Courant,* especially
since it denounced them as dull and dreary. The *Boston News Letter*
characterized its new rival as "a Notorious, Scandalous Paper . . . full
freighted with Nonsense, Unmannerliness, Railery, Prophaneness, Immorality, Arrogancy, Calumnies, Lyes, Contradictions and what not, all

---

* History would repeat itself. Jemmy turned out to be a disgruntled apprentice,
forever complaining about the poor clothes his Uncle Benjamin gave him. When
he became a full-fledged printer, Franklin offered to set him up in New Haven, but
Jemmy declined, preferring to join his mother and sisters in Newport and help
them carry on the paper started there by his father. Jemmy, too, died early, the first
in a series of young relatives and friends Franklin tried to raise and mold, almost
invariably without success.

tending to Quarrels and Divisions, and to Debauch and Corrupt the Minds and Manners of New England."[11] Unmoved, the *Courant* proceeded on its merry way. The clergy, the magistrates, the postmaster, Harvard, the rich and powerful, the whole Massachusetts establishment was considered fair game.

Boston was having its growing pains. Population had increased too fast, prices had risen, so had taxes, the poor were desperate, crime was on the upswing, political dissension was rife, and a new spirit of criticism pervaded the land. London's policy of restricting colonial manufactures and trade compounded the problems. To make things worse, just before the *Courant* began printing in the summer of 1721, there was a frightful outbreak of smallpox. Over the succeeding months 10 per cent of the city's population died.

The unprecedented severity of the epidemic led to a virulent debate as to the best means of combating it. The old remedy of isolation had not checked the disease; now a new one was proposed: inoculation. As it would be practiced throughout the eighteenth century (until superseded by Jenner's vaccination with cowpox), inoculation consisted of taking matter from fresh pustules of a person suffering from a mild case of smallpox and inserting it into the bloodstream of a healthy person through small incisions. This produced a genuine case of the disease but usually in a light form and gave long-term immunity. It was not, however, foolproof, especially when doctors misguidedly "prepared" their patients with purging, bleeding, and stiff doses of mercury or calomel. In Boston, the first to advocate the radical procedure was Cotton Mather, the Puritan divine who had dabbled in science and medicine all his life. He had heard of it initially from his African slave who claimed it had long been practiced in his homeland, then come upon reports of its use in Constantinople. For seven years he had been waiting for the chance to try it out, collecting more and more evidence from Boston's slave population that it did indeed work. Now he championed it from his pulpit as the only rational antidote to the terrible scourge. Other prominent ministers backed him, but what passed for Boston's medical profession (only one had a medical degree) rose in horror, claiming that inoculation would only spread the disease. A lone practitioner, Dr. Zabdiel Boylston, believed in him enough to inoculate his own son and slave, then others who were willing to try anything.

Mather's role in the Salem witch trials had so impaired his reputation, however, that the skeptical coterie around the *Courant* could not for a moment suspect that he might have the answer. They attacked him viciously and irresponsibly. In a fury, Mather dubbed James Franklin and his friends the "Hell-Fire Club." Undeterred by a bomb hurled into his house at the height of the controversy, he poured out his spleen in his diary: "The Town is become almost an Hell upon Earth, a City full of Lies, and Murders, and Blasphemies, as far as Wishes and Speeches can render it so; Satan seems to take a strange Possession of it, in the epidemic Rage against that notable and successful Way of saving the Lives of People from the Dangers of Small-Pox."[12]

For a sixteen year old in the process of shedding the beliefs of early childhood, beginning even to "doubt of Revelation itself,"[13] all this irreverence and uproar was huge fun. Benjamin was dying to join the fray. He felt he had mastered the style of the *Courant's* writing staff. His arduous process of self-education was beginning to pay off. Skipping meals to buy books, skipping prayers to read them, skipping sleep to practice his prose, clawing for knowledge as only a child of poverty has to claw, Benjamin had done exactly what Samuel Johnson would recommend some sixty years later to those anxious to attain an English style "familiar but not coarse, elegant but not ostentatious":[14] He had immersed himself in those issues of the *Spectator* which James had brought back from London.*

Under the first of many pen names he would use through life, that of Mrs. Silence Dogood, Benjamin sneaked an essay of his own under the shop door. Never suspecting that this was the work of the apprentice, James and his friends liked it and published it. Thirteen more followed. Sprinkling her thoughts with Benjamin's freshly acquired quotations from Cicero and Defoe, Silence Dogood, that busybody of a widow, made fun of women's hoop petticoats, pleaded for freedom of speech, attacked "religious hypocrites," upbraided the town drunkards, suggested compensation insurance for widows and spinsters, advocated education for girls, and gave vent to the feelings of generosity, outrage, and high morality of a very young and brash person suddenly finding a tribune. When the author's "small Fund of Sense for such Performance was pretty well exhausted,"[15] he stopped. And James, upon discovering the truth, was peeved.

But James was soon in trouble himself. In June 1722, his paper insinuated that the Massachusetts authorities were not trying hard enough to capture a pirate vessel off the coast. This charge was considered a "high Affront" and James was sent to jail. Benjamin managed the paper efficiently in his absence. Some fifty years later he remembered with glee that he had "made bold to give our Rulers some Rubs in it, which my Brother took very kindly, while others began to con-

---

* Brought out by Joseph Addison and Richard Steele from 1711 to 1712, the *Spectator* exerted an influence on English letters out of all proportion to its brief life-span.

sider me . . . as a young Genius that had a Turn for Libelling and Satyr."[16] Josiah and Abiah must have shuddered more than once at the boldness of these two, their youngest and brightest sons.

James, who seems to have been under some compulsion to get himself arrested and rearrested, was eventually forbidden to print or publish his paper, or any other paper or pamphlet, without previous authorization from the Secretary of the Province. To circumvent this difficulty, he made Benjamin the nominal publisher of the *Courant*—which implied, of course, a rescinding of the indenture contract. Benjamin knew very well this was only a ruse to fool the authorities, and, in fact, had secretly signed a new indenture to James for the rest of his term, but he wanted to take advantage of the subterfuge and win his freedom at once. He had tasted independence, he had savored leadership, he was seventeen and in full rebellion. Not only against James "for the Blows his Passion too often urg'd him to bestow upon me, tho' he was otherwise not an ill-natur'd Man."[17]* Not only against his father, who usually sided with him when called upon to arbitrate their quarrels, but this time told him he had no right to leave James. Benjamin's rebellion was above all against the stifling atmosphere of Boston, where his "indiscrete Disputations about Religion" had already begun to make him "pointed at with good people as an infidel or Atheist."[19]

His lifelong fight against "arbitrary power" began right there. In defiance of father, brother, and contract, he ran away, all the way to Philadelphia. Here he landed in a state of exhaustion, dirty, disheveled, almost penniless, happy. Within a few hours, he had met his future wife. Within a few days, he had found work. Within a few weeks, the fugitive, forever anxious lest his shabby clothes, his hunger betray him to the town fathers, had become the prototype of the American boy whose chief asset is self-reliance.

Another asset: People could not help liking him. A Dr. Browne, at whose inn near Burlington he had stopped in the course of his flight, remained in correspondence with him for years to come. An old woman from whom he had bought gingerbread offered him hospitality in her house (which now serves as headquarters for the local chapter of the Daughters of the American Revolution), fed him dinner—ox cheek, as he gratefully remembered—and tried to persuade him to settle down in

---

* He was to take a more casual view of the beaten apprentice's plight some thirty years later when he told his sister Jane that of course her son was chastised by his master, and rightly so. "And I think the correction very light, and not likely to be very effectual, if the strokes left no mark."[18]

Burlington as a printer. And Deborah Read, soon, was to like him very much.

It is part of the American lore now, crystallized in iconography: Deborah Read, standing on her doorstep, amused as the awkward runaway, his pockets bulging with shirts and socks, trundled up Market Street, two puffy rolls under his arms while he munched on a third. Few runaways ever re-entered the world of work and self-discipline as fast as this one. But the memory of his great adventure, of being soaked, almost drowned, exhausted, feverish, ravenous, yet pushing on, never left him. For all his high-flown talk of *errata* and atonement, the zest with which he recounts his flight is so obvious, his relish in the re-telling of those early hardships is so lively, that his story at this point fairly jumps with exhilaration.

Within a few years Benjamin would be on excellent terms again with his father and brother, never quite with Boston. He kept returning to the city for visits and spoke longingly, at times, of his native New England. In his will he bequeathed one thousand pounds to Boston to be given in low-interest loans to young married artisans who had —unlike him—served the whole of their apprenticeship in the town.* But an undercurrent of resentment remained, confined to the theological realm and generally expressed in terms of irony rather than bitterness. Writing to his brothers and sisters in later years, Franklin rarely missed a chance to take a poke at Boston and Boston ways. His temper would find a far more congenial climate in Quaker Philadelphia. Here, much as one might fault the dominant oligarchy on a certain drabness of life-style, there was hardly any attempt to force religious conformism and even less preoccupation with theology. "Everyone who acknowledges God to be the Creator, preserver and ruler of all things, and teaches or undertakes nothing against the state or against the common peace," marveled a Swedish visitor, "is at liberty to settle, stay and carry on his trade here, be his religious principles ever so strange."[20]

---

* He left a similar amount for the same purpose to Philadelphia. But neither human nature nor the economy lived up to his opinion of them: the fund is still sixteen million dollars short of the seventeen million he expected by 1990.

II

Errata Committed,
Errata Corrected

The kind hand of Providence or some guardian Angel . . . preserved me (thro'
this dangerous Time of Youth and . . . sometimes among Strangers, remote from
the Eye and Advice of my Father) without any *wilful* gross Immorality or Injustice
that might have been expected from my Want of Religion.

—Autobiography

THE YOUTH was still raw and so was the town. Created out of the wilderness by William Penn's surveyor in 1681, twenty-five years before Benjamin's birth, Philadelphia had become a lodestone for the ambitious and oppressed of Europe and of the other American colonies. With its fine port on the Delaware and its fertile hinterland, it had grown to a city of about ten thousand, living along the neatly laid out streets that its founder called Walnut, Pine, and Chestnut to honor the forest from which it sprang.

Life was cheaper here—those three puffy rolls had been handed to Benjamin by the baker for the three cents a single roll would have cost in Boston—and it was also freer. On his first day, a Sunday, he had followed a crowd and ended up in a Quaker meeting. In the peaceful silence he fell asleep. Instead of being rudely jabbed by the sexton, as would have been the case in Massachusetts, he was gently awakened at the end of the service. Thus began his lifelong amity with the Quakers who had given Philadelphia its somewhat more relaxed tone and its mercantile prosperity.

The town was still so small that Franklin and his companions, as they rowed down the Delaware on the night he first arrived, feared they had passed beyond without noticing it. (Looking back on this period in his old age, a Philadelphian reminisced, with perhaps only slight exaggeration, that he had known "every person, white and black, men, women and children in the city of Philadelphia by name."[1]) The town was still so young that the first child born there, in a cave, survived until 1767, forty-four years after Franklin's arrival. And the wilderness was still so close that bears might be found roaming in Germantown. Small as it was, young as it was, Philadelphia was the second largest city in North America, and her market the largest in the colonies. Her captains were competing with Boston for the coastal trade and expanding their commerce with the West Indies and Europe. On the homeward voyage from the Old World, they brought the German and Scotch-Irish immigrants who were putting their stamp on the once-Quaker colony.

INTO THESE HOSPITABLE SURROUNDINGS Benjamin settled with such speed and ease that it looked as if the successful course of his life had been, as the Puritans were wont to say, predestined. He found employment at his own trade. He spent his Sundays with intelligent, ambitious young men, who walked in the woods and read poems to one another. He paid court to his landlord's daughter, Deborah Read, and she was not unresponsive: "I had great Respect and Affection for her, and had some Reason to believe she had the same for me."[2] He had intended to let nobody in Boston know where he was, but a seafaring brother-in-law heard of his whereabouts, offered to smooth things over, and pushed him to make peace with his family. The governor of Pennsylvania invited him to borrow capital and become the province's official printer. At seventeen, his future seemed all mapped out.

It was not. During the seven years that followed there was to be no steady progress in business and no harmonious development of character. Far from his parents' eye, without the anchor of wife and children, he went through a tortuous succession of false starts, partly through bad luck, partly through bad judgment. As it unfolds in the *Autobiography*, the only source for those early years, his story is that of an adolescent oscillating between generosity and callousness, bewilderment and cockiness, prudence and rashness—with only one steady passion, his ever-deepening love of books.

Flattered that the governor should take notice of him, he brushed aside his father's warning against relying on a high official who would entrust one so young with such heavy responsibilities. Had he but asked around, he would have found out that Governor Keith had the reputation of being a well-meaning but wholly unreliable man, apt to give expectations because he had nothing else to give. But at eighteen Benjamin was impulsive, his head a little turned by such august patronage, and he sailed jauntily for London to buy all the equipment for a printing press. Fond goodbys were exchanged with Deborah. There was vague talk of marriage, but Mrs. Read—head of the family since her husband's recent death—thought it imprudent for people so young "to go too far"[3] with a long separation looming. There took place nevertheless what the *Autobiography* calls "an interchange of promises."[4] With Franklin went the aspiring poet James Ralph, a "pretty Talker"[5] and the most talented member of his circle in Philadelphia.

Upon arriving in England, Benjamin discovered that the governor had sent him on a wild goose chase, that he had not forwarded any of the promised letters of credit, indeed did not have the slightest credit to bestow. And another breach of faith was taking place right under his eyes: Ralph announced he had no intention of going back to the wife and child left behind in Philadelphia. As soon as he had recovered from his initial panic at finding himself "a poor ignorant boy"[6] stranded in London without work, without connections, without money to pay for his passage home, Benjamin, too, broke a pledge: Having written to Deborah that he was not likely to return soon, he never wrote again and proceeded "by degrees" to forget her.[7] He found work. He and Ralph became inseparable companions. The two of them launched into a joyous season of sowing wild oats.

As if such irresponsibility and self-indulgence were not bad enough for a child of Puritan parents, he compounded his sins—or *errata,* as he called them with the understatement of the printer's language—by rationalizing them in an impudent little pamphlet entitled *A Dissertation on Liberty and Necessity, Pleasure and Pain,* and appropriately dedicated to Ralph. Its purpose was to prove that there could logically be no such thing as evil since whatever one does is God's will, hence good. A little later he grew so ashamed of this publication that he burned all the copies he could lay his hands on. Only two escaped. Then, as an antidote, he composed a piece sustaining the opposite thesis, but did not print it, "disgusted"[8] by the uncertainties of metaphysical speculation and determined to leave theology alone for the rest of his days, a resolution he faithfully adhered to. The glorious fling of the two comrades was brought to an abrupt end: Benjamin assumed that since he helped pay everybody's bills he was entitled to the favors of Ralph's mistress when his friend was out of town. Ralph and the mistress, an amiable milliner, thought otherwise.

It was thirty-three years before they would meet again, those two provincial bumpkins who had been so overwhelmed by the temptations of the metropolis that one forgot his fiancée, the other his wife and baby girl. The baby, grown a woman in the meantime with ten children of her own, had always wondered what had become of her flighty father and asked Franklin to ferret him out when he went back to England in

1757. Both men discovered that they had turned out much better than could have been expected. Ralph had given up poetry after a coupleted blast from Alexander Pope,* but had made a name for himself as a literary jack-of-all-trades. He specialized in writing pamphlets for politicians out of office and did it so effectively that the ministry paid him £300 a year just to keep quiet. As a sign of renewed friendship, he offered Franklin his pen and was enlisted in the Pennsylvania pamphlet wars. Now married again and the father of a daughter, Ralph had contrived to keep his English family ignorant of the American one and entreated Franklin not to give away his secret, all the while expressing, as Franklin reported without raising an eyebrow, "great affection for his daughter and grandchildren" in America.[9]

After his year of "Dissipation" in 1724 and the break with Ralph, Benjamin calmed down, started saving money, bought books, indoctrinated his fellow printers into the virtues of warm gruel for breakfast instead of the customary beer, and tried to establish contact with some of the great minds in London. He did not succeed in meeting Sir Isaac Newton, but he met Newton's successor in the presidential chair of the Royal Society, Sir Hans Sloane, to whom he sold a curiosity brought over from America, an asbestos purse now in the British Museum. He also made the acquaintance of the famous satirist Bernard Mandeville, whose *Fable of the Bees* contends that self-indulgence stimulates society to economic and technological progress, a thesis Franklin had found appealing when he was young and profligate, but would refute strenuously for the rest of his life.

Cut off from his roots, lost in the anonymity of the capital, he was free to explore, to think as he pleased, to do as he pleased, to find himself if he could. He toyed for a while with the idea of roaming about Europe, picking up work where it offered, and even with the project of opening a swimming school; his prowess in swimming the three and a half miles from Chelsea to Blackfriars, performing a few stunts on the way, had impressed enough people to guarantee him pupils.

After eighteen months in London, he decided to go back to Philadelphia, give up printing, and begin a career in trade. Writing in middle age to a romantic young lady whom he wanted to impress, Franklin ascribed his decision to the powerful pull exerted by "the cords of love and friendship"[10] (poor abandoned Deborah?) but he had in fact been motivated by more prosaic reasons. On the voyage to London he had been befriended by a Quaker merchant; now about to return home, this

---

* Silence, ye Wolves! while Ralph to Cynthia howls,
And makes Night hideous—Answer him ye Owls!
(*Dunciad*, second edition)

same merchant offered him a position as clerk with the promise to set him up in his own business when the time was ripe.

There was plenty of leisure for soul-searching during the three months of their crossing in the summer of 1726, and the twenty-year-old Benjamin was none too happy with the balance sheet he drew. Had he not frittered away his energies, squandered his money, let down some of his friends, antagonized people by his brashness? By the time he stepped off the boat he was armed with firm resolves, moral and material.

As usual, nothing proceeded according to plan. The Quaker merchant whom he had come to love as a father died shortly after their arrival and the young man found himself once again penniless and without prospects—not amid the bountiful opportunities of London, this time, but in provincial Philadelphia. There was no choice but to swallow his pride and return to his former employer, Samuel Keimer. Along with James Franklin, Keimer is one of the villains—or victims?—of the *Autobiography*. He is depicted as a slovenly and ludicrous figure, a glutton and a fool, a religious fanatic given to ecstasies, easily trapped in disputation by the clever Benjamin, in short an "odd Fish."[11] Yet the account fails to mention that this same Keimer proposed to teach blacks to read the Scriptures a quarter of a century before Franklin himself came around to the idea. Not an ungenerous man, he had hired the runaway apprentice, put up with his merciless teasing and his disloyalty in sneaking off to England, and was even willing to give him a new job when he was down and out. But their truce did not last. They quarreled within six months and Benjamin quit. His next four years would be spent floundering, his repeated attempts at launching his own business all thwarted by the lack of starting capital.

He was saddened, too, by the sight of Deborah's misery. As his absence had lengthened, she had been persuaded by friends to give up hope of his return and had married a certain John Rogers, a good potter but a poor husband who had soon run through her dowry. Unhappy from the start, she also had reason to suspect that in addition to his various faults her husband was probably a bigamist with another wife living in England. She parted from him, refused "to cohabit or bear his name,"[12] and found herself in limbo, neither free nor married. Franklin felt pangs of shame at the sight of her, the very kind of shame, he mused, that Governor Keith (now ex-Governor Keith) must have felt toward him when they met on the street.

There was no logic to his life. A stroke of luck, for instance, when all seemed particularly bleak: An acquaintance whose father was well-off proposed that they form a printing partnership. Then, when everything

should have gone well, a catastrophe: The partner's father went bankrupt, leaving the two young men heavily in debt, threatened with law-
suits and the seizure of their equipment. As Franklin did not know
where to turn, two of his friends suddenly offered him help on condition that he get rid of his partner who spent more time at the tavern
than at the shop. He did so, without a qualm, just as on previous occasions he had discarded companions who were proving to be en-
cumbrances. The promised loan came forth and Benjamin was finally
on his way. By 1729 he had his own printing press, his own newspaper,
his own stationery store. But he also had debts.

A time-honored way for a young man to establish himself in the
world is to marry a girl with a dowry. But in this undertaking, too, he
met with a series of rebuffs. It is hard in hindsight to imagine that he
was not a likely prospect: Wasn't he healthy, hard-working, pleasant,
honest, intelligent? Wasn't his budding genius evident to anyone? Apparently not. In the eyes of prudent parents, a fledgling printer, let
alone one with sizable debts, was not desirable. He records drily how
one proposed match after another fell through, leaving the reader to
guess at his feelings of humiliation or bewilderment. "I was not to expect Money with a Wife unless with such a one as I should not otherwise think agreable."[13] Marriage indeed was a contractual agreement
and the dowry universally considered part and parcel of this arrangement.

There were other reasons, too, why the time had clearly come to take
a wife. "Better to marry than to burn," St. Paul had said. Franklin was
frightened by the unruliness of his sexual drive: "That hard-to-be governed Passion of Youth had hurried me frequently into intrigues with
low Women that fell in my Way, which were attended with some Expence and great Inconvenience, besides a continual Risque to my
Health by a Distemper which of all Things I dreaded, tho' by great
good Luck I escaped it."[14] One has only to read Boswell's *London Journal* or Fielding's *Joseph Andrews* to realize how lucky he was.

The family had been the cornerstone of the social order in Puritan
New England, often taking precedence over church and state. "God
setteth the solitary in families," declared the Psalmist (68:6) and the
authorities interpreted this as an injunction to do likewise. In Massachusetts, whoever could not afford to set up a "family" of his own by
hiring servants was obliged to find a place with an existing family until
he married and established his own household. Bachelors in some
places were looked upon as virtual criminals. Seventeenth-century New
Haven taxed them. Pennsylvania had no such law regulating them
(and perhaps they were never effectively enforced even in New Eng-

land), but as early as 1697 William Penn had deplored the increasing wickedness of his city: "As to the growth of vice, wee cannot but owne as this place hath grown more populous . . . Looseness and Vice have crept in, which we lament, altho endeavours have been made to suppress it."[15] Those endeavours were soon translated into stringent laws against adultery and fornication—the latter crime carrying with it a penalty of twenty-one lashes or £10.

Franklin's thoughts at this juncture turned once more toward Deborah, now possibly a widow: Her husband had absconded to the West Indies and, rumor had it, died there in a brawl. Benjamin had remained on cordial terms with the Read family through all these vicissitudes: "I was often invited there and consulted in their Affairs, wherein I was sometimes of service." Yet, glad as he was of their "regard" for him, he still felt remorse for the moral slip which he called his great *erratum*. "I pity'd poor Miss Read's unfortunate Situation, who was generally dejected, and seldom cheerful, and avoided Company. I consider'd my Giddiness and Inconstancy when in London as in a great degree the Cause of her Unhappiness; tho' the Mother was good enough to think the Fault more her own than mine, as she had prevented our Marrying before I went thither, and persuaded the other Match in my Absence. Our mutual Affection was revived, but there were now great Objections to our Union."[16] Indeed, there were. If Rogers turned up again and it could not be proved that he had a previous wife in England, Benjamin and Deborah, had they been married under the Pennsylvania law, would be considered bigamists, liable to thirty-nine lashes on the bare back and imprisonment for life at hard labor. And even if Rogers were really dead, he had left many debts which his successor might be called upon to pay.

There was still another problem which Franklin does not mention in the *Autobiography*, though it was a very live one. A baby was on the way, or just born. Whose baby? Deborah's and Benjamin's, conceived somewhat too soon, and now presented as Benjamin's alone (with an unknown mother) in order to save Deborah's honor? Benjamin's baby by some other woman, a baby whom Deborah, only too glad to find another husband in her sad predicament, consented to raise? Long debated among historians, the problem of William Franklin's origin has been only partly solved in recent years.

For a long time the single and dubious clue was a scurrilous pamphlet composed in the heat of the election campaign of 1764, thirty-four years after the fact. It dwelt on all aspects of Franklin's alleged turpitude and built up to the charge that a prostitute by the name of Barbara was the mother of William, that she had been exploited as a servant all her life by the Franklin family, and on her recent death had been spirited away to a pauper's grave. Only a few years ago, some more light was shed on the subject. A letter was found, written in 1763 by the son of one of Franklin's close friends to a London Quaker: "In answer to your hint relative to a certain Gentleman now acting in a public Station [William was at this time governor of New Jersey], 'tis generally known here his birth is illegitimate and his Mother not in good Circumstances, but the report of her begging Bread in the Streets of this City [Philadelphia] is without the least foundation in Truth. I understand some small Provision is made by him for her, but her being none of the most agreeable Women prevents particular Notice being shown, or the Father and Son acknowledging any Connection with her."[17]

When he chose, Franklin certainly knew how to cover his tracks. Nowhere is the *Autobiography* more infuriating for what it does not tell than on the subject of William's birth. Was he in fact "the great Inconvenience" that Franklin deplored as the by-product of his consorting with those "low Women?" It would be an odd way of referring to his son. As always when he deals with feeling rather than with action, the whole section of his story having to do with his marriage is full of gaps and reticence. He must have wavered quite a bit. Two months after informing his sister that he was definitely not planning to get married, he changed his mind: "We ventured, however, over all these Difficulties and I took her to Wife on September 1, 1730."[18]

Well into his seventies, Franklin advised a grandnephew who was hesitating about a business decision to resort to "moral algebra," by listing all pro's in one column, all con's in another, weighing them against each other one by one and determining in which column the balance remained. Such a system, he said, though not mathematically exact, had been useful to him throughout life. "If you do not learn it," he concluded, "I apprehend you will never be married."[19] The grandnephew answered that he agreed as far as business was concerned, but not when it came to marriage: "Before a Man is married he must *fall* in love and this seems to be as involuntary an act as *falling* into a Well which requires something more than algebra to get out of."[20] But then he was two generations closer to the Romantic Age and one can well imagine Franklin at twenty-four balancing Deborah's lack of dowry against her willingness to raise the baby or against her good health and industriousness, then balancing the threat of Rogers's return against the wiping away of his own guilt.

When it finally took place, the marriage was neither celebrated nor recorded in church; it was a simple common-law agreement under which Deborah came to live in Franklin's house and started calling herself Mrs. Franklin, an arrangement considered perfectly adequate at the time. "None of the Inconveniences happened that we had apprehended."[21] Rogers never reappeared.

If all this sounds somewhat dispirited, with the accent on guilt and reparation ("Thus I corrected that great *Erratum* as well as I could"[22]), more than on love and joy, it should be stressed that Franklin never speculated, publicly at least, as to whether he could have done better. "Keep your eyes wide open before marriage, half-shut afterwards," says Poor Richard (1738). The frustrations in their long union can sometimes be guessed at, but from the day of their marriage the husband would underscore only his wife's good points and she would express only her affection or an admiration tinged with awe.

THE MAN Deborah had just married was planning to become perfect, no less. From the nucleus of good resolutions conceived on board ship some four years earlier he had evolved a much more sophisticated "Project of arriving at moral Perfection," a "bold and arduous"[23] undertaking that would lead him to live without committing any fault at any time. The boy who had forged his mind all by himself, in his teens, was now attempting, all by himself, to mold his character in his twenties. With one deep difference, however: Whereas his intellectual growth had been all expansion and enthusiasm, his spiritual self-education would be all retrenchment and control.

Modern readers of the *Autobiography* are apt to be most charmed by the narrative passages, the flight from Boston, the feuds with masters and competitors, the climb. But to Franklin the moralizing part (which he planned to develop some day into an "Art of Virtue") was at the core of the story, his very reason for writing it.

To begin with, he compiled a list of twelve virtues—which became a baker's dozen when, told by a friend that he suffered from inordinate pride, he added humility. They were virtues of restraint rather than exuberance or generosity, carefully chosen not only for their own sake but for their practical value, their usefulness in enhancing one's public image, so many tools for making a good impression, for getting ahead in this world—their relevance to the next is not even discussed.

Then he set up a tabulating system on the ivory pages of a special booklet and proceeded to practice each virtue systematically for one week, starting all over again when the thirteen-week cycle was complete. The deadly seriousness of this plan was perfectly in keeping with the mood of his time. One had to be rational, utilitarian, moral. Far from laughing off in later life such adolescent strivings, Franklin always carried his little book with him, long after he had given up the weekly accounting, and proclaimed at the age of seventy-eight that it had made him a better and a happier man. "If the rascals only knew all the advantages of virtue," he told his French friends, "they would become honest through sheer rascality."[24] The booklet made such an impression on his Paris admirers that well into the nineteenth century one of them would refer to it in terms of a religious relic: "We touched this precious booklet, we held it in our hands! Here was the chronological story of Franklin's soul!"[25]

The ideal one pursues is one thing, the image one projects another, the reality one lives still a third. How did Franklin fare on these various levels?

1. *Temperance. Eat not to Dullness, Drink not to Elevation.*[26] There was a marked evolution from the vegetarianism of his teens to the frugal table of his twenties to the hearty board of his middle years to the well-stocked cellars (five kinds of champagne) he would keep in Paris. Old Madeira had a special place in his affections. Drink he saw as indispensable to conviviality—he wrote several drinking songs—but there is no recorded instance of his losing control. As to tobacco, he boasted that he had never smoked or taken snuff.

2. *Silence. Speak not but what may benefit others or yourself. Avoid trifling Conversation.* This is one resolution he lived up to. Argumentative by temperament but a poor orator, as he well knew, he forced himself to listen more than to speak. Jefferson was impressed: "If he was urged to announce an opinion, he did it rather by asking questions, as if for information, or by suggesting doubts."[27] Loquacious in private conversation, he was so taciturn in larger groups that observers sometimes found him boorish or, to say the least, unsettling.

3. *Order. Let all your Things have their Places. Let each Part of your Business have its Time.* A dismal failure, by his own admission. His letters abound in references to enclosures he planned to slip in, only to confess in the last paragraph that he could not lay his hands on them. He generally managed to compensate for this lack of method by his powerful memory, but in his old age in Paris the records and accounts of the American diplomatic mission were in such a muddle that John Adams was appalled.

4. *Resolution. Resolve to perform what you ought. Perform without fail what you resolve.* A mixed record. A pragmatist rather than an ideologue, he soon discovered that some wavering is unavoidable and can even be politically useful.

5. *Frugality. Make no Expence but to do good to others or yourself: i.e. Waste nothing. And 6. Industry. Lose no Time. Be always employ'd in something useful. Cut off all unnecessary Actions.* Splendid. See next chapter.

7. *Sincerity. Use no hurtful Deceit. Think innocently and justly; and, if you speak, speak accordingly.* Coming from a man who had published his first hoax at sixteen and would pen his last on his deathbed, this may be tongue in cheek. Mystification, pseudonyms, undercover maneuvers were an integral part of his temperament, brought to a peak of perfection in the hurly-burly of public life.

8. *Justice. Wrong none, by doing Injuries or omitting the Benefits that are your Duty.* All right, with a tendency to inflexibility. William eventually considered his father cruelly unjust. Franklin's insistence on equity and reciprocity as the basis for justice made him at times unyielding and unforgiving. Rather an Old Testament view.

9. *Moderation. Avoid Extremes. Forbear resenting Injuries so much as you think they deserve. And 10. Tranquillity. Be not disturbed at Trifles, or at Accidents common or unavoidable.* Here there is a substantial discrepancy between image and inner reality. He often was much more incensed at attacks, much more hurt and resentful of injuries than he cared to admit. His political passions ran deep, even though he managed not to display them in public. To discover the emotional Franklin, one has only to read the comments he sputtered in the margins of the political pamphlets that infuriated him on the eve of the Revolution. Among his papers, too, are some very angry letters, but chances are that on cooler reflection he mailed few of them.

11. *Cleanliness. Tolerate no Uncleanness in Body, Cloaths or Habitation.* A perfect score. The Paris police, in their secret reports, marveled at the whiteness of his linen. He was addicted to fresh air, sat in the nude every morning with the window open, and kept up his swimming into old age.

12. *Chastity. Rarely use Venery but for Health or Offspring. Never to Dullness, Weakness or the Injury of your own or another's Peace or Reputation.* This primly therapeutic approach to sex infuriated D. H. Lawrence. "Never 'use' venery at all," he raged. "Follow your passional impulse, if it be answered in the other being; but never have any motive in mind, neither offspring nor health nor even pleasure, nor even service. Only know that 'venery' is of the great gods. An offering-up of yourself to the very great gods, the dark ones, and nothing else."[28]

In complete contrast to this attack on Franklin's supposed prudery is the more widespread view that he was the most lecherous of the founding fathers, that he carried on through life the sinful pattern of his unmarried youth, and that his pronouncement on chastity was sheer hypocrisy. It so happens that, apart from the existence of William (who was treated as a legitimate son), there is hardly any explicit evidence to convict Franklin either of promiscuity or its opposite. But the rumors sprang up in his own lifetime and have gained ground ever since.

The story of his "illegitimate daughter" is a case in point. In 1770, Franklin's close associate John Foxcroft married Judith Osgood in England. Franklin gave away the bride and referred to her thereafter as his "daughter" because he had acted as surrogate father at the wedding, by no means an unusual practice. Many were the women he would call wife or daughter throughout his life, in a teasing or affectionate manner without suspecting, of course, that anybody would take him literally, then or later.

The only eyewitness account of his alleged philandering is that of Charles Willson Peale. When the young painter arrived in London in 1767 without reputation or friends, he presented himself unannounced at Franklin's lodgings, since his father and Franklin had been acquainted in America. He was admitted by the maid and shown immediately into a room where the Doctor, wearing a bright blue-green suit with gilt buttons and gilt braid (the painter's eye!), was seated with a young lady on his knee. Far from sounding shocked, Peale recounted the episode fifty years later to illustrate his point that "only with men of little minds"[29] is it necessary to stand on ceremony. His small sketch, generally assumed to represent this scene, does not name the participants and their features are too unclear for identification.

A number of political enemies and humorless contemporaries dropped innuendoes about Franklin's morally offensive behavior, but none ever cited a specific name or incident, not even as gossip. John Adams, who regarded him as an unregenerate sinner, noted with evident satisfaction that "there had been great disputes in Pennsylvania formerly concerning [Franklin's] moral and political character, as there had been in England."[30] He did his best to make sure that all America knew about Franklin's supposed debaucheries as ambassador to the court of Louis XVI. These sputterings reflect, more than anything else, Adams's own blinkered view of the world.

Franklin, to be sure, always delighted in irreverent hoaxes, risqué remarks, and suggestive allusions. The century of *Tom Jones* did not hesitate to express its enjoyment of carnal pleasures and its admiration for female beauty. Dandling a young lady on a middle-aged lap was not the transgression it would later be. The proper and provincial Boston of a John Adams could not condone the London of a Boswell or the Paris of a Beaumarchais.

All of which is not to say that there is no substance to the legend. Franklin traveled a great deal once he reached his forties; he lived abroad for fifteen of the last seventeen years of his marriage. It strains credulity to imagine that so vigorous a man was never unfaithful in all that time. But whatever he may have done to another's peace, he did no injury to anyone's reputation.

13. *Humility.* A lifetime of mellowing passed between his first stern —if not very humble—motto: *Imitate Jesus and Socrates,* and his eventual appreciation of his performance: "In reality there is perhaps no one of our natural Passions so hard to subdue as *Pride.* Disguise it, struggle with it, beat it down, stifle it, mortify it as much as one pleases, it is still alive, and will every now and then peep out and show itself. . . . For even if I could conceive that I had completely overcome it, I should probably be proud of my Humility."[31]

When he wrote these lines, at seventy-eight, he had come around to the point of view that perfection on all counts is not only impossible but undesirable, "a kind of Foppery in Morals," and that "a perfect Character might be attended with the Inconvenience of being envied and hated. . . . A benevolent Man should allow a few Faults in himself, to keep his Friends in Countenance."[32]

LONG AS IT IS, Franklin's list of virtues is inadequate in one respect. It omits his chief gift, his hallmark and saving grace: humor.

Except for a D. H. Lawrence who despised him as a "snuff-colored little man"[33] or a Mark Twain who upbraided him with mock anger for having poisoned many boys' lives by setting an impossible example, most people smile when they talk about Franklin. Some smile because his name brings roguish thoughts to mind, many more because they look upon him as a fellow human, a keen, amused observer of our foibles and his own. He won more hearts by little stories he told on himself than by his profession of faith in lofty goals. A man who can relate with a wink the abandonment of a moral principle must have been a comfortable person to live with. At the time of his flight from Boston to Philadelphia, he was an ardent vegetarian and considered that eating any animal was "a kind of unprovoked Murder." On shipboard, however, his fellow passengers made a fine catch of cod. "I had formerly been a great Lover of Fish, and when this came hot out of the Frying

Pan, it smelt admirable well. I balanc'd some time between Principle and Inclination till I recollected that when the Fish were opened, I saw smaller Fish taken out of their Stomachs. Then thought I, if you eat one another, I don't see why we mayn't eat you. . . . So convenient a thing it is to be a *reasonable Creature*, since it enables one to find or make a Reason for every thing one has a mind to do."[34]

Never one to meet obstacles head-on, on Don Quixote's collision course, he was prone to seek the "reasonable" compromise that would save face for everybody. When he was old and living among the French, a little note of cynicism blended with his sense of fun: He thanked Providence for having given the name of sin to several pleasures so as to make them more enjoyable.

And even if as a morally upright young married man, he did stick to his proposed daily regimen of rising at five, addressing *Powerful Goodness* (his form of prayer), studying and planning the day until eight, working until twelve, dining and overlooking the accounts until two, working again until six, putting things in their place, having supper, music, conversation, and examination of the day until ten, Deborah must have laughed many a time in the course of those laborious hours.

III

Industry, Frugality, Fertility

Doubt not my behaving well in Wedlock, having all the Industry, Frugality, Fertility, and Skill in Oeconomy, appertaining to a good Wife's Character.
—*The Speech of Miss Polly Baker*, 1747

"She proved a good and faithful helpmate. . . . We throve together and have mutually endeavor'd to make each other happy."[1] *We throve together* is an understatement: They did splendidly. By 1732, two years after they were married, Franklin had finished paying off his debts. Under the same roof on Market Street, less than two blocks from the spot where he had first caught sight of Deborah, he ran a newspaper, a printing shop, and a general store. His *Pennsylvania Gazette* was a very staid paper, more given to news than to controversy, a far cry from James's hell-raising *New-England Courant*, now defunct. The store carried a wide range of merchandise, from the salves and ointments concocted by Deborah's mother "sufficient to remove the most inveterate itch"[2] to the "crown" soap made in Boston by Franklin's brother John according to a secret recipe. In a neat cycle of self-promotion, the newspaper advertised both the products of the press and the goods in the shop. That same year, 1732, Franklin launched his *Poor Richard's Almanac* which was eventually to sell at the rate of ten thousand copies a year, his first chance at fame and fortune. Also in 1732, Deborah gave birth to their son Francis Folger—and Philadelphia broke ground for its State House, later to become Independence Hall.

The shop was Debbie's special preserve. She sold printing and writing materials, bills of lading, servants' indentures, powers of attorney, blank books, quills, ink, ink horns and ink powders, pounce (powder to blot ink), slates, parchment, sealing wax, and spectacles. There was also a brisk trade in books, those her husband printed and those he imported from England: primers, Bibles, psalters, maps, dictionaries, grammars, ballads, the highly popular almanacs—both other authors' and the home-grown *Poor Dick,* as she called it.

A large number of entries are recorded in her hand in the Shop Book, a long, narrow folio much enlivened by her perennial feud with the English language. An almanac, some paper, an ounce of ink went to people whom Debbie identified as "cristefer the Fishman," "Mary the Papist that is at Cozen Wilkinsons," and the "seck stone [sexton] of the Church."[3] Like most women of her day, including Franklin's mother and sisters, Deborah did not know how to spell. Far from criticizing them, Franklin toyed all his life with the idea of a phonetic alphabet, but his plan was never taken seriously. By the next generation, in any case, women's spelling had improved considerably.

As time passed, the shop's inventory grew until it was a mirror of Philadelphia's cosmopolitan commerce: chocolate, coffee, tea, palm oil, saffron, linseed oil, Rhode Island cheese and codfish, mackerel by the barrel, mustard powder. On occasion, customers could also purchase scales and compasses, patent medicines, homemade lampblack, scarlet cloth, white stockings, "love" goose feathers (plucked from a live goose), iron stoves, lottery tickets, book-binding services—and slaves. Sometimes Debbie got a trifle mixed up: "Mrs. Franklin is confident that she sent 20 reams of the Paper I order'd for you, but has no Bill of Lading for it, and has forgot the Captain's name,"[4] her husband had to explain. No matter; he credited her with much of their success in business.

Franklin was always at her side, busy from morning to night. Busy and looking busy: "In order to secure my Credit and Character, I took Care not only to be in Reality industrious and frugal, but to avoid all Appearances to the contrary. I dressed plainly; I was seen at no Places of Diversion. I never went out a-fishing or shooting; a Book, indeed, sometimes debauched me from my Work, but that was seldom, snug, and gave no Scandal; and, to show that I was not above my Business, I sometimes brought home the Paper I purchased at the Stores through the Streets in a Wheelbarrow."[5] Before long, the wheelbarrow loads could be measured by the score, until in the 1740s he was probably the largest paper dealer in the English-speaking world.

Debbie's industry almost matched his. "We have an English Proverb that says, He that would thrive must ask his Wife; it was lucky for me that I had one as much dispos'd to Industry and Frugality as my self. She assisted me cheerfully in my Business, folding and stitching Pamphlets, tending Shop, purchasing old Linen Rags for the Papermakers. . . . We kept no idle Servants."[6] More than twenty years later, when he stood before the House of Commons in London answer-

ing questions about the Stamp Act, he recalled how in his young days
he had been dressed from head to toe in clothes of her weaving and
had never felt prouder in his life.

It was a source of great satisfaction to him that the women of his
family were thoroughly adept at domestic skills and willing to practice
them. When his fifteen-year-old sister Jane was about to be married, he
had thought at first of giving her a tea table but then "considered that
the character of a good housewife was far preferable to that of being
only a pretty gentlewoman" and chose a spinning wheel instead. And
when this Jane's son, in turn, was on the threshold of marriage to a girl
without a dowry, he would comment, "If she does not *bring* a fortune,
she will help to *make* one."[7]*

Not a romantic notion, that of woman as money-maker, but a very
prevalent one in his milieu. Puritan and Quaker, whatever their
differences in the meeting, saw eye to eye in the counting house. Philadelphia, struggling to overtake its older rivals, had the same hardwork-
ing, acquisitive, single-mindedly mercantile atmosphere as Boston. As
late as 1744, a visitor from the more frivolous colony of Maryland
remarked in wonder that Philadelphia shops opened at five o'clock in
the morning and lamented, "I never was in a place so populous where
the *gout* for publick gay diversions prevailed so little. There is no such
thing as assemblies of the gentry among them, either for dancing or
musick."[8]

Industry by itself was not quite enough, however. It needed its sober
twin, frugality. On this score, too, Deborah was peerless: "Frugality is
an enriching Virtue, a Virtue I could never acquire in myself but I was
lucky enough to find it in a Wife who thereby became a Fortune to
me."[9] In that respect, he maintained, women were more gifted than
men: "I and thousands more know very well that we could never
thrive till we were married. What we get the Women save."[10] He may
indeed have remembered his father's old friend, Judge Samuel Sewall,
who so despaired of ever learning to live within his income that he
handed the management of his finances to his wife.

Obversely, he could not stand the would-be genteel lady, idle and extravagant. The very first issue of *Poor Richard* launched the offensive:

> Many estates are spent in the getting
> Since women for tea forsook spinning and knitting.

---

* Jefferson, too, felt strongly that women should keep busy, but for a different
reason. Indolence, in his aristocratic Virginia experience, bred ennui and ennui in
turn led to hypochondria and hysteria.

The following year, the attack escalated:

> She that will eat her breakfast in her bed,
> And spend the morn in dressing of her head,
> And sit at dinner like a maiden bride,
> And talk of nothing all day but pride,
> God in his mercy may do much to save her,
> But what a case is he in that shall have her!

This is all the more ironic since Franklin in his old age would be accused of spending far too much time in Paris chatting with ladies for whom the notion of spinning or knitting would have been as remote and repulsive, had they ever entertained it, as working for a living. And when they wanted to please him, what did the French ladies do? They bought a tea set! A whole lifetime had passed since the day Deborah had committed—for his sake, not her own—one of her few follies, fondly remembered in later years: "My Breakfast was a long time Bread and Milk (no Tea) and I ate it out of a twopenny earthen Porringer with a Pewter Spoon. But mark how Luxury will enter Families, and make a Progress, in Spite of Principle. Being call'd one Morning to Breakfast, I found it in a China Bowl with a Spoon of Silver. They had been bought for me without my Knowledge by my Wife and had cost her the enormous Sum of three and twenty Shillings, for which she had no other Excuse or Apology to make but that she thought *her* Husband deserv'd a Silver Spoon and China Bowl as well as any of his Neighbours."[11]

Of course frugality was essential to a young couple starting out in life without capital. As time passed, Franklin saw it less as a means of amassing money than as a guarantee of independence: "An Empty Sack can hardly stand upright" (*Poor Richard,* 1750). Financial independence would enable him to live according to his principles.

As it turned out, Deborah's greatest contribution to his future fame and glory had nothing to do with her industry and her frugality, praiseworthy as he thought them. It was an unwitting and unappreciated contribution: She did not saddle him with the numerous offspring he would have liked. Who could have imagined that such a robust wife would not produce seven children like her own mother, or ten like his mother, or even twelve like sister Jane? Had she been no more than average (eight children per colonial family, as he reckoned), Franklin could not have afforded the luxury of winding up his business in his mid-forties and devoting himself to knowledge and public life as if he had been born a gentleman.

Though he never complained about the minuteness of their family, he must have felt it keenly. The society from which he sprang idealized fertility. God's earliest commandment to be fruitful and multiply had been one of the most joyously obeyed. "Lo, children are an heritage of the Lord; and the fruit of the womb is his reward. As arrows are in the hand of a mighty man, so are children of the youth. Happy is the man that hath his quiver full of them." (*Psalms* 127: 3–5) This passage was still ringing in his ears decades later when he congratulated a kinsman on his seven sons and reminded him of the "Blessing on him that has his Quiver full of them."[12] Abstinence did not rank high in the Puritan canon or in Franklin's conscience; he once described an old bachelor, pathetically dying in the knowledge that the unbroken line from Adam would end with him. He was shocked by the large number of bachelors in England. "The great Complaint," he noted, "is the excessive Expensiveness of English wives."[13] But this was hardly an excuse for rich Englishmen who shied away from matrimony at the rate of nine out of ten.

"Men," he reflected in old age, are "very badly constructed, as they are generally more easily provoked than reconciled, more disposed to do mischief to each other than to make reparation, much more easily deceived than undeceived, and having more Pride and even Pleasure in killing than in begetting one another. For without a Blush they assemble in great Armies at Noonday to destroy, and when they have killed as many as they can, they exaggerate the Number to augment the fancied Glory; but they creep into Corners or cover themselves with the Darkness of Night when they mean to beget as being ashamed of a virtuous action."[14]

Franklin did more than approve of children; he adored them. How can one talk of care in the sense of burden, he asks, when it comes to children: "I would ask any Man who has experienced it, if they are not the most delightful Cares in the World."[15] And Poor Richard (1735) declared that "A Ship under Sail and a big-bellied Woman are the handsomest things that can be seen common."

To prove his point that having children is the supreme achievement of the human race and to redress the injustice committed by society in punishing women for men's misdeeds, he gave the world in 1747 his most charming fictional creation, Polly Baker. Polly was a spunky lass who, hauled repeatedly before a Connecticut court for bearing children out of wedlock, spoke up in behalf of all seduced girls. Instead of condemning her to fines and whippings for having given birth to five illegitimate children, she declared, the judges should honor her with a statue because she had taken God's commandment to heart and helped replenish the earth. "How can it be believed that Heaven is angry at my having Children when to the little done by me towards it, God has been pleased to add his Divine Skill and admirable Workmanship in the Formation of their Bodies and crown'd it by furnishing them with rational and immortal Souls?" And what about the "great and growing Number of Batchelors . . . [who] leave unproduced (which is little better than Murder) Hundreds of their Posterity to the Thousandth Generation?"[16] Shouldn't *they* be fined and whipped? A happy ending: Polly is acquitted and the next day marries one of her judges.

So spirited was her portrait, so plausible her plea that in the course of innumerable anonymous reprintings of her speech in England, in the colonies, on the Continent, throughout the century and beyond, Polly was often mistaken for a real person. She became famous as the wronged woman par excellence, as thrilling a figure as her contemporary Moll Flanders, that archetype of the golden-hearted prostitute. Such a facetious approach to the problem of bastards was not, of course, to everyone's liking. John Adams, for one, was not amused and considered *The Speech of Miss Polly Baker* yet another of Franklin's many "Outrages to Morality and Decorum."[17] But in France she was taken quite seriously and "put to work by men who were protesting in earnest . . . against conventional morality."[18]

Translated into the language of political economy, Polly Baker's ideas became *Observations on the Increase of Mankind* (1751), one of Franklin's most influential tracts. Here, too, his premise is that a high birth rate is or should be the goal of national policy. In fully settled countries where land is scarce and labor plentiful, population virtually stabilizes because low wages discourage early marriage and large families. America, on the other hand, with its abundance of land, shortage of labor, and high wages, offers every inducement to early marriage and numerous offspring. Franklin projected with great accuracy that the population of the colonies would double every twenty years. Instead of fearing this growth, Britain should encourage it in order to provide an expanding market for her own manufactures. Warming to his favorite themes, he argued that a taste for luxury inhibits the birth rate and hence harms the country that indulges it.

Only a happily married man could have spoken of wedlock as glowingly as Franklin did. Marriage between very young people stood a better chance of success, he felt, because neither of the partners had yet become fixed in his habits. Add that "*late Children,* as the Spanish Proverb says, *are early Orphans.*" Marriage at any age, however, was preferable to remaining single. He never tired of pointing out the inferiority of the bachelor: "An odd Volume of a Set of Books, you know, is not worth its proportion of the Set"[19]—or he would compare him to the odd half of a pair of scissors, his favorite mating metaphor. Even in a piece as paradoxical and whimsical as his *Advice to a Young Man on the Choice of a Mistress* (1745), whose contention is that older women make better mistresses than young ones (more reliable, more useful, more discreet, more grateful), he speaks in earnest when it comes to the married state: "It is the man and the woman united that make the complete human being. Separate, she wants his force of body and strength of reason; he, her softness, sensibility, and acute discernment. Together they are more likely to succeed in the world. A single Man . . . is an incomplete Animal."[20]

This, of course, reflects the traditional view: Man's strong point is reason, woman's intuition. But Franklin did not necessarily rank reason *above* intuition. "All inferior animals put together do not commit as many mistakes in the course of a year as a single man within a month, even though this man be guided by reason." Addressed to a French lady he was courting in old age, these lines were meant as a belated tribute to Debbie: "This is why, as long as I was fortunate enough to have a wife, I had adopted the habit of letting myself be guided by her opinion on difficult matters, for women, I believe, have a certain feel, which is more reliable than our reasonings."[21]

At the core of his views on marriage lay the notion that there should be mutual consideration. "Treat your Wife with Respect. It will procure Respect to you, not only from her but from all that observe it." If this seems overly concerned with image, he redeems himself in the next sentence: "Never use a slighting Expression to her even in Jest; for Slights in Jest after frequent bandyings are apt to end in angry earnest."[22]

With the single exception of an outburst against her sloppy book-keeping when she was old, Franklin never put on record a word of complaint against his wife. "Don't you know that all wives are in the right?" he asked a kinsman who was having a tiff with Deborah. "It may be you don't for you are yet but a young husband."[23] Was she truly a quarrelsome woman? Yes, "a turbulent temper,"[24] said a clerk who lived for three months in the Franklin house. Yes, "a hedgehog," exclaimed a neighbor incensed by a squabble over the price of a bed, "she has shot a great many quills at me but thank heaven none of them has or can hurt me."[25] Deep in political controversy in London at the time, Franklin dismissed the neighbor's tirade with a terse "silly complaint."[26]

His wife's quick temper, if such it was, does not seem to have bothered him. Better a high-spirited woman, he felt, than a meek and whining one or a silently discontented victim. "Women of that character have generally sound and healthy constitutions, produce vigorous offspring, are active in the business of the family, special good house-wives, and very careful of their husbands' interest. As to the noise at-tending all this, 'tis but a trifle when a man is us'd to it . . . a mere habit, an exercise in which all is well meant and ought to be well taken."[27] Ten years after Deborah's death, Franklin paid tribute to her tolerance of human foibles and harmless vanities: "If People can be pleased with small Matters," he remembered her as saying, "it is a pity but they should have them."[28]

Little is known about Deborah for the first half of her life, the half during which she lived under the same roof as her husband and there was no need to correspond. After the story of her extravagant purchase of the china bowl and the silver spoon, the *Autobiography* never men-tions her again. The only portrait of her still in existence is a copy made in London by Benjamin Wilson of a small canvas, the work of an unidentified Philadelphia painter. It shows a well-dressed bourgeoise in her prime, with a look of determination on her somewhat coarse face and a piece of jewelry in her hair. Her chief physical asset is the appe-tizing décolleté of a plump woman. Such plumpness was far from displeasing her husband. He once shipped home from England a large jug for beer and accompanied it with an appreciative note: "I fell in love with it at first sight, for I thought it looked like a fat, jolly Dame, clean and tidy, with a neat blue and white Calico Gown on, good-natured and lovely, and just put me in mind of—somebody."[29] A notice in the *Gazette* mentions, among clothing stolen by a thief who broke into their house, "a woman's long scarlet cloak, almost new, with a dou-ble cape," and "a woman's gown, of printed cotton, of the sort called brocade print, very remarkable, the ground dark, with large red roses, and other large red and yellow flowers . . . and smaller blue and white flowers, with many green leaves."[30] The dress is vividly described, but as a person this industrious, frugal, and jolly dame never takes the cen-ter of the stage.

Even the major tragedy of her life, the death of their son Francis at the age of four, has come down only as lived by the father. The child succumbed to smallpox in November 1736, a fate that was all the more cruel since Franklin now believed firmly in inoculation. Fifteen years had passed since his brother James had attacked the practice so rabidly in the *Courant* and Franklin, convinced by observation of the great value of inoculation, had just written a few lines in its praise for the forthcoming issue of *Poor Richard*. He had intended to have Franky inoculated as soon as the boy recovered from the "flux," but that turned out to be too late. The procedure was still so controversial even in 1736 that Franklin felt compelled to explain at length that his child had died from the disease, not, as had been rumored, from inoculation. This made him an even more ardent advocate of prevention and he persuaded his English friend, Dr. Heberden, to write a sort of do-it-yourself inoculation manual that would bypass the expensive doctors. He contributed a preface full of statistics (338 inoculated, with only two deaths, one of which was from worm fever), a poignant piece of tabulation for a man whose own child had been a casualty of the disease.

As so often happens, the dead child was attributed virtues no living one could equal. As an old man in France, Franklin had tears in his eyes when he told a friend that he was certain Franky would have been the best of his children. Not for seven years after Franky's death would Deborah give birth to their only other child, Sarah.

Work provided the best remedy. Deborah helped her husband shoulder the burden of an important new position, that of postmaster of Philadelphia, to which he was appointed in 1737. The post office was installed right on the premises, along with the printing shop and store. It was a boon for the *Pennsylvania Gazette* whose circulation jumped as soon as its publisher had free use of the mails. Fascinating as it must have been for Debbie to be at the hub of the town's life, of its news and gossip, of its lost and found, the extra work and bookkeeping were heavy. Postage was seldom prepaid in the colonial period. Letter writing was an attribute of leisure, postage a luxury. If the addressee could not pay the charge, the postmaster would generally extend credit and try to recover the debt when he could. After sixteen years, Franklin had entered in his ledger nearly seven hundred outstanding and unpaid accounts for letters received. About to depart for London, he noted in his instructions to his successor in the office: "As Mrs. Franklin has had a great deal of Experience in the Management of the Post Office, I depend upon your paying considerable Attention to her Advice in that Matter."[31]

The press, too, kept expanding. He became the official printer for Pennsylvania, bringing out all the paper money, state documents, laws, and treaties. Soon he took on the same job for Delaware and New Jersey. He was appointed clerk of the Assembly, which meant much more work, but also more business coming his way because of the enlarged circle of his acquaintance. He taught himself some French, Italian, Spanish, and Latin, yet still found time to write for the *Gazette* and especially for *Poor Richard*—whose very title, inspired by James Franklin's *Poor Robin,* reminds one of the extent of his debt to his brother. (After James's death in 1735, his widow remained one of the largest distributors of *Poor Richard*, selling a thousand copies or more per year.)

Almanacs were a printer's gold mine: Hardly a household in the colonies was without one and often it was the only reading matter. Amid a wealth of astronomical, astrological, and meteorological information were sprinkled epigrammatic verses and improving aphorisms: "*moral* Sentences, *prudent* Maxims, and *wise* Sayings." Franklin changed the conventional format little but transformed the sayings, culled from the same anthologies as his competitors', into such nuggets of homely directness that *Poor Richard* became second only to the Bible as a source of proverbial wisdom. A rather grim wisdom it was, based on thrift, caution, an obsessive hankering for self-sufficiency. Countless school children have been nurtured on such maxims as "God helps them that help themselves," "For want of a Nail the Shoe was lost," or "The sleeping Fox catches no Poultry," indoctrinated whether they knew it or not with all the virtues that "make Fortune yield." A recipe for getting ahead, yes, laced even with a touch of irony, a joke or two inserted deliberately "since perhaps for their Sake light, airy Minds peruse the rest."[32] But there is little joy in *Poor Richard*, no expansive generosity, no room for the carefree, unpremeditated spirit. It brought its author fame but it also gave rise, this prudential wisdom, to the well-known view of Franklin as a tightwad and a moneygrubber.

At home, the atmosphere was not all that stark. For one thing, the house was warm, more efficiently heated than any other in town, at least as of 1739 when he invented the Pennsylvania Fireplace, commonly known as the Franklin stove. Economy in the use of wood, better distribution of heat, reduction of drafts and smoke—all these were possible selling points for Franklin's new product. When he launched it on the market, however, he simply did what most advertisers do today: He appealed to women's desire to keep their looks. "Women, particularly from this cause [cold air] (as they sit much in the house) get colds in the head, rheums, and defluxions, which fall into their jaws and gums, and have destroyed many a fine set of teeth in these northern colonies. Great and bright fires also do very much to contribute to damage the eyes, dry and shrivel the skin, and bring on early the appearance of old age."[33]

Philadelphia women had come a long way from the original settlers who had made do in sod caves along the Delaware. Franklin's stove was widely sold in New England by his brothers John and Peter. It later made the clammy winters at Monticello bearable for Jefferson who hated the cold. Franklin could have made a fortune from his invention, as did a London merchant who adapted it, but he refused to patent it, just as a decade later he refused to patent his electrical discoveries.

He was a gregarious man and the house hummed with friends. Few people have believed as fervently as Franklin in the glory of teamwork, the value and stimulation of human intercourse. He would have been in total disagreement with the currently fashionable view that communication among people, let alone among generations, is well-nigh impossible and that we are all doomed to the icy wastes of alienation. Far from it: He had hit upon the perfect combination of sociability and adult education when he had organized some of his "ingenious Acquaintance into a Club for mutual Improvement, . . . call'd the Junto."[34]

The earliest members of the Junto were artisans, clerks, surveyors—"leather-apron men" for the most part, all with a taste for books and a yearning to improve themselves. Their conversation ranged from discussions on the order of the universe to blueprints for the organization of Philadelphia's first fire companies and earliest subscription library. Some of the members wrote pieces for the *Gazette,* all made a point of steering business Franklin's way. In time Debbie was entering into her account books the names of many local political leaders and rich merchants: Governor George Thomas; James Logan, secretary to the Penns and a notable classicist; Isaac Norris, speaker of the Assembly ("for a set of Votes"); William Allen, later chief justice; Benjamin Lay, the abolitionist (who opposed both slavery and tea drinking); Conrad Weiser, Indian interpreter and explorer; Gustave Hesselius, the limner who later painted portraits of the Franklin family. Even the Proprietor, Thomas Penn, bought and charged a cake of crown soap. Many of these men became Franklin's friends and political allies, some his implacable enemies.

His world was expanding. Before long it would encompass more than the shop and printing house where he and Debbie had worked side by side for the first eighteen years of their married life. Did he love this wife who incarnated so many of the desirable virtues? It was an age that did not necessarily expect people to marry for love, but trusted that love would come and grow after marriage. In Franklin's case, there seems to be little doubt that it did. Toward forty, when many men become restless with what the French call the devil of high noon, *le démon du midi,* he sounded some of his most uxorious notes in a warm, loving, if unromantic poem, sung in Deborah's honor at one of the annual banquets of the Junto. The fashion of the times called for Arcadia, the praise of a woman whose identity remained hidden under the name of a Greek nymph. Franklin would have none of this nonsense. His nymph was his wife, and he simply called her Joan:

Of their Chloes and Phylisses poets may prate,
    I sing my plain country Joan,
These twelve years my wife, still the joy of my life;
    Blest day that I made her my own. . . .
Not a word of her face, or her shape, or her eyes
    Or of flames or of darts you shall hear;
Tho' I beauty admire 'tis virtue I prize,
    That fades not in seventy years. . . .
Am I loaded with care, she takes off a large share,
    That the burden ne'er makes me to reel;
Does good fortune arrive, the joy of my wife
    Quite doubles the pleasure I feel. . . .
Some faults have we all, and so has my Joan,
    But then they're exceedingly small;
And now I'm grown used to them, so like my own,
    I scarce can see them at all. . . .
Were the fairest young princess, with million in purse
    To be had in exchange for my Joan,
She could not be a better Wife, mought be a worse,
    So I'd stick to my Joggy alone
                  My dear Friends
I'd cling to my lovely ould Joan.[35]

IV

Out of the Home
and into the World

I am in a fair Way of having no other Tasks than such as I shall like to give my
Self, and of enjoying what I look upon as a great Happiness, Leisure to read, make
Experiments, and Converse at large with such ingenious and worthy Men as are
pleas'd to honour me with their Acquaintance.
                    —Franklin to Cadwallader Colden, September 29, 1748

FAR FROM EXPERIENCING the period of depression so often associated
with middle age, Franklin in his forties blossomed into a new person,
more exuberant, more joyous and creative, leaping from a new self-
confidence into a new freedom. At forty-two, halfway through his life,
he retired from business. The merchant closed shop—and the scientist
emerged. The printer put down his tools—and the civic leader came
forth. The local postmaster quit—and the deputy postmaster-general
took office. Three new careers for Franklin but the end of an era for his
wife. From now on, more of a spectator than a collaborator, she could
no longer play a decisive role in their partnership.

After eighteen arduous years of publishing, printing, and selling, the
frugal and industrious couple had become rich enough to give up the
shop and the press. The annual incomes from the capital Franklin had
invested in various printing partnerships, from his position as postmaster, his real estate in Philadelphia, and his savings must have
amounted to almost two thousand pounds, as much as the salary of
Pennsylvania's governor. The penny-pinching period dating back to his
indenture at the age of twelve was over. The family moved to a more
spacious house further from the din of the market, acquired slaves, and
adopted a more elegant way of life. And just about the time he decided
that the moment had come to please himself, Philadelphia, too, began
to discover other pleasures, a taste for gay diversions, social
refinements, and a more disinterested pursuit of learning. The first

troop of traveling players braved Quaker disapproval and gave performances in the city; music invaded both church and tavern; the well-to-do started immortalizing themselves in portraiture.

The world beyond the confines of home and shop had always fascinated Franklin. He had time now to correspond with friends the length and breadth of the colonies, to give rein to his bursting curiosity, and exchange views on a huge range of topics, from fortifications and geology to theories of blood circulation, perspiration, and body temperature, from speculations on the direction of northeasters to the fine points of hemp-raising. Henceforth the highest accolade he would bestow on men would be "ingenious." (Praiseworthy women, however, would be called "discreet," or, in extreme cases, "notable.")

Science was not new to Franklin, of course. He had been hankering for it all his life, waiting for the right moment. On his crossing back from England at twenty he had noted the change in the dolphins' color after they came out of the water; he had studied the tiny crabs growing on seaweed, preserved them in jars, and pondered the mystery of their generation. Even within his own household he liked to set up experiments. He left an earthenware pot of molasses, one day, in Debbie's pantry, without closing it tightly and returned to find it crawling with ants. He got rid of all the ants but one, then secured the pot to a string hanging from the ceiling, led the string across the ceiling, down the wall, and waited. The lone ant, after gorging itself, eventually figured the way out along the string and disappeared. Within half an hour, the pot was once again black with ants all traveling the string route. Question: By what kind of language had the first one informed all the others? Same story with the pigeon boxes nailed to his house. Where others would have been content to listen to the birds cooing, he observed their population level (the strong adults driving out the young and weak) and experimented with new boxes until he was satisfied he had understood how pigeons govern their habitat.

No longer content to observe nature, he wanted to tinker with it. The time had come for "Philosophical Studies and Amusements"[1]—philosophy, of course, meaning natural science. The key word is "amusements": This fresh departure in Franklin's life started as a game, a marvelous, gregarious game carried out right at home in the presence of a worried wife, excited children, gaping neighbors, and cheering friends. Not for him the specialized, sterilized, often secretive research of the modern laboratory; science in the Enlightenment was a chummy affair, often dilettantishly, recklessly haphazard, warmly international.

The first spark came from an unlikely quarter. On a visit to Boston in 1743, Franklin met an itinerant showman-savant from Scotland, Dr. Archibald Spencer, who had begun his career as a male midwife and would end it as a clergyman. Somewhere in between he mastered a repertoire of tricks in electrostatics; the most spectacular consisted of suspending a little boy from the ceiling by silken threads while drawing sparks from his hands and feet, a demonstration which was to become a classic with all "electricians." Franklin was "surpriz'd and pleas'd"[2] with what he witnessed but lacked the equipment to perform experiments on his own. A few years later, Spencer turned up in Philadelphia and sold him all his paraphernalia, at just about the time a decisive stimulus was coming from another direction.

From London came the gift for the Library Company of Philadelphia of a glass tube, along with instructions and pamphlets on electricity. The sender was Peter Collinson, a wealthy Quaker merchant turned botanist who took delight in fostering the exchange of plants between England and America and in cross-fertilizing minds all over the civilized world by circulating discoveries from friend to friend. He spread ideas like a bee spreads pollen. With Collinson's steady encouragement Franklin's hobby flared into a passion: "I never was before engaged in any study that so totally engrossed my attention and my time as this has lately done. What with making experiments when I can be alone, and repeating them to my Friends and Acquaintances who, from the novelty of the thing, come continually in crowds to see them, I have, during some months past, had little leisure for anything else."[3] For those friends who wanted an active part in the game, he provided glass tubes. The friends, too, experimented and compared notes. Second only to Franklin in enthusiasm and inventiveness was Ebenezer Kinnersley, an unemployed Baptist minister who was to find his métier not in the pulpit but on the lecture circuit.

The initial apparatus had been makeshift, partly purloined from Debbie's household: a salt cellar, thimbles, a vinegar cruet, a cake of wax, a pump handle, the gold leaf on a book binding. With the discovery in Holland of the Leyden jar ("that wonderful bottle . . . that miraculous jar!"[4]), electrical equipment became more sophisticated, far greater charges could be accumulated, and experimenters were no longer to be compared to Rabelais's baby devils who "had only learned to thunder and lighten around the Head of a Cabbage."[5]

To console themselves that the electrical season of 1749 had not yet produced anything of much use, Franklin and his friends proposed a party of pleasure on the shores of the Schuylkill. As a stunt, spirits were to be fired by a spark sent from bank to bank without any other conductor than the water. The *pièce de résistance* was to be a turkey killed "by the Electric shock, and roasted by the electrical Jack before a Fire kindled by the Electrified Bottle. . . . The Healths of all the famous Electricians in England, France and Germany, are to be drank in Electrified Bumpers, under the Discharge of Guns from the Electrical Battery." The electrical bumper was a practical joke, a glass filled with wine that would give the drinker a slight shock "if the Party be close shaved."[6] Killing turkeys electrically, with the pleasant side effect that it made them uncommonly tender, was the first practical application that had been found for electricity. Throughout the following months, Franklin endeavored to perfect the technique; he was able to answer queries from London with the information that while hens could easily be put to death by electricity, turkeys had a tendency to faint and then recover consciousness a short time later unless administered a much stronger dose. Many years later, not surprisingly, the French were still pursuing the idea of putting electricity at the service of gastronomy. They wondered if it might not be used to speed up the tenderizing of large animals, but Franklin discouraged the notion.

An interesting by-product of these experiments was Franklin's accidental discovery that a man could survive a far greater electrical shock than previously believed. To his brother John he described how close Deborah had come to being widowed:

> Being about to kill a turkey from the shock of two large glass jars, containing as much electrical fire as forty common phials, I inadvertently took the whole through my own arms and body, by receiving the fire from the united top wires with one hand, while the other held a chain connected with the outsides of both jars. The company present (whose talking to me, and to one another, I suppose occasioned my inattention to what I was about) say that the flash was very great and the crack as loud as a pistol: yet, my senses being instantly gone, I neither saw the one nor heard the other; nor did I feel the stroke on my hands. . . . I then felt what I know not well how to describe, a universal blow throughout my whole body from head to foot, which seemed within as well as without; after which the first thing I took notice of was a violent quick shaking of my body, which gradually remitting, my senses as gradually returned.[7]

Franklin was neither the first nor the last scientist to be thus rudely shaken up. The popularizer of the Leyden jar, Peter van Musschenbroek, received so great a shock during an experiment that he thought his end had come and vowed he would not experience such a jolt again for the whole kingdom of France. His all-too-human sentiments brought him a stern rebuke from Joseph Priestley, the first historian of electricity, who compared the "cowardly professor" of Leyden to the "magnanimous Mr. Boze, who with a truly philosophic heroism worthy of Empedocles, said he wished he might die by electric shock, that the account of his death might furnish an article to the memoirs of the French Academy of Sciences. But it is not given to every electrician to die the death of the justly envied Richmann"[8]—Richmann being a Swedish physicist who had the ill-fortune to become electricity's first martyr through inadequate grounding.

Step by step, Franklin set down his progress in a series of letters to Collinson. He enriched the new science's vocabulary (*battery, conductor, armature, brush, condense,* for instance) and produced a coherent theory, that of the positive and negative states of a single electric fluid. His discoveries were couched in a tone of diffidence, for he always feared that what he was writing might already be known in Europe. He was conscious of being a provincial, on the periphery of the community of philosophers, and also aware that sometimes his speculations turned out to be wrong: "If there is no other Use discover'd of Electricity, this, however, is something considerable, that it may *help to make a vain Man humble.*"[9] At other times he reproached himself for too strong a penchant for the building of hypotheses to the detriment of slow, painstaking observation. Worried about his shortcomings in higher mathematics, he compared himself to a man searching for something in a dark room where he could only grope and guess.

Collinson received his letters with enthusiasm and communicated them to the Royal Society of which he was a fellow, but though the American contribution was duly applauded, there was no immediate follow-up in England. Not to be discouraged, Collinson published the letters as an eighty-six page booklet, *Experiments and Observations on Electricity* (1751), which was promptly translated into French and circulated on the Continent. It was in France that Franklin's ideas created the greatest excitement. The French, too, had been having spectacular fun with electricity before becoming engrossed with its serious side. The Abbé Nollet, official court electrician to Louis XV, once lined up one hundred and eighty soldiers of the guard and sent an electric shock through them, causing them to leap into the air with a simultaneity never achieved on the parade ground. Another time, he took his audience to a Carthusian monastery in Paris and assembled a human electrical circuit of seven hundred monks who performed with equal precision when the current was applied.

Within months of the publication of the "Philadelphia experiments," two French scientists, spurred on by their royal patron, set out separately to test the validity of Franklin's central thesis: that electricity was a fundamental force of nature, not just a product of the laboratory. Franklin, to be sure, had not been the first to suggest the identity of lightning and electricity, but he was the first to design the experiment that actually proved it.

The physicist Thomas-François d'Alibard beat his colleague by one week. His account of this turning point in the history of science reads like a vignette of French village life, the village in this case being Marly-la-Ville on the outskirts of Paris. Too impatient to hang around waiting for thunderstorms (or slightly apprehensive?), he entrusted the execution of the experiment to an "intelligent" and intrepid former dragoon. At the first sign of a storm, the dragoon was to rush out to the sentry box above which towered a forty-foot iron rod (set on a stool supported by three wine bottles), observe if a spray of St. Elmo's fire was visible at the pointed top of the rod, and try to draw sparks from its lower portion; equally important, he was to send immediately for the village priest.

Which is exactly what the faithful dragoon did. On May 10, 1752, at 2:20 in the afternoon, as thunder rumbled in the sky and sparks crackled in the sentry box, according to plan, a little boy dispatched for the priest found him already on his way, running through the hailstorm. At the sight of their pastor's haste, the villagers thought the dragoon had been killed and spread the alarm. Arriving on the spot and "seeing there was no danger," the priest, too, began drawing sparks from the iron rod: six times at least within four minutes, and each time "for the duration of a *pater* and an *ave*"[10]—a Lord's Prayer and a Hail Mary. All this in a state of such high excitement that he scarcely noticed the strange but severe bruises encircling his arm. Nor did he notice the strong smell of sulphur that emanated from his person and startled both the vicar and the schoolmaster whom he met on the way home. In conclusion, d'Alibard proclaimed that Mr. Franklin's idea was no longer a hypothesis, it was a reality.

Collinson, with more than usual Quaker economy of words, wrote his friend: "Thou has sett the French to Work."[11] Some weeks later, as the sensational discovery reverberated through Europe and as the British, trying desperately to duplicate the French success, were frustrated by a cold, wet summer, Collinson waxed almost eloquent: "All Europe is in Agitation on Verifying Electrical Experiments on points. All commends the Thought of the Inventor. More I dare not saye least I offend Chast Ears."[12] Less solicitous of chaste ears, Immanuel Kant simply called Franklin the Prometheus of modern times. There was no need to worry about bruising his modesty. When laurels were eventually showered on him, an honorary degree from Harvard (the first ever granted to a nonmember of its faculty), then one from Yale ("Thus without studying in any College I came to partake of their Honours."[13]), then the Copley Medal from the Royal Society, and congratulations from the King of France, he was unabashedly delighted and compared himself to the little girl who was holding her head higher because, unknown to anybody but herself, she was wearing a new pair of silk garters.

But all this acclaim was only to come a year later. For the better part of the summer of 1752, Franklin was unaware that the French had vindicated his hypothesis one month before he tested it himself in June. He had not tried to do so earlier because he felt he needed a high steeple and Philadelphia had none tall enough for his purpose. At last he hit upon an alternative means of plucking electricity out of the clouds: his famous kite. Do-it-yourself, make do with whatever is at hand, operate—almost literally—on a shoestring, Franklin's procedure was as intensely American as d'Alibard's had been French. No excited villagers dashing about—only a deserted field on a rainy night, for he did not want any witnesses, fearful of ridicule if he should fail; no specially constructed sentry box—only a shed that happened to be there; no loyal dragoon to bear the early tedium and take the final risk in his place—only his own William, not the child traditionally depicted in the Currier and Ives prints but a young man of about twenty-two who helped his father raise the silken kite and shared his initial disappointment when a "very promising cloud"[14] passed over without any effect. When at last the loose threads on the wet string stood erect and that first spark flew from the key at the end of the string to Franklin's knuckle, there was no immediate outburst of publicity but a long pause to reflect on the best means of transposing the theoretical into the practical and of bringing the practical into everybody's life.

In September he put up a lightning rod on the roof of his own home. In October, he communicated his discovery to the American world in the *Poor Richard* for 1753. The announcement is moving in its simplicity: "It has pleased God in his goodness to mankind at length to discover to them the means of securing their habitations and other buildings from mischief by thunder and lightning. The method is this . . ."[15] Such wording must have greatly pleased his Boston relatives who always worried that he did not give God enough credit. Even so, the lightning rod met with fearful opposition on theological grounds: "Oh! There is no getting out of the mighty hand of God,"[16] thundered the Reverend Thomas Prince of the Old South Church. Franklin argued that it was not unduly presumptuous on the part of man to guard himself: "Surely the Thunder of Heaven is no more supernatural than the Rain, Hail or Sunshine of Heaven, against the Inconveniences of which we guard by Roofs and Shades without Scruple."[17]

The populace in general seemed inclined to stick with ringing church bells rather than putting up lightning rods, even though Pope Benedict XIV felt the two were not incompatible. On scientific, or rather pseudo-scientific grounds, it was feared that rods would attract lightning that might otherwise have kept its distance or, worse yet, that rods would cause lightning to accumulate in the bowels of the earth until it all burst out in a dreadful earthquake. A little like the inoculation controversy all over again, it would take time. In France, a young lawyer named Maximilien de Robespierre made a name for himself by winning a landmark court decision confirming the right of an individual to put a rod on his house however much the neighbors might object.

As for the Franklin family itself, it must have soon come to consider electricity almost as a new member of the household. From a rod about nine feet high affixed to the top of the chimney came a wire that went down through the well of the staircase to the iron spear of a pump:

> On the staircase opposite to my chamber door the wire was divided; the ends separated about six inches, a little bell on each end; and between the bells a little brass ball suspended by a silk thread, to play between and strike the bells when clouds passed with electricity in them. After having frequently drawn sparks and charged bottles from the bell of the upper wire, I was one night awaked by loud cracks on the staircase. Starting up and opening the door, I perceived that the brass ball, instead of vibrating as usual between the bells, was repelled and kept at a distance from both; while the fire passed . . . sometimes in a continued, dense, white stream, seemingly as large as my finger, whereby the whole staircase was inlightened as with sunshine, so that one might see to pick a pin.[18]

It takes a stout-hearted woman to pick up her pins by that kind of light, and one does not envy a wife whose house starts ringing with bells whenever an electrically charged cloud passes overhead. One spring when Franklin was often away from home, he instructed his family to catch lightning in his phials every time the bells rang and to store it until his return. No wonder Deborah often complained of headaches. Years later, those bells were still ringing. "If the ringing frightens you," he wrote from London, "tie a Piece of Wire from one Bell to the other, and that will conduct the lightning without ringing or snapping, but silently. Tho' I think it best the bells should be at liberty to ring, that you may know when the wire is electrify'd and, if you are afraid, may keep at a distance."[19]

William shared his father's fascination with the vagaries of electricity. A meticulous observer rather than an imaginative thinker, he charted inch by inch the course of a bolt of lightning that had struck a house in Philadelphia and concluded that it did not follow the shortest route but detoured to reach metal fixtures at various points. Franklin was pleased with his report and felt it suggested a new hypothesis about the direction of lightning.

It was hoped for a while that electricity might be useful in medicine for the treatment of some forms of palsy, paralysis, and deafness. Results turned out to be disappointing, but Franklin seems to have worked one remarkable cure on a young woman who for ten years had suffered from violent convulsions: "Tortured almost to madness with a cramp in different parts of the body, then with more general convulsions of the extremities, . . . and at times with almost the whole train of hysteric symptoms," she sought him out as a last resort before killing herself. He gave her "200 strokes of the wheel" morning and evening. It was shock therapy in every sense of the word. She gradually improved. After two weeks he sent her home with her own apparatus and instructions to electrify herself every day for three months. Eventually she could report that she enjoyed such health "as I would have given all the world for this time two years."[20]

Trained physicians were few and licensing did not exist in America; hence it is not strange that Franklin's relatives also turned to him for medical advice. He tried to help, all the while insisting on the limitations of his knowledge. As early as 1731, hearing that his older sister Mary had breast cancer, he, the arch-rationalist, had been moved to suggest a desperate last resort: "We have here in town a kind of shell made of some wood, cut at a proper time, by some man of great skill (as they say) which has done wonders in that disease among us, being worn for some time on the breast. I am not apt to be superstitiously fond of believing such things, but the instances are so well attested as sufficiently to convince the most incredulous."[21] (But he had also pointed out that the disease was "often thought incurable"; and in fact his sister died that year.) To his parents, he wrote that he was not keen on "prescribing and meddling in the Dr.'s sphere"[22]—especially as he himself employed a doctor—but he proceeded nevertheless to discuss the medicinal properties of various salts and to recommend salt of lee mixed with turpentine as the best defense against gravel and stone. Years later, when his brother John was in agony with the stone, Franklin had a flexible catheter fashioned according to the latest model devised by an Italian doctor, and sat next to the silversmith while he was making it to see that his instructions were properly carried out. He also sent John a recipe for onion pottage which he regarded as a dissolvent of calcarious matter.

Long reconciled with his Boston family, Franklin was beginning to act as its head. Both siblings and parents sound a little in awe of him.

They expressed worry about their spelling and style, but he reassured his mother, "I never met with a Word in your letters but what I could not readily understand."[23] He was on respectful if somewhat formal terms with his parents who could see that, while his religious principles were not exactly what they would have wanted, he had not done badly. His letters to them are those of a dutiful son, sending money so his mother might hire a chaise to "ride warm to meetings this Winter,"[24] chatting about the doings of his own little family and the many cousins moving in and out of the area, giving glimpses of Debbie's efforts to make all newcomers feel welcome and comfortable, encouraging his father to set down all he could remember about the Franklins in England and about his own early life ("there was nine children of us who were happy in our parents, who took great care . . . to breed us up in a religious way,"[25] the old man inserted pointedly in the midst of the genealogy).

His father died in 1745. His mother survived until May 8, 1752, two days before d'Alibard's experiment at Marly-la-Ville which launched her son's great fame. She lived long enough, however, to see him elected alderman of Philadelphia. Not unlike Napoleon's mother who would sigh wistfully about her son's career, "May it only last!" (*"Pourvu que ça dure!"*), Abiah does not seem to have been carried away by maternal pride: "I am glad to hear you are so well respected in your toun for them to chuse you alderman alltho I dont know what it means nor what the better you will be of it beside the honer of it. I hope you will look up to God and thank him for all his good providences toward you."[26]*

He took her death calmly, as he was wont to do in the case of older people. He thanked his sister Jane for her continued care of their mother in old age and sickness. "Our distance made it impracticable for us to attend her but you have supplied all. She has lived a good life, as well as a long one, and is happy."[27] Whereupon he changed the subject.

His mind was engrossed with other concerns. The preceding eight years had been filled not only with the quiet pursuit of science but also with a growing involvement in an array of civic projects and in the defense of the country. In the age-old conflict over the best use of one's talents—whether they should be allowed to bloom in unfettered leisure or be subordinated to the immediate public weal—eighteenth-century opinion fluctuated. Franklin opted unequivocally for the priority of

---

* George Washington's mother took an even more negative view of her son's public life, upbraiding him for not staying home to take care of her and openly expressing her tory sympathies during the Revolution.

public interest: "Let not your Love of Philosophical Amusement have more than its due Weight with you," he admonished a fellow scientist who was pining for retirement. "Had Newton been Pilot of but a single Ship, the finest of his Discoveries would scarce have excused or atoned for his abandoning the helm one hour in time of danger; how much less if she carried the fate of the commonwealth!"[28] Jefferson, on the other hand, held out for the private man: "Nobody can conceive that nature ever intended to throw away a Newton upon the occupations of a crown."[29] The opposite view would prevail once again in the course of the French Revolution. According to tradition, the president of the Revolutionary Tribunal sent the chemist Lavoisier to the scaffold with the observation, "The Republic has no need of scientists."[30]

The crisis of 1747, when French and Spanish privateers raided up the Delaware and threatened Philadelphia itself, launched Franklin once and for all into public life. Much as he might protest, he would soon find pleasure in the hurly-burly of the arena and would come to relish the taste of power. His first initiative was to organize a voluntary militia, having cleverly bypassed both the pacifist reluctance of the Quaker-dominated Assembly and the inertia of the provincial government. Popular response was enthusiastic: A public subscription collected funds, women sewed flags, volunteers flocked to the standards. They elected their own officers. The Philadelphia companies chose Franklin as their regimental colonel, but he wisely declined, well aware that his sudden popularity and influence were causing serious alarm in some quarters. In London, Thomas Penn, son of the colony's founder and owner of three-fourths of the proprietary rights, viewed Franklin as a dangerous man: "I should be very glad he inhabited any other Country." But Penn added cautiously that since Franklin was a "Sort of Tribune of the People, he must be treated with Regard."[31]

The conclusion of peace in 1748 freed the tribune to devote more of his attention to schemes for health and education. Some of these schemes were not originally his creation but owed their fruition to his organizing and fund-raising genius—the Pennsylvania Hospital, for instance, on which he kept a close eye as historian, public relations man, and president of managers. Some brought him heartaches—the Academy of Philadelphia most of all (later the University of Pennsylvania), for which he drew an elaborate blueprint (emphasizing modern as well as classical studies), and served as the first president of the board of trustees, only to lose his influence to a high-church faction. Some matured very slowly—the American Philosophical Society, for example, which took more than twenty years to evolve from his original concept of an intercolonial network for the exchange of ideas to its eventual format as a society "for the promotion of useful knowledge."[32]*

Placing the best means of communication at the service of "all lovers of useful knowledge" was one of the incentives, though not the only one, that led Franklin to take what was for him an unusual step: soliciting a public office, that of deputy postmaster-general. He did not even wait for the incumbent to be quite dead before asking the ever-obliging Collinson to help his candidacy among men of influence in London. The incumbent died and Collinson carried out his mission successfully. Franklin and a fellow printer, William Hunter, were put in charge of the whole colonial postal service in 1753. The office was worth only £150 a year, but Franklin was willing to spend up to three hundred pounds to obtain it. Actually it turned out to be a good business proposition besides serving the scholars. After a few years in the red (Franklin and Hunter invested some £900 of their own in its redesigning for greater efficiency), it began operating at a sizable profit. By 1774, when Franklin was abruptly dismissed after twenty-one years because of his political activities, the annual revenue had been raised to £1,500 for the postmaster and £3,000 for the British Treasury, which had never received a penny from his predecessors.

No sooner did he take office than he set out for a ten-week inspection tour of New England. The following year he visited all the post offices in the northern colonies; in 1756 it was the turn of Virginia, then the southernmost extension of the mail service. This and other trips for which the political situation provided ample pretext kept him away from home a total of at least fourteen months in four years. And they were only a prelude to the next thirty-three years that would see him at home during less than nine of them! From the start, Franklin welcomed the opportunity to travel, to see new places, expand his already large circle of friends while improving the haphazard and very limited mail service he had found. Indeed, he thrived so much on his travels that they became a physical need, almost an addiction. No matter how bad the roads or how rough the waters, he counted on his journeys, in America and later abroad, to restore both body and spirit. As to Deborah, she was reluctant even to cross the Delaware. She could only watch helplessly as the adventurous spirit that had lain dormant in her husband

* Franklin's efforts "inspired" a well-intentioned anonymous poet to rhapsodize:
Who bid Yon Academick structure rise?
"Behold the Man!" each lisping babe replies.
Who schemed Yon Hospital for the helpless poor?
And op'd to charitable use each folding door.[33]

for a quarter of a century now reappeared, her most insidious and dangerous rival.

The promotion to postmaster-general proved a rich source of plums for Franklin's relatives. Extremes of nepotism that would be unthinkable today were accepted as perfectly natural in colonial America. The post office was a business and businesses were kept as much as possible in the family. Difficulties arose only when there were more kin than jobs.

Franklin's first appointment was that of William to take his place in the Philadelphia post office; the following year he made William comptroller of the whole system. When the two of them departed for England, the Philadelphia postmastership stayed in the family, passing to William Dunlap, a printer who had married Deborah's niece. Dunlap kept careful records but defaulted abysmally in his payments. His debt to the post office piled up to over a thousand pounds; when Franklin tried to collect it, Dunlap turned on him in a fit of rage, accusing his uncle of "merciless Oppression" and declaring that Franklin would be satisfied with nothing short of the "entire Destruction of a poor Helpless Family." Dramatizing his self-pity, Dunlap offered his heart's blood to the executioner: "Whet your Poynard, Sir, and it is ready for you."[34] Dismissing this "extraordinary Letter," Franklin calmly proposed the matter be arbitrated by "indifferent men."[35] Dunlap subsequently became an ordained minister but was generally considered a better printer than preacher.

After the Dunlap disaster, the Philadelphia post office passed to Franklin's brother Peter, a retired merchant and shipmaster from Newport. Fourteen years older than Benjamin and a man of intelligence and scientific curiosity, he was the recipient of some of Franklin's most interesting speculations. One letter theorized that the earth's water may originally have been salty and that salt mines are the residue of receding seas; another described the best means of securing a powder magazine from lightning. In response to a ballad composed by Peter on the unlikely theme of "discountenancing expensive foppery and encouraging industry and frugality,"[36] Franklin, while applauding the content, hinted that the ballad was impossible to sing. He proceeded to a long exposition of his musical taste, stressing that simple tunes were preferable to complex ones and that modern composers were guilty of unintelligible phrasing.

When Peter took over the post office, he was already past seventy and in frail health. He filled his post loyally for two years and paid methodical attention to records in which "mail" is invariably spelled "male." His death brought to an end a thirty-year spell (from 1737 to

1766) during which the Philadelphia postal system never left the hands of the Franklin family. William suggested Cousin Josiah Davenport as Peter's successor but Franklin replied that the post had been promised to the brother of his fellow deputy-postmaster.

The Boston post office, too, remained a Franklin fief for many years. John Franklin, financially the most successful member of his generation after Benjamin, lived there. He had followed their father in the soap and candle business and turned the crown soap, stamped with the family coat of arms, into a product of high quality. Then he branched out into small industry and started a bottle and window factory in Braintree, Massachusetts, putting to good use the skills of a community of German artisans. John and Benjamin had long maintained a fond and bantering relationship. Benjamin delighted in teasing his older brother (there were sixteen years between them) by aiming elaborate barbs at the inflexibility of the Puritan faith. John answered briefly, hating "Prolixity and all his Works."[37]

When Franklin offered him the postmastership of Boston during a Christmas visit in 1754, John was living in a substantial mansion graced by an unusually rich library and located in the elegant Cornhill part of town, only a few steps from the spot where James and Benjamin had published the *New-England Courant* some thirty years earlier. John died soon after taking over his new responsibilities. He had no children of his own, only stepchildren. The postmastership was assigned to one of them, Tuthill Hubbart, to the vividly expressed anger of Franklin's sister, Jane Mecom. Blood is thicker than water, hinted Jane, who had a son Benny, far more entitled, she felt, to this position than a mere stepson. Franklin did not yield, though he later compensated Benny Mecom with the postmastership of New Haven, and Tuthill Hubbart remained postmaster of Boston until the Revolution.

It was in the course of his 1754 stay in Boston in his brother's house that Franklin met Catharine Ray, who had come to visit one of her sisters, married to a Hubbart son. A classical situation: a man nearly fifty, at the height of his scientific glory, well on his way to political fame, euphoric among his admiring relatives, basking in his newly discovered powers to impress and to charm; a girl in her early twenties, euphoric too on one of her rare trips away from aging parents and windswept Block Island, vivacious, romantic, glorying in the impact she was making on that celebrated man. She chatted away and Franklin listened, really listened. She made sugar plums and he claimed they were the best he had ever tasted. He "guessed her thoughts" and she called him a "conjurer."

On December 30, they set out together for Newport where

Catharine was to stay with another married sister. When they reached
an icy hill, their horses, improperly shod by a dishonest smith in Boston, kept falling on their noses and knees, "no more able to stand than
if they had been shod on skates."[38] Yet they would both remember with
delight, for years to come, how they had talked away the hours "on a
winter journey, a wrong road and a soaking shower,"[39] and in middle
age she would assert that a great part of her life's happiness was due to
the pleasing lessons he had given her on that journey.

What lessons? His later letters tease her about her supposed refusal
to learn ("I would gladly have taught you myself," he writes about
marital *multiplication*, "but you thought it was time enough and would
not learn"[40]), but they also reveal a powerful mutual attraction ("You
have spun a long thread, 5022 yards! . . . I wish I had hold of one end
of it to pull you to me."[41]). How hard he had really pressed during
their days together, how strenuously she had really demurred will
remain forever their secret.

A few more days in Newport, a few in Westerly, and then she had
to rush home to the bedside of a sick parent. He watched her sail. "I
thought too much was hazarded when I saw you put off to sea in that
very little skiff, tossed by every wave. . . . I stood on the shore and
looked after you till I could no longer distinguish you even with my
glass." He could not bring himself to leave. After an absence of almost
six months he lingered some more in New England. "I almost forgot I
had a home till I was more than halfway towards it."

He had barely reached Philadelphia when her first letter arrived.
That day he thought the northeast wind the gayest wind that blew
since it brought him her kisses, as promised, her kisses all mixed with
snowflakes, "pure as your virgin innocence, white as your lovely bosom,
and—as cold."[42]

A romance? Yes, but a romance in the Franklinian manner, somewhat risqué, somewhat avuncular, taking a bold step forward and an
ironic step backward, implying that he is tempted as a man but respectful as a friend. Of all shades of feeling, this one, the one the French
call *amitié amoureuse*—a little beyond the platonic but short of the
grand passion—is perhaps the most exquisite. It is a flattering relationship (where is the woman who wants to be appreciated solely for her
virtue?) and yet, circumscribed as it is, it will not lead to final
heartbreak. Franklin never lost a female friendship. And with his many
reminders that he could easily be his correspondent's father, the woman
must have felt young, always. No wonder the French ladies, quick to
sense the delightful possibilities of flirting with one's own father, called
him *papa*.

His first letter to Catharine is typical. One moment of folly: "I almost forgot I had a home." But it does not last: "Then like an old man who, having buried all he loved in this world, begins to think of heaven, I began to think of and wish for home; and, as I drew nearer, I found the attraction stronger and stronger. My diligence and speed increased with my impatience. I drove on violently and made such long stretches that a very few days brought me to my own house and to the arms of my good old wife and children where I remain, thanks to God, at present well and happy."[43] Saved! Reason has prevailed.

More than once, when meeting a fresh young face, or still better an eager young mind, Franklin would forget all about good old Deborah, intent as he was on teasing, wooing, and teaching his new friend with a warmth, a sophistication, a sureness of touch, an intensity of personal interest that few men could match. But given a little time, a little reflection, he would pull back. He pulled back gently, not in a hasty retreat nor in a disavowal of feeling that would leave the girl bewildered and hurt. When the situation became too passionate, he would simply put it back into perspective in such a way that his correspondent could have no doubt about his desire for her, spiritual *and* carnal, yet no delusion about his being totally carried away. And what can be more unimpeachable in appearance yet more sobering in effect than a pleasant, casual mention of one's dear mate? There never was to be a letter to "Katy," even a flirtatious one, without some reference to Deborah:

> The cheeses, particularly one of them, were excellent. All our friends have tasted it, and all agree that it exceeds any English cheese they ever tasted. Mrs. Franklin was very proud that a young lady should have so much regard for her old husband as to send him such a present. We talk of you every time it comes to table. She is sure you are a sensible girl, and a notable housewife, and talks of bequeathing me to you as a legacy, but I ought to wish you a better, and hope she will live these hundred years; for we are grown old together, and if she has any faults I am so used to 'em that I don't perceive 'em. . . . Indeed, I begin to think she has none, as I think of you. And since she is willing I should love you as much as you are willing to be loved by me, let us join in wishing the old lady a long life and a happy.[44]

Catharine felt no such marital compunction and remembered Debbie only in polite postscripts. She wrote breathlessly, effusively ("Absence rather increases than lessens my affections. . . . love me one thousandth Part So well as I do you."[45]), poured out her soul then feared she had been indiscreet, shed many tears when he did not answer her, promised to reform and begged Franklin to destroy her letters or send them back. He reassured her, promised that nobody would see them but himself; he also hinted that since even the most innocent expressions of friendship between persons of different sexes are liable to be misinterpreted by suspicious minds, he would be cautious, "and therefore though you say more, I say less than I think."[46]

A born coquette, she consulted him on affairs of her heart, sent him —supposedly for translation—the love messages a young Spaniard had written her, with the incongruous result that among Franklin's political tracts and philosophical pamphlets there appears an English rendering, in his hand, of the ardent lines once penned by Don Laureano Donado de el Castillo to his "dear Heart." Entertained ("The Pleasure I receive from one of your letters is more than you can have from two of mine"),[47] flattered ("You have complimented me so much . . . that I could not show your Letters without being justly thought a vain Coxcomb"),[48] he took it all in good spirit, encouraged her to tell him more about her pretty mischief, but refused to help her choose among her suitors, even though he made it clear that he favored any worthy Englishman over the Spaniard.

Finally, he advised her to lead a good Christian life, get married, and surround herself with "clusters of plump, juicy, blushing, pretty little rogues like their Mama."[49] Which is just what Catharine eventually did. The next time Franklin met her she was Mrs. William Greene, wife of the future governor of Rhode Island, to whom she had already borne the first two of their six children.

They remained friends till the end. Even though they did not recapture the magic of that first encounter, the spark never quite went out of their letters, nor their gratitude toward life which had given them that much and no more, the warmth of the embers without the devastation of the flame. To Catharine Ray Greene the world is indebted for some of Franklin's most poetic letters, written in a vein of humor and tenderness seldom found in his correspondence with Deborah and Sally.

V

"Much of a Beau"

... a base born Brat.
—John Adams, *Autobiography*

The whole Circumstances of his Life render him too despicable for Notice.
—Reverend Mr. William Smith, May 20, 1756

Two PSYCHIC DRIVES dominated William Franklin's life: a hankering for respectability because he was illegitimate, a hankering for power because power meant both communion with his father and proof of his own worth.

To be a bastard was by no means as damaging in eighteenth-century America as in Victorian England, but in British law (unlike Roman or canon law) the subsequent marriage of his parents could not legitimize a child born out of wedlock. Only a baby born after marriage might be called legitimate. Was this the case with William? Not only is the identity of his mother unknown but even the date of his birth is cloudy. It is generally ascribed to 1731 because Franklin wrote to his mother in April 1750 that William was nineteen, and William in July 1812 referred to himself as being in his eighty-second year. But this may have been no more than a face-saving date, meant to put his birth a few months at least, if not quite nine, after the date of Franklin's marriage, September 1, 1730. The chief objection to 1731 is the fact that William was commissioned an ensign in 1746, and fifteen seems an extraordinarily early age even in the days of abbreviated adolescence. When he found out about his status is not known; but once his father's political enemies got hold of this piece of information, they never let William forget it.

As if to make up for what he could not give his first-born child, Franklin lavished money and attention on his education. Compared to the struggles of Benjamin's own childhood, William had every advantage. He was not taken out of school after a meager two years, but put in the best that Philadelphia had to offer, first with Theophilus Grew, a well-known astronomer, mathematician, and author of almanacs, then with Alexander Annand by whom he was initiated into the mysteries of Latin, the mark of the educated gentleman. He did not have to skip meals in order to buy books; the books he needed were ordered from London: Ovid's *Metamorphoses*, Aesop's *Fables*, Sterling's *System of Rhetoric*. He did not have to derive all his athletic pleasure from prowess in the water: He owned a horse; and when the horse was lost, an advertisement in the *Pennsylvania Gazette* offered a free ride to whoever would bring it back. Whereas his various cousins were trained as bakers and goldsmiths, saddlers and printers, it was understood from the start that William would never be called upon to dirty his hands. While praising his own father's stern pedagogic methods, Franklin proceeded to behave in exactly the opposite way when it came to his son.

Yet William's home life cannot have been an entirely happy one. Even though they always referred to each other as mother and son, Deborah, it would seem, did not like him. Those were reticent days where private feelings were concerned, but there are straws in the wind. A Franklin great-granddaughter, recording what she had heard from her mother, speaks of Debbie's reluctance to bring William into the household: "the tenderness of her husband towards herself at last overcame her objections and her only child, Sarah . . . was brought up to call him brother."[1] When William was in his twenties, an Englishman from Virginia by the name of Daniel Fisher worked for three months as Franklin's clerk, boarded with the family, and kept a diary. He had been warned, he said, of dissension in the home and those warnings were amply borne out. Deborah and William did not even speak to one another. Mrs. Franklin accused her husband of "having too great an esteem for his son in prejudice of herself and daughter, a young woman of about 12 or 13 Years of Age, for whom it was visible Mr. Franklin had no less esteem than for his son. One day, as I was sitting with her in the passage when the young gentleman came by, she exclaimed to me (he not hearing): 'Mr. Fisher, there goes the greatest villain upon earth!' This greatly confounded and perplexed me, but did not hinder her from pursuing her invectives in the foulest terms I ever heard from a gentlewoman."[2] Even though William did not live at home at the time, the tension was so great that Fisher decided against staying on.

On one occasion only, and that when he was a grown man, did William allow his personal feelings to surface. Accused by his father of having taken part in a family quarrel, he replied that on the contrary it had been the endeavor of his life to avoid such clashes. "I have not only pass'd over quietly what I have been told by others, but Things of the most provoking Nature which I have seen and heard in Person. A Regard to your Peace and Happiness has prevented your being acquainted with these Matters."[3]

As a teen-ager William had run away from home, bent on seeking his fortune aboard a privateer. Franklin, while fetching him back, had taken a benign view of the escapade. Hadn't he too as a youngster dreamed of going off to sea? All boys, he wrote to his sister, get carried away when they see "prizes brought in, and quantities of money shared among the men, and their gay living. It fills their heads with notions that half distract them and put them quite out of conceit with trades and the dull ways of getting money by working. No one imagined it was hard usage at home that made him do this. Every one who knows me thinks I am too indulgent a parent as well as master."[4]

Still restless, William enlisted for a proposed expedition against French Canada and spent the bitterly cold winter of 1746 in Albany waiting for supplies that never arrived, the military leaders being guilty, in the words of a New Jersey commissioner, of "gross misman-agement, criminal negligence, and corruption."[5] Nevertheless, William's martial inclinations, which his father had hoped "would have cooled"[6] remained as fervent as ever. Although none too happy about it, Franklin let him have his way. He noted with some pride that William's captain and brother officers gave a good account of him and he allowed his son to use the columns of the *Pennsylvania Gazette* to advertise a reward of three pounds a head for the return of seventeen deserters.

He was relieved two years later when William's military career came to an end. "As Peace cuts off his Prospect of Advancement in that way, he will apply himself to other Business."[7] Peace, of course, did not end all chances for adventure. Still in his teens, William journeyed to the back country of Western Pennsylvania with a delegation sent to negoti-ate a trade treaty with the Indians. He traveled on foot and by canoe beyond the confluence of the Allegheny and Ohio Rivers where Fort Pitt would soon be built and sat in on the great councils of the Indian chiefs. If the leader of the expedition is to be believed, the villages on the bluffs above greeted the white men with "great joy."[8] William re-turned home fired with the conviction that the way to wealth lay through these vast and fertile territories now held by the Indians but sure to fall to the enormous American appetite for land speculation and settlement. When a friend inquired from London about the American hinterland, Franklin sent him William's journal and referred to his son as the expert on the question.

The Indian trip, however, had no immediate sequel, and William was again at loose ends—not really an unpleasant condition for "a tall and proper Youth, and much of a Beau," in his father's words, now free to devote his full attention to girls and dancing assemblies. As often happens with sons of self-made men, he was something of a snob. His well-thumbed copy of *The True Conduct of Persons of Quality,* still in existence, bears witness to that. Such hankering after gentility was not uncommon in the younger generation: At the age of thirteen or fourteen, Washington copied out 110 "Rules of Civility and Decent Behaviour." These dealt less with virtue as Franklin understood it than with polite conduct, advising against scratching in public, spitting at the table, or cleaning one's teeth with the tablecloth, as well as stressing respect for age, rank, and merit. They ended on a more inspiring note: "Labor to keep alive in your Breast that little Spark of Celestial fire Called Conscience."[9]

Franklin confided to his mother his fear that William had acquired a habit of idleness in the army and fancied he might live on his father's money, "but I have assured him that I intend to spend what little I have myself . . . and as he by no means wants Sense, he can see by my going on that I am like to be as good as my Word."[10] Around twenty, William was sent on a trip to Boston to meet his New England relations, especially his aunt Jane Mecom to whom he was introduced as a "discreet and sober lad"[11] in need of her motherly advice. He made a good impression all around and Franklin received flattering comments on his son's accomplishment and gentlemanly behavior.

This was the period of Franklin's ascension up the ladder of power. As he left the lower rungs, William replaced him. The father had been clerk of the Assembly for fifteen years. In 1751 he took his seat as a member and William inherited the clerkship—much to Franklin's relief, for he had found the job so tedious that he resorted to playing with magic squares and circles to while away the time. He had held onto it nevertheless because it brought so much business to his printing firm. But when William took it over, *he* was expected to remain alert "to everything," especially on those occasions when his father could not attend the sessions. His political education thus started at the roots. The process of stepping into his father's shoes was repeated with the postmastership of Philadelphia, to which the comptrollership of the whole colonial postal system was to be added the following year.

Much more interesting to William with his early taste of Indian diplomacy, he was taken along on one of the most important missions of his father's political career, the Albany Congress of the early summer of 1754. Here he met commissioners from the other northern colonies, Indian chiefs, and sachems summoned to refurbish the badly tarnished chain of friendship and concert plans for defense against French expansion. French sallies into the Ohio Valley that spring had marked the opening scene of what would be known as the French and Indian War, a war for mastery of the entire North American continent. Confined to the eastern seaboard, the English colonies found their access to the fur trade and the rich land beyond the Appalachians blocked by French expansion southward from Canada and northward from Louisiana. Caught in the middle were the Indians, eagerly sought as allies by both sides, trying to exploit for their own survival the struggle of the imperialist powers.

Franklin, and others with him, felt that the colonies must at last unite or face destruction ("Join, or Die" read the caption of his famous "Snake," the first American political cartoon). He brought to Albany his "Short Hints towards a Scheme for a General Union of the British Colonies on the Continent," although his instructions from the Pennsylvania Assembly had called for nothing of the sort. After days of heated debate, a plan of union, based largely on his scheme, was adopted by the Congress. It provided for an executive appointed by the crown and a council elected by the colonial legislatures. To this union the individual colonies would surrender their power to make war and conclude treaties, their management of the Indian trade, and the right to purchase and settle Indian lands beyond their own boundaries. It was a bold plan, both bold and premature, as Franklin and his backers were aware. They pinned their hopes for its implementation on an act of Parliament, knowing full well that none of the colonial governments, with the possible exception of Massachusetts, was likely to approve it, so strong were their mutual suspicions even in times of gravest danger. But their hopes were disappointed: The British government vetoed it on the grounds, Franklin observed, that it smacked too much of popular sovereignty. In spite of the ultimate failure of the plan, Franklin's promotion of it taught his son an invaluable lesson in the art of lobbying.

When the war spread to Pennsylvania, it gave William a chance to display his expertise in the only field in which he was more competent than his father. Franklin was sent in 1755 to confer with General Edward Braddock, the British commander in chief, and William accompanied him. In order to obtain wagons and supplies for Braddock's army, Franklin pledged his own property to upward of twenty thousand pounds—and narrowly missed losing it all. William, empowered to enter into contracts for the transport and commissariat of the expedition, issued an appeal for wagons to the farmers and drew up a list of foodstuffs to be packed; the list shows that he had had enough army experience to include in each parcel two dozen bottles of old Madeira and two gallons of Jamaica spirits. The whole family was pressed into action: Deborah's brother, John Read, served as wagon master and Debbie herself proudly notified Franklin's correspondents that her husband was busy near the front line contracting for military supplies, "which tho' so much out of his Way, he was obliged to undertake, for preventing some Inconveniencies that might have attended so many raw Hands sent us from Europe."[12] The disaster that befell Braddock's expeditionary force, ambushed and massacred, was much less the fault of those "raw Hands" than that of their commander who, despite Franklin's repeated warnings, felt confident that the local "savages" would be no match for "the King's regular and disciplined troops."[13]

Franklin's fiftieth birthday, in January 1756, was cold, wet, and exhilarating. He and his son were in action, building defenses against the Indians around a tiny settlement near Bethlehem, supervising the erection of stockades (which would be captured and destroyed a few months later), galloping over hard terrain, relishing every minute of their joint new life at its roughest. It was good to be away from the women for a while, especially since the women sent warm underwear and gastronomic treats: "We have enjoyed your roast beef and this day began the roast veal. All agreed that they are the best that ever were of the kind. Your citizens, that have their dinners hot and hot, know nothing of good eating. We find it in more greater perfection when the kitchen is four score miles from the dining room. The apples are extremely welcome and do bravely eat after our salt pork; the minced pies are not yet come to hand."[14] A few days later, trying to write Debbie a longer letter on a rainy day but being constantly interrupted, Franklin sent her the compliments of all the gentlemen: "They drink your health at every meal, having always something on the table to put them in mind of you."[15]

In high spirits when she sent goodies, he was somewhat upset when messengers came empty-handed, but not beyond a mock chiding: "Not a scrap for poor us. So I had a good mind not to write you by this opportunity; but I never can be ill-natured enough. . . . I think I wont tell you that we are well, nor that we expect to return about the middle of the week, nor will I send you a word of news; that's poz. I am your *loving* husband, B. Franklin. P.S. I have *scratched out the loving words*, being writ in haste by mistake when I *forgot I was angry*."[16]

All considered, the military skirmishes on the frontier were rather an exciting diversion. But they were about to be overshadowed by a long and bitter political battle within Pennsylvania. By intensifying the need for men and funds, the French and Indian War had brought to a critical point the smoldering animosity between the Assembly and the descendants of the humanitarian founder of the colony, William Penn. Living mostly in England while represented in America by a governor of their choice, the Penn family, known as the Proprietors, tended to consider Pennsylvania no longer as a "holy experiment" meant to provide asylum for Quakers and other men of good will, but almost as a personal domain to be exploited for their own profit. They had abandoned the Quakerism of their father in favor of the Church of England, hence had no religious scruples against a war being waged in defense of the colony but were dead set against paying taxes on their enormous personal landholdings. Their governor had clear instructions to hold firm on that issue. On the other hand, the Quaker-dominated Assembly, because of its pacifist convictions had traditionally shied away from supporting a military force. Eventually the Quakers were persuaded to drop their objections to others forming a militia, but the central question remained: Where was the money for defense to come from?

Franklin, who was on fairly good terms with the governor and had close ties with many of the Assembly leaders, tried to play a mediating role between the deadlocked parties but ran into more frustrations than success. In a moment of exasperation he confided to his friend Collinson in London that he liked neither the governor's conduct nor the Assembly's. The governor's vacillations reminded him of those signs showing St. George spurring with both heels while reining in with both hands, "always a Horseback and never going on."[17]

When he realized that a compromise solution was impossible, he sided unequivocally with the Assembly's assertion of its rights to tax the estates of the absentee landlords. From Magna Carta to the seventeenth-century revolutions, Englishmen had viewed unfair taxation as the greatest infringement of their liberty and in his eyes the inherited privileges of the Penns were a blatant instance of that "arbitrary power" he had started fighting at seventeen.

Thomas Penn, in London, was uneasy. Back in 1748 he had not liked the formation of a Philadelphia militia, electing its own officers, that upstart printer in particular. Now, in 1756, Franklin seemed more dangerous than ever. The new militia was far larger than the previous one, and it, too, had elected him colonel. Obviously elated with his taste of action, he had accepted. Was he, in fact, scheming to "assume full personal power in the province,"[18] as rumors reaching Penn hinted broadly?

Penn was not the only one to be worried. Franklin's friend and fellow scientist, Cadwallader Colden, alerted Collinson, "Mr. Franklin's conduct is the most surprising. . . . I can no way account for it so as to give my mind satisfaction consistent with the esteem I had of him."[19] The loyal Collinson was still more upset when word reached him of an episode that seemed to have almost Caesarist implications. Twenty officers and thirty grenadiers of Franklin's regiment had improvised a parade in his honor and escorted him with drawn swords the full length of his street as he was setting out for Virginia. This was a serious *faux pas,* far too high a tribute for one of his rank—"as if he had been a member of the Royal Family,"[20] sputtered a report to the Penns. Professing not to understand Collinson's concern, Franklin dismissed the incident as nothing more than an embarrassing trifle: "The People happen to love me. Perhaps that's my Fault."* He reveled in popularity and enjoyed power. He once claimed that he wielded more real power than the Penns because he had the "Affections and Confidence of their People, and of course some Command of the Peoples' Purses."[22] But did he really meditate a coup? It seems very unlikely. At any rate an order from England disallowed the militia and put an end to his brief military career.

The battle between Franklin and the Penns was joined. To the end of his days he would be primarily a political man. The shop and the printing press had already receded in the background. He would soon stop writing for *Poor Richard.* The civic projects had been launched, the great discoveries in electricity had been made, the post office reorganized. He now threw most of his energy into public life and in so doing stepped out of his home, first in spirit then in person. Where there had been nothing but friends and conviviality there would be partisans and detractors, malicious gossip and attacks, a constant marshaling of assets. Deborah and Sally counted less, William counted more.

On Franklin's side was the alliance of Philadelphia-based Quaker merchants and German immigrants, an alliance that had dominated provincial affairs from the early years of the colony. Hard-working and prosperous, this group was acutely suspicious of any attempt to curb the rights to self-government granted by William Penn's charter, including the right to tax. On the Penns' side, the Proprietary party was a less homogeneous collection of those who had personal ties to the Penn

---

* Some of them certainly did. An anonymous songwriter enthused:
    Who was the Man brave Braddock did record?
    "The only man that with him keep his word."
    'Twas He, whose name the good and just will sound
    While patriot deeds on faithful records stand.[21]

family or grievances against the governing oligarchy. It made political bedfellows of the Anglican upper class and many of the newer immigrants, especially the Presbyterian Scotch-Irish who felt underrepresented in the government and underprotected on the frontiers where most of them had settled.

Spokesman and chief polemicist for the Proprietors was William Smith, a man who would loom large and sinister in Franklin's life. Smith had come to New York from his native Scotland in 1751 as a penniless schoolmaster but had quickly made a name for himself as a man of letters. A tract of his stressing citizenship in education and the importance of mechanical arts had caught Franklin's eye at a time he was looking for bright teachers to staff the budding Academy of Philadelphia. When they met, Franklin was so taken with this brilliant, driving, belligerent young man, equally at home among poets, philosophers, and politicians, that he pressed him to settle in Philadelphia, soon had him teaching at the Academy, and considered him something akin to a spiritual son.

Rather abruptly in the fall of 1753, Smith decided to go to England to be ordained an Anglican minister and win support for both the Academy and the German charity schools that he and Franklin believed would help Americanize the unassimilated mass of German immigrants pouring into the colony and threatening to swamp its English culture. Enthusiastic reports came back from England: Smith, it was said, had taken literary circles by storm. A more significant and more ominous conquest was Thomas Penn whom he wooed so effectively that the Proprietor promised lavish aid for the Academy.

Far from suspecting that Smith was already embarked on his singleminded pursuit of a bishopric and had decided that total allegiance to the Penns would best serve his personal interest, Franklin had only one worry about his protégé. He hoped that the young reverend would refrain from wearing his gown around the Academy after returning to America: Too strong an odor of Anglicanism might offend its Quaker and Presbyterian backers. No sooner had Smith reached America than an anonymous pamphlet was circulated in England concerning the current troubles in Pennsylvania. It put the blame squarely on the Quakers and the Germans. Dismissing rumors that it was Smith's handiwork, Franklin ascribed this vicious attack to the Pennsylvania governor, whom he was soon to label "half a Madman."[23] But at this very time his beloved Smith was writing behind his back to Thomas Penn and boasting that he enjoyed as much of Franklin's confidence as "he gives any Body."[24]

By the spring of 1756, Franklin and Smith were no longer on speaking terms. The precise circumstances of the break are not known.

Franklin's only explanation is very unsatisfactory: "I made that Man my Enemy by doing him too much Kindness."[25] Having committed an initial mistake in judgment, he compounded it by underestimating his new enemy's power and tenacity. After Smith had taken his stand openly and indulged his love of polemic in another tirade against the Quakers and the Assembly, Franklin snapped hopefully, "He has scribbled himself into universal Dislike here."[26] But that was far from the case. Smith may have drunk too much, failed to pay his debts, and neglected his appearance, but his influence was growing. Soon he was able to oust Franklin from the presidency of the Academy's Board of Trustees (although he remained a member of it) and to impose an Anglican coloration on the institution. This was but the first round in a lifelong duel between the two men. William, too, detested the "miscreant Parson,"[27] who, in turn, felt no compunction about capitalizing on William's illegitimate birth, remarking with supreme disdain that "the whole Circumstances of his Life render him too despicable for Notice."[28]

Early in February 1757, the Assembly, realizing that local pressure would never force the Proprietors to pay their share of taxation, resolved to petition the king and chose Franklin as its agent in England. He agreed to "go home," as the colonists put it. In the eyes of his political enemies, he did not merely agree, he jumped at the chance. They saw his mission as ominous for the Penns and predicted that heaven and earth would be moved against the Proprietors. Thomas Penn dismissed the threat, minimizing Franklin's reputation and potential influence in England. But he did not realize the depth of his opponent's political passion. For all his genial manner and cultivated appearance of detachment, Franklin was totally involved: "[His] face at times turns white as the driven snow with the extreams of wrath,"[29] remarked an observer.

A whiff of real power can be more intoxicating than the joys of the family or the blandishments of sex. In this context, Deborah's loud complaints to Daniel Fisher in the summer of 1755 about Franklin and his son being engrossed in their common pursuits while neglecting Sally and herself are more understandable. She may have chosen to direct her venom against William rather than admit the change in her husband. Catharine Ray, too, must have been taken aback when the man who one year earlier had exclaimed, "Begone, Business, for an Hour at least, and let me chat a little with my Katy"[30] (the "little" meaning four pages) now sent his Katy a brief farewell message, the gist of which was, Begone, Katy, and let me tend to Business.

By the first week of April he had made out his will, a power of attorney to his wife, and left town accompanied by William, who had been enrolled some years earlier in the Middle Temple, one of London's four colleges or inns of court famous for the study of law. This brisk departure was followed by three months of protracted farewells due to the chronic indecision of the British commander in chief responsible for dispatching the packet boats. While her father's frustrations mounted, thirteen-year-old Sally, summoned to his side, enjoyed a few weeks' sightseeing in New Jersey and New York.

William was gloomy. He was nursing his private heartache. Just like his father more than thirty years earlier, William was courting a young lady of eighteen and pressing her to marry him before he left America's shores. But this particular young lady came from a much more distinguished background than Deborah Read. Elizabeth Graeme's mother was the stepdaughter of that very Governor Keith who had sent young Benjamin Franklin on a fool's errand to London in 1724. Graeme Park, with its three-hundred-acre deer reserve, was the most elegant country estate in the area. Whether Elizabeth's parents objected to William's birth is not known—they may well have been told of the secret by Smith—but there certainly were social and political difficulties on the horizon, since the Graemes, being landed gentry and Anglican, favored the Penns. Plans for marriage had been postponed. William proposed an elopement but Elizabeth demurred. The messages he rained on his "dearest Betsy" during those last days are brimming with clichés and flourishes. A sample: "The Morning of our Love, my dear Betsy, has been and is still overcast, threat'ning a wrecking Storm; who knows but kind Heav'n may graciously permit a clearing Sun to scatter those Clouds of Difficulties which hang over us and afford a Noon and Evening of Life calm and serene. I trust our Conduct will be such as to deserve this Mark of Divine Goodness."[31] The strongest note of sincerity was struck in his daydreams of retirement and country life as master of Graeme Park.

Father and son sailed in June 1757 with their two slaves Peter and King. As soon as they were on the high seas their spirits revived. Back in Philadelphia, Deborah, afflicted with a bad cold and fever, poured out her anguish and misery to a friend, moaning that she was "very weak indeed . . . not able to bear the least thing in the world."[32] Sally, a joyous and chatty girl, tried to comfort her. Mother and daughter braced themselves for an absence that was expected to last several months. As it turned out, they would not see their men for a full five years.

VI

"The Seeds of
Every Female Virtue"

My Son is my Son
'Til he takes him a Wife:
But my Daughter's my Daughter
All the Days of my Life.
    —Franklin to Mather Byles, June 1, 1788

EDUCATING A BOY was one proposition, bringing up a girl an entirely different one. The question of the "Propriety of educating the Female Sex in Learning, and their Abilities for Study" had been the very first of various topics debated between the adolescent Benjamin and another "bookish Lad in the Town" when they were both trying to sharpen their wits. The other bookish lad was of the opinion that it was improper to educate women, since they were "naturally unequal to it." Benjamin took the contrary side, not so much out of conviction, as he admits, but "for Dispute sake."[1] His arguments soon found their way into one of the letters he smuggled into his brother's paper under the pseudonym of Silence Dogood. He bolstered them with a quotation from Daniel Defoe protesting the barbarous custom of not educating women: "Their Youth is spent to teach them to stitch and sew, or make Baubles: they are taught to read indeed, and perhaps to write their Names, or so; and that is the Height of a Woman's Education. . . . What has the Woman done to forfeit the Priviledge of being taught? . . . Why did we not let her learn, that she might have had more Wit? Shall we upbraid Women with Folly when 'tis only the Error of this inhumane Custom that hindered them being made wiser?"[2]

Half a century elapsed between the moment those brave new views were expressed and the time Franklin was called upon to put them into practice with his own daughter. What did he do, when that day came, to develop her intellect? Precious little. He did not intend to open up to her the full Pandora's box of knowledge, but mainly the useful, the functional skills: reading and writing—he insisted on proper spelling but did not intimate, as Jefferson did with his daughters, that he would love her less if she made mistakes—arithmetic and some bookkeeping. Much the same assets that Deborah was putting at his service but with the hope that Sally would be still more proficient than her mother. He was impressed with the Dutch custom of teaching daughters accounting, an accomplishment that stood them in good stead if they were active partners in their husbands' business and even more so if they were widowed and exposed to the "Imposition of crafty Men."[3]

Still, most of Franklin's references to Sally as a growing girl have to do with her amiable disposition, her willingness to please, not with any achievements beyond the purely domestic. When sick away from home, he longed for his "little Sally with her ready Hands and Feet, to do, and go, and come, and get."[4] Of his daughter at eleven, he said that she was an honest, good girl, as dutiful and sweet-tempered as one could wish. "I promise myself much Comfort in her when I grow old."[5] Already he was foreseeing the woman who would in fact take care of him "dutifully" in his final years, even though through most of her life he had been absent.

While a pioneer in many other fields, he was, when it came to woman's role, a man of his time. Not everybody in his time went as far as the Philadelphia clergyman who asked heaven to spare him from learned daughters, but a local schoolmaster did feel impelled to assure the public that his curriculum would not prevent young ladies from getting husbands. The goal was exclusively to prepare them for their future roles as wives, mothers, mistresses of the household and—as the most widely read ladies' manual put it with disarming thoroughness—widows.

Women had no place in Franklin's elaborate curriculum for the Pennsylvania Academy (just as they had no place in Jefferson's plans for the University of Virginia), and many years later when his young friend Polly Stevenson showed signs of devoting herself too seriously to the study of philosophy, he warned her, "There is . . . a prudent Moderation to be used in Studies of this kind. The Knowledge of Nature may be ornamental, and it may be useful, but if to attain Eminence in that we neglect the Knowledge and Practice of essential Duties, we deserve Reprehension. For there is no Rank in natural Knowledge of equal Dignity and Importance with that of being a good Parent, a good Child, a good Husband or Wife."[6] His initial delight in Polly's eagerness to learn from him had turned to alarm when she talked of renouncing marriage altogether and devoting herself to study. A spinster, even a wealthy spinster he considered an incomplete woman.

Such a view was not seriously challenged in his day, not even by contemporary women. Abigail Adams, as strong-minded a lady as one could wish, lamented the lack of decent educational opportunities for girls but declared emphatically that "to be the strength, the inmost joy of a man who . . . seems to you a hero at every turn—there is no happiness more penetrating than this."[7] Her feelings were echoed by such achievers as Eliza Pinckney, who almost singlehandedly launched the South Carolina indigo industry, and by Mercy Otis Warren, historian of the Revolution.

Still, there were well-educated women right in the Franklins' own circle. Cadwallader Colden, a close friend, trained his daughter Jane to be such a skilled botanist that she identified a number of plants for the first time. And Susannah Wright's example could have provided inspiration for Sally. Susannah did not marry; instead, she devoted her long life to an awe-inspiring range of interests and activities. She supervised a farm on the banks of the Susquehanna, experimenting with flax and silkworms, was famous for her homemade medicines and skill in tending the sick, drew up legal documents when the occasion arose, and corresponded not only with Franklin but with other prominent Pennsylvanians on business and public affairs. She was well read in science, knew several languages, wrote poetry (some of which was published), and painted creditably. Books were one of her greatest joys and she had a large library at Hempfield, her domain in the wilderness.

Little Sally made her appearance in the Franklin household shortly before electricity, in 1743. She was barely more than a toddler when the initial experiments were taking place, six when the electric picnic with all its pranks was held on the banks of the Schuylkill, ten when the first lightning rod in America was installed on her house. She had no competitors: William was already thirteen when she was born, Franky long dead. The house was warm and full of fun, her father as proud of her as any father. "Your granddaughter is the greatest lover of her book and school of any child I ever knew,"[8] he boasted to his mother. A cross-stitched purse made by Sally at the age of five was sent to grandmother Abiah in Boston and thanks to good New England thrift was still being used—relined—by a relative in Nantucket after the Revolution. (Grandmother Abiah's reaction when she heard about dancing classes may not have been quite so delighted: In her own Puritan childhood the pulpits had rung with denunciations of dancing and all it led to.) Sally was to spend many hours on the pastimes thought proper for a lady of good family, that "dreary succession of hair-work, feather-work, wax flowers, shell-work, the crystallization with various domestic minerals and gums of dried leaves and grasses, . . . yarn and worsted monstrosities."[9] When, in her early years of marriage, she sent a present of American shells to her father's friend in London, Polly Stevenson, Polly, who was much more of a bluestocking, answered almost indignantly, "I hope you do not expect me to make a Grotto or Flowers of them; I never had a Taste for that sort of Work and now I could not find Time to do it; . . . I shall admire their natural Beauty."[10]

Along with her initiation into spinning, knitting, and embroidering—her father even hired a tailor to teach her to make buttonholes properly—Sally's commercial apprenticeship began early. When she was only eight, Franklin's London agent was sending her some books to sell: weighty treatises in Latin, dictionaries and grammars, a few collections of fables at which she may have stolen a look, eventually magazines, and a cask of Sheffield goods. A woman in business was far from unusual in colonial America. Peter Faneuil, the Boston merchant and donor of Faneuil Hall (the "Cradle of American Liberty"), dealt with many tradeswomen, some of whom purchased thousands of pounds' worth of imports annually. In Franklin's own Philadelphia, local directories listed "Margaret Duncan, Merchant, No. 1 South Water St."[11] This merchant had an extraordinary story to tell. She was shipwrecked on a voyage home from Scotland, and chosen by lot, with others, to be eaten by her starving fellow travelers. The Delaware capes were sighted just in time to spare her that fate. She had vowed to build a church if Providence answered her prayers, and true to her word, left money for the construction of the Presbyterian "Vow Church" of Philadelphia. Many of these enterprising women were widows who came into their own after their husbands' death. The Widow De Vries of New Amsterdam, who often shipped out on her own vessel, is a notable example.

Had Sally been born while her father was still active in printing, she might have been initiated into that profession, one in which women played a distinguished role. When Franklin's brother and erstwhile master James died in Newport, his widow Anne carried on the business, aided by her two daughters whom their father had taught to be skilled compositors. They published the *Newport Mercury* and served as official printers for Rhode Island. On the side they printed "linen, calicoes, silks, etc. in figures very lively and durable colors, and without the offensive smell which commonly attends linen printing."[12] Anne had many counterparts the length of the Atlantic seaboard, from the Widow Draper in Boston to Elizabeth Timothy in Charleston, the widow of Franklin's partner there. On occasion, the printer's wife would furnish her husband with a text eminently suitable for publication: Mrs. Ezekiel Russel, endowed with a "ready pen and a biddable muse," turned out scores of ballads on passing events, the most popular being inspired by tragedies and deaths, and printed with a "nice border of woodcuts of coffins and death heads."[13] These ballads sold long and profitably under the Liberty Tree in Boston.

Sally had no biddable muse. Not an aspiring poet nor by any means as motivated an adolescent as Franklin had been, she contented herself with being a sweet-tempered girl, no beauty but pleasantly fair-haired and blue-eyed, somewhat tending to plumpness. She was of such a talkative disposition that her father sometimes resorted to bribes to keep her silent, as she fondly reminded him when she found herself the mother of a chatterbox. Deprived throughout her teens of the mental stimulation provided by her father and brother, she did not push herself intellectually as far as she could have. In the case of French, for instance, she started out with great impetus at the moment of Franklin's departure for England and talked him into letting her have private lessons though Deborah expressed no enthusiasm for the project. Somewhat prematurely for the level she had reached, her father sent her a French translation of Richardson's *Pamela*—but also a rebuff because a letter in French she had sent him had obviously been corrected by her teacher. Her zeal soon collapsed. As an adult she does not seem to have remembered any of her French, in spite of her close friendship with France's minister in Philadelphia. When her boy, studying in Europe, wrote to her in French, she promptly instructed him to relearn his English.

Her commitment to that other permissible frill, music, was deeper, and so was the moral support she received. Francis Hopkinson (often, though erroneously, called the first American composer) thought she had real talent and urged Franklin to procure her a good harpsichord in England. He did. In her music she could be more than pliantly dutiful, satisfactorily domestic: She could meet her father as a peer. The joy of playing duets with him on the harpsichord and the glass armonica may have given her a slight savoring of the thrills William had known in Franklin's company. William, too, took an interest in her musical progress and sent her scores as well as the latest London songs.

He also sent Sally pretty clothes, a scarlet feather, a muff and tippet (a kind of stole), some fashionable linen. Nothing would do in William's eyes if not in the latest mode. When his sister shipped him a pair of painstakingly embroidered ruffles, he thanked her for her good intentions but explained in great sartorial detail why it would be out of the question for him to wear them as they were.

While willing to make his daughter an occasional gift of silk and satin, Franklin was primarily concerned with her spiritual welfare: "Read over and over the Whole Duty of Man and the Ladies' Library."[14] Poor Sally, no force on earth could make a modern fourteen year old read those books once, let alone over and over. But they were among the most frequently reprinted in the eighteenth century and Franklin, who had sold them back in Philadelphia, was familiar with their contents. The *Whole Duty of Man* was a manual for the care of the soul against the "dangers of the World, the Flesh and the Devil."[15] Its seventeen chapters, meant to be read and pondered, one every Sunday, were variations on the theme of duty: duty to God, to oneself, and to one's family and neighbors, including a detailed itemization of all that is owed to parents by their children. Dreary as it was, it did not, at least, dwell on the tortures of the damned, an improvement over the grim *Day of Doom* which Puritan children of the preceding generation had been expected to learn by heart.

The *Ladies' Library* was in the same vein, but addressed to an exclusively female audience and running on to nearly twelve hundred pages of instruction in unmitigated virtue. Covering every aspect of woman's life from the cradle to the grave, it left nothing to imagination or chance. While the author did not condemn pleasure entirely, she enveloped it in so many caveats that it seemed scarcely worth the effort. Even wit could be a curse to women, especially if joined to beauty: "Ladies of a lively active Spirit are very apt to turn it to Intrigue; which, perhaps, may begin in Frolick only, but too often ends in Shame."[16] Some points in the manual must have been particularly appealing to Franklin: its double-barreled attack on idleness ("not only the Road to all Sin, but a damnable Sin in itself"[17]), its emphasis on good works, its stress on the importance of arithmetic for ladies. He may have been less impressed by its warning against music and painting: "The Fancy is often too quick in them, and the Soul too much affected by the Senses. Music especially so softens that it enervates it, and exposes it to be conquer'd by the first Temptation which invades it."[18] Happily the author realized that banning music altogether would give it the appeal of forbidden fruit; the solution was to divert the would-be musician to church music and hymns.

Gradually the air of London made Franklin realize that his growing daughter needed something to leaven the heavy diet of inspirational literature he had prescribed, and he sent her sets of the *World* and the *Connoisseur*, weekly magazines of the mid-1750s modeled after the *Tatler* and *Spectator*. Worldly but proper, they gave her a glimpse of the London that was opening up to her father and brother. The magazines steered clear of politics and religion but otherwise ranged "with novelty and good-humour" over "the fashions, follies, vices, and absurdities of that part of the human species which calls itself the World . . . to trace it through all its business, pleasures, and amusements."[19] The tone was bemused, the social satire gentle. Women's fashions were a favorite target. There were even tidbits of boudoir history (French, of course), but nothing injurious to morals. Franklin no doubt wanted to broaden his daughter's provincial horizons and initiate her into the world that might one day be her own.

It might be her own because her father had a friend in London, William Strahan, with whom he had been playing the matchmaking game ever since Strahan's son was a little boy and Sally a baby. They had been business correspondents for years before they would finally meet in person. Strahan, who according to Samuel Johnson ran England's greatest printing house, was the son of an Edinburgh solicitor. He had come to London to seek his fortune, married young, produced a numerous progeny, and done extremely well, even before becoming printer to the king. Several of the most prestigious books of the century were published by him: Johnson's *Dictionary*, Gibbon's *Decline and Fall of the Roman Empire*, Adam Smith's *Wealth of Nations*. A wholesale exporter of books to America, he was invaluable to Franklin who, trusting his judgment, soon gave him a blanket order for all current works he thought worth sending, omitting only those on theology which he had vowed to steer clear of. Strahan supplied him with general merchandise, too, and acted as his banker abroad, while Franklin tried to collect Strahan's bad debts in the colonies and shipped off to England "philosophical packets" containing his latest speculations along with the crown soap manufactured by his relatives.

Before long business and personal matters were criss-crossing their letters, going beyond the two printers to embrace their entire families. It was Strahan who enrolled William in the Middle Temple, who sent Sally her first consignment of books and a full-length mirror that did not survive transportation on the salty seas. ("Suppress all vain complacency in looking in the Glass," she would read in the *Ladies' Library*.)[20] Half-facetiously, half-seriously, Franklin's emphasis on a proper housewifely education, on forming a dutiful, amiable, modest, and religious character was soon aimed at supplying William Strahan, Jr., with the ideal mate.

When Sally was not yet seven and her "fiancé" about ten, Franklin wrote his friend, "I am glad to hear so good a Character of my Son-in-Law. Please to acquaint him that his Spouse grows finely, and will probably have an agreeable Person. That with the best Natural Disposition in the World, she discovers daily the Seeds and Tokens of Industry, Oeconomy, and in short, of every Female Virtue, which her Parents will endeavour to cultivate for him; and if Success answers their fond Wishes and Expectations, she will, in the true Sense of the Word, be worth a great deal of Money, and consequently a great Fortune"[21]— the inevitable equation of good wives and money. In his letters Sally became almost exclusively "our Daughter," Billy Strahan "my Son."

All this had something of a royal betrothal. Not once was any reference made to the feelings of Billy Strahan or Sally Franklin.

VII

London

Of all the enviable Things England has, I envy most its People.
    —Franklin to Polly Stevenson, March 25, 1763

IMAGINE DEBORAH in mid-winter 1758. She is about to turn fifty. Her husband has been gone for half a year and there is no mention yet of his return. Communication between them is haphazard, at the mercy of gales, captains' whims, French privateers roaming the Atlantic, the pressure of his business. She keeps writing by every opportunity, roughly once a week, but receives few answers. She knows that Franklin and William have landed safely in late July and that they have rented four comfortable rooms in the London house of Margaret Stevenson, a widow living on Craven Street near the Houses of Parliament.* She also knows that Franklin soon fell ill, quite seriously, for more than two months, but that he is now on his way to recovery, though still weak and dizzy. He has told her of the many bleedings he has undergone, the huge quantities of bark infusion he has swallowed, all to little avail, and he has stressed that though his landlady gave him the best care she could, he did miss his wife's devotion and Sally's ministrations.

And now a letter has come from London, a long letter. It is not from Franklin. It is from their old friend, the printer William Strahan whom he has at last met face to face. "Look out sharp," Franklin had written on the eve of his departure "and if a fat old fellow should come to your printing house and request a little smouting [part-time work], depend upon it, 'tis your affectionate friend and humble servant."[1] On

---

* Craven Street, earlier known as Spur Alley, is a little lane off the lower end of the Strand, just around the corner from Trafalgar Square and cheek by jowl with the south side of Charing Cross Station. Neither square nor station existed in Franklin's day, nor had the street yet been cut through to the Thames Embankment, but its proximity to Whitehall and Parliament, to say nothing of Garrick's theater in the Haymarket, made it an ideal location for Franklin during his many years in London.

their first morning in London, Strahan had rushed to greet Franklin and his son.

There is every reason for Debbie to settle down and open this letter with happy anticipation. But it is a strange message indeed. Hard to follow, flowery, convoluted, the exact opposite of her husband's sparse style. Even a more literary soul than Deborah could be swamped by a sentence such as this:

> But as all who know me, know that I cannot help speaking my sentiments freely, on any subject that strikes me in a great degree, so I choose to write my mind in regard to Mr. Franklin, before all others to you, because you are the most unexceptionable judge of the truth and propriety of what I say, and because I am persuaded you will listen to me, not only with patience but with pleasure; and indeed, whatever your own personal qualities may be, however amiable and engaging in my mind, your being the choice of such a man, must add greatly to your honour, to be the wife of one who has so much ability, inclination, and success, if you view him in a public capacity, in being eminently useful to his country, must necessarily confer on you great reputation, and to be the bosom friend of one who is equally fitted to promote any kind of domestic happiness, must as necessarily be the constant spring of the most substantial comfort to you.

What on earth is Strahan driving at? The next paragraph, however, is terse and clear: "For my own part, I never saw a man who was, in every respect, so perfectly agreeable to me. Some are amiable in one view, some in another, he in all. Now madam as I know the ladies here consider him in exactly the same light I do, upon my word I think you should come over, with all convenient speed to look after your interest; not but that I think him as faithful to his Joan, as any man breathing; but who knows what repeated and strong temptation, may in time, and while he is at so great a distance from you, accomplish."

Will Debbie burst into tears at this point? Or will she burst into fury? Will she merely shrug and laugh it off? Will she reproach herself for her invincible fear of the sea?

The sea is worse in apprehension than in reality, says Strahan. In his memory not a soul has been lost between Philadelphia and England. And what a marvelous experience for Sally whom they all long to meet! Finally, after a few more flourishes, he informs Debbie both that her husband will not come home nearly as soon as planned and that some female rival may already be lurking in the wings: "But I cannot take my leave of you without informing you that Mr. Fr. has the good fortune to lodge with a very discreet good gentlewoman, who is particularly careful of him, who attended him during a severe cold he was some time ago seized with, with an assiduity, concern, and tenderness, which perhaps only yourself could equal: so that I don't think you could have a better substitute till you come over, to take him under your own protection."[2]

Deborah must have wondered, as we still do, whether this attempt to arouse her jealousy had been inspired by Franklin himself, in a bid to prevail on her to join him, or whether Strahan, genuinely looking out for her interests though not for her peace of mind, was acting on his own. Could Franklin have known that Strahan was writing?

He knew. He may not have seen the letter itself before it was sent, but he was aware of its purpose. "Strahan has offered to lay me a considerable wager, that a letter he has wrote to you will bring you immediately over here; but I tell him I will not pick his pocket, for I am sure there is no inducement strong enough to prevail with you to cross the seas."[3] As Franklin thus presents it, about a month later, it was nothing more than a bet. And he does not specify his part in that rather crude joke, nor does he comment on it—whether to express hope that it will produce the desired effect or worry that she might have taken it amiss. He simply states he knew all along that the ploy would not work.

Debbie's answer to Strahan is lost, but Franklin's comments on it show that both her fear of the ocean and her trust in his ultimate fidelity remained unshaken: "Your answer to Mr. Strahan was just as it should be; I was much pleas'd with it. He fancy'd his Rhetoric and Art would certainly bring you over."[4] On the same day, Strahan gave some indication that his warning had been more in earnest than Franklin would have his wife believe. He wrote to David Hall, his former journeyman who had emigrated to Philadelphia, married Deborah's second cousin, and become Franklin's partner, "I have received Mrs. Franklin's letter; to whom I beg you would give my sincere Respects, and tell her I am sorry she dreads the Sea so much that she cannot prevail on herself to come to this fine Place, even tho' her Husband is before her. There are many ladies here that would make no Objection to sailing twice as far after him; but there is no overcoming Prejudices of that Kind."[5]

Whether Debbie's faith in Franklin's loyalty was well founded or not, her terror of the sea was neither unique nor totally irrational. The New Jersey poet Annis Boudinot refused to accompany her husband on a voyage to Europe in 1766: Thinking of her children, she saw no reason to "venture both their parents in one bottom."[6] Martha Jefferson hated any form of travel so much she could not even be persuaded to move from Monticello to Philadelphia for the Continental Congress. And Franklin's own ship barely missed being wrecked on the shoals of the Scilly Islands: "Were I a Roman Catholic," he had quipped on landing, "I should on this Occation vow to build a Chapel to some Saint; but as I am not, if I were to vow at all, it should be to build a Light-house."[7] Even William had been thoroughly shaken by the crossing. Two hours after setting foot on English soil, he moaned, "Altho' our Passage cannot, when compar'd to most others be deem'd a very disagreeable one, yet I cannot but be of Opinion that let the Pleasures of this Country be ever so great, they are dearly earn'd by a Voyage across the Atlantick. Few are the Inducements that will tempt me to pass the Ocean again, if ever I am so happy as to return to my native Country."[8]

Addressed to his fiancée, Elizabeth Graeme, these lines, glum as they were, undoubtedly provoked less distress in her heart than the letter that followed, after an inexplicable five months of silence. This long, incredibly callous letter, elaborated not upon how much William was yearning for her but on how much he was enjoying himself in "this bewitching Country." Sightseeing in the English countryside, visiting Windsor Castle, admiring Vauxhall with its lighted trees and artificial waterfall, listening to ravishing music, watching the great Garrick on the stage, meeting "politicians, philosophers, and men of business," all those fascinating occupations had entirely engrossed his attention, so much so that he was writing at two o'clock in the morning because he could find no other time. The heartlessness of such ravings was hardly mitigated by his mentioning *en passant* that he wished she were at his side.

Turning to politics, he played up the part he was taking in the stormy negotiations with the Penns whom he accused of poisoning the political atmosphere. He sent her a copy of an article published under his name in a London paper in answer to the Proprietors' charges. The ideas were his father's but the words were his. Choosing to ignore that Elizabeth's family was in sympathy with the Penns, William blandly asked her to let him know the reaction at home to his debut in political journalism. At the very end of the letter, as if remembering belatedly that this young woman was in love with him and that he was supposed to be in love with her, he added one personal touch: He was sending her, he said, "one of the newest fashion'd Muffs and Tippetts worn by the gayest Ladies of Quality at this End of Town."[9]

Elizabeth did not reply at once. She may have hoped that William's December message would soon be superseded by some other, more effusive. The following May, at last, she tired of waiting and poured out her bitterness in a letter that William did not open until late October, on his return to London from a long trip. It was an outburst of rage. William's answer, frigidly polite, was not sent to Elizabeth but to a third party, a Mrs. Abercrombie. He contrived to place the responsibility for the break entirely on "Miss Graeme," he being the steadfast lover, she the fickle young thing. Elizabeth, it appears, had called his muff and tippet "a gawdy Gewgaw," had branded his political friends a "collection of party malice,"[10] and had protested that she was neither humble nor abject enough to accept him, William, as a partner for life. Affecting not to sense the frustrated passion under those expressions, William quoted them as proof that she no longer cared for him. His conclusion, that he would not mind—nay, that he would be glad—to see her find happiness with another man, was the unkindest cut of all.

While William's engagement was breaking up, Sally's intended betrothal was prospering. The bonds of friendship between Franklin and the whole Strahan family were growing tighter. One of the little girls had declared she would marry only him, another daughter delighted him with her musical abilities, and he thought highly of the three young sons. Two years after the failure of his initial effort to bring Deborah and Sally over to London, Strahan thought the time was ripe for a concrete proposal. Franklin, who by then had ceased even to mention the date of his return, forwarded it to his wife:

> I receiv'd the Enclos'd some time since from Mr. Strahan. I afterwards spent an evening in Conversation with him on the Subject. He was very urgent with me to stay in England and prevail with you to remove hither with Sally. He propos'd several advantageous Schemes to me which appear'd reasonably founded. His Family is a very agreeable one; Mrs. Strahan a sensible and good Woman, the Children of amiable Characters and particularly the young Man, who is sober, ingenious and industrious, and a desirable Person. In Point of Circumstances there can be no Objection, Mr. Strahan being in so thriving a Way, as to lay up a Thousand Pounds every Year from the Profits of his Business, after maintaining his Family and paying all the Charges.

Billy Strahan was indeed a good match. For Sally, then sixteen and a half, this would have meant a wealthy life in a brilliant circle. Tempted but torn, Franklin left the decision to his wife: "I gave him . . . two Reasons why I could not think of removing hither. One my Affection to Pensilvania, and long established Friendships and other Connections there. The other, your invincible Aversion to crossing the Seas. And without removing hither, I could not think of parting with my Daughter to such a Distance. I thank'd him for the Regard shown us in the Proposal; but gave him no Expectation that I should forward the Letters. So you are at Liberty to answer or not, as you think proper."[11]

Deborah's decision could have been anticipated. She remained right where she was. The age-old conflict was being re-enacted: The husband wants to move and to rise, the wife wants to stay put and dig in.

Considering the extraordinary chance Sally was missing, one wonders why Franklin did not insist more on bringing her over. Was he ashamed of his Philadelphia womenfolk? Although there is no trace of such a feeling in any of his surviving correspondence, an echo of it is perhaps to be found in a cryptic line written some years later by his landlady. After Franklin had gone home in 1762, Mrs. Stevenson, hoping for his return to England, entreated him thus, "Doe my Dear sir bring your Beter half and your dear girle and let her shine in this Country. You cant doute I doe not I am shur she has Merits and her name is Franklin."[12] Whether the good lady was referring to Deborah or Sally as having merits is not clear, but she seems to be conveying the idea that Franklin had doubts in his mind as to whether his wife and daughter would be presentable in the circles in which he moved; Debbie, too, may have sensed that she might appear provincial and prove a source of embarrassment.

For a man about whom it would so often be proclaimed that he "stole the lightning from the heavens and tore the scepter from tyrants," Franklin was a total failure when it came to matchmaking. Sally did not marry young Strahan. William did not marry his father's choice for him, Polly Stevenson. One generation later, grandson Temple did not marry Cunégonde Brillon, the daughter of Franklin's closest friends in Paris. Neither did Benny Bache, his other grandson, marry Elizabeth Hewson, daughter of that same Polly Stevenson.

Polly Stevenson. There is no way of telling the story of Franklin's family without weaving her in. She was eighteen when they met in London for the first time, fifty when she stood by his deathbed in Philadelphia. And during that whole span it was to be, as he put it, "all clear sunshine"[13] between them. Polly was the remarkably well-educated daughter of his landlady. Since she did not live at home but in Kensington with an aunt from whom she was expected to inherit a fortune, the many many things Polly and her mother's lodger wanted to tell each other had to be written down. One hundred and seventy of their letters have survived.

They are intensely affectionate letters in which Franklin displays the best, the warmest, the wittiest side of his nature. He wrote poems for Polly, he sent her little notes of tenderness when her own mother was too busy to write, he explained in terms of luminous simplicity the quintessence of his scientific thought. He rejoiced almost lyrically in the quality of her mind, in the words of a friend, "the most logical Head of any Woman he ever knew,"[14] and in his own words, "a Mind thirsty after Knowledge and capable of receiving it."[15] She was only too eager to cultivate that thirst since her greatest ambition, she admitted, was to render herself "amiable" in his eyes. But he drew the line at a certain point: He did not want her to be carried away by intellectual enthusiasm to the point of becoming a bluestocking and rejecting marriage and motherhood.

He always called her his dear good girl—once, his dear little philosopher; she called him her dear preceptor—once, her ever dear saint. When he experimented with a new system of phonetic spelling, his maiden flight was a letter to her and she was one of his very few ardent disciples in that doomed undertaking. When she knit him garters, he proclaimed they were the only comfortable ones he owned and sent a model to Philadelphia for Debbie's friend Goody Smith's "fat knees."[16]

Were they ever lovers? Some historians think they were. They argue that Franklin seemed upset and downcast at the time of Polly's wedding, that when she was widowed he talked her into joining him in Paris, later into following him to Philadelphia. They point to some roguish passages in his letters such as the one in which he alludes to the properties of the Spanish fly or the time he tells her she has forgotten one important particular in her list of resemblances between her first child (his godson) and himself. All this is true but an argument just as strong, if not stronger, can be made for the opposite view. Polly was a prim girl: The only fault she ever chided Franklin for was his coolness toward the outward practices of religion. Her style is demure, worshipful, never erotic; the only time she ever showed passion in her letters was when she met her future husband or talked about him after his death. Could the relationship with Mrs. Stevenson have remained as placid as it did if Franklin had been conducting an affair with her unmarried daughter? Would he have been chosen to give Polly away? Aren't his expressions at the time she marries very clearly those of mock despair? Is there no place in life for the vibrant but unfulfilled?

With the ardent Catharine Ray he had played the role of the mature but still tantalizing male, the naughty uncle. The much more levelheaded and cultivated Polly he wanted as a daughter, as a wife for William. This fatherless girl soon took in his heart the place of the absent Sally, five years her junior. Indeed he lavished much more time and emotion on the London substitute daughter than on the real one in Philadelphia.

As for Polly's mother, in some respects she reminds one of Debbie. They both spelled atrociously but cooked splendidly and saw to it that the man under their roof was well cared for, his shirts aired, his linen impeccable, his tastes catered to, and his freedom respected. Mrs.

Stevenson, about whom absolutely nothing is known prior to Franklin's settling in Craven Street, must have spent her life in more elegant circumstances than Debbie. Her guest, still a raw provincial when he arrived, was quick to notice and adopt certain refinements and promptly communicated them to his wife. He sent home "six coarse diaper Breakfast Cloths," explaining that they should be spread on the tea table, "for no body breakfasts here on the naked Table." Under Mrs. Stevenson's tutelage he developed a taste for fine crystal, fine china, fine silver. Always keen on spreading knowledge, he made sure to include in his purchases some samples "from all the China works in England, to show the Difference of Workmanship."[17] And in a postscript he urged Deborah to put on her glasses and look closely at the figures on the china bowl and coffee cups.

Some of his gifts to his wife are touching in their thoughtfulness: a Common Prayer Book with the print so large she might be "repriev'd from the Use of Spectacles in Church a little longer,"[18] a candle screen to save her eyes, a reading glass set in a "pretty pattern"[19] of silver and tortoise shell. Crate upon crate of quality goods left London for Philadelphia. He shipped carpeting and bedding, damask tablecloths, fifty-six yards of an interesting new kind of cotton printed from copper plates for bed and window curtains, upholstery material, two pairs of "large, superfine blankets," and a novelty, silk blankets taken as a war prize on a French ship. He sent choice glassware and silverware as well as little curiosities, a gadget to core apples, another to make small turnips out of big ones, a new kind of snuffer, some crystal salt "of a peculiar nice Flavour, for the Table, not to be powder'd."[20]

This was only a beginning. He sent shoes, pins, needles, Persian lining, gloves, silver gilt cups unexpectedly struck off to him at an auction, "fit for nothing but to give Drams to Indian Kings,"[21] saucepans bought in Sheffield about which he said he would be very disappointed if Deborah were not "much taken with them,"[22] and much more.

Gone were the days when he felt a pewter spoon was good enough for his breakfast porridge. The middle-aged Franklin, as generous and expansive as the young Franklin had been tight and guarded, sent presents left and right, a fine edition of Virgil to Harvard, fancy objects to friends. It was as if, in love with London, in love with life, he had wanted to scatter the elegance of England all over the colonies.

Ironically, while ship after ship plied the Atlantic carrying the cream of London's shops to his Philadelphia home, Franklin's name was becoming a universal watchword for thrift. The first English printing of *Father Abraham's Speech*, later known as *The Way to Wealth* appeared in March 1758. This brief work did as much for his reputation as a sage as the invention of the lightning rod had done for his fame as a scientist. It fixed his image forever as the patron saint of savings banks, the culmination of the Protestant ethic. Composed as he whiled away the time waiting to sail for England, it was his swansong as Poor Richard, stitching together a hundred-odd maxims culled from a quarter-century of the almanac, all of them directed exclusively to the theme of making money and holding onto it. By the end of the century it would have been reprinted at least 145 times, translated into French, German, Italian, Dutch, Gaelic, and Swedish—later into Catalan, Chinese, Greek, Hungarian, Welsh, and Russian. Franklin may have been surprised to see his gospel of industry and frugality raised almost to the level of Holy Writ, surprised and amused because he had just turned his back on that whole moneygrubbing period of his life. Henceforth he would still be industrious but certainly no longer frugal.

He was even inclined to take a more benign view of occasional lapses in industry. The time had passed when the full weight of his reprobation fell upon the woman who did not rise at dawn or the one who put frivolous diversions ahead of the austere joys of spinning. He would explain facetiously to Polly that her mother could not write during the day because she was "laying abed in the Morning," while in the evening her eyes were bad "from playing at Cards."[23]

No wonder Mrs. Stevenson was exhausted after the shopping sprees she volunteered for or was pressed into. Not only did she undertake the long-distance redecorating of the Franklin household, but she also shopped for Debbie herself: "A crimson satin cloak for you, the newest fashion. . . . Seven yards of printed Cotton, blue Ground to make you a Gown; I bought it by Candlelight and liked it then, but not so well afterwards; if you do not fancy it, send it as a present from me to Sister Jenny. There is a better Gown for you of flower'd Tissue, sixteen yards, of Mrs. Stevenson's Fancy, cost nine Guineas and I think it a great Beauty. There was no more of the Sort or you should have had enough for a Negligee or Suit."[24] In return, Mrs. Stevenson appreciated the comestible gifts from America, the dried venison and bacon that Deborah sent: "Some Rashers of it yesterday relish'd a Dish of Green Pease. Mrs. Stevenson thinks there never was any in England so good."[25] Cranberries, small hams, smoked beef, and buckskins were most welcome. Especially praised were American apples, Newton Pippins in particular.

Was there anything more than a warm friendship between Franklin and the ever-obliging Margaret Stevenson? Did their many years of cohabitation under the same roof (five years at a stretch, then ten) lead them to a closer physical relationship? It is quite possible; people fell into a habit of inviting them together or sending greetings to both. But if such was the case, their liaison remained discreet and provoked no raised eyebrows, no comments on the part of friends or enemies. True, some unidentified rumors reached Deborah's ears, but one cannot tell whether they had anything to do with Mrs. Stevenson. All that has survived is Franklin's reaction, in a brief passage to his wife: "I am concern'd that so much Trouble should be given you by idle Reports concerning me. Be satisfied, my dear, that while I have my Senses, and God vouchsafes me his Protection, I shall do nothing unworthy the Character of an honest Man and one that loves his Family."[26]

The impression conveyed by Franklin's letters of the late fifties is one of intense personal happiness in spite of the frustrations and delays encountered in his political mission. Six months after his arrival in London, he had been granted an interview with the Penn brothers, Thomas and Richard, in the course of which Thomas had maintained that he was entitled to revoke any of Pennsylvania's rights that he saw fit, for his father had lured immigrants with promises he was not legally empowered to keep. In other words, William Penn had cheated the unsuspecting colonists, and "if they were deceived, it was their own Fault." When Franklin saw with what "triumphing laughing Insolence" Thomas Penn not only mocked the duped colonists but defamed his own father's character, he conceived "a more cordial and thorough contempt" than he had ever before felt for any man living. In his confidential report of the conversation to a committee of the Pennsylvania Assembly he compared the Proprietor to a "low Jockey" who was amused when a "purchaser complained that he had been cheated in a Horse."[27]

This intemperate simile was promptly leaked back to the Penns. When he was made aware of this, Franklin did not much repent, he said, feeling it was time for the Proprietors to be "gibbeted up as they deserved, to rot and to stink in the nostrils of posterity."[28] The Penns, it seems, had not sensed the depth of his hatred during that fateful interview and had continued signing themselves "your affectionate Friends." Once they found out what he had said about them, they refused to have any more direct dealings with him. Nevertheless, after three years of debate and two hearings before the Privy Council, an agreement was hammered out by the lawyers for the two sides. The king approved the Pennsylvania Assembly's bill taxing the Proprietary estates at the same rate as other property of the same description, and exempting only their unsurveyed wastelands.

To Deborah, Franklin wrote little about his mission, nothing about the political climate. Neither did he say one word about the plays he saw, the concerts he attended, the interesting people he was meeting. Rather than the pleasures, he tended to stress the inconveniences of London. He described his trouble in finding even a dirty hackney coach in his part of town. The man who had once been proud of pushing his own wheelbarrow along the streets of Philadelphia now felt that the public carriages were so shabby that "one would be ashamed to get out of them at any Gentleman's Door."[29] Such an expensive city, he complained, and so dirty! The streets of London were such an eyesore that he wished to do for them what he had done for Philadelphia's: Clean them up. He observed a poor old woman sweeping Craven Street; reflecting upon the various modes of accomplishing such a task, he came up with a complete proposal involving teams of broom-equipped workers and lattice-bottomed carts for the drainage and disposal of mud. "Human Felicity," he mused, "is produc'd not so much by great Pieces of good Fortune that seldom happen, as by little Advantages that occur every Day."[30]

His description of the city's air pollution strikes quite a contemporary note: "The whole Town is one great smoky House and every Street a Chimney, the Air full of floating Coal Soot, and you never get a sweet Breath of it that is pure without riding some Miles for it into the Country." He dwelt on the miserable English climate and sighed that it was hard to keep warm in bed. He now wore a "short Callico Bedgown with close Sleeves, and Flannel close-footed Trowsers"[31]—a passage omitted in early editions of his letters because the editors felt such details were indelicate or unworthy of a Father of the Country. Jumping as usual from complaint to remedy, he perfected with a sliding shutter the London coal-burning version of his Pennsylvania wood-burning stove.

The chief topic when writing back home was, understandably, his quest for all the English relatives he could locate. On a summer ramble with William he went back to Ecton, the village where his father, grandfather, and great-grandfather had lived, and many more generations before them. The American Franklins saw the ancestral house, a decayed stone building, converted into a school, but still known as the Franklin house. They met the rector of the parish, whose wife, "a goodnatured chatty old lady," remembered a great deal about the family and took the visitors to the graveyard. Peter, the slave, scrubbed the moss-covered stones while William copied the inscriptions and Franklin gathered information about dead uncles and still-living cousins. What he heard, or chose to relate, gave him immense pleasure, offering as it did a multifaceted preview of his own best qualities. Uncle Thomas, for instance, had been a leader. He had "set on foot a subscription for erecting chimes in their steeple, and completed it, and we heard them play."[32] He had found a method for saving the village meadows from being flooded and his method was still in use. In case Deborah had not yet exclaimed, "But this is exactly like my own Benjamin!" he added that Uncle Thomas's advice and opinion had been sought by all manner of people and that he was looked upon as something of a conjurer.

A conjurer! The very word Catharine Ray had used about him! He made a special note that his uncle had died four years to the day before he, Benjamin, was born. "Had he died on the same Day," remarked William, "one might have suppos'd a Transmigration."[33]

In this happy frame of mind, Franklin soon established cordial relations with his surviving cousins, notably a Mrs. Fisher, eighty-five, weak with age, but "smart and sensible," with whom he was so enchanted that as soon as he returned to London he sent her, along with some Madeira, a letter full of genealogical information. "You have taken more care to preserve the memory of our family than any other person that ever belonged to it!" exclaimed the old lady. In turn, she gave him the nicest gift she could, a vignette of his background: "And tho' I believe our family never made any great Figure in this County, yet it did what was much better, it acted that Part well in which Providence had placed it and for two hundred Years all the Descendants of it have lived with Credit and are to this Day without any Blot in their Escutcheon, which is more than some of the best Families, i.e. the richest and highest in title can pretend to."[34]

Franklin also looked up Deborah's relatives—button makers, most of them, in the neighborhood of Birmingham. He gave her an ample account of the hours spent in their company, stressing their joviality and high spirits: "Mrs. Salt is a jolly, lively dame, both Billy and myself agree that she was extremely like you, her whole face has the same turn, and exactly the same little blue Birmingham eyes. . . . We had a very genteel dinner, and were verry cherry [sic], drinking mother's health, yours, Sally's and all our relations in Pennsylvania; they talk of the presents they had received from mother, of buckskins and the like, and one has still preserved a pair of gloves sent some thirty years ago."

So much enthusiasm was generated on both sides that a relative who had heard too late of the Americans' arrival followed them out of town "to have his name put down in my book." And Franklin summed up, "They are industrious, ingenious, working people and think themselves vastly happy that they live in dear old England."

Hunting for ancestors and relatives was not their only summer pursuit. Father and son also went sight-seeing, the father often collecting honors on the way. In 1758, it was a reception at Cambridge with "particular Regard shown by the chancellor and vice-chancellor."[35] In 1759, a trip to Scotland that reads like a triumphal progress: Edinburgh made Franklin a burgher and gild brother of the city on September 5; Glasgow paid him the same tribute on September 19; St. Andrews gave him the freedom of the burgh on October 2. No longer was it plain Mr. Franklin who was thus honored, it was *Doctor* Franklin, for he had received an honorary degree of Doctor of Laws from the University of St. Andrews the preceding February and now bore the title he would be addressed by for the rest of his life. No wonder he would refer to the summer of 1759 as "six weeks of the densest happiness"[36] he had known. Scotland always retained a special place in his affections. Scottish melodies, as he often proclaimed, were his favorite music. Many of his closest friends were Scots: Strahan, the publisher; Lord Kames, the jurist; Alexander Dick, the physician; David Hume, the philosopher who offered Franklin a graceful compliment, "America has sent us many good things, gold, silver, sugar, tobacco, indigo . . . but you are the first philosopher, and indeed the first great man of letters, for whom we are beholden to her."[37] The one flamboyant exception was the Reverend Mr. William Smith, his bitter foe.

Parson Smith had crossed the ocean and the duel between them now shifted to England. Soon after Franklin's departure from America, Smith had become embroiled in a new battle with the Pennsylvania Assembly, had been charged with libeling the elected government, and landed in jail. From his cell he had conducted his Academy classes through the spring of 1758 and, barely released, had gone over to England to appeal his case. He won this round. He was exonerated by the Privy Council while the Assembly which Franklin had tried to defend was reprimanded for its highhanded tactics. Smith put his time and his English connections to good use by scoring a few extra points. When given an honorary Doctor of Divinity degree by Oxford, he took advantage of the occasion to blacken Franklin's reputation and did it so effectively that Oxford hesitated until 1762 before conferring on Benjamin and William the honorary degrees of Doctor of Laws and Master of Arts respectively.

What could Debbie possibly report from Philadelphia that might match such excitement? News from home, even the best-intentioned news, was bound to sound grim and dreary. Entrusted with her husband's power of attorney, she had to carry on business for him—he still maintained his printing partnerships, the deputy postmastership, and some part of the wholesale paper trade. This meant collecting money from debtors which, in turn, meant coping with a flood of sob stories when they could not pay. Except for the letters from her husband,

Deborah's mail was sheer gloom. Rather than cheery messages, the fashion of the times called for litanies of tribulation as if the writers had feared a jealous divinity watching over their shoulder. Illnesses and sorrows supplied the basic stuff most communications were made of, with at the end an invariable profession of submission to the will of God. In this chorus of laments, Franklin, with whom cheerfulness was a way of life and almost a moral imperative (a bad mood, he said, denotes an unclean soul) struck a refreshing note. One of his friends once asked him for a few lines as a remedy against depression: His letters, like his "facetious discourse," had "a magical power of dispelling melancholy fumes."[38]

Whatever time was not given to business was given to good deeds, an activity so completely taken for granted that Debbie could not even expect applause for her selflessness. "I need not tell you to assist Godmother in her Difficulties," wrote her husband, "for I know you will think of it as agreeable to me as it is to your own good Disposition."[39] Whether her disposition really pushed her in that direction or whether she was merely obeying the dictates of the society she lived in, she performed acts of kindness for various relatives, helped at the hospital, and sat up with the sick, apparently unafraid of contagion. (A man sent her a gift of fish for having taken care of him when he had smallpox.)

There is no flesh and blood Debbie for this period. Not a single one of those letters which, Franklin said, gave him "fresh pleasure" every time he reread them has survived, and she is to be found only in hints and echoes. Having refused to follow her husband overseas, Deborah could not even indulge in complaining. Her mood was described by a Quaker friend as one of resignation and "Christian spirit,"[40] yet the friend hinted that Franklin's absence had lasted long enough. She must have scanned his letters for the most fleeting trace of homesickness. She found some at first. He eagerly asked for portraits of Sally and herself, even thought of commissioning a London artist to execute a family "conversation piece."[41] And he expressed nostalgia: "You may think perhaps that I can find many amusements here to pass the time agreeable. 'Tis true, the regard and friendship I meet with from persons of worth . . . give me no small pleasure; but at this time of life, domestic comforts afford the most solid satisfaction, and my uneasiness at being absent from my family and longing desire to be with them make me often sigh in the midst of cheerful company."[42]

With the passing years, however, his writing became ever more perfunctory. Even an event as tragic as the death of Deborah's mother who fell into the fire in the course of a fit elicited no more than a conventional reaction. To be sure, the news of his own mother's death ten years earlier had not prompted a more emotional response. Was it death itself that he wanted to keep at arm's length or was he simply incapable of feeling strongly for people from whom he was separated? His French friends would tease him one day for forgetting them as soon as they were out of sight. It may have been the secret of his remarkable adaptability, this knack of making himself a home in new places, building the cocoon of new "families" when his own was not available. For Debbie, who had spent virtually her entire life within a few blocks of her childhood home, amid old friends and relatives, and whose longest recorded journeys were to Woodbridge, New Jersey, and Lancaster, Pennsylvania, such adaptability must have been incomprehensible.

The fact of the matter is that Franklin could have sailed home as early as 1760. Why he tarried in England another two years is something of a mystery.

VIII

Homecoming, Homesickness

We have often wished that we could put Great Britain under sail, bring it over to this country and anchor it near us.
—William Franklin to William Strahan, April 25, 1763

THE MYSTERY of why Franklin tarried in England two years longer than necessary is probably connected with William. William, who had won Strahan's praise for being "one of the prettiest young gentlemen"[1] he had ever known from America, had completed his legal studies at the Middle Temple, put on his lawyer's gown, and been called to the bar in Westminster Hall. He was a young man of charm and polish, expensively dressed, well-traveled. Cambridge, Oxford, Scotland, the Netherlands—wherever his father went, he went too. His father's friends were his friends. The two of them were looked upon, said Strahan, as brothers, intimate and easy companions. Well aware of his father's extraordinary devotion, William was moved on one occasion to blurt out his own: "I am extremely oblig'd to you for your Care in supplying me with Money and shall ever have a grateful Sense of . . . the numberless Indulgencies I have receiv'd from your paternal Affection. I shall be ready to return to America, or to go to any other Part of the World, whenever you think it necessary."[2]

Now that William was in his thirties, his education complete, it was time to settle him in the world. Franklin entered a prolonged and secretive period of political maneuvering. He could count on a number of influential friends on the Board of Trade and the Privy Council. There were many in government circles who felt it would be wise to strengthen the father's loyalty to the crown by giving the son a position in government. In the summer of 1762, William was abruptly catapulted into the limelight: He was made royal governor of New Jersey.

Franklin never cared to divulge whatever role he had played in the appointment but according to John Penn, nephew of Proprietor Thomas, the whole business was transacted so rapidly that "not a tittle of it escaped until it was seen in the public papers; so that there was no opportunity of counteracting or, indeed, doing one single thing that might put a stop to this shameful affair."[3] Forty years later, John Adams, still sputtering over such hanky-panky, declared that "without the Supposition of some kind of Backstairs Intrigues it is difficult to account for that mortification of the pride, affront to the dignity and Insult to the Morals of America, the Elevation to the Government of New Jersey of a base born Brat."[4]

Had Adams but known, another "base born Brat" had just come into the picture, who would be the only one to affirm that William owed his appointment solely to his personal merit and the services rendered during the French and Indian War. William—repeating here as well the paternal example—had recently fathered an illegitimate son. He, too, recognized his paternity, while keeping the mother's identity a secret (an oyster woman, claimed his enemies with no particular evidence). Unlike Franklin, however, he did not raise the child himself and did not give him his own name until many years later: Officially called William Temple, the little boy would be referred to simply as Temple. His tombstone in the Père Lachaise cemetery in Paris gives the date of his birth as February 22, 1762, but all references to his age in family correspondence point to 1760 as the year he was born. Such was the inauspicious beginning of one who would become the most blindly beloved of Franklin's grandchildren.

Did Franklin know about this child? Did he hope that William would settle down and marry Polly Stevenson as he himself had married Deborah, talking her perhaps into raising the baby as he had done with his own wife? Was it his dream to bring back to America his son the governor and his Polly as first lady of New Jersey? If so, he was in for bitter disappointment.

William, in an unexpected assertion of independence, announced he was marrying someone else. The woman of his choice was the frail daughter of a Barbados planter, thirty-four-year-old Elizabeth Downes, known to his friends as "his old flame from St. James's Street."[5] No document has survived to prove or disprove that Franklin opposed this union, but he left England abruptly less than three weeks before his son's wedding.

From Portsmouth, his port of embarkation, Franklin sent Polly a heartbroken farewell:

> This is the best Paper I can get at this wretched Inn, but it will convey what is intrusted to it as faithfully as the finest. It will tell my Polly how much her Friend is afflicted that he must, perhaps never again, see one for whom he has so sincere an Affection, join'd to so perfect an Esteem; whom he once

flatter'd himself might become his own in the tender Relation of a Child; but can now entertain such pleasing Hopes no more. Will it tell *how much* he is afflicted? No, it cannot. Adieu, my dearest Child: I will call you so; why should I not call you so, since I love you with all the Tenderness, all the Fondness of a Father? Adieu. May the God of all Goodness shower down his choicest Blessings upon you, and make you infinitely happier than that Event could have made you. Adieu.[6]

Never again was William's name to be mentioned in all the letters exchanged between Franklin and the Stevensons in later years, an omission which, given the formality of the times, cries out louder than any curse. Judging by his correspondence, Franklin was to adopt an attitude of correct politeness toward his daughter-in-law, to whom he consistently sent "love," never less, never more, whereas she invariably sent her "duty," never more, never less. In the absence of feeling, ritual will do.

After five glorious years, Franklin was leaving England in an anguished frame of mind. His famous composure, his famous irony and detachment had deserted him He spoke of his "extreme regret"[7] even though he was going back to a country he loved. Well aware that Parson Smith was gleefully spreading reports that he had fallen from grace during his long absence, he compared his emotions—a mixture of grief, fear, and hope—to those of the dying. He stressed that the attraction of reason was pulling him toward America but that his inclination was for England, not a very flattering remark for his family back home. Finally, he consoled himself with the often-repeated promise that he would come back soon. "I shall probably make but this one Vibration and settle here forever. Nothing will prevent it if I can, as I hope I can, prevail with Mrs. F. to accompany me."[8]

The news of her husband's imminent return prompted Mrs. F. to make a last desperate attempt to bring up to date the account book he had given her on the eve of his departure five years earlier. In a fit of initial zeal, Deborah had made her first entry the day before he left Philadelphia. Thereafter, she gamely recorded "a pair of purpill shoes for Sally—7 shillings, 6 pence," "a pound of anchovise, 3 shillings, 6 pence." But she had soon become a little erratic and had forgotten to put down the date on which she had paid the ironing woman or the man who split wood and cleared the cellar. Several pages were left blank. Some entries reflected her state of mind: "laid out fullishly, 10 shillings . . . and generously 10 shillings"; others, her failings: "my cash did not quite hold ought this month," and finally her bewilderment: "September the 1st took for famely expenses in Cash £6.0.0 as I am not abell to put down every penney." In May 1762, she had pulled herself together and recorded such frivolous purchases as "a Blew necklis for Salley and a Jet Necklase for my Selef," and had ended, virtuously, with £6.3.9. spent for "goodeys for my pappy 2 Jars." At the top of the eleventh page, a laconic entry in Franklin's hand: "Nov. 1. 1762. I arrived home from England. B.F."[9]

In spite of the Reverend Mr. Smith's dire predictions about "the diminution of his Friends,"[10] Franklin came back to the warmest welcome. Far from having turned hostile in his absence, the Assembly, to which he had been re-elected *in absentia* every year for five years, now examined his accounts, approved them even though they did not make a very clear distinction between public service and private pursuits, and voted him a retroactive salary of five hundred pounds per annum for his work in England. Such a sum was to be branded as exorbitant by William Smith as soon as he caught up again with Franklin on the American side of the Atlantic; it was indeed a token of the Assembly's faith in its agent since Thomas Penn had spread the word far and wide that Franklin had lived luxuriously in England and embezzled public funds.

Judging by the number of times he assured his English friends that his popularity was higher than ever, Franklin's apprehension must have been great indeed. Had he not disappointed his fellow citizens in America by coming privately to town before they heard of his landing, he reported, they would have met him "with 500 Horse."[11] He was so busy describing, in letter after letter, the flow of well-wishers coming to his house "from morning to night" that he hardly mentioned Deborah or Sally, even to such intimate and interested parties as Collinson or the Strahans. "My little Family is well" is all he ever said. Only some years later would he recollect that he had found his daughter a young woman "of many amiable Accomplishments."[12]

For all the enthusiasm of his welcome, Franklin's letters to England were immensely nostalgic; he talked much of going back as soon as his affairs were settled, "provided we can persuade the good Woman to cross the Seas. That will be the great Difficulty."[13] The good woman, once again, was not to be persuaded. There is no way of telling how prolonged or how intense was the discussion between the spouses, whether it ended in complete amity or left scars. Deborah did not keep a journal and Franklin did not confide. The records only reveal rather contradictory data. On April 6, 1763, five months after his return, he made a payment of ninety-six pounds to a carpenter "towards my House," which would indicate that Debbie had won out and that a new home would root her husband in town. On the other hand, writing to Strahan a few months later, he was still making plans to cross the Atlantic: "No Friend can wish me more in England than I do my self. But before I go, everything I am concern'd in must be settled here as to make another Return to America unnecessary."[14] He may have been ashamed to admit to Strahan that his wife's will had prevailed after all, and that Strahan's prediction—that their separation would be *endless*—had, it seemed, proved correct.

He missed England. Compared to the wits of London his compatriots sounded pedestrian: "Why should that petty Island, which compar'd to America is but like a stepping Stone in a Brook, scarce enough of it above Water to keep one's Shoes dry; why, I say, should that little Island enjoy in almost every Neighbourhood, more sensible, virtuous and elegant Minds, than we can collect in ranging 100 Leagues of our vast Forests?" After the bustle of London's thoroughfares, dusty and muddy as they were, even the streets of Philadelphia, so lovingly paved, lighted, and swept by his civic zeal, looked empty now. Everywhere he turned his eyes, he saw England's superiority. He trusted that America would catch up: "in time you will improve us. After the first Cares for the Necessaries of Life are over, we shall come to think of the Embellishments. Already some of our young Geniuses begin to lisp Attempts at Painting, Poetry and Musick."[15]

He sent Polly Stevenson some of those lisping attempts for her comments and improvements. Polly was depressed. Her dear preceptor had gone to America. Her closest friend had gone to Jamaica. Another good friend, Dorothea Blunt, who had so happily flirted with Franklin, was dangerously ill. Every time something went wrong her mother reproached her for having advised against following the beloved lodger to Philadelphia as he had proposed; but Polly still felt her advice had been sound. In Franklin's honor, Mrs. Stevenson overcame her horror of putting pen to paper and launched into a tortuous missive which started sadly with a description of her various ailments (constant slow pain, hissing in the head), proceeded with the assertion that he would not know his old landlady if he saw her, gathered enough momentum to inform him that she would welcome more American lodgers, went on from there to describe the latest embellishments to her house, and wound up in a burst of good cheer over a cranberry tart served at her table, a surprise and novelty to her guests, due to Deborah's kindness: "Pray Sir thank you Dear good Woman for them and her kind letter not in the common Mood of thanks, but what truly flows from a gratful harit. I hope one day to tell Mrs. Franklin I Love her Dearly and truly."[16] For all their phonetic spelling and sometimes illegible scrawl, Deborah Franklin and Margaret Stevenson shared an *art de vivre* based on taking life as it came, unfair as it was, and grabbing at every straw of good fellowship.

True to habit, Franklin had Mrs. Stevenson running errands for him all over London. She did it with fervor. Along with his requests she sent him bits of gossip, a whiff of the life he had known. Every Monday, he said, he wished himself back at the "George and Vulture" (of later Dickensian fame) and hoped that his friends, feeling his presence in spirit, would order a chair for him and caution one another not to tread on his toes. He begged Strahan to keep him abreast of all the political goings on and to supply the whys and wherefores. Five years away from home are unsettling and Franklin must have felt a measure of culture shock even though he was coming back to his own.

One of his greatest comforts in this period of restlessness was the rediscovery of Sally, now nineteen. Father and daughter played duets, she on the harpsichord, he on the new instrument he had perfected during his years in England and brought back to America: the glass armonica, of all his inventions perhaps the one that gave him the keenest personal enjoyment. An ingenious adaptation of already existing but clumsy sets of tuned glasses, it produced tones, "incomparably sweet beyond those of any other"[17] and especially well suited to the plaintive Scottish airs he loved so well. Both Mozart and Beethoven composed for the new instrument and its star performer, Marianne Davies, made a number of triumphal tours of the Continent. Toward the end of the century, the glass armonica (later spelled harmonica or called glassychord) fell into disrepute when rumor had it that its performers went mad, presumably from excessive nervous stimulation in the tips of their fingers.

Franklin liked to show off his latest brain child. On one occasion, just a month after his return, its "soft warblings rolling smooth and clear"[18] helped relieve the tension of an otherwise difficult afternoon. Mrs. Ann Graeme, the mother of William's jilted fiancée Elizabeth, had come on a visit. She probably felt the need to pay a social call since her daughter had stormed into the Franklin household a few days earlier in a state of near hysteria brought about by the news of William's marriage and impending return. In spite of the bitter exchange of letters between them three years previously, Elizabeth, it seems, did not consider that the engagement had been broken.

What could Franklin say? He used whatever soothing expressions came to mind. Elizabeth, in later years, made cryptic references to some "fond letters" he had written her "when he wished me to have been a member of his family"[19] (letters written earlier in anticipation? letters written later in regret?). Even if William had still been free, the politi-

cal gap between the families had grown enormous: Elizabeth had stood
godmother to William Smith's first daughter, the Graemes were more
wholeheartedly than ever on the side of the Penns. William, anyway,
had already been married three months by December 1762 and it was
pointless for the tempestuous young woman to exhibit her "perturba-
tion of mind."

Mrs. Graeme was relieved at least to be able to inform her daughter,
now resting in the country, that Franklin and Deborah had tactfully
refrained from any comment and that the conversation had been polite
and "easy."[20] Still, as she sat by the Doctor's chair while he played the
armonica, the mother had felt deep anguish, she said, for her distraught
child who in that very room had been so torn by conflicting emotions.
Aside from the thought, shared by Dr. Graeme, that such a one as
William would never have made their Elizabeth happy, she could only
offer the solace of religion. But Elizabeth was not to be comforted in
the conventional way. She went into an alarming decline and her parents, in a panic, packed her off to England.

William, meanwhile, the object of all this commotion, had been happily making preparations for the future. He drew up a will making provisions for his little son Temple whom he had decided to leave in England and entrusted it to his friend William Strahan. He then spent
quite some time worrying about the proper wording of his wedding announcement, to be published in Strahan's *London Chronicle*. A meticulous person, William chose the title of "new appointed Governor of
New Jersey" over that of "Excellency" since he had not yet "kissed
hands" to receive his investiture. Finally, he was able to report
roguishly to Strahan on the great day (September 4, 1762) that he had
"arrived in the land of matrimony and (to continue the seaman's
phrase) hopes to get safe into harbour this night."[21] In an effort to pro-
pitiate Franklin, Strahan sent word to a common friend in Philadelphia
that the bride was "very agreeable, sensible and good-natured . . . a
Favourite with all who know her."[22]

Franklin did not see fit to mention the marriage at all in his first letters after his arrival home. But when his sister Jane, having read about
it in the Boston papers, along with the news of William's appointment
as governor, sent her congratulations, he replied in stilted fashion: "As
to the Promotion and Marriage you mention, I shall now only say that
the Lady is of so amiable a Character that the latter gives me more
Pleasure than the former, tho' I have no doubt but that he will make as
good a Governor as Husband: for he has good Principles and good Dis-
positions, and I think is not deficient in good Understanding."[23]

As he was writing these guardedly optimistic lines, the young couple was fighting storms and gales in an epic crossing that took three months. They had to go back to port once, they rescued the crew of a sinking ship, they thought their last hour had come in the Bay of Biscay, and when at last they reached the mouth of the Delaware they found the river so choked with ice that they could not sail up to Philadelphia. It was an ordeal William would not have wished, he said, "on the devil, nay Parson S[mith]." But his wife, though dreadfully seasick, had behaved much beyond his expectations and seemed "to have forgot her fatigue, as a wife, when delivered of a fine girl or boy, forgets the pain of labor."[24]

The last leg of the journey had to be made in an open carriage. Finally, on February 19, 1763, the frozen newlyweds were cheered by the sight of a welcoming party that came from Philadelphia headed by Franklin and Sally. Elizabeth found in Deborah a willing listener to her stories about the perils of the deep. "My mother is so averse to going to sea that I believe my father will never be induc'd to see England again,"[25] William told Strahan.

Leaving Elizabeth to recover from the harrowing voyage, Franklin and William hurried off to New Jersey, the two of them together as in the old days. Franklin watched his son escorted to Perth Amboy by several "Gentlemen in Sleighs" and greeted by the outgoing governor; he witnessed his taking the oath; he accompanied him to Princeton and listened to an address by the president of the College of New Jersey; he was in Burlington to see William received "with great demonstrations of joy"; they dined with the City Corporation, William's commission was "opened and declared."[26] After fifteen days of traveling and feasting, father and son rejoined their women in Philadelphia. With much satisfaction and not a little relief, William could report that his reception by the former governor "was extremely genteel, and that from all ranks of people in New Jersey was equal to my most sanguine wishes."[27] He had solid grounds for apprehension since the former governor, recalled after less than one year in office, had been very popular, and Parson Smith had predicted the worst.

The first decision now confronting William was whether he would reside in Perth Amboy, capital of East Jersey, or Burlington, capital of West Jersey. He opted for Burlington probably because it was less than twenty miles up the river from Philadelphia and offered a more luxurious mansion. Soon he was learning to walk the tightrope between the demands of his superiors in England and the wishes of his constituents as expressed in the Assembly. London had the power to fire him but the Assembly held the purse strings and voted his salary—a salary he immediately judged inadequate. His first legislative victory was to have it raised from one thousand to twelve hundred pounds sterling per year.

He assumed the governorship at the very moment when, for the first time, all of North America east of the Mississippi had come under the British flag. The year 1763 started triumphantly for England and the colonies. The Treaty of Paris, signed February 10, wiped out the vast French holdings in Canada while returning to France a few commercially important but tiny Caribbean islands. Voltaire spurned the Canadian wastes ("a few acres of snow") and most of the colonists begrudged their military and financial assistance in that direction; but Franklin, as early as 1760, had contended that *The Interest of Great Britain Considered* was to retain Canada rather than the sugar islands. A further consequence he did not foresee was clearly perceived by Comte de Vergennes, then French ambassador to Turkey, later France's foreign minister: "England will soon repent of having removed the only check that could keep the colonies in awe. They stand no longer in need of her protection. She will call on them to contribute towards supporting the burdens . . . and they will answer by striking off all dependence."[28]

But this was in the future. For the present, Franklin was concerned with improving the postal service in the colonies and extending it to newly won Canada. As soon as the weather broke after the miserably cold and snowy spring of 1763, he undertook a series of inspection tours. His plan was to expedite communication between Boston and New York (as he had already done between New York and Philadelphia) by making the mails travel by night as well as by day, a novelty for America. Whereas it had taken three weeks for a man writing from Philadelphia to receive an answer from Boston, Franklin figured that with the new system it would take only six days. His superiors in London were also clamoring for the drawing of detailed maps. After a month in Virginia, he came back to Philadelphia, tried to talk Debbie into accompanying him to New England and, failing as usual to dislodge her from home, took off on an extended trip with Sally and his fellow postmaster-general. To Strahan, who had teased him for becoming sedentary, he emphasized that the itinerary of his postal inspection was to cover some 1,780 miles.

The trip started splendidly in early June 1763 with a stay in New Jersey. The governor and his lady took Sally on an expedition to the Passaic Falls and included her in various social functions while her father carried on his business. Still dreaming about England, Franklin stole "a spare half hour" to send a brief message to Polly: "The Ease, the Smoothness, the Purity of Diction, and Delicacy of Sentiment that

always appear in your Letters never fail to delight me; but the tender
filial Regard you constantly express for your old Friend is particularly
engaging."[29] To Deborah he wrote that she was welcome to open all
the mail that would arrive from England "as it must give you Pleasure
to see that People who knew me there so long and so intimately retain
so sincere a Regard for me."[30]

From New York, father and daughter proceeded by packet boat to
Newport, skipping Connecticut because the July weather was too hot.
(Legends nevertheless have sprung up in several Connecticut towns
which would have Franklin traveling through them with Sally, laying
milestones along Route 1 and performing useful deeds as he went.) In
Newport they visited Ezra Stiles, future president of Yale, whom they
found greatly relieved because his three thousand silkworms had just
surmounted a distemper in the course of which "they lost Appetite, became livid or rather purple, and seemed irrevocably lost."[31] Now the
worms were beginning to cocoon and had turned so voracious that
Stiles and his slave had all they could manage to procure the five bush-
els of mulberry leaves needed for their daily diet.

The next stop in Rhode Island was with Catharine Ray whom
Franklin had not seen since their carefree encounter in Boston eight
years earlier. Catharine had become Mrs. Greene and the mother of
two little girls. Was it an anticlimax for both of them, this friendship in
a sober key? To make it worse, Catharine had to nurse him instead of
flirting with him, for shortly before reaching her house he suffered a
bad fall and dislocated his shoulder. Still, the visit had its charm and
Sally would have loved to stay longer but her father was pressing on to
Massachusetts. It was in his native Boston that she celebrated her twen-
tieth birthday.

Going back to Boston . . . He had done it so often, somewhat richer,
somewhat more important and famous every time. But each time there
had been fewer of his relatives to greet him. Gone were his father and
mother; they had both lived into their eighties and he had seen to it
that a proper inscription in the Old Granary burial ground immor-
talized their virtues and his filial piety. Gone was brother Josiah, lost at
sea so many years ago; gone was sister Ann Harris and gone, too, sister
Mary Homes whose husband had discovered the runaway Benjamin in
Philadelphia and talked him into getting in touch with his family.
Mary had worried in her day about "not writing polite enough" but
Benjamin had reassured her, protesting that politeness was not "necessary to make Letters between Brothers and Sisters agreeable."[32] Gone
was brother James whose apprentice he had been. Gone, so young,
James's son, that Jemmy to whom he, in turn, had taught the art of

printing. Gone was sister Sarah Davenport, the first to reopen correspondence with him after he had left the paternal roof; she was the next oldest to Benjamin, probably entrusted with his care when they were little.

All his half-brothers and half-sisters had died. He had never called them "half," of course. He would always refer to them as brothers and sisters, just as a son-in-law was called son and a sister-in-law sister. The all-embracing family of the eighteenth century had no use for the legalistic little hedges that the modern mind erects between its members. The last survivor of that early group had been Elizabeth, better known as sister Douse, born twenty-eight years before Benjamin. When sister Douse, a widow, was turning old and infirm, it was suggested that for the sake of economy her furniture should be sold and she be put to board in someone's house. But Franklin would have none of it: "As having their own Way is one of the greatest Comforts of Life to old People, I think their Friends should endeavour to accommodate them in that as well as in anything else. When they have long liv'd in a House, it becomes natural to them, they are almost as closely connected with it as the Tortoise with his Shell, they die if you tear them out of it. Old Folks and old Trees, if you remove them, 'tis ten to one that you kill them. So let our good old Sister be no more importun'd on that head."[33] Sister Douse was allowed to live out her days in the relative comfort of the little house on Unity Street; she survived just long enough to hear that Franklin had met in England a relative of theirs who remembered her as a little girl sailing away with her parents.

Even sister Lydia Scott who was younger than he had died while he was away. And his brother John in whose comfortable house he had stayed on his previous visit—a visit made so joyous by Catharine Ray and her young friends—had succumbed to his painful kidney malady. Of the thirteen siblings that Franklin remembered sitting around the family table, there remained but three: Peter, whom he now visited in Newport and to whom he offered the postmastership of Philadelphia (just as he had offered the Boston postmastership to John eight years earlier), Jane Mecom, and himself. "As our Number diminishes, let our Affection to each other rather increase"[34] he had written to Jane. He planned to spend most of the summer with her. Sally was to lodge with their cousin Jonathan Williams, "as there is a Harpsichord and I would not have her lose her Practice; and then I shall be more with my dear Sister."[35]

IX

Faith or Deeds?

Serving God is doing good to Man, but praying is thought
an easier Service and therefore more easily chosen.
—Poor Richard, 1753

JANE HAD ALWAYS BEEN his "peculiar favorite"[1] and remained so for the
more than sixty years that they corresponded. He was the youngest of
the Franklin boys, she was the youngest of the girls, and they outlived
all the others. Separated from the older children by a gap of several
years, Benjamin, Lydia, and Jane made up the last unit of the enormous family. Lydia seems to have been colorless, but Benjamin and
Jane were of the same cast: intelligent, vital, unsinkable. In her seventies, after a life of drudgery in the course of which she had buried
eleven of her twelve children and a large number of grandchildren, had
been forced to flee her home during the Revolution, and was currently
struggling to support the ne'er-do-well husband of her only surviving
daughter, she remarked with a touch of wonder, "I am still cheerful for
that is my natural temper."[2]

They were alike in many ways, Jane and Benjamin, but where he
had managed to rise, she never had a chance. Married at fifteen to an
almost illiterate saddler, Edward Mecom, whose health was always
shaky, whose children were afflicted with a mysterious languor. Was it
tuberculosis? Was it syphilis? Did she mean to imply anything when
she commented that her husband had suffered much by "sin and sorrow,"[3] or was she merely using a Puritan formula? She wanted so
much to stretch her mind, to read, to converse, but she was forever
cramped, spiritually and physically, squeezed in for years in her parents' house where she nursed the old and tended the young, then in
her own home where poverty compelled her to take in lodgers.

Jane had a huge source of strength, her faith, and a huge source of
joy, her brother Benjamin. He never let her down. He gave her much
more than the money, clothes, flour, and wood recorded in their letters.

He gave her a feeling of her own importance and of the very real need he had "of her good opinion." Their correspondence is woven with all the threads of the brother-sister relationship: a rough, teasing loyalty; an undercurrent of squabbling; a shared nostalgia for the world of their childhood, that scented world of soap and candles, of secret family recipes for dyeing silk. They both had a drive to dominate, transmuted on his part into an urge to protect, on hers into a fretful wish to interfere, criticize, and reform. Not an easy woman to deal with, Jane, in spite of her adoration for him: She was emotional and possessive, demanding yet worried about giving offense, quick to take offense herself where none was meant—"miffy," as he said. For Franklin, visiting her was a bittersweet experience, a return to the Boston he had fled, the childhood he had transcended, the ideals of the parents he had honored but not really listened to. The bone of contention between them was always the same: faith.

Having lost the faith of his childhood, he had come close to atheism, then moved back to a sort of ethically fortified deism, optimistic and comfortable. This was not enough to satisfy the more committed Christians among his friends, such as the chemist Joseph Priestley who regretted that Franklin used his great influence to make unbelievers of others. Stung by the reproach, Franklin promised to do some serious theological reading, provided the works were not too long.

Like many spirits of the Enlightenment, he had become more concerned with the definition and achievement of virtue than with salvation, preoccupied not so much with the City of God as with the City of Man. Franklin's God created and governed the universe, but man was exuberantly his own master while on earth. Though he maintained he believed in God and had composed his personal liturgy, he was lukewarm about church attendance, at least as far as he himself was concerned, feeling that the sermons were meant "rather to make us Presbyterians than good Citizens." (Franklin always referred to his family as Presbyterians although they were, strictly speaking, Congregationalists. In New England, both groups were lumped under the rubric "Puritan" and both took their theological inspiration from John Calvin but divided on questions of church government and organization.)

In late life Franklin stretched his tolerance to embrace any form of honest dissent: "I think all the heretics I have known have been virtuous men. They have the virtue of fortitude, or they would not venture to own their heresy; and they cannot afford to be deficient in any of the other virtues, as that would give advantage to their many enemies; and they have not, like orthodox sinners, such a number of friends to excuse or justify them."[4]

But his parents' religion, and Jane's, was rooted in the Puritanism of the previous century. Not for them the rational humanism of the new age or its broad-minded deism. In the face of heresies on all sides, Puritan theologians were walking a fine line in declaring on the one hand that man could do nothing to earn grace, which was entirely the gift of God, while on the other insisting that good deeds would naturally follow the bestowal of grace. Much as Franklin's relatives deferred to his intelligence and admired his worldly success, they could not keep silent about the serious errors that threatened his soul.

When his parents voiced their worry about a possible lapse in his spiritual values, he defended himself with all the respect of a dutiful son. Hearing in his early thirties that mother Abiah grieved because "one of her sons is an Arian, another an Arminian," he apologized for the uneasiness he had caused: "If it were a thing possible for one to alter his opinions in order to please another, I know none whom I ought more willingly to oblige in that respect than yourselves. But, since it is no more in a Man's Power to *think* than to *look* like another, methinks all that should be expected from me is to keep my Mind open to conviction. . . . In the mean time your Care and Concern for me is what I am very thankful for." He assured her that the Freemasons were "a very harmless sort of People" (though they might be wrong in refusing admission to women) and claimed that he hardly knew what Arians and Arminians were. Whereupon he unwittingly demonstrated his ignorance of those fine theological points by quoting Scripture to the effect that "at the last day we shall not be examin'd what we *thought*, but what we *did* . . . to our Fellow Creatures,"[5] which is precisely what the heresy of Arminius was about. It consisted in believing that good works could be an inducement for God to bestow His saving grace.* Abiah, however, remembering perhaps that her own father had defended liberty of conscience for Quakers and Anabaptists against intolerant orthodoxy, was reassured by her son's letter and expressed her satisfaction.

When it came to his brother John, Franklin could indulge more freely in poking fun at New England righteousness. In 1745, a volunteer force from Massachusetts besieged the French fortress of Louisbourg, in Canada, and a day of fast and prayer was ordered in support of the expedition. Franklin computed that five hundred thousand special "petitions" from New England, added to the prayers of every fam-

---

* Even though Franklin was sufficiently familiar with the Bible to invent a "new" chapter of Genesis that fooled many of his friends, William Robertson, principal of the University of Edinburgh, remarked, "Theology, I believe, is of all the Sciences the only one in which I suspect he is not perfectly sound."[6]

ily morning and evening and multiplied by the number of days since January 25, made forty-five million prayers, "which, set against the prayers of a few priests in the garrison to the Virgin Mary gave a vast balance in your favor. If you do not succeed, I fear I shall have but an indifferent opinion of Presbyterian prayers in such cases." Back to his favorite theme: "Indeed, in attacking strong towns I should have more dependence on *works* than on *faith*."[7] (Whether by faith or works, the volunteers did conquer that "citadel of Popish darkness,"[8] as it was called by the clergyman who preached the first Protestant sermon in captured Louisbourg.)

Franklin simply could not share the vehement hatred of Catholicism that was an article of political and religious faith among contemporary Protestants. Twitting an old friend about the rigidity of Puritanism still surviving in mid-century Connecticut—no travel on the Sabbath, no form of amusement whatsoever—he described the earthy *joie de vivre* of a Sunday in Flanders: "In the Afternoon both high and low went to the Play or the Opera, where there was plenty of Singing, Fiddling and Dancing. I look'd round for God's Judgments but saw no Signs of them. The Cities were well built and full of Inhabitants, the Markets fill'd with Plenty, the People well favour'd and well clothed; the Fields well till'd; the Cattle fat and strong; the Fences, Houses and Windows all in Repair." All of which made him suspect that the "Deity is not so angry at that Offense as a New England Justice."[9]

He could joke this way with John or some of his friends but not so easily with Jane who clung tenaciously to the Puritanism of her parents, unaffected by new currents in eighteenth-century Boston. One of Franklin's earliest extant letters to his sister, written right after a visit to her in 1743, contains the essence of their lifelong debate. In answer to an "admonition" from Jane, he vehemently denied that he was "against worshipping of God" and that he believed good works alone would merit Heaven. Then he pleaded for tolerance: "There are some things in your New England Doctrines and Worship which I do not agree with, but I do not therefore condemn them, or desire to shake your Belief or Practice of them." But in the end he could not refrain from slipping in a few words in support of good works: "When you judge of others, if you can perceive the Fruit to be good, don't terrify yourself that the Tree may be evil . . . for you know who has said, *Men do not gather Grapes of Thorns or Figs of Thistles*."[10] None of this did much to convince Jane. Even poor Debbie, who had imprudently praised good works, was suspected of having meant to hurt the feelings of the Boston relatives she had never met.

The biblical theme of the tree to be judged by its fruit is one that

Franklin would come back to in earnest. Writing in full maturity to an obscure "zealous religionist," he spelled out the intensity of his commitment to the public good and formulated his credo:

"I wish [faith] were more productive of Good Works than I have generally seen it; I mean real good Works, Works of Kindness, Charity, Mercy and Publick Spirit; not Holiday-keeping, Sermon-Reading or Hearing, performing Church Ceremonies, or making long Prayers, fill'd with Flatteries and Compliments, despis'd even by wise Men, and much less capable of pleasing the Deity. The Worship of God is a Duty, the hearing and reading of Sermons may be useful; but if Men rest in Hearing and Praying, as too many do, it is as if a Tree should value itself on being water'd and putting forth Leaves, tho' it never produc'd any Fruit."[11]

Did he imagine at some point that Jane was relenting? Or was it the freer climate of London and the fact that their mother was dead six years now and beyond offense? He thought the time had come for a little levity and raised the topic again in a flippant mood. Under the guise of playful comment upon a pietistic short poem written by their Uncle Benjamin and brought to his attention by one of their English relatives, he teased his "dearly beloved Jenny" about choosing to stress the lowest of the three theological virtues—faith—instead of reaching for the third step on the ladder—charity. Kind words, he asserted, "are the rank Growth of every Soil, and choke the good Plants of Benevolence and Beneficence." As if all this were not shocking enough, he reminded Jane of a distich they had learned in their childhood: "A Man of Words and not of Deeds/Is like a Garden full of Weeds," and supposed that a bigot might invert it to read, "A Man of Deeds and not of Words Is like a Garden full of . . ." "I have forgot the Rhime," he concluded, "but remember 'tis something the very Reverse of Perfume."[12]

Jane's reaction, now lost, must have been such a howl of protest that sixteen months later Franklin was still apologizing and insisting that he had "not meant any personal Censure on you or any body. If anything, it was a general Reflection on our Sect; we zealous Presbyterians being too apt to think ourselves alone in the right, and that besides all the Heathens, Mahometans and Papists, whom we give to Satan in a lump, other Sects of Christian Protestants that do not agree with us, will hardly escape Perdition."[13]

They never found a meeting ground in religion; still they remained immensely fond of each other, and Franklin's tone grew more gentle as Jane's life grew more tragic. He enjoyed doing favors for his relatives and playing the patriarch—a compensation perhaps for having been the youngest—and Jane's family was the greatest beneficiary of his paternalism. It was certainly needed in their case.

Of Jane's four daughters, one had died as a baby. The other three were still living at the time of Franklin's visit in 1763, but the health of Sarah was already impaired. Within a year she would be dead, at the age of twenty-seven, leaving four small children to her mother's care. The two younger girls were at home, Polly languishing but keeping her symptoms to herself, and Jenny, the one who would eventually outlive all the others, exasperating her parents by what was interpreted as moods and laziness while it probably indicated depression and disease.

Of Jane's eight sons, four had already died: James and Josiah in infancy; Edward, a saddler, at twenty-seven; Ebenezer, a baker, also at twenty-seven. What was unusual was not the mortality rate—only two of Jefferson's seven children survived infancy, only two of Cotton Mather's fifteen outlived their father—but the fact that Jane had to watch most of her children go into a long decline before they died in their twenties.

The four surviving sons were far from contented and prosperous. Only one was living at home, Josiah (a second Josiah), who had been trained as a saddler and helped his father. John, a goldsmith, had established himself in New York. He was estranged from his family—out of touch to the point of unwittingly getting married on the very day of his father's death two years later. John Mecom's health, too, failed early and he spent some miserable years in Philadelphia living more or less off Debbie, who must have been known in the family as a soft heart, though possibly a sharp tongue.

On the other two sons, Peter and Benjamin, the hopes of the Mecom family had once rested. Those two seemed endowed with more brains and vitality. They had been raised by prosperous uncles who gave them a better start in life. They both ended insane—crushed perhaps by the futility of their efforts to meet unattainable goals, more probably by some hereditary flaw in the family.

Peter had been apprenticed to his uncle John Franklin who taught him the family trade of tallow chandling and initiated him into the secrets of making crown soap. He was considered lucky: Uncle John was the wealthiest of the Boston Franklins, seemed fond of him, and did not forget him in his will. The uncle died when Peter Mecom was not quite seventeen, but Peter's portion was to come to him only after his aunt's death. He soon quarreled with her, left her house, and joined another soap boiler to whom he revealed the precious recipe for crown soap. Within months, John Franklin's widow advertised in the Boston papers that some impostor was passing off as crown soap a product vastly inferior in quality, and that the only true crown soap was carried by her, Mrs. Elizabeth Franklin. A bitter family feud ensued, in which Jane took up the cudgels for her son and put pressure on Franklin to back up his own blood against those nasty in-laws. But Franklin, who was in New York at the time, waiting for his ship to sail for England, turned her down. "Above all things I dislike family quarrels, and when they happen among my relations, nothing gives me more pain. . . . What can I say between you, but that I wish you were reconciled, and that I will love that side best that is most ready to forgive and oblige the other."[14]

Peter Mecom did not stay long with soapmaking anyway. At the age of twenty-two he was showing signs of mental disturbance judged at first by his family to denote a lack of willpower. By the time of Franklin's 1763 visit, poor Peter had already been sent to the country as a helpless boarder in a woman's home. He was to vegetate there for eighteen years, Franklin footing the bill.

Even Benny, the smartest of the Mecom boys, was becoming by 1763 a source of worry. At age thirteen, he had been apprenticed to Franklin's partner in New York, James Parker, and advised "to be very cheerful and ready to do everything he is bid, and endeavour to oblige everybody, for that is the true way to get friends."[15] At that time (1745) his mother may well have hoped that Benjamin, her third son, might eventually prove that he bore worthily the same name as his brilliant uncle.

He certainly showed no inclination to be cheerful. Soon he complained to Jane and to third parties that he was being ill-used. He had not been properly taken care of when afflicted with smallpox; he was not provided with decent clothes; he was sent on petty errands; indeed, he was so unhappy that he had tried to run off to sea on a privateer. Thrown into a panic by this last piece of news, Jane appealed to Franklin. His answer, a long letter meant to reassure her, shows how the middle-aged man can minimize the problems of the adolescent he once was. Boys are just given to fretting, he said, witness his other nephew Jemmy who was never satisfied with the clothes given him when he was Franklin's apprentice. (Being the only item the apprentice received for his work, clothes inevitably became a point of friction.) Benny might well have had his own purpose in mind when he alleged that Parker was not outfitting him properly:

> I heard both his master and mistress call upon him on Sunday morning to
> get ready to go to meeting, and tell him of his frequently delaying and shuf-
> fling till it was too late, and he made not the least objection about his clothes.
> I did not think it anything extraordinary that he should be sometimes will-

ing to evade going to meeting, for I believe it is the case with all boys, or almost all. I have brought up four or five myself, and have frequently observed that if their shoes were bad they would say nothing of a new pair till Sunday morning, just as the bell rung, when, if you asked them why they did not get ready, the answer was prepared: "I have no shoes" and so of other things, hats and the like; or if they know of anything that wanted mending, it was a secret till Sunday morning, and sometimes I believe they would rather tear a little than be without the excuse.

Whereupon he proceeded to counterattack and to list some of Parker's grievances, without ever mentioning, however, that Parker in his youth had run away from his own master just as he, Franklin, had. Benny, it appeared, was staying out nights, sometimes all night, refusing to give an account of where he spent his time or in what company. This was something that Jane had been aware of, said Franklin, but had not related. He felt it was quite proper, indeed indispensable for Parker to chastise his apprentice. "If he was my son, I should think his master did not do his duty by him if he omitted it, for to be sure it is the high road to destruction."[16] Rescinding Benny's contract was out of the question; it would only unsettle the youth still further. He concluded, however, with a promise of arbitration and an appraisal of Benny as a basically very promising youngster whose only shortcomings were those of his age—the first of many evaluations of her son he would send to Jane in a decrescendo of optimism and hope.

In the spring of 1748, at the very time he was writing those lines of cold comfort, Franklin opened a printing house in Antigua and entrusted it to the care of a "sober, honest and diligent young man,"[17] whom he highly recommended to Strahan as a distributor of London books in the West Indies. Four years later, no longer diligent and sober but grown careless and "got to sitting up late in taverns,"[18] the young man was dead. Franklin sent Benny, not quite twenty, to replace him; Parker gave his former apprentice some "handsome apparel," and let him go, perhaps with relief, one year ahead of the expiration of his contract.

To his anguished sister, Franklin explained that Antigua was reckoned one of the healthiest islands in the West Indies, that Benny would find the business already settled, an established newspaper, no other printing house on any of the Leeward Islands to interfere with him or beat down his prices, higher than those on the continent. "Industry and frugality" was all he needed to make his fortune. Benny had been recommended to some gentlemen for their patronage and advice, and cautioned against sitting up in taverns like his predecessor. Still, Franklin took concrete steps to prevent his nephew from yielding to recklessness, and warned Strahan not to extend him more than limited credit.

Benny sailed to Antigua in August 1752. By late November, Franklin was having second thoughts: "I fear I have been too forward in cracking the shell and producing the chick to the air before its time."[19] But he still felt that if Benny could but be prevailed on to behave steadily, all might be well. What had happened to make him doubt the wisdom of his decision? Both Benny's letters and his mother's are lost. But a tug of war had started between the uncle who wanted to hold on to the reins for a while before relinquishing the entire ownership of his printing house and the nephew who clamored for immediate independence. Benny also turned down an alternate plan under which, staying in Antigua, he would have sent his parents a small annual sum to help them toward their rent, and would have supplied the Franklin household in Philadelphia with rum and sugar in exchange for financial backing from his uncle. Rejected, too, was the offer of the New Haven printing office which Franklin had outfitted with the latest equipment from London. With all due respect and protestations of love, Benny was determined to be his own man. If Franklin was disappointed, he never said so. He let the young man have his way.

With Benny's letters came sweetmeats, oranges, and a whiff of exoticism. Writing to his aunt Deborah, he described a tropical hurricane, stressed the heavy mortality among the white community, and told of the way in which notice of such deaths was transmitted: The bell tolled hierarchically, nine times for a man, six for a woman, three for a boy, two for a girl.

After four years, Benny suddenly left Antigua. "I shall be very glad to hear he does better in another Place," sighed Franklin, "but I fear he will not for some Years be cur'd of his Fickleness and get fix'd to any purpose. However we must hope for the best, as with this Fault he has many good Qualities and Virtues."[20] The Antigua press, now purchased and paid for by Benny, was dismantled and sent to Boston.

What may have prompted his return was the death of his uncle John, postmaster of Boston, early in 1756. Here was a post he felt himself sufficiently qualified to occupy. But Franklin had promptly conferred it upon John's stepson, and Jane was upset. The letter in which she deplored that Franklin was not helping her son Peter against John's widow and stepchildren in the controversy about the crown soap also asserted that Benny had more right to the postmastership than a nonkinsman. Franklin, however, would not hear of her request. It was not his policy, he said, to remove from office someone who was doing well and kept regular accounts. He had shown no "backwardness"[21] in

assisting Benny and would think of him as soon as he gave signs of settling down, should any vacancy occur. (Benny did obtain the postmastership of New Haven some years later.) Well aware of the resentment
such a statement would provoke in Jane, Franklin urged Debbie not to
take part in this family quarrel but to write "Sister Jenny and recommend a Reconciliation."[22]

With a loan from his uncle, Benny made a fresh start in Boston and
for a while all went well. He married Elizabeth Ross, daughter of the
former mayor of Elizabeth Town, a girl both Franklin and Deborah
had long known and were very fond of. One of his little girls was
named after Debbie "in grateful remembrance of [her] numerous
kindnesses."[23] From London, Franklin sent him printing equipment,
stationery, paper, a trunk of books to sell—and reams of good advice.
Well thought of as a printer, Benny was considered eccentric as a person. Unlike his uncle, who had taken pains to be seen in the streets
pushing his wheelbarrow, he went to work—and operated the press—in
a powdered wig, ruffles, and gloves. "Dandified," people called him.
Were Jane's children, handicapped as they were by poor health, unsettled still further by the glamour of their uncle's fame and their
cousins' relative opulence? No matter how hard he tried, Benny could
never measure up. Even such a scoop as being the first in America to
publish his uncle's *Father Abraham's Speech* as a separate pamphlet
was not enough to keep him afloat. A magazine he attempted to launch
folded after three issues.

By the time Franklin arrived home from England, in 1762, Benny
was in full crisis again, determined to leave Boston and open up shop
in New York. He traveled down to Philadelphia to consult his uncle. It
is easy to imagine the lecture he was treated to on "rolling stones gath-
ering no moss," but he moved to New York all the same. Franklin
visited him there the following year on his way to Boston, and reported
to Strahan (who was fretting over some money Benny owed him) that
he was beginning to fear things were "going wrong" with Mecom.[24]
Benny's next venture, the *New-York Pacquet*, appeared only seven
times.

There was plenty of time to discuss the Mecoms' problems in the
course of that summer of 1763, for Franklin had suffered a second fall
from his horse while on a postal inspection in New Hampshire,
dislocated his shoulder again, and was forced to spend many weeks re-
cuperating at his sister's home. It gave him a chance to re-establish contact with his fellow Bostonians. Much as he liked poking fun at them,
he adored being back for a while among his own: "Besides their general good sense which I value, the Boston manner, turn of phrase, and

even tone of voice and accent in pronunciation all please and seem to refresh and revive me."[25] Those words were to be written nostalgically in old age when Franklin knew he would never see Boston again. When he sat in Jane's little parlor, however, he could not have guessed that even though he still had twenty-seven years to live, this was his last visit to his native city.

For Jane, the summer of 1763 was altogether an uneasy one. Yes, she had her illustrious brother under her roof, many of the famous people in town flocked to her house, and the conversation was such that she would feast on her memories for years to come. Still, how could she fail to draw a parallel between her sickly, restless sons and the glamorous William with his law degree, his refined bride, his prestigious position? How could she not compare her own daughters' struggle against shabbiness and fatigue with Sally's radiant health, her good clothes, her musical accomplishments? When Sally was a little girl, Franklin had expressed the hope that she would prove "an ingenious sensible notable and worthy woman, like her aunt Jenny."[26] Here she was, truly a well-educated young lady, whereas Aunt Jenny had been stifled from the start.

As Sally played the harpsichord, accompanied by her father on the glass armonica (he had sent one to Boston, too), Jane must have tried once more to disentangle her rejoicing in her brother's success from her anguish over her own family's failure. Perhaps it was asking too much. On one occasion, years earlier, she had been interrupted in the midst of a great wash by the news—a false rumor as it turned out—that Franklin had been made a baronet in London. Urged by her husband to congratulate Debbie without delay, even though she wanted to proceed with the wash, Jane struggled to produce a few lines of cheer to "her Ladyship." She could not keep up the pretense of shared happiness through a whole sentence. Her congratulations were sandwiched between the news that her own daughter Sarah was "still sick," and a sad allusion to her son Edward spitting blood and not having done "won stroke of work this month."[27] As the Philadelphia Franklins' good fortune was underscored by the Boston Mecoms' ill-fortune, Jane's half-ironic obsequiousness unavoidably took on an almost acid quality.

This tension in Jane found its outlet in an exaggerated concern for her brother's health and comfort and in undue emphasis on the nursing of his sore shoulder. So much solicitude irritated him and in his thanks for her hospitality he included a few barbs: "I am . . . very happy in being at home, where I am allow'd to know when I have eat enough and drank enough, am warm enough, and sit in a Place that I like, and no body pretends to know what I feel better than I do myself."[28]

One more instance of rather rough brotherly teasing, but it was to be the last. The blows that struck Jane shortly after that summer were too cruel and the courage with which she accepted them was too great to allow for anything but respect.

With lapidary impact her "Book of Ages" tells the story of one woman's life in Puritan New England—the early marriage, the relentless pregnancies, the avalanche of deaths humbly accepted as her supreme homage to the divine will: "The Lord Giveth & the Lord taketh away oh may I never be so Rebelious as to Refuse Acquesing & saying from my hart Blessed be the Name of the Lord."[29]

X

The Dream and
the Nightmare

At Present I am here as much the Butt of Party Rage and Malice, express'd in Pamphlets and Prints, and have as many pelted at my Head in proportion, as if I had the Misfortune of being your Prime Minister.
—Franklin to Strahan, September 1, 1764

DEBORAH HAD WAITED FIVE YEARS and five months for her husband to come back from England. Then she had waited six weeks for him to return from his postal inspection tour through the southern states. Then she had waited five months while he was traveling through New England with Sally. In November 1763, at last, he was home, physically and spiritually at home. The worst of his nostalgia for England had abated. Much to her relief, he talked complacently of the indolence of old age, of "bustling" as better left to the young, of the danger of uprooting old trees. Indeed, he used that metaphor so often that Polly Stevenson informed him she had seen some fine tall firs removed from Kensington to the Queen's Palace without injury, "and why should not the valuable North American plants flourish here?"[1]

In their mid-fifties, Deborah and Franklin planned, for the first time in their lives, to build a home. It was to stand just a few steps from the spot where she had caught sight of that ragged runaway of seventeen munching on his loaf: a three-story brick house, thirty-four feet by thirty-four, in the center of a deep and narrow lot fronting on Market Street. The land had been pieced together over the years by adding to Deborah's original inheritance strips acquired from her sister, her brother, and neighbors. After a series of rented houses—half a dozen at least—none of them large enough to accommodate servants, apprentices, and boarders, this, at last, would be a fitting showcase for the elegant appurtenances shipped from London; for Franklin's pride and joy, the armonica; for Sally's harpsichord; for the electrical instruments. Here was a chance to install the latest model of the Franklin stove, the cleverest systems for disposing of steam, smell, and smoke, the ultimate in kitchen appliances—a glorious marriage of European refinement with American practicality.

Work had started in the spring, with the high hopes and good will that generally attend the beginning of such ventures. From New York, Franklin had sent love to Mr. Rhoads, the builder, and requested him to make up an invoice for the locks and hinges that could not be found in Philadelphia. Upon his return from New England he paid bills for sand (to go in the pavement) and some iron work. One is surprised to find how little had been accomplished in six months; the building boom then taking place in Philadelphia may account for such slow progress. Franklin's adopted city had more than doubled in population from the day of his first arrival and was on its way to becoming the second largest in the British Empire. Most of the elegant building, to be sure, took place in the surrounding countryside where the local gentry escaped urban chaos as well as the devastating Philadelphia summers, but Franklin, unlike Washington and Jefferson, was a city boy through and through, and could not imagine residing anywhere but near the market place, the firehouse, and his fellow citizens.

As a counterpoint to the happy sound of hammers there was, still very far away, the rumble of trouble on the frontier. Lured by the hope of French support, Pontiac, the chief of the Ottawas, had attacked Detroit in May 1763, giving the signal for Indian uprisings from the Great Lakes to the Gulf of Mexico. In June, the *Pennsylvania Gazette* reported from Fort Pitt the "most melancholy Accounts"[2] of the murder of a family, of attacks on soldiers, of scalpings. Through the summer and fall, the papers were full of the ever-more audacious forays carried out on the sparsely settled far reaches of Pennsylvania where the Scotch-Irish settlers, less mindful of Indian sensitivities than their Quaker and Moravian predecessors, had settled lands to which they did not have treaty rights. The small number of armed men authorized by the Assembly were quite inadequate to cope with the Indian raiding parties. Rage and frustration grew on the frontier.

As often happens, the innocent were made to pay for the guilty. The innocent, in this case, were the remnants of a tribe of peaceful Indians established among the whites at the Penns' Conestoga Manor near Lancaster. A mob from nearby Paxton attacked those Indians and killed the six that they found at home. This was on December 14, 1763. Two days after Christmas the Paxton Boys, as they called themselves, stormed the workhouse at Lancaster where the remaining fourteen

Conestoga Indians had been taken for safety. They murdered them all. The British troops stationed in the town had received no orders and did not interfere. Franklin, appalled, reported to an English friend that "the Spirit of killing all Indians, Friends and Foe, spread amazingly thro' the whole Country." The rioters, "almost universally approved of by the common People . . . projected coming down to this City [of Philadelphia], 1000 in Number, arm'd, to destroy 140 Moravian and Quaker Indians."[3] As the tide of hatred mounted, he tried to stem it with a barrage of words—his long and impassioned "Narrative of the Late Massacres," the most vibrant manifesto he ever wrote. In an attempt to save those 140 Moravian Indians, herded in terror on Province Island at the mouth of the Schuylkill, he appealed to human decency, to the age-old and universal law of hospitality, to reason, to emotion, to every rhetorical device at his command.*

Did it help? He thought it did. "It would perhaps be Vanity in me to imagine so slight a thing could have any extraordinary Effect. But however that may be, there was a sudden and very remarkable Change; and above 1000 of our Citizens took Arms to support the Government in the Protection of those poor Wretches."[4]

The Paxton Boys, armed with rifles and tomahawks, gathered their forces to march on Philadelphia—three hundred men, perhaps, with more to follow. On the eve of the confrontation, the newly arrived governor, John Penn (son of Richard and nephew of Thomas), came rushing to Franklin, on whom the delicious irony of the situation was not lost: "And, would you think it, this Proprietary Governor did me the Honour, on an Alarm, to run to my House at Midnight, with his Counsellors at his Heels, for Advice, and made it his Head Quarters for some time."[5]

Franklin's advice was to stand firm. When, on the morning of February 6, 1764, the Paxton Boys crossed the Schuylkill, marched through Chestnut Hill and into Germantown, they were met by a delegation of clergymen who informed them that the city was prepared for defense, that even many Quakers had taken up arms, and that there would be bloodshed. "The Fighting Face we put on made them more willing to hear Reason."[6] The rioters paused in Germantown. The following day, a delegation of prominent citizens, including Franklin, went out to talk to them and listen to their grievances. An agreement was reached, "and within four and twenty Hours, your old Friend was a common Soldier,

---

* Toward Pontiac and his cobelligerents, however, he urged a hard line. Without going to the extreme of General Amherst's suggestion to send them smallpox-infested blankets, Franklin thought that fighting the rebel Indians with bloodhounds would be a good idea.

a Counsellor, a kind of Dictator, an Ambassador to the Country Mob, and on their returning home, *Nobody*, again."[7]

The Moravian Indians had been saved . . . after a fashion. They were resettled on the upper Susquehanna but not before their numbers had dwindled from 140 to 83 through smallpox and dysentery during their year's stay in the Philadelphia barracks. Franklin's long-standing distrust of the Proprietors only intensified, however. He suspected they were selling out to the rioters and would never bring to justice the murderers of the Conestoga Indians. Worse yet, he predicted that under what he felt was a parasitical stewardship, the whole of Pennsylvania was heading toward disaster. There was no point on which Franklin and John Penn saw eye to eye: not on taxation or proprietary estates, hence not on the formation of a militia and not on ways to raise and spend monies. And beyond the issues there was an irreversible conflict of personalities: "I don't love the Proprietary, and . . . he does not love me. Our totally different Tempers forbid it."[8]

As the land thawed and burst into bloom, positions hardened, tempers rose, and the city of brotherly love became anything but brotherly. Voltaire who had just proclaimed that in Quaker Philadelphia "Discord [and] Controversy are unknown"[9] would have recanted, had he only known. Wrote Franklin about Penn, "All regard for him in the Assembly is lost; all Hopes of Happiness under a Proprietary Government are at an End. . . . Every thing seems in this Country . . . to be running fast into Anarchy and Confusion."[10] Wrote Penn about Franklin, "There will never be any prospect of ease and happiness while that villain has the liberty of spreading about the poison of that inveterate malice and ill nature which is deeply implanted in his own black heart."[11] Franklin conceived the somewhat naïve conviction that if only Pennsylvania could be put directly under the control of the crown, all would be well. Others, too, wondered if the moment had not come to get rid of the Penns.

If Debbie had imagined that with the winding down of the Paxton episode her household—for two hectic nights the seat of government— would return to placid domesticity and serene plans for the future, she must soon have come to realize that the new conflict developing between her husband and the Penns would obliterate her dream. True, two hundred pounds were advanced to the carpenter for building expenditures, but nobody's heart was in the new house. It had been engulfed by current events. In late May, Franklin became acting speaker of the Assembly, and the petition he had drafted to ask the king to take over Pennsylvania's government was adopted with slight revisions, signed, and sent out. By June 25, he feared the worst: "I doubt the Year will scarce pass without some civil Bloodshed."[12]

Elections were approaching. He ran for assemblyman from Philadelphia. The old Franklin home, to which the neighborhood had once flocked to gape at the jolly marvels of electricity, now served as campaign headquarters. One of the nastiest campaigns ever witnessed by the colonies, that of 1764, was appropriately described by contemporaries as "scurrilous." The vogue was to hurl insults at one another under the guise of fake epitaphs. Using this "lapidary style," Franklin's partisans dealt as many low blows as they received, each side depicting itself, of course, as on the defensive.

"I bore the personal Abuse of five scurrilous Pamphlets, and three Copperplate Prints from the Proprietary Party before I made the smallest Return,"[13] lamented Franklin. But the real losers in political campaigns are usually the women of the family, lucky if they are only ignored, but more often dragged into a brutal limelight. The campaign of 1764 was no exception. A sordid pamphlet, *What is Sauce for the Goose is also a Sauce for the Gander,* used the mysterious circumstances of William's birth to smear the whole Franklin household:

> HIS PRINCIPAL ESTATE, SEEMING TO CONSIST—TILL VERY LATELY—IN HIS HAND MAID BARBARA—A MOST VALUABLE SLAVE—THE FOSTER-MOTHER—OF HIS LAST OFFSPRING—WHO DID HIS DIRTY WORK—AND IN TWO ANGELIC FEMALES—WHOM BARBARA ALSO SERVED—AS KITCHEN WENCH AND GOLD FINDER *—BUT ALAS THE LOSS—PROVIDENCE FOR WISE THO' SECRET ENDS—LATELY DEPRIV'D HIM OF THE MOTHER—OF EXCELLENCY **—HIS FORTUNE WAS NOT HOWEVER IMPAIR'D—FOR HE PIOUSLY WITHHELD FROM HER—MANES—THE PITIFUL STIPEND OF TEN POUNDS PER ANNUM—ON WHICH HE HAD CRUELLY SUFFERED HER—TO STARVE—THEN STOLE HER TO THE GRAVE IN SILENCE—WITHOUT A PALL THE COVERING DUE TO HER DIGNITY—WITHOUT A GROAN A SIGN OR A TEAR—WITHOUT A TOMB OR EVEN—A MONUMENTAL INSCRIPTION[14]

Judged by the anger it provoked in Franklin's camp, this heavy-handed effort, humorless and obscure as it now appears, must have hurt. Believing (probably in error) that it was the work of their old enemy, the Reverend Mr. Smith, his allies counterattacked with an equally coarse broadside referring to the "sinister cunning," the "brazen Effront'ry," and the "Heart bloated with infernal Malice" of "this irreverent Parson."[15]

It was, all in all, a miserable summer. Work continued on the new

---

* "A genteel name for him whose business is to empty privies," according to a dictionary to which the pamphlet's author refers.

** "Your Excellency" was of course, the title of William as governor of New Jersey.

house, albeit at a sluggish pace—the plasterers were paid in August—but Franklin was perplexed about his future. "The Proprietary Party . . . will . . . either demolish me or I them."[16] He started toying again with the idea of leaving Pennsylvania and becoming a Londoner for the rest of his days.

The election was held on October 1. While his party won a majority in the Assembly, Franklin was defeated on the county as well as on the city lists (it was permissible to run on both). Some of the Scotch-Irish had not forgiven him for branding them "Christian white savages" in his account of the Lancaster massacres; some Germans had not forgotten that he had called them "Palatine boors" less than a decade earlier in an essay with unfelicitous racist overtones (*On the Increase of Mankind*); some were incensed by the sexual indiscretions of his youth and the rise to power of his bastard son; some simply could not stomach the unbroken series of his successes. Outwardly he kept his composure— "Mr. Franklin died like a Philosopher"[17]—but the humiliation was searing. On the county list his name had come next to last. From speaker to nothing, it was quite a tumble.

Yet loss of face did not mean loss of power. In London, Thomas Penn was soon informed that "Franklin . . . and others tho' excluded have had the entire direction of Matters within Doors. The measure and plan of each day's proceedings being settled by them every Evening at private meetings and cabals held with their Friends in the House."[18] Indeed, as soon as it sat, on October 15, 1764, the Assembly voted to send to England a delegate who would forward the cause of Pennsylvania versus the Penns; a few days later, as everyone had anticipated, it chose Franklin for that mission, by nineteen votes to eleven. Another few days and he embarked, cheered on by three hundred friends and supporters who accompanied him to Chester, fired their cannon, sang an anthem calling on God to save George III and Franklin, and, as he would proudly recall, filled his sails with their good wishes. Brisk winds carried him to England in a record thirty days. When Mrs. Stevenson came home from shopping on December 10, she found her old lodger sitting in the parlor.

For him, the relief of distance, the welcome of friends, the elation of action. For the family, the frustration of living in a polarized climate where the adulation of some does not make up for the hostility of those who spy on your every move and misinterpret your every gesture. Of this, Franklin was not unaware. In a last message to Sally from a little island in the Delaware, he had asked her to keep a low profile: "You know I have many Enemies (all indeed on the Public Account, for I cannot recollect that I have in a private Capacity given just cause for offense to any one whatever) yet they are Enemies and very bitter ones; and you must expect their Enmity will extend in some degree to you, so that your slightest Indiscretions will be magnified into crimes, in order the more sensibly to wound and afflict me. It is therefore the more necessary for you to be extreamly circumspect in all your Behaviour that no Advantage may be given to their Malevolence." Such is the usual advice politicians give their families, and it sounds depressing but reasonable enough.

But then, refusing to admit that Sally could have a mind of her own, that she was no longer clay to be molded, he forbade her to leave the church even though she had expressed her intention to do so. (She had been brought up an Anglican and, like her mother, was a member of Christ Church.) "Go constantly to Church whoever preaches. The Acts of Devotion in the common Prayer Book are your principal Business there; and if properly attended to, will do more towards mending the Heart than Sermons generally can do." Sally knew very well her father had never thought highly of the sermons he heard on his rare visits to church. Anticipating her objections, and with the Reverend Mr. Smith much on his mind, he elaborated, "I do not mean that you should despise Sermons even of the Preachers you dislike, for the Discourse is often much better than the Man, as sweet and clear Waters come to us thro' very dirty Earth."[19]

Poor Sally. For a brief moment she had been given to hope that it would be her turn, this time, to accompany her father to England. Instead, she was being told to watch her step, go to church whether she liked it or not, improve her bookkeeping by setting a few hours aside each day for study and solitude—and, since she was endowed with "goodness of Heart," to show herself "attentively dutiful and tender" toward her good mama in order to earn favor with her father and with God.

The "good Mama" thus entrusted to her daughter's care now comes into focus for the first time. Finally we have *her* letters; she speaks in her own voice, in a cascade of unpunctuated pages addressed to her "dear child" as she called him and signed "your a feck shonet wife": long, rambling, chaotic, hard to decipher and interpret, but intensely human letters. They are unpretentious and warm, alive with compassion, chatty, comfortable, courageous in an everyday way, shining with her loyalty to him, overflowing with her love for him, a love tinged with deference and awe. Those biographers of Franklin who have simply dismissed Debbie as "illiterate" cannot have read her letters. Her husband loved them, missed them when they failed to arrive, and told her many times that she was his best correspondent.

While he was settling down again to the familiar London routine, Philadelphia struggled through one of the worst winters in its history. Debbie writes of the frozen river on which taverns had opened and ox roasting took place, of the huge snowdrifts swallowing up the landmarks, of her own fingers too stiff to hold the pen, and, of course, of the unfinished house at a standstill. To make matters yet a little more grim, she had accepted as permanent house guest an Englishwoman by the name of Ann Hardy. Ann ("Nanny"), a former maid of Mrs. Stevenson, obviously not made of pioneering stuff, was cold in spite of Debbie's wrapping her in a double gown; Nanny longed for London's coal fires and had no use for wood-burning stoves; Nanny suffered a bad attack of jaundice but refused the ministrations of Philadelphia's famous Dr. Bond since she would trust none but an English physician; Nanny spurned the one-horse chair in which Deborah took her out to speed her recovery and raise her morale. It was in vain that she urged Nanny to be "contente and good-youmerred."[20]

Deborah herself tried hard to be good-humored, in keeping with the promise she had made on the eve of her husband's departure, and she related whatever cheerful news she could: Their marble fireplace had arrived from England in good shape, she had been able to put up a visitor in the guest room even though the new house was not ready for occupancy; their friends did not desert her—indeed, there was such a stream of them that her writing was constantly interrupted. Most of all, she strove to please Franklin by insisting that she was discreet and cautious, not giving any ground for offense: "We have nothing stiring amoungst us but phaemlits [pamphlets] and Scurrilitey but I have never sed or dun aney thing or aney of our famely you may depend on it nor shall we. . . . I partake of none of the divershons I stay at home and flatter myself that the next packit will bring me a letter from you."[21]

It took a long time before she heard from him—five months. When news of his safe arrival finally reached Philadelphia in mid-March, the bells rang through most of the night and libations were poured. As Governor Penn noted sourly in a letter to his uncle Thomas, the Quakers ran about like madmen to acquaint their crew of the joyous tidings. "People as they met in the street shook hands and wished one another joy upon this great event."[22] Deborah recounted the scene in homely terms: She was at table with William, Elizabeth, and some friends, she had told her company that there was no fancy dessert but, who knows, she might be able to treat them with something from England. A few minutes later a neighbor came running with the news that the post had come, bringing Franklin's first letter, "so I had the pleshuer of treeting quite grand-indeed, and our little Companey as cherful and hapey as aney in the world none excepted o my dear hough hapey am I to hear that you air safe and well. Hough dus your armes doe . . . o I long to know."[23]

Distance seemed to rekindle Franklin's enthusiasm for the new house; throughout the spring his letters were full of eager inquiries and no end of advice. Presuming that she had already moved in—which would not be the case for several months—he gave detailed instructions on the way to hang "the blue mohair stuff"[24] he meant as curtains for the blue chamber; he wished he had given orders not to start painting until his return; he approved of her buying a sizable new lot next to theirs although he thought the price rather steep; he fretted over the installation of the new kitchen (which was in the cellar), not quite trusting her to understand its intricacies, "as it is a mere Machine, and being new to you, I think you will scarce know how to work it. You mention nothing of the Furnace. If that Iron one is not set, let it alone until my Return, when I shall bring a more convenient copper one."[25] Like anyone who has ever built a house, he was indignant over the delays. How about the well? Was it dug, at last? When would she be able to start gardening? The rubbish, he supposed, had not yet been removed, nor the fences put up. The workmen, he sighed, had been unkind to keep her so long unsettled.

She moved in May 1765. A group of their friends gathered in the new dining room. Franklin had expected an avalanche of compliments but was disappointed: "You tell me only of a Fault they found with the House, that it was too little, and not a Word of any thing they lik'd in it: not how the Kitchin Chimneys perform; so I suppose you spare me some Mortification, which is kind."[26] She rushed to reassure him, asserting that when it would please God to restore him to his own house he would be very pleased with the looks of it: "it dos make a fine Squair and an equil spaise on each sid."[27] Such a meager description only whetted his appetite. In August, while announcing he would not be able to come home until the following spring, he again bombarded her with recommendations. Never be without tubs to catch the rain water lest the foundations suffer—be careful with the fires—don't oil the floors until my return—tell me about your baking in the iron oven—send me a draft of the newly purchased lot—send me measurements of windows, chimneys, buffet—be sure and lock up my books and papers—and finally the tangible homesickness: "What Room have you chosen to sleep in? What Colours are they painted? I wish you would give me a particular Account of every Room, who and what is in it, 'twould make me seem a little at home."[28]

The paradox that spring and summer of 1765 was that Franklin put the accent on the domestic, Debbie on the political. Being so far away, he had somehow lost touch with the state of mind of Philadelphia, where the Penns were no longer the crucial concern. The city, indeed all the colonies, were now quivering with excitement and indignation over a new issue, the Stamp Act, and Franklin failed for a time to grasp that in his countrymen's minds this transcended all others: "The Subject now is the Stamp act and nothing else is talked of, the Dutch talk of the stompt ack, the Negroes of the tamp, in short every body has something to say,"[29] reported Sally.

The imposition of a stamp tax had been a foregone conclusion since the previous summer but was not actually passed until February 1765, to take effect the following November first. Under its terms, pre-stamped paper in appropriate denominations would have to be used for all legal and official transactions, for newspapers and their advertisements, even for wrapping playing cards. It was strictly a revenue measure, designed to make the colonies shoulder more of the enormous debt left over from the French and Indian War and the continuing presence of ten thousand troops in America—as it was, Americans paid far less in taxes than the average Englishman.

The long delay gave the colonists ample time to organize their opposition. Franklin, though he lobbied long and hard against the measure when he belatedly realized how sensitive a nerve had been touched, mistakenly assumed it would be met in the end with grudging compliance. Preventing it, he wrote, was like trying to hinder the sun from setting. "Since [the sun is] down . . . and it may be long before it rises again, let us make as good a Night of it as we can. We may still light Candles. Frugality and Industry will go a great way towards indemnifying us. Idleness and Pride tax with a heavier Hand than Kings and Parliaments."[30] In 1765, however, Father Abraham's words fell on deaf ears. Self-reliance had its limits. The colonists refused to allow Parliament to tax them because they were not represented in it; only their own elected assemblies, they maintained, had the right of taxation.

When the ministry determined to have the Stamp Act administered by native American agents rather than the usual incompetent absentee customs officials, Franklin, quick to grasp a chance for political gain, suggested his friend, John Hughes, as agent for Pennsylvania. This appointment was a tactical victory but a strategic blunder: The more far-sighted Penns, who had at first intended to press their own candidate, were now scurrying in the opposite direction, eager to disassociate themselves completely from the act. Franklin kept reassuring Hughes that though his new office might make him unpopular for a while, cool execution and firm loyalty to the crown would carry him through. Some years later he insisted that cooperating with the ministry in naming agents had never signified approval of the act, but he ruefully admitted that had he foreseen the trouble in store he would not have put forward his friend's name. Jane Mecom, whose political sense was acute, professed herself amazed when she heard that Hughes's appointment had been her brother's doing, "but even this I concluded must have some good Reasons for which others could not see into."[31] Jane's loyalty was unshakable.

If Franklin was slow in realizing the depth of feeling back home, Hughes never did quite comprehend that this was more than another conspiracy hatched by the Penns and the Presbyterians. In fact, the furor provoked by the impending act went beyond provincial boundaries and local interests as nothing had ever done before. The Virginia Resolves of late May 1765 marked the beginning of open resistance and touched off a chain of similar resolves by other assemblies, asserting their exclusive right to tax. In Boston, the colonial tinderbox, mobs took to the streets in August, hanged the stamp officer and lieutenant governor in effigy, and smashed their houses. Violence and rumor of violence spread. Before long, most of the stamp officers had resigned or fled without ever having issued a piece of stamped paper.

William Franklin kept a tight rein on his New Jersey government and for a time seemed to be riding out the storm: There were no riots, no resolves, and initially no interest in participating in the Stamp Act Congress that several of the other colonies were planning for October. But New Jersey could not entirely escape the contagion and was finally stirred to resistance. William blamed the trouble on the meddling of outside newspapers (the state had none of its own) which ridiculed the people of New Jersey for their docility, hinting that the governor had lulled them with "a Dose of Poppies and laudanum."[32] The New Jersey stamp agent who had been appointed through Franklin's influence resigned in terror at what was going on in neighboring colonies, even though it meant forfeiting a sizable bond. William was furious but had enough political acumen to yield: "For any Man to set himself up as an Advocate of the Stamp Act . . . is a sheer Piece of Quixotism."[33] Later, however, after the act had been repealed, he would deprecate the "superpatriots" who wanted to keep the argument going after it had been won.

Like his son, Franklin was walking a fragile tightrope. In London he defended American rights, but in his few surviving letters to trusted friends back home he condemned the "Madness of the Populace or their blind Leaders" who provoked "greater Burthens by Acts of rebellious Tendency"[34] and made the struggle for repeal that much more difficult. Bitter as the attacks of his enemies had been through the past year and a half, he was still able in the summer of 1765 to dismiss them philosophically as "Arrows . . . like those that Rabelais speaks of which were headed with Butter harden'd in the Sun."[35] He blandly advised Debbie not to let anyone make her uneasy with their "idle or malicious Stories or Scribblings," but to enjoy her friends, "and the Comforts of Life that God has bestow'd on you, with a cheerful Heart. Let Sally divert you with her Music. Put her on practising on the Armonica."[36]

Anyone living in Philadelphia in those days would have found it hard to share his detachment. His enemies accused Franklin of having taken part in framing the Stamp Act and of plotting to become governor of Pennsylvania. "I wish you was on the Spot and yet I should be afraid of your Safety,"[37] sighed his printing partner David Hall to whom, in an early attempt to circumvent the tax, Franklin had shipped a large quantity of what proved to be unusable and expensive paper.

Tension mounted through the second week of September. On the eighth, John Hughes, who as stamp agent felt particularly threatened, warned Franklin that any letter, henceforth, might be the last he would receive from his old friend. "When a Mob is on foot, my Life and Interest may fall a Sacrifice to an infatuated Multitude."[38] On the twelfth, Hughes was informed that his house would soon be torn down. On the night of the sixteenth, a mob assembled and he felt that his last hour had come. He kept a running diary: on his guard and well-armed at eight o'clock; told at nine that his friends were patrolling the streets; in hopes at midnight that the rabble was dispersing; thankful to God in the morning to find that he was "yet in the land of the living"[39] and his property safe.

Not a word, in Hughes's melodramatic recital, about Deborah Franklin who was running the same risks. Her account of that momentous night, written one week later, is in sharp and delightful contrast with Hughes's. For nine days, she says, she had been under pressure to leave her house but she did not feel that it would be proper to show any anxiety, so she had merely sent Sally to stay with William in Burlington. On the fateful sixteenth, their cousin Josiah Davenport had appeared at her door, having been told by more than twenty people that it was his duty to be with her. "I sed I was plesed to reseve Civility from aney bodey so he staid with me." As rumors of an impending attack were mounting, she had asked the cousin to fetch a gun or two, since they had none in the house. She also called for her brother (meaning either her own brother John Read or Franklin's brother Peter, then postmaster at Philadelphia) and with the gun he brought they turned one room into a magazine. "I ordored sum sorte of defens up Stairs such as I cold manaig my selef."

There she was, the woman who did not dare set foot on a ship. Not for one moment did she yield to panic. ("Your indignation must have exceeded your fear!" exclaimed Jane.[40]) When urged once more to move out, she declared that her husband had not done anything to hurt anybody, nor had she given offense to anyone. She was not going to be made uneasy, she stated, nor would she stir, "but if aney one came to disturbe me I wold show a proper resentement and I shold be very much afrunted." Intimidated by such firmness and by the eight hundred citizens who had taken to the streets to see that peace was kept, the would-be rioters had second thoughts about affronting her, and the night ended quietly.

Like Cincinnatus returning to his plough, Deborah in her next paragraph went back to matters concerning their house: She had hoped to tell him that the lot was settled and the wall finished but there was some boundary dispute and she did not feel, as she never tired of repeating, that this was the moment to give offense to anybody. "I contente my self with thinking what ever is, is beste." By the last line of this unassuming account of what may have been her finest hour, her thoughts were centered once again on the faraway husband: "god bles you and keep you is the prayer of yours forever D Franklin."[41]

This letter, when he read it two months later, moved him to pay her tribute: "I honour much the Spirit and Courage you show'd and the prudent Preparations you made in that Time of Danger. The Woman deserves a good House that is determined to defend it." And he vowed never to forget those relatives, friends, and neighbors who had rallied to her side. Knowing that his words would not be seen by Jane, he allowed himself an outburst against a Presbyterian clergyman who had excited the mob by spreading word that he, Franklin, had planned the Stamp Act: "I thank him he does not charge me (as they do their God) with having plann'd Adam's Fall and the Damnation of Mankind."[42]

As all parties in the colonies braced for what was called "the dreadful November first," the day the Stamp Act was to go in effect, Deborah tried to cope with her tensions by keeping busy. She dusted shelves, stored away books and papers, "as it did imploy my mind."[43] She strove (on his instructions?) not to discuss current events in her letters but found it almost impossible: "I have wrote several letters to you one almoste everey day but then I cold not forbair saying sumthing

This portrait of Deborah Franklin was copied by the English painter and scientist Benjamin Wilson from a small original sent from Philadelphia, probably the work of the limner John Hesselius. It is the only Franklin portrait to have remained in the family, though it did not always receive the best of care, justifying Sally's gloomy remark that "It was great nonsense for a woman to have her portrait taken; she was sure to find herself, by the next generation, in a garret window grinning at a north wester." Oil, ca. 1759. American Philosophical Society.

This painting of William Franklin is the work of Mather Brown, Boston born grandson of Franklin's old friend, Mather Byles, and dates from about 1790 when William was in exile in London. Oil. Mrs. Manderson Castle.

Sarah (Sally) Bache had her portrait painted by John Hoppner during the Baches' trip to England in 1791, a trip financed by the sale of the diamonds surrounding the king of France's miniature given to her father when he returned home from his mission. Oil. Metropolitan Museum, Wolfe Fund.

Franklin met Mary Stevenson Hewson, or Polly, as he always called her, when he first settled into her mother's house in Craven Street in 1757. She quickly became a second daughter to him and was at his bedside in Philadelphia when he died over thirty years later. Artist unknown. Pastel. Miss Katherine Bradford.

William Temple Franklin, painted by John Trumbull. "He is just fit to be employed in a court," commented Polly Hewson, "and to be the gallant of the French ladies, nothing else." Oil on panel, 1790. Yale University Art Gallery, Trumbull Collection.

B. Franklin inv. J. Ferguson delin.   J. Mynde sc.

A magic square of squares. Much as he might admonish his son to be unswervingly attentive as clerk of the Pennsylvania Assembly, Franklin himself had often found the debates "so unentertaining that I was induc'd to amuse myself with making magic Squares or Circles, or any thing to avoid Weariness." Later these squares and circles were considered worthy of publication in his scientific works. Printed in James Ferguson, *Tables and Tracts* (London, 1767). Yale University, Franklin Collection.

Franklin's glass armonica. Franklin found the tones of this instrument (which h[e] perfected) "incomparably sweet beyond those of any other" and for a time enjoyed a great vogue in England and on the Continent. Mesmer found it wel[l] suited to his therapy, but others were convinced that it led to madness in thos[e] who performed on it. Engraving from Barbeu-Dubourg's French edition [of] Franklin's *Oeuvres* (Paris, 1773). Yale University, Franklin Collection.

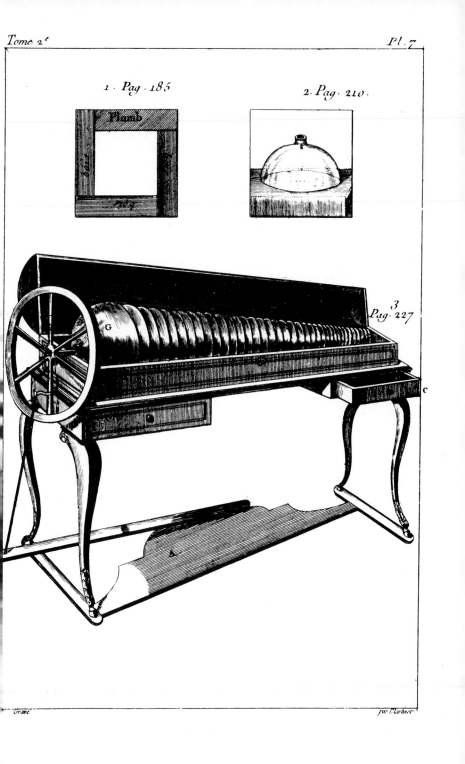

1 . Pag . 185   2 . Pag . 210 .

Plumb

3
Pag . 227

Franklin was amused by this print "which tho' a copy of that by Chamberlain,"
he wrote Deborah, "has got so French a Countenance that you would take me for
one of that lively Nation." It shows even more clearly than the original the bell
he had rigged up in his house and the electrical storm raging outside. Engraving
after Mason Chamberlain, 1773. Yale University, Franklin Collection.

This letter to Polly Stevenson of July 20, 1768, is Franklin's earliest known use of the phonetic alphabet that had fascinated him for years. The devoted Polly made valiant efforts to master it but was not quite ready to renounce her linguistic past. Temple's schoolmaster James Elphinston uzd a simplr verzun al hiz lyf. American Philosophical Society.

Margaret Stevenson to Franklin, probably 1763. Though writing was an "od-dieus task" to Franklin's London landlady, she overcame her aversion to entreat him to return with his wife and daughter, attempting to reassure him in this passage that they would not be out of place in the genteel society of the capital. American Philosophical Society.

Deborah's last letter to her husband, October 29, 1773, closed, typically, with an anecdote about her beloved Kingbird. Though she lived for another fourteen months, she was apparently too infirm to write. American Philosophical Society.

to you a bought publick afairs then I wold distroy it and then begin a gen and burn it a gen and so on."[44]

So, on a fine October day, she decided to answer all his "dear questions" about their home to the best of what she felt were her very limited writing abilities. Debbie's talents lay more in narration—where lack of punctuation, jumbling of time, gushes of feeling combine to give her stories a breathless rush—than in description. Clumsy and flat as it is, her presentation of their house manages to convey her prime emotion about it, not pride of ownership but nostalgia for the absent master: "O my Child there is graite odds between a mans being at home and a broad as every bodey is a fraid thay shall doe wrong so everey thing is lefte undun."

She starts off with his room containing his "armonekey maid like a Deske," the boxes of glasses "for the Elicktresatecy,"[45] his writings, his pictures not yet hung since she does not dare drive nails without his approval. About Nanny's room she could not say much, for Nanny kept it locked at all times and Deborah only got a peek at it when the occupant was ill.

The showpiece was the music room, referred to as the blue room, featuring another armonica and Sally's harpsichord. It was an elegant chamber, graced with gilt, carvings, an ornamental chimney, decorative chairs and screen, but it fell short of expectations "Billey dont like the Blew room at all."[46] But Franklin, with extraordinary self-assurance for a man more than three thousand miles away, told her exactly how to rescue this room he had never seen: "I suppose the Blue room is too blue, the Wood being of the same Colour with the Paper, and so looks too dark. I would have you finish it as soon as you can, thus. Paint the Wainscot a dead White; paper the Walls blue; and tack the gilt Border round just above the Surbase and under the Cornish. If the Paper is not equal coloured when pasted on, let it be brushed over again with the same Colour: and let the Papier Machée figures be tack'd to the middle of the Ceiling; when this is done, I think it will look very well."[47]

Deborah's own room, shared with her maid Susannah, was of Spartan simplicity, while Sally's was full of books. The guest room was embellished with the pieces Franklin had sent from England a few years earlier. The elaborate dining room could seat twelve: Debbie had covered the chairs with a horsehair that looked fully as fine as heavy silk, she thought.

The insurance survey, dry as it is, fills out some decorative detail omitted by Debbie: ornate interior walls with fluted columns, half-pilasters and fretted woodwork. Overlooking all this, pictures of the king and queen, of the Earl of Bute, of brother John Franklin. Underfoot, some secondhand Scotch carpets, one of which did not meet with the approval of their friends. The hanging of the curtains would await his return, as he knew just how he wanted them. So would the placing of his clock.

Even though she did not forget to tell him, in answer to his queries, that the chimney worked well and that she had baked successfully in the new oven, Debbie's letter is a rather despondent one. Asked to list what was still needed, she mentioned drinking glasses, one or two tablecloths, perhaps a pair of silver canisters, a "turkey carpet" if he met with one. Basically, she did not care. "All thees things air be cume quite indifrent to me at this time."[48]

A few days later, she received what must have been a particularly affectionate letter from London and her spirits revived. "I cole it a *husbands Love letter*. Hough am I plesed to read it over and over a gen." She gave him news of John Hughes who had been seriously ill ever since the night of the near-riot. Hughes was in a tight spot: A ship had arrived from England on October 5, bringing the stamped paper and his commission. A new mob had collected and, to the sound of muffled bells, had sent him two drummers with the news "that thay was a Coming and wold be thair in a minit and all moste terreyfi his wife and Children to deth."[49]* In her partisan zeal and with the oversimplification of absolute loyalty, Deborah had nothing but contempt for the "mob." The carpenter's daughter pointed out with pride to the soap boiler's son that the agitators were led by two or three parsons and two or three doctors—those who call themselves "the better sorte," whereas six or seven hundred "hones good traidesmen"[51] kept them in check.

In this climate of terror, Debbie did what she knew how to do: She took care of the sick. Sally was sick. Nanny was very sick and very dissatisfied, though she staunchly refused to go back to England. Benny Mecom's former master James Parker had blamed his bad fit of gout on his heart but Debbie knew it was due to the Stamp Act. "Thanke God I have bin so favered that I have bin abel to nurse them all."[52] She still found time to run to the dock and supervise the loading of the apples and cranberries she was shipping to London.

On October 31, the *Pennsylvania Gazette* came out with a black border. It carried an announcement to the effect that as of the "Fatal To-

---

* Hughes promised in writing not to carry the Stamp Act into execution in Pennsylvania until this was done in the neighboring colonies. This way he did not have to resign and was considered by some to have parried with skill and courage the attacks mounted against him; others thought him foolhardy and entreated Debbie to prevail on him to resign unequivocally. Eventually he moved out of town, "disgusted with his Friends and all the World."[50]

morrow," the publishers, unable to bear the burden of the tax, would stop publishing the paper for a while and search for methods of escaping "the insupportable slavery." Three days later, Debbie expressed her immense relief that the first of November had come and gone without as much disorder as dreaded. Some friends had dropped in and she had baked the best buckwheat cakes of her life. "Thay sed I had ought dun my one ought doings"[53] ("outdone my own outdoings"). Incidentally, the flour for those supercakes came from a farm bought from the father of Daniel Boone.

Deborah was willing to entertain a constant flow of guests—the teapot never seems to have run dry—but she hardly ever went visiting. "I keep my self to my self"[54] is the leitmotiv of her letters. She did not wear her good clothes in her husband's absence, she did not antagonize anybody, she had not even spoken to their new tenant on the recently purchased lot. Having noted that Franklin had been away for exactly one year, she assured him once again that almost everybody in Philadelphia loved him.

Not everybody did. Many were those who were still convinced that he had favored the Stamp Act. The chief justice, for one. He declared in the Assembly that he knew for sure Franklin was opposed to the repeal of the odious tax. Exclaimed Benjamin Rush—not yet the famous physician or Franklin's good friend—"O Franklin, Franklin, thou curse to Pennsylvania and America, may the most accumulated vengeance burst speedily on thy guilty head!"[55] William received a warning that his father might be hanged in effigy on the following market day. This did not happen, but the prospect had been disturbing since William well knew that when Hughes's effigy had hung on the market place for a full twenty-four hours, not a single magistrate had interfered.

Confusion prevailed. "We are not more than one degree from open Rebellion,"[56] wrote Governor Penn. Forbidden by public outrage to use the stamps, forbidden by the government *not* to use them, the courts of justice came to a standstill, debtors flouted their creditors, the harbors filled up with immobilized ships, commerce was paralyzed.

Commerce was paralyzed. That was the turning point. On both sides of the Atlantic businessmen suffered heavy losses. They quickly mobilized to force Parliament to reverse its position. On the American side, a boycott of English goods. On the English side, a torrent of petitions detailing the merchants' distress. From his unofficial but influential pedestal, William Pitt, the Great Commoner, spoke out vehemently in favor of the colonies. "I rejoice," he thundered, "that America has resisted."[57] The new ministry had already determined on repeal, but how could Parliament be won over without loss of face?

Franklin now saw his course. He embarked on a massive campaign of public relations against the Stamp Act, "that Mother of Mischiefs." He lobbied day and night. "Besides opposing the Act before it was made, I never in my Life labour'd any Point more heartily than I did that of obtaining the Repeal."[58] He printed hundreds of copies of a political cartoon of his own design and used it as his stationery: in a bleak landscape, a dismembered woman, Magna Britannia, her severed legs (New England and Virginia) and arms (Pennsylvania and New York) strewn around her. She is begging. Ships in the background display brooms on their masts, a sign that they are for sale. Just in case the message was not clear enough, the recipient of the card was supplied with an "Explanation" and a "Moral."

Above all, Franklin used his best weapon: the written word. Under a rich variety of pseudonyms, he bombarded the London press with letters, each "selling" a facet of the American cause or of the American way of life. Hardly a minute was left to dispatch the briefest personal messages to his family, but many of his propaganda pieces were reprinted by the American papers, and William, who was in the know, could point out to Deborah that "NN," "Pacificus," "Secundus," "FB," "Homespun," were as many pen names of her husband.

Of this range of incarnations, "Homespun" must have spoken most directly to her. Keeping clear of political theory, taxation, and legislation, but making a case for American self-sufficiency, "Homespun" argued against a letter to the editor that had ridiculed Indian corn. On the contrary, he maintained, green ears of corn, roasted, are a delicacy beyond expression; "*samp, hominy, succatash,* and *nokehock,* made of it, are so many pleasing varieties; and a *johny* or *hoecake,* hot from the fire, is better than a Yorkshire muffin. But if Indian corn were as *disagreeable* and *indigestible* as the Stamp Act, does he imagine we can get nothing else for breakfast?" Whereupon "Homespun" launched into a panegyric of American produce, from the splendid array of cereals and rice to the delights of home-grown teas. "We have sage and bawm in our gardens, the young leaves of the sweet white hickory or walnut, and, above all, the buds of our pine, infinitely preferable to any tea from the Indies."[59] Debbie's buckwheat cakes, it seems, carried more political clout than she realized.

Franklin's great day came on February 13, 1766. Of the forty-odd merchants, colonial agents, and visiting Americans appearing before the House of Commons, all testifying to the evil consequences of the Stamp Act, he was the star performer. He dwelt on the docility of the colonies before the recent acts of Parliament: "They were governed by this country at the expence only of a little pen, ink and paper. They were led by a thread." They loved England, Englishmen, and English goods. But now all that was "very much altered." In an effort to play down ideological issues, he stated that the colonies did not object to all taxes, but only to those levied internally, which was less than candid, for he must have known that his countrymen were moving toward more radical views.

Many of the 174 questions put to him were sympathetic, not to say rehearsed, and provided a fine opportunity to insist that there was not "a single article imported into the Northern Colonies, but what they can either do without, or make themselves,"[60] an assertion calculated to send a chill through the audience. His thoughts at that moment turned to Deborah, as he later told her. He felt strong and secure in the knowledge that should trade between the two countries cease altogether, he could, once again, be clothed from head to foot "in Woollen and Linnen of my Wife's Manufacture."[61]

Repeal was carried on February 22 at 2:00 A.M., after days and nights of tumultuous debate. London church bells rang, West India ships on the Thames broke out their colors. Within hours Franklin was telling his wife, "Tho' I cannot by this Opportunity write to others, I must not omit a Line to you who kindly write me so many. I am well; 'tis all I can say at present, except that I am just now made very happy by a Vote of the Commons for the Repeal of the Stamp Act. Your ever loving Husband."[62]

Still very tired and "almost blind" from so much writing, he scribbled a few more lines to Deborah five days later. Domesticity washed over his letter, a wave of relief after so much public tension. He sent "some curious Beans"[63] (possibly bush beans) for her garden. Remembering that he had turned sixty—an occurrence she had celebrated by serving punch to his friends on January 17—he congratulated her and himself on the great share of health they both enjoyed while entering the fourth score of their life, a compliment not quite fair to Debbie who was only fifty-eight if one can trust the dates on her tombstone (1708–1774). Curiously, however, all of Franklin's references to his wife's age imply that it was the same as his own.

He had wanted her to be the first in America to hear about the repeal, but, as it happened, premature rumors of the good news had reached Philadelphia before his letter, triggering wild rejoicing. "The bells rang," wrote Sally, "we had bonfires and one house was illumanited [sic], indeed I never heard so much noise all my life the very Children were distracted. I hope and pray the news may be true."[64] It did become true, and the concurrent vote of the House of Lords made it final on March 18.

As details of Franklin's examination before the House of Commons trickled back to Philadelphia, his stock rose, through April and May, till at last his friends could reassure him that the eyes of many who had thought ill of him were now open. Quoting Pope, one of his correspondents commented that his remaining enemies were still "willing to wound, and yet afraid to strike."[65] Franklin professed indifference to the ups and downs of his popularity. To Jane Mecom he remarked with a shrug, "These are the Operations of Nature. It sometimes is cloudy, it rains, it hails; again 'tis clear and pleasant, and the Sun shines on us. Take one thing with another, and the World is a pretty good sort of World. . . . One's true Happiness depends more upon one's own Judgement of oneself, on a Consciousness of Rectitude in Action and Intention, and in the Approbation of those few who judge impartially, than upon the Applause of the unthinking undiscerning Multitude, who are apt to cry Hosanna today, and tomorrow, crucify him."[66] Jane indignantly disagreed: "Their treatment of you . . . makes the world apear a misereable world to me notwithstanding your good opinyon of it. When a grat Deal of Durt is flung some is got to stick."[67] By coincidence, Franklin was using the same image that very day, but with considerably more optimism: "Dirt thrown on a Mud-Wall may stick and incorporate; but it will not long adhere to polish'd Marble."[68]

When it came to his wife, his celebration of the happy outcome of events took a less philosophical and more concrete turn. He sent her a new gown and fourteen yards of "pompadour satin." To Sally he shipped fancy négligées and petticoats, two dozen pairs of gloves (none, she had lamented, were ever quite large enough in the forearm), and four bottles of lavender water. For the house there were damask tablecloths, curtains, and the "Turky carpet" Deborah had requested. Of all this bounty nothing gave her as much joy as the promise of a box of three fine cheeses, for her husband had added, "Perhaps a Bit of them may be left when I come home."[69]

He would be home soon, then. The nightmare of politics and discord, of absence and anguish was dissipating. Even though Deborah had discovered "that when a house is dun thair is much to be dun after,"[70] the house, any day now, would be theirs to share and enjoy.

But one month later, when he sent his report to the Assembly, he mentioned only that he was much fatigued and in need of a summer journey of six or eight weeks, after which he proposed to apply himself in earnest to the interests of the province—that is, to his original mission of securing the removal of the Penns. Another winter, he hoped, would bring Pennsylvania's affairs to a satisfactory conclusion. Hence he requested leave to return home the following spring.

For Deborah, this meant that her vigil would last another year.

XI

Father of the Bride

As a Daughter is neither to anticipate nor contradict the Will of her Parent, so, to hang the Balance even . . . she is not oblig'd to force her own by marrying where she cannot love.

—*Ladies Library*, 3:34

DEBORAH PUT SO MUCH STRESS on her policy of staying at home and keeping out of the limelight that Franklin eventually started to worry about the effect such a retiring life would have on his daughter's social activities. She was now well into her twenties. Knowing that "my dear Papa likes to hear of Weddings," Sally sent him lists of her acquaintances who had "entered the matrimonial state"[1] since he left. Yes, but what about her? Did she at least increase the number of her friends?

Indeed she did, came Deborah's ever-obliging answer. That very morning, for instance, Sally was still asleep because she had danced so late at the assembly the previous night. City assemblies were prestigious and decorous affairs in the course of which, sustained by tea and rusks, some fifty ladies and as many gentlemen from the best families, Anglican and Proprietary, danced with each other, partners being drawn by lot. So long as the Stamp Act had not been repealed, Franklin had turned a deaf ear to his women's hints about Sally's having to wear her mother's gown on such occasions, for lack of a proper one of her own. As soon as the American boycott of English goods was lifted, he resumed his shipments and even filled some rather frivolous requests transmitted by Sally but originating with her more urbane and elegant sister-in-law Elizabeth who pined for the London shops. The governor's wife was taking Sally in tow; Debbie's letters, once she felt free to mention social events, fill up with references to her daughter's trips to New Jersey. One "Twelef night" Sally was driven across the frozen Delaware in a "Chariot in four" by James Logan, Jr., son of William Penn's longtime secretary. She was old enough to "answer for her self,"[2] as

Debbie reminded her husband, lest he wonder at a young lady traveling unchaperoned.

Yet it was not at the governor's mansion that Sally met her mate. It
was under sad circumstances, at the bedside of her closest friend, Peggy
Ross. Peggy was engaged to a thirty-year-old Englishman, Richard
Bache, who had settled in Philadelphia a few years previously. But she
fell ill. "She bore a long and lingering fit of sickness with *Patience,* and
met the King of Terrors with that *Fortitude* and *Resignation* which *Innocence* ever inspires."[3] At the approach of death, Peggy had asked
Richard Bache "to marry her intimate friend Sally Franklin, which
. . . he obligingly did."[4] So goes the family traditions as related in her
Book of Remembrance by Sally's granddaughter, Mrs. Elizabeth Duane
Gillespie.*

Richard Bache had been lured to America in 1760 by the success of
his older brother who ran a thriving import and marine insurance business in New York. Promptly admitted into the best circles of Philadelphia, Richard is listed in 1762 among the members of the Mount
Regale Fishing Company, along with Penns, Shippens, Morgans,
Chews, and other leading citizens. The Company gathered ostensibly
for fishing, mostly for sociability. On one such outing, Bache and a
fellow member supplied "Beefsteaks, 6 chickens, 1 ham, 1 breast veal, 2
tongues, 2 chicken pies, 1 quarter lamb, 2 sheeps' heads, peas, salad,
radishes, cream cheese, gooseberry pies, strawberries, 2 gallons spirits
and 25 lemons."[6]

For a time he seems to have prospered every bit as much as his
brother. The entries in his "Day Book" for the years 1762 and 1763

* Mrs. Gillespie was gratefully aware that were it not for this twist of fate, she
would not have been descended from the great Benjamin Franklin. She would not
have met Germany's chancellor Bismarck and he would not have grasped her hand
in both of his, exclaiming that he was proud to touch Franklin's blood. In a moment of elation, she proposed a family picnic to be held on the hundredth anniversary of Peggy's timely death. The idea was rejected, but the doggerel composed
for the occasion lives on:

> Maiden whose bones have crumbled long ago,
> Above thy tomb we bend, yet not in woe;
> Regrets we have none that an early call
> Grim Death made thee; he comes for all,
> And taking thee, he left us cause for mirth.
> Reaching far back, aye, even from our birth,
> Each one of us was glad, for thy finale
> 'Twas that which made us flesh and blood with Sally.
>
> Requiems we sing not, for they're rather dull;
> Odes we will write with praises ever full;
> Sonnets and verses to thy name we'll pen.
> Sally's our grandma, she's the child of Ben.[5]

end with a well satisfied and elegantly calligraphed "Laus Deo."[7] Then his affairs took a turn for the worse. He spent most of 1765 in England acting as agent for his brother and trying to improve his own connections since an American importer had to depend heavily on reliable contacts and creditors in the mother country, given the chronic lack of currency and lopsided balance of payments in the colonies. Once back in Philadelphia, he opened a dry-goods store on Chestnut Street and advertised in the *Pennsylvania Gazette* a "neat assortment of European and East-India goods," newly arrived.

After Peggy's death in August 1766, Sally asked her father to send her a mourning ring to wear in loving memory of her friend. By the time the ring arrived—and along with it an epitaph he had composed at the request of the dead girl's father—Sally and Richard had informed Franklin of the depth of their feelings for each other. Their letters, now lost, were promptly followed by one from Debbie, fairly quivering with apprehension. After chatting along for a few uneasy pages, she finally took the plunge and confirmed that Sally had indeed been adding to the number of her friends. She, Deborah, was not taking the situation lightly. "Obliged to be father and mother," she was acting for the best. And the best way, she felt, was to treat the young man as a friend (which he deserved) and allow his visits, lest she drive Sally to see him elsewhere. "I hope I ackte to your Satisfackshon."[8] Two of their closest friends, consulted on the matter, felt Debbie was following a wise course. There followed a description of Sally's social life, teas, card games, balls, a seat in young Penn's carriage (a surprise considering the animosity between Franklin and the Penns), all obviously meant to show it was not for lack of connections with the most prominent Philadelphia families that Sally wanted to link her life to that of a man who ran a dry-goods store on Chestnut Street.

Franklin's reply, in May 1767, sounds strangely aloof. He left the matter, he said, to Deborah and to William "for at this Distance I could neither make any Enquiries into his Character and Circumstances, nor form any Judgment, and as I am in doubt whether I shall be able to return this Summer, I would not occasion a Delay in her Happiness if you thought the Match a proper one."[9] Whereupon he announced the shipment of two summer hats to Sally and moved on to other news. Clearly, he was disappointed at what appeared an unexciting choice, given Sally's opportunities.

Some weeks later, still indicating no enthusiasm, he confirmed his faith in Deborah's judgment about their daughter's match: "If you think it a suitable one, I suppose the sooner it is compleated, the better." He was certain by then that he would not come home that summer. Having to miss his only daughter's wedding elicited no comment on his part. His main concern was that his wife should not splurge. Well aware that Philadelphia weddings were generally sumptuous and long-drawn-out affairs, involving large parties given by the bride, punch parties by the groom every evening for a week, he cautioned Deborah not to "make an expensive feasting Wedding, but conduct every thing with Frugality and Oeconomy." He emphasized that their income had diminished considerably and that for his part he was being as frugal as possible in London, contenting himself with a single dish when he dined at home and "making no Dinners for anybody."[10]

Actually Franklin had some cause to relapse into his old anguish about money. The partnership with David Hall which had provided him with a comfortable income for eighteen years had expired and there was real danger that he might lose his position as postmaster general. He was still a rich man, however, about to take a splendid trip to Paris that summer, and he did not need to torment the already worried Deborah by raising the specter of a poverty-stricken old age with their money melting "like Butter in the Sunshine" unless they paid attention. Bache, he warned, should have no expectation of a dowry. "I can only say, that if he proves a good Husband to her, and a good Son to me, he shall find me as good a Father as I can be but at present I suppose you would agree with me that we cannot do more than fit her out handsomely in Cloaths and Furniture, not exceeding in the whole Five Hundred Pounds Value. For the rest, they must depend as you and I did, on their own Industry and Care."[11]

Fortune hunters were much on his mind at the time, for Polly Stevenson's engagement, concluded somewhat before Sally's, had just been broken. The fiancé, Franklin reported indignantly, had proved "a mean-spirited mercenary Fellow, not worthy so valuable a Girl as she is in every Respect, Person, Fortune, Temper and excellent Understanding."[12] And now "a mere fortune hunter"[13] were the very words applied to Bache in a confidential message William sent his father during that tense spring of 1767.

Richard Bache, as he himself informed Franklin, had suffered a business misfortune that may not have been his fault but was of catastrophic proportions nevertheless. In the early spring of 1766 when his affairs had been foundering in the general slump caused by the Stamp Act, he had made himself owner of the *Charlestown*, a ship of 110 tons, large by Philadelphia standards, which had been cast away in Delaware Bay. He had it repaired and fitted out for a long trading voyage to Jamaica, then on to the Bay of Biscay and Rotterdam or London. Confidently he debited all the expenses of the venture to one Edward

Green in London with whom he had, or thought he had, a clear understanding. When the bills fell due, Green reneged and Bache was left liable for every farthing, "he having refused to pay any of my Bills which were drawn on him on Acct. of said Ship, she is therefore, contrary to my Expectations, thrown upon my own hands."[14] His indebtedness was staggering, even after the ship was sold. Eventually he worked out a settlement which obliged him to sign bonds, due in five years at 7 per cent interest, totaling £3620.0.4. William had legitimate grounds for concern.

Bache's letter to Franklin—an appeal for help?—is lost. William's alarmed message dispatched somewhat later throws little light on the disaster. Feeling responsible for his sister's welfare, William had inquired about his prospective brother-in-law and he had received so many contradictory opinions that he wound up more puzzled than ever. Without knowing the full story of the *Charlestown,* he had learned that the amounts of Bache's bills far exceeded his ability to pay, even if he were worth as much as he said he was, which to William seemed doubtful. John Ross, the late Peggy's father, asserted flatly that Bache wanted to better his circumstances by marrying into a family that would support him. "If Sally marries him," William warned, "they must both be entirely on you for their Subsistence." Then, worried that his sister might consider him a traitor, he ended his letter with the (obviously disregarded) admonition: *Do burn this.*[15]

And Sally? Sally's sole concern was to comfort Richard Bache. Bolstered by love, she emerges at last as a full-fledged woman, no longer the "dutiful" girl who hides behind polite formulas aimed only at her elders' approval. Her letters to her fiancé radiate with her trust in him and with the solidity, the loyalty that would be her trademark: "I would by no means have you think too much on a misfortune which no human prudence could prevent, for nothing is worse for the health and spirits than reflecting for a long time on one subject. You ask me how I keep up my spirits; let me tell you that while I think you love me, it is out of the power of misfortune to make me truly unhappy."[16] Still, unconcerned as she tried to appear, she looked pale and sick, said her mother. Tension mounted in Philadelphia as the family awaited Franklin's reaction to the bad news.

His answer to Bache arrived in September. Its language was mild but its message was a firm *no:*

Sir

I received yours of the 21st of May and am truly sorry to hear of your misfortune. It must however be a consolation to you that it cannot be imputed to any imprudence of your own, and that being yet in the early part of life, industry and good management may in a few years replace what you have lost. But in the mean time your own discretion will suggest to you how far it will be right to charge yourself with the expense of a family which if undertaken before you recover yourself, may forever prevent your emerging. I love my daughter perhaps as well as ever parent did a child, but I have told you before that my estate is small, scarce a sufficiency for the support of me and my wife, who are growing old and cannot now bustle for a living as we have done; that little can therefore be spared out of it while we live, and how far the profits of any business you are in or may expect after a total loss of your stock will go in housekeeping you can best judge.

I am obliged to you for the regard and preference you express for my child and wish you all prosperity; but unless you can convince her friends of the probability of your being able to maintain her properly, I hope you will not persist in a proceeding that may be attended with ruinous consequences to you both.

I am Sir Your most obedient humble Servant.[17]

Very much the kind of language Franklin must have heard from all those fathers who had not wanted *him* for a son-in-law. Very much the kind of language Richard Bache would use when his own daughter Debby planned to marry against his will. Rather unperturbed, it seems, at having quashed his daughter's fond plans, Franklin, that very day, turned his attention to what he thought were elephants' tusks, belonging in reality to mastodons, and sent some remarks on elephants to the friend who had shipped him the fossilized discoveries from Big Bone Lick (Kentucky). To the modern reader, his apparent indifference to Sally's feelings is disturbing, just as in the earlier matchmaking episode with Strahan; but Franklin did suggest to his wife that she send their daughter to join him in London—provided the captain's wife were on board. Such a trip, he thought, might be of "some amusement" to Sally and would "improve"[18] her. This was the standard remedy for lovesick maidens.

Was he still dreaming his old dream? Curiously, neither Strahan nor her father had so much as mentioned Sally's name during Franklin's two years back in America. Billy Strahan was as yet unattached (he never did marry) and a better prospect than ever now that he had been taken into full partnership by his father. If Sally listened to paternal advice now and married him, she could still meet David Hume and Samuel Johnson, James Boswell and the rest of the Strahan circle; she could travel to Scotland, to Bath, to the Continent; best of all, she would enter a family Franklin adored, from the impetuous father to the frail mother, from daughter Rachel who played the armonica so well to young Peggy whom he called his little wife, from William to George to Andrew, all destined by their father to the world of publishing, but all fated, as it turned out, to go their individual ways.

But Sally wanted Richard Bache.

She had the women on her side. In the darkest hour of crisis, Elizabeth still offered a toast to "brother Bache,"[19] probably unaware of the unflattering portrait her husband was painting of brother Bache in the mistaken trust that the document would be burned.

Debbie had felt comfortable with Bache from the very beginning. She even thought he looked like Franklin, a coincidence joyfully commented upon by one and all in those pre-Freudian days. More than anything, Debbie loved Sally with a gritty vehemence. With every passing month, she discovered new facets to be admired in her daughter. Sally knew just how to behave when the governor entertained dignitaries; Sally rushed to her brother's side when it was feared William would be challenged to a duel ("she is a mere champion, that daughter of ours!");[20] Sally who already as a child had eased her mother's headaches with her "little hands"[21] now knew how to steady her mother's moods. Surviving without Sally "one more day" was impossible . . .

Another ally across the seas: Mrs. Stevenson, inebriated at the thought of a wedding and all the lovely shopping it entailed, but held in check by Franklin who assured her there would be no marriage. She sat down in mid-September and wrote to Debbie, mother to mother, puzzled companion to awed wife. What was happening, she wondered. No news from Philadelphia. Franklin complaining that he was left in the dark. At all events, she had bought some silk and had it made up into a fashionable négligée "not out of character for your Daughter as Miss Franklin" (probably meaning for your daughter even if she remains Miss Franklin). She had planned a much more sumptuous outfit for the bride "but your goodman forbid it." She was bewildered and Franklin appeared in a terrible mood. He had left for France, "his Back full of small blind boils, so-call'd," and now he had written that his ill-humor had still found no vent and that he had a great mind to vent it upon her. She really did not know why she should deserve his anger, she moaned, "but he is the best Judg." Bending like a reed in the tempest and presuming Debbie did the same, Mrs. Stevenson sighed that she wished they could sit in a room together and chat. In her chaotic way she was trying to tell Deborah that great men—all men?—are sometimes hard to live with. And also that she understood Debbie's loneliness: "I truly think your expectations of seeing Mr. F. from time to time has bin to much for a tender affeciont wiff to bear, but I make no dote as his abacens is for the good of the country in generalle."[22]

Franklin came back to England the first week of October in very high spirits. Charmed by French manners, intrigued by French ladies, thrilled by his reception in the Parisian scientific world, impressed—up to a point—by Versailles, flattered by the affability of the royal family, he poured all his renewed *joie de vivre* into a letter to Polly, one of his most exquisitely young and vivacious letters. To his family he wrote upon the day of his return, promising a full description of the voyage when he found time. If he sent it, it has left no trace.

From them he found awaiting him a batch of prudent, nebulous letters: political news from William, family news from Debbie ranging from the ravages wrought by the moths to the death of Polly Mecom, Jane's youngest and most beloved daughter. About Sally, one word only: She and Mr. Bache were "disappointed."[23]

By mid-November, as he worriedly asked Deborah what was happening, his daughter's destiny had already been sanctioned and sanctified for more than two weeks: "Last Thursday Evening [October 29, 1767] Mr. Richard Bache, of this City, Merchant, was married to Miss Sally Franklin, the only Daughter of the celebrated Doctor Franklin, a young Lady of distinguished Merit. The next Day all the Shipping in the Harbour displayed their Colours on the happy Occasion."[24]

The ships were happy but Father was not. A thunderous silence emanated from London. In December, Jane Mecom sent cautious congratulations. Setting aside for a moment her own despair over her Polly's death, she wished her brother lasting pleasure from his daughter's marriage "to a worthy Gentleman whom she loves and the only won that can make her Happy."[25] His answer was icy: "She has pleas'd herself and her Mother, and I hope she will do well: but I think they should have seen some better Prospect."[26] A year later, knowing the weight that Jane's opinion carried in her brother's mind, Deborah slyly forwarded to London a letter in which Jane (who in the meantime had met Richard Bache) expressed her favorable impression of him. To no avail. Franklin saw through the little stratagem and answered with a dry, "I am glad you approve the Choice they have made."[27] His love, in his letters home, was invariably sent to Sally alone. Bache's name was not even mentioned and his several overtures to his father-in-law went unanswered.

Sally's victory was dearly paid for by her mother and herself. Where, one wonders, had they found the courage to fly in the face of paternal authority? What had they written in self-defense? Thrown into the fire, perhaps, by the angry hand of the recipient, or suppressed by the zealous hand of a descendant, or else simply destroyed by accident, all references to the wedding have disappeared. One does not even know whether William attended. A letter he sent his father five days after the event does not refer to it.

After a brief honeymoon in New York, Bache took off for Jamaica for several months in the hope of mending his affairs; Sally, lonely and sad, stayed home—her parents' home, the only one she would have for most of her life. Gloom spread in the beautiful new house on Market Street. The rifts tearing the family apart can be guessed at from a letter William wrote his father in May 1768. One can do no more than guess because William was in such a defensive mood that his style became quite convoluted and his meaning hard to grasp. Franklin, in a letter now lost, must have accused his son of listening to "whispers and Makebates [trouble-makers]"[28] and of getting involved in a family quarrel. William insisted that, on the contrary, his whole life had been spent trying to avoid confrontation even when he had been amply provoked. He did not specify what this particular quarrel was about. As far as one can tell, it had to do with Deborah's being angry with their friends for not approving Sally's match. She may have written to her husband that she was not angry, said William, but such was not the case: "Be assur'd, Sir, that you are greatly mistaken in thinking that my Mother was not angry." (Deborah, it will be remembered, had been dubbed "a hedge-hog" by her neighbor; here was the hedgehog, quills out, defending her child, much to the horror of the royal governor of New Jersey.) William decided, however, to end his disturbing message on a note of serenity. With the pseudo kindness of people who hint that everything is going to rack and ruin but that they will not destroy their correspondent's peace of mind by giving unpleasant details, he assured his father that he would persevere in his policy of not acquainting him with those miserable stories, "for as to what other People may think it is a Matter of no Consequence."[29]

But it was, of course, a matter of consequence. And Franklin decided that his displeasure had been felt long enough. In the summer of 1768, almost a full year after the marriage, he at last admitted his son-in-law into the fold. Since the young couple was then visiting in Boston, Debbie was the ecstatic transmitter of the good news: The pathetic height of her joy reflects the depth of her anxiety. "The post horn is blowing now and I am quite in a flutter until I know what news; I hope it will be good. . . . Well, the post brought letters from the packet; and now, Mr. Bache (or my son Bache) I give you joy: although there are no fine speeches, as some people would make, your father (or so I will call him) and you, I hope, will have many happy days together."[30]*

* The longer passages of Deborah's letters have been modernized.

"No fine speeches" was indeed an understatement. Although his first letter to Bache opened with the words "Loving Son," Franklin reiterated his charge of irresponsibility in marrying Sally before he could support her. "In this Situation of my Mind, you should not wonder that I did not answer your Letters. I could say nothing agreeable: I did not chuse to write what I thought, being unwilling to give Pain where I could not give Pleasure." He added, however, that time had made him easier, as well as Bache's accounts of happier prospects. "If you prove a good Husband and Son, you will find in me an Affectionate Father."[31]

A cold-sounding letter, yet one the family was to treasure down the generations. Mrs. Gillespie comments that "it shows plainly the power Franklin had for keeping his feelings under restraint and not committing himself in words until composure was restored to him. It was a great joy to his daughter who showed in many ways her sorrow at having caused her father distress."[32] It certainly sent Debbie into raptures. Now she knew that Mr. Bache could make himself agreeable to his father-in-law. "And then I hope my heart will be more at rest than it has been for some time past."[33] Franklin was expected home any minute (he had been away almost four years) and Debbie urged the young Baches to be back in Philadelphia in time to greet him.

Franklin did not return. To Debbie who, after this last disappointment, no longer tried to conceal her despair, he wrote in a conciliatory vein that he was glad she found so much reason to be satisfied with Mr. Bache. "I hope all will prove for the best."[34] Thawing a little further, he volunteered a few months later that Bache's sister, who had paid him a visit in London, appeared "a very agreable, genteel, sensible young Woman."[35] By the spring of 1769, the news of Sally's pregnancy moved him to send her six caudle cups and saucers "of great beauty." (Caudle was a warm drink of wine or ale, bread, sugar, spices, and sometimes eggs, given to a woman in childbed and offered to her visitors.) Mrs. Stevenson, he reported, was so excited at the prospect of Sally's baby "that she keeps talking as much as would fill . . ."[36] Some irreverent mouse has nibbled from the manuscript the name of the receptacle that Mrs. Stevenson's chatter would have filled.

The baby, of course, provided a marvelous opportunity for further reconciliation and no chance was overlooked. He was named Benjamin Franklin Bache and his grandmother made a point of referring to him by his full name—a distant caress to that other Benjamin Franklin she would never see again. She stressed his resemblance to their little dead Franky and his resemblance to his illustrious namesake. Grandfather was thanked for his interest in the child's inoculation and assured that all had been carried out in compliance with his instructions. Sally who, according to her mother, was the perfect nurse and educator, took pains to convince her father that she was still his girl and that if he did not want her and her husband to settle in Jamaica, they would not do it: "No, Sir, your child will not give you pain. She will stay, and prove to you through life what she really is, your dutiful and affectionate daughter."[37]

In spite of these overtures and the generally cordial tone of Franklin's answers, Deborah and Sally were quite uneasy when Bache, four years after his marriage, took off for England in the fall of 1771 to visit his family, to meet his formidable father-in-law, and possibly to obtain his help. Sally had wanted to accompany him but had been prevailed upon by her husband and William to stay at home—once again. She fretted that Bache might not be diplomatic enough: "I trust you met with an agreable reception from Papa, I am indeed anxious to hear; if it should not be as cordial as I could wish at first, yet I know when you consider it is my Father, your goodness to, and afection for me, will make you try a little to gain his esteem and friendship, but I need not tell my dearest Lad how much happier I should be to hear he had receiv'd you with afection."[38]

When her "dearest Lad" arrived in London in October, he found that Franklin was still away on one of his summer jaunts, this time to Ireland, but Mrs. Stevenson received him like a son, giving free rein to her exuberant cordiality in the absence of her sometimes critical lodger. Her daughter Polly had reasons of her own to sympathize with young love. On a visit to Margate with her ancient aunt in the summer of 1769, she had lost her heart to a promising pathologist, William Hewson, and served notice to Franklin that she might very well run off with this man: "To be sure it would be an imprudent Step at the discreet Age of Thirty, but there is no saying what one should do, if sollicited by a Man of an insinuating Address & good Person, tho' he may be too young for one & not yet establish'd in his Profession."[39] In contrast to Sally's, this match was warmly approved by all of her relatives, and by Franklin, her *de facto* father, who gave her away on July 10, 1770.

By the time of Bache's visit, Polly was the happy mother of a baby boy. She took an immediate liking to Sally's husband and to further his cause wrote Franklin a letter that could not fail to enchant him at a time when, in his sixties, he may have felt that he had lost both Sally and Polly to their new lives. No more queries about natural science. Polly, with marriage and motherhood, seems to have lost all interest in such lofty topics (although her husband was a brilliant scientist), but she still knew how to go straight to "her dear philosopher's" heart—or his vanity: "Welcome! my dear and honour'd Friend! Welcome once more to our Island! The Wind may blow now without making our Hearts ache. You were constantly in our Thoughts during the late stormy Weather. I have pray'd for you at Midnight when I have been suckling my little Boy and heard the Window Sashes rattle." The whole letter goes on the same way, cajoling, tender, flattering. As soon as he read that "Mr. Bache is at Preston where he will wait with the pleasing Expectation of seeing you in your Return, we were all very much pleas'd with him,"[40] Franklin rushed to Preston and opened his arms to Richard Bache.

"He receiv'd me . . . with a degree of affection that I did not expect to be sensible at our first meeting,"[41] reported an almost incredulous Bache who, in his hour of elation, was thoughtful enough to write a long account to the anxious Debbie. His letter overflows with gratitude to Mrs. Stevenson and with a lively affection for Deborah, shown in his perfect choice of topics: his own resemblance to Franklin, noticed by all their acquaintances as it had first been by her ("I should be glad to be like him in any respect"), his games with the little Hewson boy. At a time when memories of her husband and her immense love of children were the only bright spots in Debbie's life, he knew how to give her warmth.

Short as it was, the stay at Preston was a great success all around. Richard's mother and four sisters vied with one another in wooing the great man. Franklin in turn took a liking to Mrs. Bache, who henceforth addressed him as "brother." From London he sent her a present of oysters and, what was still more appreciated, a portrait of himself. Purred Mrs. Bache, "It is so like the original you cannot imagine with what pleasure we look at it, as we can perceive in it the likeness of my Son, as well as your Self. . . . You are sometimes in the dining room, and other times in the parlor."[42]

Traveling together back to Craven Street, the two men became better acquainted. "I very much like his Behaviour,"[43] Franklin commented to Jane Mecom. Indeed, he was sufficiently impressed with his son-in-law's integrity and business ability to give him a joint power of attorney with Debbie for the purpose of collecting debts.

A happy ending, one might say. The age-old female technique of bowing one's head while having one's way had been vindicated. Passion had prevailed over reason. And now reason was almost admitting that passion had not been so blind after all. Richard Bache, in early 1772, was sailing home with something akin to paternal blessing.

Yet it was not such a happy ending. Richard Bache was coming home almost empty-handed, his hopes for a new start unfulfilled. He had wanted to change careers, had brought along £1,000 to acquire some public office with his father-in-law's backing. But Franklin, whose disaffection from the crown was growing rapidly, did not wish to see yet another member of his family dependent upon governmental patronage, particularly in the kinds of jobs open to Americans. He advised Bache to be his own man, a merchant in Philadelphia, selling only for ready cash. Bache had to be content with a gift of £200 for some additional cargo ("that his Voyage hither might not be quite fruitless"), the loan of another £60, and the comforting thought that by being industrious and frugal he would eventually "pay his debts and be clear of the world."[44] Selling for ready cash was a piece of advice Franklin bestowed on several young relatives. Sound as it appears, it must have been almost impossible to put into practice in an economy forced to operate on credit because it was always short of currency.

Franklin communicated his views to both William and Sally. The moral about being supported by one's own industry rather than by government made only a limited impression on William: A year later he was still trying to find a comfortable sinecure for an impecunious relative and asked Franklin to use his influence to have the man appointed customs collector for the port of Burlington. His timing could not have been worse. Franklin retorted angrily that he "could not ask that office, trifling as it is, for any Relation of mine. And detesting as I do the whole System of American Customs, believing they will one Day bring on a Break through the Indiscretion and Indolence of those concern'd in the Collection, I should never wish to see one so near to me engaged in that Business."[45] Sally received no such blast about Richard Bache's application, and for that she must have been relieved. But if she had hoped for an appraisal of her husband's character, for some comment beyond the strictly financial, she was disappointed. Money and money alone was discussed.

As for herself, she was told with a trace of contempt that if her husband kept a store she might prove as serviceable to him as her mother had been to her father, for she was not deficient in capacity and, he hoped, "not too proud." She might easily learn some accounting (a theme Franklin had been harping on for years) and she could copy letters. Upon occasion she even wrote them very well, he admitted. Friendly on the surface, his letter really amounted to a blunt refusal to lift the Baches out of their predicament and help them attain a standard of living more in keeping with the education Sally had received and with the style maintained by the governor and his wife. As a bonus, she was allowed to stay on with her mother and save the rent of a separate establishment: "Indeed it seems to be your Duty to attend her as she grows infirm."

Sally was not "too proud." Before her husband arrived home, she had already fitted out a store on the ground floor of one of Franklin's tenant houses on Market Street, "an excellent Stand for dry goods."[46] By May 1772 the Baches were advertising *for cash only* a variety of textiles endowed with such exotic names as humhums, silk pullicats, and Ozenbrigs. But the business did not thrive; a "sorry concern" Bache was calling it less than a year later. He was anxious to try another line, the wine and grocery business, "which few have failed in."[47]

Sally did not meet with much better fortune in the domestic sphere. As her mother grew frailer, she had offered to take over many of the household cares. Franklin had applauded this initiative: "Remember, for your Encouragement in good oeconomy, that whatever a Child saves of its Parents' Money, *will be its own another Day.* Study Poor Richard a little, and you may find some Benefit from his Instructions."[48] Still, he knew his wife well enough to suspect that she would not readily give up the reins. Sure enough, six months after her brave beginning, Sally admitted defeat: "I am no longer house keeper; it gave my dear Mama so much uneasiness."[49] Debbie was now so afraid of spending too much that she would only allow Sally driblets of money, never enough to buy in quantity and more economically.

A husband chronically in debt, a mother ailing and set in her ways, a perennially absent father, no home of her own, these were the harsh realities of Sally's life. But she also had her little Ben, another baby on the way, and a nature both placid and cheerful. Above all she had an unshakable love for her Mr. Bache.

XII

The Patriarch
of Craven Street

Lend then, my dear Paternal Friend, a pitying ear to my Griefs.
—Amelia Barry to Franklin, December 7, 1781

I am gratly obliged to you for the trouble I give you.
—Martha Johnson to Franklin, February 15, 1768

. . . the best Friend I ever had.
—Hannah Walker to Franklin, July 17, 1769

I don't mean . . . to give you too much concern
or troble with my Sons, tho' . . .
—Jonathan Williams Sr. to Franklin, August 27, 1770

DYERS, BAKERS, LACEMAKERS, tavernkeepers, seamen, printers, laughing children, anguished widows, gifted nephews, ne'er-do-well nephews . . . so many humble people who would have left no visible trace had they not been Franklin's kin. Yet in his life they mattered. They were the counterweight to the lords of high politics and the princes of science, Hillsborough and Priestley, Shelburne and Pringle. They anchored him to reality and to his past, gave him the feeling of his power and his kindness, the essential comfort of belonging. He rarely turned his back on them or ignored their needs. True to Puritan tradition, he unhesitatingly accepted his responsibilities as patriarch of a sprawling family: women in distress, youngsters in need of a home, relatives from America to be steered through the perils of London, and, back home, the perennially troubled members of the Mecom family.

Take, for instance, the case of Amelia Evans, not even a relative by birth. Born a year after Sally, she was Deborah's goddaughter, and the only child of Lewis Evans, one of the most eminent cartographers of colonial America, a man of many talents and interests who had drawn the diagrams for the Franklin stove, joined with its inventor in an early insurance scheme, and lectured on electricity. Amelia's life was to be one of "adventure and misfortune."[1] Her mother died when she was three, her father when she was eleven, leaving her the copper plates to his maps and not much else. She received an excellent education but, as she admitted, did not listen to Deborah, her "revered Godmama," and was for a time "too eagerly bent on the pursuit of new acquaintance and a life of dissipation."[2] Eventually she found her way to England (where she borrowed five guineas from Franklin on the pledge of the copper plates) and thence to Tunis to serve as governess in the family of the British consul. There she met and married David Barry, an Irish captain engaged in the Turkey trade.

In 1773 the Barrys settled for a time in a little house just outside London. Enchanted by an evening spent there, Franklin wrote Debbie that her goddaughter was "a great Traveller, having now been in all the 4 Quarters of the World." It was a cozy evening, Amelia suckling her "Giant Boy,"[3] born in Smyrna, while his two-year-old sister doted on the elderly guest. Pleased with the charm he always exerted on children, Franklin related how the little girl, usually shy, ran to him with a smile, then stayed by his side the whole time and refused to let anyone else come near.

A year later the Barrys, back in Tunis, had a third child. "Amelia has now some Connection I think with the whole Globe, being born herself in America, and having her first child in Asia, her second in Europe and now her third in Africa."[4*] Captain Barry quit the sea and went into grain export, staking everything on continued war between Turkey and Russia. Peace came instead, followed by years of drought, and he was ruined. As the Barry fortunes began to go downhill, Amelia's letters became more frantic. Whereas in happier times she had beseeched Franklin to send her a lock of his hair as "perhaps . . . the last request I may ever make of you,"[5] she now bombarded him with entreaties she called effusions of her heart. She wanted him to rescue her helpless family by procuring Mr. Barry a United States consulship, by settling her claims on some property in Philadelphia, and by arranging payment of the profits from a new edition of her father's maps. While she was at it, she also asked for inscribed copies of his works as a "Gift to 'your dear Child' (sweet epithet more delightful to me than

---

* Franklin was a little confused: the first child was born in Ireland, the second in Turkey. As time went by, their names became more extravagant: the third one, for whom Franklin was designated as godfather, was called Philotesia Janetta, the fourth Anna Africana. Anna Africana spoiled the euphony by marrying a Swiss, Johann Rudolf Schintz.

being called the Favorite of the first Prince on earth)."[6] In return, she favored him with some poetic flights of her own.

Franklin, by then in France, found time to busy himself with the promotion of her father's maps, but there already were so many pirated editions that not much was to be made on the legitimate one. In 1779, Amelia and her family moved to Italy where her husband soon died, still enmeshed in poverty. The young widow was reduced to outright begging: She hoped Franklin would send her money enough to take her and the children to England. He apparently did not. She tried another tack late in 1784, proposing that he spend the winter with her in Pisa and let her wait on him hand and foot, like a faint copy of "your little Sally"[7] (with whom she had always felt competitive). Amelia was only one of an army of suppliants in those years, yet Franklin's early fondness for her still moved him to suggest that she might return to America as he had done after a long exile. She replied that rather than becoming a burden to her friends, she was prepared to "seek some sequestered vale among the Apenines, and derive from Religion and Philosophy such aids as they extend to the meanest of their votaries . . . to submit to evils which must soon terminate."[8] But she also reminded him to look into that bit of "unlocated" property of hers in Philadelphia.

Distressed women of his own blood had a greater claim to his aid. Martha Johnson, for example. The widow of an officer and the mother of two young children, she was a niece by way of Franklin's half-sister Ann Harris. After her husband's death, her English in-laws proposed that she run a little shop in the country in partnership with them. This she did, leaving her fourteen-year-old daughter Nancy with Franklin in Craven Street, while Sammy, age eleven, was given some schooling with his financial help and then apprenticed to a Philadelphia merchant in London. Nancy was endowed with a "fine Voice, . . . a good Person and pleasing Behaviour," and Franklin thought she might well "advance herself" in music.[9] Within a year, her ill-fated mother was back in London, also living for a time with the Craven Street ménage, having been fleeced out of her widow's pension by her "cunning" relations. The outlook seemed to improve in 1770 when Nancy married a captain in the navy "said to be very rich"[10] and followed him to his native Barbados, but the husband soon died, a hurricane destroyed her house, and her inheritance was tied up in a long lawsuit.

Martha Johnson's letters during the Revolution—recitations of unalloyed woe—are graphic and touching, at times almost epic. The war had separated her from her family and friends in America and she never expected to see any of them again, "for I look on my self as a poor forsaken wanderer who has no mortal to enquire after me to see whether I am dead or alive."[11] No sooner had she recovered from a long and devastating illness than she lost her belongings and her little store of money in a fire; all she had left was a bed gown and a petticoat. She evidently received some money from Franklin in the "dreadful distress which is out of my power to describe,"[12] somehow picked up the pieces and started over. Sammy had gone to sea as a midshipman and risen to lieutenant, perhaps helped again by the distant benefactor whom Martha even in the midst of war had confidently implored to put in a good word for her son with influential English friends.

The affairs of Hannah Walker and her husband were mustier. A lacemaker, she was Franklin's first cousin once removed and one of the clan that he had sought out with such enthusiasm during his first mission to England. By his second mission, he was considered the dispenser of favors and accepted the role as naturally as it was pressed. Unfortunately the patronage of such an illustrious relation seems to have been too heady for Hannah's husband who used Franklin's name in some improper way, drew a rebuke from Mrs. Stevenson, and caused poor Hannah torments of humiliation. She pleaded for pardon, offering such a tangled account of her family troubles that it must have been easier to help her than to understand it: "I have done more than was fitting or Reasonable for a woman to do but I thought if I could save charge I would for Brewing and washing and mending and making for my family and but one woman to do everything sick or well. . . . Indeed Sir if you did know in everything what I have gone through in every thing ill nature by his Friends and Troubles in my Family innumerable and no body to comfort me but God alone you I am sure would Pity me very much and think no body could have gone through it but to give a full account in a Letter would be to Troublesome."[13]

The indefatigable Mrs. Stevenson was dispatched to look into things in the hamlet of Westbury where the Walkers lived. And things, she found, were awful, the house miserable and cold, the lodging "hard," the tea so bad she was reduced to drinking milk. But poor Mrs. Walker did her best, trying to keep her guest warm and well fed, while the parson slipped a mat under the London lady's feet.

Back in London, Mrs. Stevenson set out to find them a better house, no doubt with Franklin's encouragement, and at long last (but not before the Walkers' beer shed had caved in) found a suitable one. For the purchase price she lent them £150, to be returned at a low rate. True to form, Mr. Walker promptly squandered the money and his wife had to write once again to beseech Franklin's forgiveness. The solicitor suggested that any future contributions be made without the husband's knowledge: "I wish the man felt more distress and the woman less."[14] Indeed Mr. Walker had made such a mess of it that the bailiff was at the door. Without a timely payment by Franklin they might have lost all their possessions.

Fortunately some of the patriarchal commitments were more pleasant. Not long after he had settled once more into the comfortable surroundings of Craven Street, Franklin began to stock the house with the children whose company seemed as necessary to his happiness as that of "ingenious" adults. His cousin Thomas Franklin, a village dyer, had welcomed him back to England with the gift of a hare. A year later, in the spring of 1766, he appeared on the doorstep with his daughter Sally, a girl of about eleven whose mother had recently died and whose appeal to Mrs. Stevenson was instantaneous. For the next six years, except for occasional visits to her father, Sally was to make her home in Craven Street, acquiring "a little Schooling and improvement" under Mrs. Stevenson's solicitous eye, and making herself useful and agreeable about the house. Not as intellectual as Polly Stevenson nor as talented as Nancy Johnson, she was "sensible and of a sweet obliging Temper."[15] Mrs. Stevenson on the spot and Deborah from a distance vied in affection for the motherless child. When Sally almost died of a fever her first year in London, Mrs. Stevenson was distressed and felt guilty for having invited her to stay; when she recovered, Debbie could scarcely find adequate words to express her relief. "I love her so far as London,"[16] she exclaimed; in her heart there was room enough for two Sally Franklins.

Cousin Thomas's gratitude took the concrete form of butter, chickens, and sage cheese. When it looked as if Franklin might soon be returning to America, in 1768, he ventured to ask him to take Sally along. Debbie was enthusiastic about the plan but Franklin had doubts: "The Care of educating other People's Children is a Trust too weighty for us as we grow old."[17] He did not go home, however, and Sally stayed on in Craven Street till she was "grown up almost a woman,"[18] at which point she married a farmer's son, eliciting a sigh of regret from her guardian: "I shall miss her, as she is nimble-footed and willing to run of Errands and wait upon me, and has been very serviceable to me for some Years, so that I have not kept a Man."[19]*

There was another child, more important if less serviceable:

* The nimble-footed Sally's marriage ended with her death nine years and four children later. Eventually, Franklin's patriarchal obligations would be inherited by no less than George Washington to whom the vicar of Lutterworth appealed for congressional help in favor of the youngest boy who lived with his grandfather in indigent circumstances.

William's illegitimate son. Four years old when his grandfather returned to England, little Temple was cared for by a succession of women whose itemized bills for inoculations, haircuts, stockings, and pocket money are for a long time the only surviving proof of his existence—bills paid by Mrs. Stevenson before they made their circuitous way to New Jersey. Not before the boy turned nine did William begin to show stirrings of more fatherly concern. His own marriage was (and would remain) childless. Might it be possible to claim his son without the truth being known, without undoing the aura of respectability with which the governor had so carefully surrounded himself? "I should be glad to know your sentiments about bringing him over with you," William wrote his father early in 1769. "He might then take his proper Name, and be introduced as the Son of a poor Relation, for whom I stood God Father and intended to bring up as my own."[20] He had even picked out an Anglican clergyman to take charge of Temple's education. Nothing came of this scheme, however, since Franklin remained in England for another six years.

About the age of eight, Temple was enrolled in the Kensington boarding school run by Mrs. Strahan's brother, James Elphinston. A well-known if somewhat eccentric educator, whose system of rationalized spelling appealed to Franklin while his "foolish giggle"[21] irritated Boswell, Elphinston soon came to love Temple like a son. In fact, once the child emerges from anonymity, everybody seems to have been fond of him. He spent holidays in Craven Street, went off on jaunts with Mrs. Stevenson, attended birthday parties, and was included as a matter of course in the compliments addressed to Franklin's heterogeneous family by his correspondents. The only voice never heard in this chorus is Deborah's. Her silence might be explained as resentment against this new instance of sin in the family, an *erratum* committed by the unloved William this time, not by the almost perfect Benjamin. But it is much more likely that Deborah was never apprised of the child's existence. Not the slightest allusion to Temple appears in any of her husband's letters so rich in news about every other member of the clan, however distant. More surprising still, even Mrs. Stevenson and Polly were not let into the secret of Temple's origin. Who were they supposed to think he was? Describing to her sister-in-law a wedding in which Temple had acted as usher, Polly discreetly referred to him as "Mr. Temple, a young gentleman who is at school here and is under the care of Dr. Franklin."[22] Years later, she would refer with amusement to the game the whole family had played, pretending they had not guessed the true state of affairs.

Franklin grew increasingly charmed by his grandson: "Temple improves continually and more and more engages the regard of all that are acquainted with him, by his pleasing, sensible manly Behaviour."[23] But he was in a quandary about the boy's future. He had always intended him to follow the gentlemanly path to Eton and Oxford, but Eton and Oxford would be more than William could afford, and Franklin was not very pleased with what he heard about the "Relaxation of all Discipline, the Viciousness of the Youth, and the Extravagance of Expense" that characterized the "Great Schools."[24] On the other hand, they were supposed to offer the best training for manhood. Elphinston wanted to keep Temple at his own school. Franklin deferred any decision on the usual grounds that he would soon be coming home and could shift the boy and the problem to William. Father and grandfather, seeing that Temple had "a good Memory, quick Parts and ready Elocution,"[25] did agree that law would be the best choice of a profession, just as it had been in William's case.

Franklin's English kin would have been sufficient to tax Mrs. Stevenson's hospitality, but more came from across the sea. In 1770, two brothers arrived from Boston, Josiah and Jonathan Williams, grandsons of Franklin's half-sister Ann. Josiah was a blind musician for whom Franklin had ordered a glass armonica some years before; he now came to England to study with the organist and composer John Stanley who was also blind but who, he fervently believed, could "give him more Light . . . than any man living can see."[26] While Josiah happily filled his days with concerts, oratorios, and operas, Jonathan, a trained accountant, set Franklin's chaotic accounts in order, a service he was to repeat periodically over the next twenty years.

To the relief of their mother who had feared for their "Morrals" in such a place as London, the two young men were described by Franklin as veritable paragons. Josiah lived only for his music while Jonathan was diligent in his business, "tender of his Brother, not fond of the expensive Amusements"[27] of the city and spent all his leisure studying mathematics. Like William in the old days, Jonathan was taken along on a ramble through England. He was even left in charge of Franklin's colonial agencies for a spell. "Sober, regular, and inclined to Industry and Frugality,"[28] he reminded Franklin of his own best qualities in youth. In fact, the parallel went further: Jonathan would one day commit his own *erratum*, a child fathered out of wedlock during a subsequent stay in England.

Jonathan took back to Boston his granduncle's watch and, much more valuable, his enduring affection, an affection that would not waver through all the vicissitudes of a checkered business career. Jonathan in turn patterned himself after his illustrious relative, deliberately pursuing many of the same interests and seeking out his modes of thought more assiduously than any other young kinsman. As to Josiah, he returned home somewhat later, having fulfilled his "Heart's Desire"; within a few months he was dead of tuberculosis at the age of twenty-five. "I know the good Mrs. Stevenson whose Bowels yearned toward him will feel most pungent Grief" commented a sympathetic friend.[29]

Shortly after the departure of the Williams boys, the house on Craven Street was turned over to Polly Hewson and her family. Her husband had for some time been in partnership with Dr. William Hunter, the famous anatomist, the two of them giving highly popular lectures and demonstrations to medical students. All had worked smoothly until Hewson married; then everything seemed to go awry. Perhaps Hewson dallied too much with his bride; perhaps Hunter could not bear to lose the disciple who had lived in his house like a son. In any event, Hunter proposed to terminate the partnership, charging his younger associate with a host of trespasses: too frequent absences, insufferable rudeness, failing to ask permission before employing a man "to pick Bones out of the Tubs to fit up a Skeleton."[30]

Both sides turned to Franklin to arbitrate their differences and he arranged a truce to enable them to complete the term. Then Hewson struck out on his own, demolishing one end of the Craven Street house and remodeling it as an amphitheater. By the time he had moved in his family, his skeletons, his "prepar'd fetuses," and all the other paraphernalia of his trade, the old house must have been stretched to the bursting point. Mrs. Stevenson found another home for herself and her lodger a few doors away and made the move during the fall of 1772, while Franklin was visiting in the country.

Nothing better illustrates the comfortably uxorious quality of their relationship than a nasty letter he sent her shortly after the move—even though he had been spared most of its confusion. Feeling as unappreciated, harassed, and exhausted as any woman would under the circumstances, Mrs. Stevenson had gone off in a huff to stay with friends, the painter Benjamin West and his wife. Franklin reminded her bluntly that guests become tiresome after three days. "My Advice to you is to return with the Stage tomorrow." But then, lest she imagine that he was summoning her back because he could not manage without her, he spelled out his contentment at being left alone in the company of Nanny* and the cat—better still if Nanny were not there either to

---

* This was the very Nanny who had been such a trial to Debbie in Philadelphia, now sadder and poorer than ever. She had returned to England to collect a small inheritance and had married a "worthless fellow"[31] who had squandered it.

ask him what he wanted for dinner and if the cat would go away, too, rather than bother him with mewing requests to be let in or out. Oh, for the enjoyment of an empty house! "This Happiness however is perhaps too great to be conferr'd on any but Saints and holy Hermits. Sinners like me, I might have said US, are condemn'd to live together and tease one another."[32]

In truth, he had found in England a family that he was perilously close to preferring to the one in America. Mrs. Stevenson was livelier than Debbie, Polly was brighter than Sally, William Hewson more distinguished than Richard Bache. There were the Hewson grandchildren to make up for his own that he had never seen. It was a household devoted to his comfort and interests, and also full of fun and high spirits. During one of Mrs. Stevenson's beloved jaunts, Franklin, Polly, and Hewson put together the *Craven Street Gazette*, detailing domestic events for the absent "Queen Margaret" in the style of the court calendar. Franklin even viewed his landlady's passion for smuggling ("She is a Smuggler upon Principle")[33] with an indulgent amusement he would scarcely have accorded anyone else. Polly sought his advice on everything, from coping with her difficult aunt to raising her children. Mrs. Stevenson would continue to entrust him with her investments long after he returned to Philadelphia.

In such happy and loving surroundings, it is not surprising that a friend visiting Craven Street reported that "Doctor Franklin looks heartier than I ever knew him in America."[34]

Forced to re-enter Mrs. Stevenson's service, she remained nostalgic for Philadelphia.

XIII

"Sorrows Roll upon Me Like the Waves of the Sea"

I never can forget that you have not only been the best of Brothers but as a tender Father to me and mine.
—Jane Mecom to Franklin, December 30, 1765

THREE THOUSAND MILES OF OCEAN were not enough to insulate Franklin from the continuing misfortunes of the Mecoms. Unlike his Boston cousins, Jonathan and Josiah Williams, Benny Mecom, the problem nephew, had no capacity for sustained work—only a firm trust that the great man would somehow descend like a deity to reverse the downward saga of his life.

After his years in Antigua and his brief success in Boston, Benny, forever restless though married and many times a father, had decided in 1763 to try his luck as a newspaper publisher in New York. Within a year he was bankrupt and his uncle had the unpleasant task of informing Strahan that after the sale of Benny's assets (including the press brought back from Antigua), the creditors would be lucky to receive four shillings out of every pound owed them. "He seems so dejected and spiritless that I fear little will be got of him."[1]

Still, Franklin felt it incumbent upon him to bail out his nephew and help him make a fresh start, this time in New Haven. Benny's former master, James Parker, had been promoted from postmaster of New Haven to comptroller of the whole colonial system, and Benny was given the vacant postmastership. He also took a four-year lease on the printing office his uncle had equipped for him years earlier and had then sold to Parker when it became apparent that neither Benny nor Jemmy Franklin wanted it.

Thus Benny who had hated Parker in the days of his apprenticeship and had escaped from under his yoke by going to Antigua was again submitted to the authority of his old master. While Franklin who had intertwined their lives from the start was off in London, those two remained locked in a corrosive pattern of animosity. Parker was a dour man, honest, punctilious, exasperating, torn between self-pity and self-contempt, seeing himself as a new Job fully as tormented as the biblical one. Benny . . . what was he? A born failure, probably a manic-depressive, forever wavering between grandiose schemes and near-paralysis, a disturbed personality made still more troubled by being constantly accused of laziness. Deliberately or not, he drove Parker to distraction: by not answering his frantic messages, by not sending in the post office accounts, by promising to pay his rent without ever doing so ("not a copper for those four years! not a copper!"), by the sheer weight of his spinelessness and his passivity.

In a stream of querulous letters to Franklin, letters running sometimes to twenty pages and covering the whole range of human dissatisfaction, Parker, when he came to Benny, exhausted the vocabulary of bewilderment, frustration, stammering rage. Benny was "indifferent . . . lethargic . . . indolent . . . sluggish . . . on the going-back road . . . irrecoverable." Trying to change him was "as vain as washing the Blackmoor white." One could not "quicken his motions any more than a dead man's."[2] After his cries of anger, the older man felt pangs of guilt: "He must live. And yet I know not what to do with him."[3] Two years of this nagging brought Parker a hollow victory: "My dunning B. Mecom about the Post-Office has occasioned him to resign his commission."[4] Going one step further, he advised Benny against trying to continue as a master; given his temperament, he had better content himself with being someone's journeyman. But Benny, who was no less arrogant than ineffectual, reacted with indignation. From Parker came more prophecies of doom, soon fulfilled: A rival paper, the *Connecticut Journal*, elbowed out Benny's *Connecticut Gazette*. Parker noted it smugly, took back his press, and leased it to the competitor—who did pay the rental and was quite successful. By 1768 Benny's New Haven venture had ended in disaster.

He went to Philadelphia, straight to Debbie. Of course she tried to help. She introduced him to the Reverend Dr. Allison but reported to her husband, with a twinkle, that this doctor of divinity, vice-provost of the College of Philadelphia, was not orthodox enough to suit Jane's son: When the Presbyterian clergyman expressed the opinion that God in His mercy had made the road to Heaven so wide that some of all religious denominations could go there abreast, Benny had been upset and shocked. These quirks amused Deborah more than they irritated her. She championed her nephew's cause and lashed into Parker with such vehemence that he sent long defensive letters to London insisting that charity begins at home and that he was overwhelmed with his own family obligations—specifically with a host of recently orphaned nephews to feed and raise. Not much later, still struggling, still industrious and upright, as unendearing as ever, Parker died, an event he had been announcing as imminent for the last twenty years.

Benny's Philadelphia period started in high spirits. He found work with another printer—only journeywork, to be sure, but it fetched a good salary and he expected to be set up in his own printing shop as soon as Franklin returned, William told his father. Deborah felt nothing but compassion for the struggling young family. While professing submission to God's will, she could not help thinking that Benny's wife Betsy, a charming young woman, had been afflicted with an unwarranted share of bad luck. She knew better than to mention lending the Mecoms any money and spoke only of inviting Betsy and her five little girls to tea. Franklin was alarmed anyway. He wondered how "so very sluggish a Creature as Ben Mecom . . . can maintain in Philadelphia so large a Family. I hope they do not hang upon you; for really as we grow old and must grow helpless, we shall find we have nothing to spare."[5]

Within the next few months, Benny justified the general lack of faith in him. He promptly quarreled with his employer, quit several other jobs, and slid ever faster toward total ruin. "Coz. Ben Mecom is starving at Philadelphia," reported William, "and would have been, I suppose, in Gaol by this Time if it had not been for the Assistance my Mother and I have afforded him and his Family. . . . His Pride and Laziness are beyond any Thing I ever knew, and he seems determin'd rather to sink than to strike a Stroke to keep his Head above Water. . . . In short I look upon him to have a Tincture of Madness."[6] This first real insight into Benny's condition came too late to be of any help. By 1770, all ambition spent, all pride crushed, Benny applied to the town fathers of Philadelphia in his wife's name and his own for a "License to sell spirituous Liquors by small Measure. . . . We are not fond of the Prospect it affords," he admitted, but "it may contribute to support a Number of young growing Children."[7]

Except for this last document, his story has been told in many voices, Parker's, Debbie's, William's, Franklin's, never his own. And never, strangely, in his mother's. Did someone at a later time delete all references to the Mecom family's high-hope-turned-black-sheep? Did Jane feel that her own misfortunes now rated priority over her son's?

Within fifteen months of Franklin's return to England, she had lost her husband, her daughter Sarah, two of Sarah's children. "Nothing but trouble can you hear from me."[8] Indeed, Jane was almost competitive in her grief, as if by outsuffering others she had more hope of the eternal glory held out to the few as a reward for their sorrows. The Reverend Samuel Cooper, she told Debbie, had preached a special sermon for her comfort, and Debbie, impressed, reflected that the more trials she met with, the more sister Jane shone. She herself did not possess that kind of courage and would never have quoted, as Jane was fond of doing, Alexander Pope's "Whatever is, is right."

Jane decided to launch a little millinery business with the help of her two surviving daughters, Jenny and Polly. Enthusiastic about the project, Franklin soon had Mrs. Stevenson selecting London's latest fashions in ribbons, bonnets, and caps. He financed the original stock and predicted that "industry and Frugality early practis'd and long persisted in" would eventually make "the Girls grow rich." Should they think this a very small start, he reminded them that he himself had had no more to "begin the World with,"[9] forgetting that an untrained woman milliner could hardly be compared in earning power with a skilled male printer. In her search for the best ways to obtain the bright reds and greens needed to make "Flowers for the Ladyes Heads and Boosomes," Jane consulted the memorandums left by their "good old unkle Benjamin."[10] This return to the craft of her ancestors, most of whom had been dyers, lifted her spirits; she seemed to have found her métier.

All went well for a while, but in Jane's life nothing went well for long. Polly, her youngest and most cherished daughter, took sick. She had been concealing symptoms of tuberculosis and doing "so much more than she was able that it increased her disorder."[11] Hastily dispatched to Nantucket to recuperate under the care of their relatives on the island, Polly died there at the age of nineteen. This time Jane reeled from the blow. The "duble Share of Sperrites"[12] that Deborah credited her with was not enough. Biblical in its rhythm and thrust, her outcry of pain justifies Franklin's feeling that she was a natural writer: "Sorrows roll upon me like the waves of the sea. I am hardly allowed time to fetch my breath. I am broken with breach upon breach, and I have now, in the first flow of my grief, been almost ready to say, 'What have I more?' But God forbid that I should indulge that thought, though I have lost another child. God is sovereign, and I submit."[13] Some months later, trying to say something pleasant about Sally's wedding, Jane was still almost incoherent with grief: "Oh My Brother she [Polly] was everything to me. Every Word and Every Action was full of Duty and Respect, and I never Lookd on Her but with Pleasur Except when she was sick or in troble."[14]

There was nothing to do but go on for Jenny's sake, and make those

gay baubles for the "top ladies" of Boston. But even in this, her last ref-
uge, Jane met with unexpected problems. On October 28, 1767, the
Boston town meeting, in an angry reaction to the imposition of duties
on tea, glass, and paper by the British government, resolved to discourage the consumption of foreign superfluities. "It proves a Litle unlucky
for me," Jane lamented, "that our People have taken it in there Heads
to be so Exsesive Frugal at this Time." She could understand the necessity of wearing one's old clothes over again—that was her Franklin side
—but she could not help deploring this new blow to her humble industry: "I should Like to have those that do bye and can afford it should
bye what Litle I have to sell and imploy us to make it up."[15]

Franklin was of two minds, sorry for Jane whose initiative he had
warmly applauded, yet proud and happy to see his countrymen stand
up to taxation measures whose effect on Anglo-American relations was
so devastating that his prime endeavor was now to obtain their repeal
rather than the ouster of the Penns. "It is a little unlucky," he answered, echoing her words, "that the Business you are fallen into happens at present to be in Disgrace with your Town Meeting; perhaps
you may think of some other . . . if their Resolutions continue and are
regarded by the Ladies."[16] The British merchants, he confided to a
friend, thought the men might be content with homespun stuffs but
they hoped "the Women will never get the better of their Vanity and
Fondness for English Modes and Geegaws."[17] With the passage of
time, his attitude hardened and even though Mrs. Stevenson kept
filling Jane's orders he made his growing uneasiness clear to his sister.
He spoke approvingly of Boston's resolution against wearing the
"Trumpery Finery of this Country,"[18] punned on the word *goods* not
meaning anything *good*, hinted that he would be sorry to see her "en-
gag'd in a Business which happens not to coincide with the general
Interest,"[19] and was relieved eventually to hear that she was about to
give it up. Historically unimportant as it is, Jane's business fiasco was a
poignant preview of the much larger drama brewing in Franklin's life,
when the political man's views would clash head-on with the private
man's feelings. In her own simple way she expressed the helplessness of
the victims of faction and party: "It is difficult to know whether either
party is in the right. . . . I wish we had let alone strife before it was
meddled with and followed things that make for peace."[20]

In spite of her brother's material assistance and words of comfort,
Jane fell into such a spell of despondency that "all the Assistance of
Reason and Religion were scarce sufficient"[21] to keep up her spirits.
And no wonder. Her son Peter had been insane for many years;
Benny's career was plummeting once more; John, the goldsmith, was

sponging off his in-laws in New Jersey; Jenny, at home, irritated her mother by putting on airs of gentility (like Benny) and lying abed late in the morning. Jane decided the moment had come to leave Boston for the first time in her life and go visiting in Philadelphia.

Aunt Mecom's arrival was awaited with happy anticipation and not a little terror. Even Franklin in faraway London confessed to some apprehension, for he knew from experience that there was "an overquantity of touchwood [tinder]"[22] in Jane's constitution. After a stay with William in the governor's mansion in Burlington, she progressed to Philadelphia and finally met the sister-in-law with whom she had exchanged so many letters for so many years. But Deborah, whose jolly missives had given much pleasure in Boston, was no longer at her best. She had suffered a stroke and though on her way to recovery was feeling the weight of her age. Jane, some five years younger, was as sprightly as ever in her mind but far from agile: She noticed that Debbie could outwalk her easily.

With just enough rivalry between them to make life interesting, the two women enjoyed each other's company: "We are as happy as we could expect to be in your absence."[23] Indeed, Debbie breathlessly reported to her husband a piece of news so unusual she knew he would not believe it from anyone's pen but her own: They had gone to a play! She does not say what they saw in that evening of deviltry, but it might have been *Hamlet* or *Romeo and Juliet*, perhaps even such light fare as *Love à la Mode* or *The Musical Lady*, all offered by a troop of players in the course of November 1769 despite the best efforts of sober Philadelphians to ban them. Debbie had expected someone in town to remark on such wantonness of conduct, but no one did. Worse still "to some folks,"[24] she had accompanied Jane twice to Presbyterian services. In a reciprocal gesture of good will, Jane went with her to Christ Church. Franklin was so relieved to hear about this family harmony that he suggested Jane might settle in Philadelphia for good, but by the time his proposal arrived, she had already left—probably in a huff.

The reasons for her precipitous departure are not clear. Debbie wrote cryptically that she was not at liberty to talk until Jane gave her leave, which was not yet the case. A few weeks later, commenting on Jane's latest misfortune, the death of her son John, she ventured to add that Jane "thinks I don't think quite as she does but I love her and will as long as I live."[25] Franklin, who had more than once expressed his hope that Jane had not left because of some offense, guessed that the tiff might have had something to do with his sister's "aptness to interfere in other peoples' economical affairs by putting in a word now and then unasked." At any rate he was pleased when he heard at last that a good understanding had been restored between her and "the Philadelphia folks."[26]

With the death of their brother Peter in 1767, only he and Jane remained of the family that had grown up on Union Street. A new note of mellowness now creeps into their letters. She knew well, she said, that he felt brothers and sisters should love each other more as their number diminished, but her affection for him had always been so great there was no room for increase. She was wrong. As the political atmosphere of London became ever more hostile to the American agent in the seventies, as the spiritual distance between himself and William grew, Franklin poured out to his sister the feelings that he was not sharing with any other relative, certainly not with his wife and daughter with whom he was communicating only in the most perfunctory manner.

To Jane, and through Jane to Boston, he affirmed his imperviousness to attack: "One cannot behave so as to obtain the Esteem of the Wise and Good without drawing on one's self at the same time the Envy and Malice of the Foolish and Wicked. . . . The best Men have always had their Share of this Treatment."[27] To Jane he enunciated his famous dictum in regard to offices: Never ask for them, never refuse them, never resign them. To Jane he revealed the ever-deeper frustration of his attempts at Anglo-American conciliation: "I had us'd all the smooth Words I could muster, and I grew tired of Meekness when I saw it without Effect. Of late therefore I have been saucy." He had concluded that to kick a bit when imposed upon had a good effect: "A little Sturdiness when Superiors are much in the Wrong sometimes occasions Consideration."[28]

That was in 1773. When, early in 1774, he was dismissed from the postmastership, he hastened to reassure his sister, "Don't let this give you any Uneasiness. You and I have almost finish'd the Journey of Life; we are now but a little way from home, and have enough in our Pockets to pay the Post Chaises. [As it turned out he still had sixteen years to live, she twenty.] Intending to disgrace me, they have rather done me Honour."[29] His tone was no longer facetious now but choking with indignation. He strove to maintain the "good opinion" she had of him, denying as an "infamous falsehood" the rumor that he was being won over to the English side by extraordinary favors: "They may expect it till Doomsday. For God knows my Heart, I would not accept the best Office the King has to bestow while such Tyrannic Measures are taking against my Country."[30] Again, more vehemently, he protested against the report published in a Boston paper that he was being restored to royal grace: "So far from having any Promise of royal Favour, I hear of nothing but royal and ministerial Displeasure."[31]

Well aware that their letters were being tampered with (the seals were broken and badly patched up), they kept corresponding anyway. As his political fortunes reached their lowest ebb in England, her fervor raised him to Golgotha: "I think it not Profanity to compare you to our Blessed Saviour who Employed much of His time here on Earth in doing Good to the body as well as souls of men. . . . I think the comparison just. . . . Oh my dear Brother may you and I Imitate Him also in Holyness."[32]

No more the younger, poorer sister, Jane had become the comforter. As she saw it, they were communing in God, the two of them, communing in the sorrow of this world's imperfection. Deborah was dismissed in an offhand manner with the simple remark that she had not been heard from in a long time. It seems she had slipped Jane's last letter under her pillow, intending to read it later, but her grandchild had gotten hold of it and torn it to pieces. "As we know, my sister is very forgitfull."[33]

Sister was not just forgetful. She was almost dead.

XIV

"Your A Feck Shonet Wife"

I am very sorry to think that I should not have it in my power to attend on you.
When will it be in your power to come home? How I long to see you but I would
not say a word that would give you one moment's trouble. . . . If you are having the gout . . . I wish I was near enough to rub it with a light hand.
—Deborah to Franklin, August 16, 1770

WHETHER IT BE ULYSSES OR FRANKLIN, ten years away from home is a
devastating stretch. Interest wanes, time yawns, feeling becomes formula. Endless repetition serves only to empty the formula of whatever
content it once had. As Franklin liked to quip, love is governed by a
variant of the law of attraction: It diminishes in direct proportion to
distance.

It would never do nowadays, such a marriage. In our day, a wife
might ask what kind of father, instead of coming home for his only
daughter's wedding, would choose instead to burden her, the aging
mother, with the entire responsibility for it, limiting his role first to the
expression of qualms and reservations, later to an angry silence. In our
day she would not put up with a husband who was always away—five
years the first time, then ten long years abroad—while he promised
every spring he would come back in the fall, every fall that he would
sail home in the spring. Ten unbroken years, even though he had
known for the last four of them that she was desperately ill and that
she longed to see him once again before she died. He had been told she
had suffered a stroke; he could see for himself the once firm hand and
the once clear mind waver and disintegrate into a chaos of babbling
and a jumble of lines. But he did not want to see. He stayed away.

What about him, the husband? He, nowadays, would probably not
have remained married to such a wife, the plain, hardly literate wife of
his youth. He would feel that she had not grown apace with him, that
she was still a shopkeeper's wife while he had become a world-famous
scientist and statesman. He would be acutely aware that she had no

wit, no elegance, no repartee, not even the courage to cross the sea and accompany him on his missions—which might be just as well considering the kind of figure she would cut in the sophisticated circles of London.

They said nothing of the kind. It was the eighteenth century, not today. For well over forty years he called her his dear child and she called him her dear child. To the house in Philadelphia which they had started building together but would never enjoy together he continued to send the best, the most refined wares England had to offer. To his London residence she continued to send the rustic gifts of the colonies, not only to him but to his landlady, a lady for whom she may well have suspected that he entertained more than purely friendly feelings. And the landlady reciprocated by buying for the wife the prettiest gloves, ribbons, and bonnets in the London shops. Everybody thanked everybody. Everybody sent love. Rather than complain or regret, Franklin and his wife chose to gloss over life's imperfections and their partner's inadequacies with expressions of appreciation and endearment. "Let thy discontents be thy secrets," said Poor Richard (1741). "If the world knows them 'twill despise thee and increase them."

Brooding was a form of self-indulgence which the inhabitants of colonial America did not look upon kindly. With few exceptions they had not been cursed yet with the anguish of option. Too busy living, too awed by the miracle of remaining alive while death stalked all around, too concerned with the afterlife, they did not give much weight to the vagaries of day-to-day happiness. Often reminded by her husband of God's bounty toward them, Deborah dutifully voiced her gratitude or her humble submission as the case required. If she ever took time to meditate upon her fate, she probably considered herself, all in all, a lucky woman.

Had he loved Deborah? He had certainly not married her out of passion but he was fond of her. So far as one can tell, he did not fall madly, deeply in love with anyone else. Not for him the slightly absurd character of the moonstruck lover he had poked fun at under his youthful pen name of Silence Dogood. Never did his emotions imperil the equilibrium he strove to maintain, his cool detachment toward any impulse that might deflect him from his main purposes: a good name, money, knowledge, usefulness. In his drive for success he had needed a healthy partner. But when the active "country Joan" he had so vividly appreciated turned into an ailing woman, he felt no urge to be at her side; he chose first to ignore the danger signals, then to unload on their daughter the task of taking care of her.

On the eve of his departure, Deborah had promised never to complain. She kept that promise for a long, long time. As the years went by, however, her despair broke through her self-imposed restraint. It only alienated him further. To his friends he wrote of scientific and other topics in his usual crisp way. To William he sent lengthy letters of political musings. To Jane Mecom he revealed his personal reaction to events. But to Deborah, most of the time, he dispatched the kind of hurried messages a child addresses its parents from summer camp: all's well . . . no time to write more . . . mailman about to leave . . . love to everybody. Reading those dull, perfunctory notes, nobody would guess what a witty, brilliant correspondent Franklin could be. Nor would one get an inkling of the exciting life he was leading in London, a life of political frustration, to be sure, but vibrant with friends, travel, honors, an entertaining family circle and the thrill of being at the center of action.

Once their house had been completed and the Stamp Act riots weathered, Deborah's correspondence reverted to the humdrum of a life in which nursing the sick was the most noteworthy event. In July 1766, an epidemic form of dysentery ravaged Philadelphia with such ferocity that her letters read like a death roll of their friends and relations. She tried to keep Sally out of town; as to herself, unwilling to leave the house untended, she never budged.

Among the victims of the disease was Mary Franklin whose husband, Franklin's brother Peter, had died six weeks earlier. Even though Debbie had known her sister-in-law for only two years (Mary had spent the rest of her life in Rhode Island), she tried to help to the limit of her strength, in spite of a heat wave, thanking God for keeping her "up and well": "Poor Dear Sister is dead. . . . For 8 nights I had four hours rest a night and the last night I sat up all night although I had a nurse the last 4 days. It was impossible I could do myself any longer for I was not able to bear my weight on my feet. . . . And I have the satisfaction to say I did all in my power to oblige and serve her, and she did me the justice to say to several of the good folks that visited her after brother's death that she found her sister a mother."[1]

When Peter and Mary, a childless couple, had come to Philadelphia to take over the post office, they had brought their foster son, Ephraim Brown. They planned to adopt him legally, but never got around to doing it. Upon hearing of Peter's death, Franklin promptly made arrangements from London for the young man to enter a printing partnership with his widowed "mother" and support them both. But Mary in turn died so soon that Ephraim was left with only her verbal assurance that she intended him as her heir. Deborah raised no objections, indeed was probably relieved when Ephraim departed for Boston, taking along the family maid and some of the late Franklins' property.

But in Boston Jane Mecom rose up in arms. Frustrated once already when her well-to-do brother John's inheritance had gone to his stepchildren, she could not sit back and watch Peter's earthly goods benefit outsiders while her own brood was in need. She was outraged to see the maid parading about town in Mary's purple chintz gown, a gown "vastly finer" than any she, Jane, had ever owned. She was shocked to hear rumors that the maid hoped to marry Ephraim and that the luggage of the pair included a chestful of dollars plus nearly everything valuable that had belonged to Peter and Mary. All her life Jane had known, and probably envied, Mary Franklin as a woman who kept herself "full of good Living," a woman blessed with an abundance of fine shifts, aprons, handkerchiefs and lace caps—never did Mary wear a plain cap, it was said. How naïve of Debbie to swallow Ephraim's story! With more than a trace of contempt, Jane told her so: "My thought is they two pilfered of all kinds that they thought you could not detect them in."[2] She herself subjected the alleged culprits to a stern cross-examination.

It was lucky that some of Mary's wardrobe had remained in Philadelphia; Debbie sent it on to mollify her sister-in-law. Better yet, the saucy maid met with her comeuppance: Ephraim Brown took off for England without her. She came back to Debbie hoping for employment, but Debbie did not take her in because she was given to "fits." And so, clad in her possibly ill-gotten purple, the maid disappears from the story while Ephraim surfaces in London. Here, a skilled printer, he found work with Strahan and quartered himself—of course—in the Craven Street house. But something went wrong. He moved to Oxford, fell ill, and died there, leaving Franklin his medical and funeral expenses to pay.

Still another vignette of colonial life is to be culled from Deborah's rambling reports: the ordeal of childbirth, as lived by her motherless niece Debby Dunlap, the wife of that eccentric former postmaster of Philadelphia who had once accused Franklin of wanting to stab him with a "poynard" in the heart. The pregnancy had been hard, young Debby had been obliged to keep to her bed for two months; on the day of the delivery her husband was brought back from Maryland, dangerously ill. The "poor little mother" did not have enough milk, the baby howled. A poignant scene comes alive in Deborah's clumsy account: her kindness, Debby's pain, everybody's helplessness: "She lay in continual pain screaming and crying with what the doctors call a spasmodical disorder in her head, and all her joints so bad as to turn her eyes quite crooked; and to start them right it hurt her sight and threw her into fits and disjointed her eyes, so that her chin fell down on her breast and she has been deprived of her senses. And she is so haunted with such dreadful ugly things of the imagination."

In the midst of her delirium, the young woman cried out for Franklin: "The night before last she was in great distress, calling on her uncle and said if he was here she would not be treated in such a manner. I sat by her and folded her in my arms and told her that I would take as much care of her as though you were there, and held her for two hours. And Sally sat at her feet and wrapped them up and had a thing to heat them with. At last she fell asleep and was yesterday as happy as we could expect."[3]

Five months later Debby was reported in rather better health "and restored to her reason in some" but "blind still."[4] Deborah herself sounded for the first time a note of heavy discouragement: "It is very hard on me, now more than 60 years old. . . . I am father and mother to our own, and so I must be to poor Debby by inclination and for credit's sake."[5] The strain on Deborah had been greater than she suspected. The following winter, during Sally's first pregnancy, she suffered a stroke.

The seriousness of her condition did not escape the family doctor and friend, Thomas Bond, America's foremost professor of medicine. In June 1769, he sent an alarming message to London: "Your good Mrs. Franklin was affected . . . with a partial Palsy in the Tongue and a sudden Loss of Memory, but she soon recovered from them, tho' her constitution in general appears impaired. These are bad Symptoms in advanced Life and augur Danger of further Injury on the nervous System."[6]

Franklin immediately consulted Sir John Pringle, physician to the Queen, and forwarded the luminary's advice (no longer extant) to Philadelphia. As soon as she had sufficiently recovered to write, Debbie thanked husband and doctor for their solicitude but disagreed with their diagnosis. She put the blame for her illness on what would now be called psychosomatic causes: loneliness, depression, worries about the two young women who looked to her for emotional support—the unfortunate Debby Dunlap and the no less unfortunate Betsy Mecom, wife of the perennially troubled Benny. Above all, she underscored her "dissatisfied distress" at Franklin's staying away so much longer. It had been such a dismal winter. She could not eat, she could not sleep, she had lost all her "resolution." Hers had not been a real illness, she insisted. "I was only unable to bear any more and so I fell and could not get up again."[7]

To this pointed allusion he never gave any reply. Did he ever stop to think how often he had raised her hopes only to dash them? His return had seemed imminent at first, so imminent that he had instructed her to postpone many of the decisions about the new house because he expected to be back any day and make them himself. But after two years of delays, doubt had begun to creep into Deborah's mind. Some of her neighbors gave out that Franklin would surely come home that summer, others said he would not. As to herself, "I can't say anything as I am in the dark and my life of old age is one continued state of suspense."[8] The following year, however, certainty had returned. She was positive he would sail on the August packet. When he did not, she no longer put much stock in his repeated assurances that a few more months would allow him to bring Pennsylvania's affairs to a happy conclusion. Then came her stroke.

With the birth of Sally's little boy in the summer of 1769, Deborah found a new reason for living. Though still very shaky, she was just well enough to attend the christening and provided Franklin with enthusiastic descriptions of her "Kingbird." Incapable at such a distance of matching her fervor, he rejoiced sedately in her delight and hoped that "having such an Amusement"[9] would be beneficial to her health. Inoculation, of course, was the first order of the day and for one brief moment the memory of their dead Franky held them together.

Franklin was pleasantly surprised to hear that his wife had not interfered when the baby—not quite a year old—had been whipped for a tantrum. He told her the story of two boys in the street: "One was crying bitterly; the other came to him to ask what was the Matter? I have been, says he, for a Pennyworth of Vinegar and I have broken the Glass and spilt the Vinegar, and my Mother will whip me. *No, she won't whip you*, says the other. Indeed she will, says he. *What*, says the other, *have you then got ne'er a Grandmother?*"[10]

Such firm pedagogical principles were soon eroded when he was presented with a godson of his own to fondle and spoil. Polly's first child, Billy Hewson, born two years after Benny Bache, furnished Franklin with a welcome topic to fill up his letters home. A note of competition soon crept in: *Your* grandson, he would say, *my* godson . . . Exactly one year after recommending sternness to his womenfolk in Philadelphia, he was advising Polly to humor her offspring: "Pray let him have everything he likes; I think it of great Consequence while the Features of the Countenance are forming. It gives them a pleasant Air, and that being once become natural and fix'd by Habit, the Face is ever after the handsomer for it, and on that much of a Person's good Fortune and Success in Life may depend. Had I been cross'd as much in my Infant Likings and Inclinations as you know I have been of late Years, I should have been, I was going to say not near so handsome, but as the Vanity of that Expression would offend other Folks Vanity, I change it out of Regard to them, and say a great deal more homely."[11]

To Benny's varied accomplishments he countered Billy's sagacious look and manliness in the cold bath, that cornerstone of eighteenth-century child rearing. Sally did not even score a point when she produced a second son (Willy), for Polly, making up for a late start, already had a second son (Tom). Mrs. Stevenson, who preferred girls, felt sorry for Deborah and herself, eliciting a spirited rejoinder from Sally: She would not, she declared, exchange her Willy for twelve girls.

It was all gentle banter, helping to conceal the grim reality—Deborah's mind was slipping. She was no longer able to handle efficiently her husband's affairs in America. In an outburst of irritation, two years after her stroke, he scolded her harshly for not keeping an exact account of her expenses: "You were not very attentive to Money-matters in your best Days, and I apprehend that your Memory is too much impaired for the Management of unlimited Sums without Danger of injuring the future Fortune of your Daughter and Grandson."[12]

To tax her with never having been attentive to money matters, whereas he himself had paid tribute to her frugality more than once—and when his own accounts were kept haphazardly—was unfair. To hint that she was endangering her beloved Benny's inheritance was cruel, coming from one who lived most comfortably in London and engaged every summer in extensive travel. A few months after his tongue-lashing, mollified by the profuse explanations she sent, he wrote that he did not wish to see every receipt, only an account of the larger sums. Eventually he gave a power of attorney to Richard Bache and the financial problem was resolved to everyone's relief. But the larger problem of her decline remained and to that he was impervious.

When she lamented that she was no longer able to walk about and was losing her memory, he countered that a month-long journey through Cumberland had given a new spring to his health and spirits: He had ascended a high mountain and gone down eighty fathoms under the sea in the coal mines. When she moaned that she was "growing very feeble very fast"[13] with only the meager consolation that her headaches had diminished, he chose to ignore the first part of her sentence and rejoice at the vanishing pains. When she explained that her right hand had become so weak that she found it difficult to put on her clothes, he retorted that they both had great reason to be thankful that "so great a Share of Health and Strength remains as to render Life yet comfortable."[14]

He had once inquired what neighbors came to call, to which she answered simply, "very few come to see us."[15] How different his own "agreeable" situation, lionized by Englishmen of science and affairs, sought out by visiting dignitaries from abroad, "my company so much desired that I seldom dine at home in winter and could spend the whole summer in the country houses of inviting friends if I chose it."[16] Whatever affectionate greeting he concluded with, however often he expressed his wish to see his home again, his feelings were ambivalent; sometimes he was even thoughtless enough to reveal this: "I am afraid, when I come home, I shall find myself a Stranger in my own Country . . . and leaving so many Friends here, it will seem leaving Home to go there."[17] He was still haunted by the old longing to settle for good in England.

The last time she wrote him was on October 29, 1773. It was a brief, shaky letter, containing as usual a Kingbird story. "My grandchildren are the best in the world," she concluded. "I can't write any more. I am your a feck shonet wife."

It was many months before he realized that their dialogue had become a monologue. "My dear Love," he began in April 1774, "I hoped to have been on the Sea in my Return by this time, but find I must stay a few Weeks longer, perhaps for the Summer ships. Thanks to God I continue well and hearty, and hope to find you so when I have the Happiness once more of seeing you."[18] Was she still lucid enough to appreciate the "dear love" instead of the usual "dear Debbie" or "dear Child?" There is no telling.

Throughout 1774 he was puzzled at her silence. In May: "It is now a very long time indeed since I have had the Pleasure of a Line from you. I hope that you are as well as I am, thanks to God."[19]

In July: "I have had no Line from you by several late Opportunities: I flatter myself it is owing not to Indisposition but to the Opinion of my having left England, which indeed I hope soon to do."[20]

In September: "It is now nine long months since I received a Line from my dear Debby. I have supposed it owing to your continual Expectation of my Return; I have feared that some Indisposition had rendered you unable to write; I have imagined any thing rather than admit a Supposition that your kind Attention towards me was abated. And yet when so many other old Friends have dropt a Line to me now and then at a Venture, taking the Chance of its finding me here or not as it might happen, why might I not have expected the same Comfort from you who used to be so diligent and faithful a Correspondent, as to omit scarce an Opportunity?"[21]

"On Monday, the 19th instant, died in an advanced Age, Mrs. Deborah Franklin, wife of Dr. Benjamin Franklin; and on the Thursday following her Remains were interred in Christ-Church Burying-Ground."[22] On Christmas Eve William sent word to his father:

> I came here on Thursday last to attend the Funeral of my poor old Mother who died the Monday Noon preceding. Mr. Bache sent his Clerk Express to me on the Occasion, who reached Amboy on Tuesday Evening, and I set out early the next Morning, but the Weather being very severe, and snowing hard, I was not able to reach here till about 4 o'clock on Thursday Afternoon, about half an Hour before the Corpse was to be moved for Interment. Mr. Bache and I followed as Chief Mourners . . . and a very respectable Number of Inhabitants were at the Funeral. . . . Her Death was no more than might be reasonably expected after the paralytic Stroke she received some Time ago, which greatly affected her Memory and Understanding. She told me, when I took Leave of her, on my Removal to Amboy, that she never expected to see you unless you returned this Winter, for that she was sure she should not live till next Summer. I heartily wish you had happened to have come over in the Fall, as I think her Disappointment in that respect preyed a good deal on her Spirits.[23]

Franklin received the news in late February 1775. One month later, accompanied by Temple, he sailed home.

Did he feel sad? Did he feel relieved? Did he feel guilty? Except for a matter-of-fact remark that his wife's death required him to wind up his current negotiations speedily in order to take over the management of affairs in Philadelphia, there is absolutely no surviving trace of his reaction. It should be said in all fairness that 1774 had been the most harrowing year of Franklin's life. Humiliated in public, stripped of all effectiveness, deprived of a major source of income, forced to face the fact that ten years of diplomatic effort had been for nought, he had also suffered through the personal tragedy of the Stevenson family: Infected in the course of an autopsy, Dr. Hewson had succumbed to septicemia, leaving Polly pregnant with their third child. The letters in which Franklin had related—to a Deborah who did not answer anymore—the ups and downs of the young doctor's agony are among the most moving he wrote.

Death on all sides, failure on all sides, an almost-estranged son, the infirmities of age close on the horizon, the threat of a jail sentence . . . Deborah's disappearance may not have loomed much larger than the other catastrophes engulfing him. And his conscience had long been disciplined to the dogma that public affairs come first.

There is no evidence that, as time went by, he ever thought he should have behaved differently toward Deborah. He spoke of his dead wife with the comfortable affection one feels for a valiant comrade. "I have lately lost my old and faithful Companion," he wrote some three years later, "and I every day become more sensible of the greatness of that Loss which cannot now be repair'd."[24]

Eventually a note of fun crept into his reminiscences. In his seventies he toyed with the idea of marrying the elderly Madame Helvétius, the widow of the philosopher. His tongue-in-cheek proposal took the form of a facetious piece entitled *The Elysian Fields*. It showed the late Debbie and the late Monsieur Helvétius happily married to each other in the nether-world, oblivious of their former earthly connections. What better course, then, for their surviving spouses than to marry one another—as a just revenge?

His very last mention of Deborah came shortly before his death. He had gone back, in his eighties, to end his days in Philadelphia. A French friend, Madame Lavoisier, wife of the famous chemist, sent from Paris a portrait she had painted of Franklin. He thanked her in that half-humorous, half-nostalgic style that was the trademark of his old age: "Our English Enemies when they were in Possession of this City and of my House made a Prisoner of my Portrait and carried it off with them, leaving that of its Companion, my Wife, by itself, a kind of Widow. You have replaced the Husband and the Lady seems to smile, as well pleased."[25]

The lady, in his memory, was smiling and well pleased.

XV

Steering through Storms

I for the most part kept my sentiments to myself and only endeavoured to steer my little bark quietly through all the storms of political contest with which I was every where surrounded.

—William Franklin to William Strahan, June 18, 1771

IN AN OUTBURST of filial gratitude, William Franklin had once assured his father that he was prepared to follow him to the ends of the earth. But he was not, as it turned out, prepared to follow him along the ideological path to independence. In 1775, William was an officer of the crown every bit as much as he had been when he had "kissed hands" in 1762. While Benjamin Franklin tacked and trimmed his way through the decade between the repeal of the Stamp Act and the Declaration of Independence, his son attempted to carry out the instructions of His Majesty's government even when he detested its ministers and deplored its policies. However much one may fault him for lack of imagination, for failing to see that the world was changing, one cannot accuse him of a breach of faith or a lack of consistency.

For over twelve years—far longer than any of his fellow governors—William administered New Jersey as successfully as a man of good will, considerable industry, and adequate intelligence could be expected to do in difficult circumstances. Were it not for the Revolution, he might be remembered chiefly for his efforts to improve roads in his province and alleviate the condition of debtors in its prisons. The twin capitals of his little domain were the sleepy river ports of Burlington and Perth Amboy, on opposite sides of the colony. The early Proprietors of East Jersey had fixed on Ambo Point as "a sweet, wholesome and delightful place, proper for trade,"[1] and the same description could have served for Burlington, the capital of West Jersey. Neither fulfilled the commercial expectations of its Quaker settlers, though Burlington had a brief heyday as a shipbuilding and trade center between the Delaware and the West Indies before being eclipsed by Philadelphia, eighteen

miles down river. The Proprietors of the two Jersies squabbled so inter-
minably that the crown took over in 1702 and united them; thereafter
the provincial government shuttled back and forth between the two
towns.

New Jersey was not one of the more volatile colonies. Its population
was largely rural (even the capitals numbered scarcely more than one
thousand souls and did not rate a post office), and there were no local
newspapers to inflame political passions, no firebrands the likes of Sam
Adams or Patrick Henry. On the eve of the Revolution, New Jersey was
hardly more stirred by differences with England than by purely local
concerns. The British government found the colony so insignificant
that it often took years before getting around to reading and disallow-
ing objectionable bills passed by the provincial Assembly. In the long
run, it must have been galling for a man of William's ego and ambition
to stagnate in one of the backwaters of the Empire, largely unnoticed
and unappreciated, to find all avenues of advancement closed, not because he lacked ability but because his father, from whose shadow he
never seemed to escape, was fast becoming identified in English eyes
with all that was odious in American behavior.

The beginning, however, had been full of promise. Life in New Jersey was pleasant and relaxed. William built himself an imposing three-
story brick house at the water's edge in Burlington, kept a stable of fine
horses, and bought a farm at nearby Rancocas. He mixed with the best
society the province had to offer, mostly Anglican gentry. Over the
years he would even become "very sociable"[2] with Governor Penn—a
colleague, after all, not merely his family's inveterate enemy. But the
sociability with Penn did not sprout for a good ten years. Long after
Franklin's return to England, William was still devoting his energy to
defending his father against the attacks of the Proprietary party in
Pennsylvania and those of the Reverend Mr. Smith—attacks that
would, he declared, "make even Devils blush."[3]

William and his father also joined forces in the great American pastime, land speculation. Far from having shady overtones, land speculation attracted almost everyone, from Virginia planter to Philadelphia
merchant to New England lawyer, along with the contentious army of
Indian traders and adventurers. The journey into the wilderness he had
made at eighteen left an enduring impression on William. Franklin,
too, as early as 1756, had fancied himself and the evangelist George
Whitefield as joint leaders into a new Promised Land: "I sometimes
wish that you and I were jointly employ'd by the Crown to settle a
Colony on the Ohio. . . . What a glorious Thing it would be, to settle
in that fine Country a large strong Body of Religious and Industrious

People! . . . In such an Enterprize I could spend the Remainder of Life with Success."[4]

These lands were not precisely empty. They belonged to a host of Indian tribes and had been claimed by France as well as by several American colonies. It may seem incongruous to twentieth-century sensibilities that fervent imperialists like Franklin should consider themselves genuinely sympathetic to the Indians and their culture. Again and again Franklin would refer with fascination to the simplicity of the Indians' way of life, the dignity of their social relations, and the flavor of their speech; he was indignant about the unjust treatment they had received at the hands of their "civilized" neighbors ("almost every war between the Indians and whites has been occasioned by some injustice of the latter towards the former")[5] and the despicable behavior of those who traded with them, "the most vicious and abandoned Wretches of our Nation."[6] And yet he never doubted that it was the American destiny to settle from sea to sea on lands which the Indians had hunted and fished for countless centuries. This assumption had been one of the mainsprings of his prophetic if stillborn Albany Plan of Union in 1754, proposing that the colonies federate not only to protect themselves against Indian and French attack, but also to help the "establishing of new colonies westward."[7]

By 1763, French claims east of the Mississippi had been extinguished by war; there remained problems between Indians and colonists, to be settled by persuasion. A group of Pennsylvania merchants who had suffered heavy losses during the French and Indian War, and later during Pontiac's uprising, had been pressing loudly for monetary compensation from the British government. When they saw that this was out of the question they asked for a land grant instead. These "suffering traders" gave impetus to western colonization ventures which attracted a flock of speculators on both sides of the Atlantic. William soon became involved in some of these projects through his ties with many traders and in the hope that such investments offered a more pleasant path to wealth than industry and frugality.

His hopes soared at the signing of the Treaty of Fort Stanwix (1768) by which the Indians ceded to the British government the vast territory south of the Ohio River. He had spent three months at the fort hammering out the agreement. An excellent reputation preceded him for he had prosecuted the murderers of two Indian women in his province and invited Indian notables to the hanging. In gratitude he was given the name of Sagorighweyoghsta, "the Dispenser of Justice."[8] The conclusion of the treaty emboldened him and his friends to form the Grand Ohio Company, with a stellar array of financial backers from both England and America, and to petition for almost 25 million acres. There was some talk of William's being placed at the head of the new colony to be established on that land. He was confident that with a little nudging the British government would give its blessing to the scheme and counted on his father to do the nudging. Franklin himself was as enthusiastic a shareholder as his son and stood well with Lord Shelburne, the minister in whose purlieu the American colonies fell in the mid-sixties.

Because of the competing claims of other speculators, speedy approval was of the essence. At times it seemed almost within reach, then new complications would arise, new postponements, panic among the investors. The sympathetic Shelburne was succeeded by Lord Hillsborough, decidedly hostile to American expansion. The petition bogged down hopelessly in the Board of Trade, an eighteenth-century equivalent of Dickens' "Circumlocution Office." Franklin was no longer an effective lobbyist, having become too closely identified with American resistance to taxation and parliamentary authority. Furthermore, he seemed to have lost his drive. Strahan confided to William in some dismay, "His Temper is grown so very reserved . . . that there is no getting him to take part in anything."[9]

Another swing of the pendulum in 1772: Hillsborough fell from grace and was replaced by the more amenable Lord Dartmouth. The Privy Council approved the colony under a new name: Vandalia, in honor of Queen Charlotte who claimed descent from Vandal kings.* The future looked rosy. There still was, however, the process of ratification—so long and so slow that Franklin was reminded of a sailors' story: "They were handing a Cable out of a store into a ship, and one of 'em said: 'Tis a long, heavy Cable. I wish we could see the End of it.' 'D—n me,' says another, 'if I believe it has any End; somebody has cut it off.' "[10]

The pendulum swung once more. When the storm broke out between Britain and her colonies, the Treaty of Fort Stanwix had not yet been ratified; it never would be. Vandalia was fated to remain a mirage. William found himself up to his ears in debt after almost a decade of fruitless lobbying and petitioning. Land speculation was an expensive business: Some of his partners had gone bankrupt, owing him money he would never collect; others had become his enemies in the wrangles over liability for the mounting costs. As always, Franklin stood creditor to his son, patient but exacting.

---

* The Queen came from Mecklenburg in the region of Germany traditionally known as Vandalia; in the eighteenth century the Vandals enjoyed a better reputation than in later days.

Even without land schemes, William would have lived beyond his income. His own notions of the style befitting the gubernatorial dignity were reinforced by his wife's taste for fashion and luxury. They both dressed elegantly and furnished their residence with the finest that London had to offer: The silver tankard had to be made by the crown's goldsmith; the silk damask bed in which a visitor slept was so elaborate that the guest "could hardly find himself"[11] the next morning. The governor and his lady attended the races in Philadelphia, endowed the Anglican Church in Burlington with silk as fine as that used in the mansion, and entertained lavishly. George Washington, a shareholder of the Vandalia Company, certainly dined (and may have slept) at the governor's home. William prided himself on his extensive library which included a choice collection of works on agriculture. By his own statement, he had "entered far into the spirit of farming,"[12] probably the only branch of science that really interested him, and wanted nothing but the latest equipment for his farm. Most of it he ordered through his father in England ("I know you love to encourage whatever has a useful Tendency").[13]

Since New Jersey was, or was believed to be, one of the poorest provinces, the Assembly kept the purse strings tight: It granted him no raise after the initial one. Nor was any money to be made from patronage; lower officials were so badly paid it was difficult to get anyone even to take the jobs. William complained that to avoid the expense of a license, one of the few fees that were his due, people were getting married in church (for which no license was required). How he longed for a more rewarding governorship—Barbados, for instance, his wife's native island, which paid twice as much as New Jersey! When it fell vacant in 1766 he promptly informed his father, but the plum went to somebody else. On the tenth anniversary of his installation, William lamented that he had now served longer than any of his fellow governors but had lost money while most of the others had made fortunes. To no avail. Could the crown at least make him independent of the good will of the Assembly by paying all of his salary? No.

Fortunately there was good will aplenty in New Jersey during his first years. He had disarmed critics with his charm, his political skill, and his thorough knowledge of his calling. By leading an irreproachable personal life he had stilled those who recoiled at the blemish of his birth. Nothing could have been wider of the mark, or more ironic as it turned out, than the prediction made by Governor Hamilton of Pennsylvania that William "would certainly make wild work without his Father's experience and good Understanding to check and moderate his

Passion."[14] In fact, his instincts were infinitely more cautious than his father's, his passions solidly in check.

William soon grasped the temper of his people, what they would put up with and what they would not. Patiently, he tried to enlighten ministers in England who did not want to be enlightened, only obeyed. Relentlessly, he tried to cajole, harangue, or threaten his Assembly into compliance with the mother country's laws and regulations without giving up hope of having them changed where they made no sense to him.

The paper money issue is an example. The shortage of currency was an abiding source of financial and economic embarrassment for the Americans. The colonies wanted to issue their own paper money but Parliament had forbidden it in 1764. William repeatedly complained about this prohibition, the New Jersey Assembly practiced obstructionism by stalling on supply bills needed to pay the costs of quartering His Majesty's troops in the province, Franklin wrote pamphlets—all in vain. But where Franklin would fume, "I am weary of suggesting . . . to so many different inattentive heads,"[15] William never forgot that he was an agent of the crown, not like his father a spokesman for the colonies. He knew his superiors would judge him by the docility of New Jersey and he proudly reported in the summer of 1765 that the Assembly had never before passed so many bills submitted to it. When the Assembly pleaded poverty in order to refuse new appropriations, William privately assured the ministry that the colony was in a more flourishing condition than ever and that the public coffers were almost overflowing.

During the Stamp Act troubles he kept a tight rein, annoyed with the government's bungling of the whole affair, but determined that, come what might, the ministry would have nothing to reproach him for. The only governor who persuaded his Assembly to protest against the act but to obey it, he felt answerable for his people as a nursemaid might for unruly children to a distant father: "I am in hopes," he wrote after the repeal, "that the People of the Colonies, particularly Persons of Property, will conduct themselves so as to give great Satisfaction to the present Ministry."[16]

Though less burdensome, the Townshend Acts reopened in 1767 the wounds caused by the Stamp Act. Once again, here was taxation without representation, and once again the reaction in the colonies was noncompliance in the form of consumer boycotts of English goods and nonimportation agreements. As if the acts were not grievance enough, Lord Hillsborough, no friend of America, was appointed to the newly created post of secretary of state for the colonies, a post he would hold for four and a half crucial years, from 1768 to 1772. Franklin summed up Hillsborough's character as "Conceit, Wrongheadedness, Obstinacy and Passion,"[17] and installed him in his private demonology as a worthy and, alas, more powerful successor to the Reverend Mr. Smith and the Penns.

A few months after taking office, the new secretary sent William a scathing letter, condemning him for "entire Ignorance of what was passing in the Assembly," "a very blameable Inattention to Duty," a "Disrespect to a Correspondence directed by the King himself"[18]—all this because William had not stopped his Assembly from discussing a Massachusetts proposal to petition the king for redress of grievances, and because a bill passed to support troops in the colony fell a little short of British expectations.

No matter how devoted, no self-respecting royal servant could accept such a tongue-lashing. William's reply, one of the most eloquent expositions he would ever make of the colonial position, fills thirty-one printed pages. He reminded Hillsborough that petitioning the king was a traditional right of Englishmen, not a crime, and that the New Jersey Assembly was far from alone in questioning Parliament's authority to tax the colonies: Every "House of Representatives on the Continent" felt the same way. If Hillsborough thought otherwise, he was woefully misinformed. While deploring the "scandalous riots" and attacks on officers of the government (William never could abide mobs or violent protests), while admitting that the troops sent over would probably accomplish the immediate purpose of restoring order, he insisted that this did not remove the principal difficulty. "Men's Minds are sour'd, a sullen Discontent prevails, and, in my Opinion, no Force on Earth is sufficient to make the Assemblies acknowledge, by any Act of theirs, that the Parliament has a Right to impose Taxes on America."[19] Britain, he added, stood to lose far more by American boycotts than she could possibly gain by revenue from duties. As for his personal conduct of affairs, he reviewed his whole past record of service dating back to the Braddock campaign with his father and reminded Hillsborough that his skill in steering New Jersey through the recent Stamp Act troubles had won him the praise of his superiors.

To his father, William poured out the full measure of his resentment against Hillsborough: "There is a Meanness in this Kind of Conduct extremely unbecoming in one of his Station." The secretary had slighted him even in his choice of closing formula—not the customary "I am with great Truth and Regard, Sir . . ." but just "I am, Sir . . ."[20] Franklin would understand: These were years, brief years, when he and William worked together intimately and smoothly, united

A Crescendo of Misunderstanding

1767   The Townshend Acts, imposing duties on glass, paper, tea, and other imports, coupled with an invasion of overzealous and frequently corrupt customs officials instructed to carry out to the letter all regulations against smuggling. Suspension of the New York Assembly as a result of the conflict over quartering British troops.

1768   The dispatch of British troops to quell riots in Boston. Franklin becomes agent for Georgia in addition to Pennsylvania.

1769   The threatened revival of a statute of Henry VIII allowing those indicted for crimes in the colonies to be transported to England for trial. Franklin becomes agent for New Jersey.

1770   The Boston Massacre: Crowds pelt the redcoats with snowballs, the redcoats open fire, five civilians are killed and six wounded.

1771   The repeal of the Townshend Acts except for the duty on tea. Franklin becomes agent for Massachusetts.

1772   The burning of the British customs schooner Gaspee in retaliation for the unfair treatment of American merchants and captains; the formation of committees of correspondence to coordinate colonial resistance.

1773   The Tea Act, giving the East India Company a monopoly on tea imports, leading seven months later to the Boston Tea Party.

1774   The Coercive Acts punishing Massachusetts for the Boston Tea Party and in turn provoking the meeting of the First Continental Congress.

1775   April: the battles of Lexington and Concord.

in their objectives and strategy if occasionally disagreeing on minor tactical details. So profound, almost pathetic, was William's dependence that he fell into the habit of sending Franklin all of Hillsborough's communications and all of his own replies, asking his father to forward these replies to the secretary if he approved them or to rewrite them, using presigned blanks, if he did not. Sometimes William even enclosed alternative drafts, leaving the choice to Franklin. Hillsborough found out about this practice, suspected a conspiracy, and reprimanded the governor sharply. By this time, however, Franklin was the duly appointed agent for New Jersey and William retorted that an agent had a perfect right to know what he would be called upon to advocate.

As Franklin saw it, the best defensive weapon in the American arsenal was nonimportation. Neither illegal nor violent, it gave a patriotic boost to his beloved "Industry and Frugality," the exact reverse of the English avidity for "Luxury, Licentiousness, Power, Places, Pensions and Plunder."[21] Nonimportation might, of course, invite an English counterboycott of American goods, but "something must be try'd and some Risque run, rather than sit down quietly."[22] Long a believer in the Italian proverb that he who turns himself into a sheep is soon eaten by the wolf, he preached firmness and discipline. Let the English withdraw to their pre-Stamp Act position, when Parliament limited its interference to regulating colonial trade and manufactures. That would satisfy most reasonable people and leave the hotheads unheeded; but should the London government persist in its stubborn defiance, "mutual Provocation will go on to complete Separation; and instead of that cordial Affection that once and so long existed . . . an implacable Malice and Mutual Hatred . . . will take place."[23]

These gloomy words were the climax of a tract in the form of questions and answers written in November 1769 at the request of William Strahan, perhaps with a view to publication in his *London Chronicle*. Not published until several years later, it was circulated among influential Englishmen to build up the case for repeal of the Townshend Acts. This was to be the last episode in the political partnership, though not in the personal friendship, between the two printers who for so long had seen eye to eye on almost everything, had hoped to merge their families, and still had a common stake in the outcome of the land grant. Strahan, about to become King's Printer (and later elected to Parliament) never deviated from his original conviction that English and American interests "are and ought to be mutual and inseparable."[24]

The repeal of most of the Townshend duties the following year, rather than strengthening the Franklin-Strahan alliance, brought out the first signs of strain. Where Franklin focused his dissatisfaction on the fact that England had not waived the right she claimed to tax the colonies—indeed was still taxing tea—Strahan denounced the "absurd and groundless Complaints" of America's "Bill of Rights Gentlemen" and was beginning to feel that many American grievances were "mere Bagatelles,"[25] blown up out of all proportion. How could the mother country afford the staggering expense of defending the whole empire, he argued, if Parliament was denied the power to tax all parts of it? By late 1770, Strahan admitted that he "differed widely" from Franklin in his assessment of American politics. "But though we *differ* we do not *disagree*," he insisted, "and must ever be good Friends, as I trust we aim at the same End, tho' we differ in the Means."[26] Franklin, too, professed that the old friendship continued as before, but added bitterly, "our Friend Strahan is grown a great Courtier."[27]

The first notes of discord between Franklin and his son, early intimations of a more serious break to come, appear at the same time. Like Strahan, William was concerned with the growing tendency of Americans to resort to illegal forms of protest, not only against taxation measures but against all assertions of British authority. "I think that all Laws until they are repealed ought to be obeyed and that it is the Duty of those who are entrusted with the Executive Part of Government to see that they are so."[28]

How does one tell the story of this parting of the ways? There was no clear-cut dividing line, no marshaling of arguments, no dramatic confrontation until it was too late, but rather a tortuous process, slowed down by the mutual affection of father and son, their reluctance to admit they were drifting apart. Little survives of their correspondence for the pivotal years: For 1769 only a two-sentence extract of a letter from Franklin to William and five letters from William to his father; for 1770, from each to the other, a single brief note. The son was becoming so guarded, the father so volatile in his moods and assessments that the growing polarization of their views cannot be charted.

One is tempted to show Franklin, the man of the people, the searching mind, undergoing an irreversible radicalization while William, the snob, the petty civil servant, clings to his conservative bias. But that would ignore the honest convictions of very many Americans—not all of them snobbish and petty—for whom loyalty outweighed any sense of grievance and an oath of allegiance was a sacred compact.

It would also disregard the infinite complexities of Franklin's character and the ambivalence imposed on him by his dual role as agent of the colonies and of the British government. More than once he complained that he was suspected "in England of being too much an American, and in America of being too much an Englishman."[29] Both charges indeed were justified up to a point. As agent for several colonies he had to be an advocate of the American point of view, but as deputy-postmaster general for North America he was, like William, an officer of the crown. Having almost lost the postmastership in 1768 because of his outspoken opposition to the Townshend Acts, he was determined to hold onto his office as long as possible. Then, too, he was still negotiating with the government on two delicate fronts, trying to win approval both for the Ohio land grant and for the petition to oust the Penns. He needed all the shrewdness he could muster, all the diplomacy, all the flexibility. Hence the confusing alternation between the inflammatory denunciations of British policies in the press, that earned him the appellation of "Judas . . . in Craven Street," and counsels of moderation to both parties. Were it not for the furiously scribbled comments in the margins of his huge collection of political pamphlets, one would have no inkling of his private thoughts. Here and only here is his posture consistent: Anything even slightly derogatory about the Americans provokes an outburst of rage.

The fundamental differences in political outlook between father and son were brought into the open for the first time when Franklin was elected agent for Massachusetts, late in 1770. Massachusetts was the most combustible of the colonies and quite a few members of its Assembly had misgivings about appointing a man they considered too moderate. Their deputy agent in London, Arthur Lee, had reported ominously, "The possession of a profitable office at will, the having a son in a high post at pleasure . . . joined with the temporizing conduct he has always held in American affairs preclude every rational hope that in an open contest . . . Dr. F. can be a faithful advocate."[30] Franklin, having once obtained this new agency, would be automatically pushed into a more openly aggressive stance.

As one more effort to put the colonial houses of representatives in their place, Hillsborough had decreed that henceforth no appointment of an agent by an assembly would be valid unless it also received the approval of the governor of the province. But Massachusetts had long been at odds with its governors and was not about to give in on this point; jealous of its prerogatives, it went ahead and appointed Franklin on its own.

When, early in 1771, he tried to present his credentials, Hillsborough refused to recognize or even to look at them. Franklin, as he tells the story in his journal, claimed that he did not know of the new instructions for appointment nor that Governor Hutchinson of Massachusetts had refused his assent. Hillsborough took no notice of his protestations and treated him with sneers and mockery. Franklin—still in his own account—behaved with perfect correctness throughout the stormy interview. Yet his anger at last got the better of him and, as he was about to take his leave, he remarked that whether his appointment was acknowledged or not did not really make much difference, since he did not think that an agent could "*at present* be of any use to any of the Colonies."[31] This was a dangerous taunt to the man who had the fate of the colonies in his hands, but Franklin did not regret his audacity. Indeed he reported with undisguised satisfaction that Hillsborough had found his last words extremely rude and abusive: "He assured a Friend of mine that they were equivalent to telling him to his Face that the Colonies could expect neither Favour nor Justice during his Administration. I find he did not mistake me."[32]

The friend of Franklin's to whom Hillsborough confided his anger may well have been Strahan who was on easy terms with the secretary. Still quite fond of William with whom he carried on an extensive correspondence, Strahan felt the moment had come to give the governor a warning: "Your Father . . . is not only on bad terms with Lord Hillsborough, but with the Ministry in general. . . . *But all this to yourself. My Sole Motive* for writing you thus freely is to *put you upon your Guard*, & to induce you to be as circumspect in your Conduct as possible, as it is imagined here that you entertain the same political Opinions with your Father, and are actuated by the same motives with regard to Britain and America."[33]

William must have groaned when he read the letter. Farewell, dreams of advancement! Farewell, hopes of a higher income! In an effort to pull what chestnuts he could out of the fire, he defended his position in a long answer to Strahan, counting on his friend to make judicious use of it in future conversations with the secretary. Hillsborough, he declared, "has no reason (other than the natural connexion between us) to imagine that I entertain the same political opinion with my father with regard to the dispute between Britain & America. My Sentiments are really in many respects different from those which have yet been published on either side of the question." Without elaborating on his personal views, he merely added that as he could not expect the voice of an individual to be listened to, given the temper of both parties, he was keeping his feelings to himself and "steering his little bark" as best he could through the turbulent waters. "I have on no occasion given up a single point of the Crown's Prerogative, nor have I ever attempted the least infringement of the People's Privileges."[34]

When the time came, later in 1771, to reappoint his father as agent of New Jersey, William, anxious to underscore his independence, insisted on carrying out the procedure to the letter of the law: The choice of the Assembly had to be submitted for *his* approval as governor. He met with furious resistance, not because there was any disagreement over the nominee but because the representatives were unwilling to yield on their prerogatives. They retaliated by withholding his salary. He won out in the end, only to have to face his father's displeasure. Franklin, in fact, had hinted he might resign rather than acquiesce to such an infringement of popular rights, but when the news of his reappointment reached him his mood had mellowed, his mind was excited by new concerns, and he accepted it without protest.

A strange year in Franklin's life, 1771 started in gloom and ended in serenity. His clash with Hillsborough had undoubtedly been much more upsetting than he cared to admit. He was in an irritable mood throughout the spring, out of sorts not just with the ministry but with almost everyone. The heartless upbraiding of Debbie for her loss of memory and careless accounting was only one of a spate of untypically ill-humored letters: to the painter Jeremiah Meyer who had been tardy (eight years tardy!) in delivering promised miniatures; to William who forwarded an improperly worded bill from his Assembly; to the daughter of a Philadelphia neighbor, causing her to remark on the "Manner and Shortness"[35] of his style.

He knew the remedy: movement. All his life he was a firm believer in exercise as an antidote to depression and illness. To women he recommended pleasant walks and climbing stairs, to men more energetic activities such as raising one's body heat by lifting dumbbells. His own preferred form of therapy was travel. After months of sedentary, tension-ridden life in the polluted air of the capital, he never failed to experience a physical and spiritual lift from discovering new sights and visiting old friends.

His stay at Twyford that summer with Bishop Shipley and his family completely restored his mood. Warmed by their affection, stimulated by their admiration, he dashed off the story of his adventurous youth, the first and sprightliest part of his *Autobiography,* a monument to optimism, a tribute to man's power and potential that came forth, paradoxically, at a moment of personal and national crisis.

Prevailed upon to tarry one more day in August in order to celebrate from afar Benny Bache's second birthday in true Shipley style with their dessert for special occasions, a floating island, he toasted his grandson's health in an atmosphere of flattering banter. The savory details were communicated to Debbie in two exuberantly jovial letters—in the course of which he even granted her absolution for the poorly kept accounts!*

The trip back to London, in company with the youngest Shipley girl, eleven-year-old Kitty, inspired the most delightful letter Franklin ever wrote, the account of their conversation in the carriage. It ranged from haunted houses to considerations on marriage. They had ample time to settle the matrimonial futures of her four sisters while Kitty herself insisted she would have none but an old husband, preferably a retired general of seventy or eighty. Her views were solicited by Franklin without condescension, listened to seriously, discussed with interest. Is there a better way to a child's heart? Kitty herself never married and none of her sisters followed the path she and Franklin had laid out for them, but the little girl's chatter, the way in which she "cut up the Chicken pretty handily (with a little Direction) and help'd me in a very womanly Manner",[37] her grace all along the way have been captured forever.

In high spirits, Franklin set out a few weeks later on a richly rewarding tour of Ireland and Scotland. A pleasant surprise awaited him on the way: a complete shift in Lord Hillsborough's behavior toward him. Sensing perhaps that he had gone too far in antagonizing the colonies and their agent, the earl was transformed from overbearing superior into gracious host at his family castle in Ireland. As puzzled as he was relieved, Franklin enjoyed the détente but remained on his guard. He was in such an elevated mood by the time his trip was over that when, on his way back to London, he met his son-in-law Richard Bache for the first time, he greeted him with unexpected cordiality and gave his belated blessing to his daughter's marriage.

* Always anxious to become a member of her husband's new "families," Deborah sent the Shipleys an American squirrel, the celebrated Mungo who became their prize pet and whose death was memorialized by Franklin in an epitaph "in the monumental style and measure."[36]

XVI

"You Are a Thorough Courtier"

I have often thought that it will hereafter be considered as Lucifer's Masterpiece in human Affairs—the effecting so great a Misunderstanding between two Countries, that *every Consideration* should [inspire] to Love and Confidence in each other.

—John Temple to William Franklin, April 6, 1769

A WELCOME LULL in the conflict between American claims and British pretensions gave Franklin some time in 1772 for other than political pursuits. Appointed to a committee of the Royal Society to study means of protecting the Purfleet gunpowder magazines from lightning, he recommended the use of pointed conductors. The committee followed his advice, with only one dissenting member who claimed that pointed rods would "collect the lightning in too powerful a manner"[1] and proposed knobby conductors instead. But since pointed rods were so closely identified with Franklin and Franklin with the wrongheaded colonies, the controversy took on political overtones once the atmosphere heated up again in the following years.

Franklin stayed out of the scientific row, trusting that experience would ultimately settle the dispute. (It was to prove that there is no great difference between knobs and points.) King George III, however, eventually had his palace wired with knobby conductors; a rumor arose that he tried to force Sir John Pringle, the president of the Royal Society, to reverse the Society's earlier vote and reject the report, and that Pringle replied the king could change the laws of the land but not those of nature.* A day would come, during the American Revolution,

---

* At the height of the furor, an irreverent epigram made the rounds:

> While you, great George, for safety hunt,
> And sharp conductors change for blunt,
> The nation's out of joint:

> Franklin a wiser course pursues,
> And all your thunder fearless views,
> By keeping to the *point*.[2]

when Franklin expressed regret that the king had not done without lightning rods altogether!

For the man who in 1763 had predicted a "glorious, cloudless reign" for the "virtuous young King,"[3] who in 1768 had described George III as the "best King . . . any nation was ever blest with,"[4] and had continued to defend him until he seemed absolutely indefensible, this was the end of a reluctant evolution. As late as 1773, Franklin clung to the idea of a commonwealth with the king at its head as the only workable compromise in the conflict over parliamentary authority, arguing that the king alone, and not "the King, Lords, and Commons collectively"[5] should be the sovereign and legislator along with the colonial assemblies.

Indeed, he always had a weakness for kings. When the king of Denmark, Christian VII, who was drinking himself into softheadedness, invited him to lunch in the course of a visit to London, Franklin sent William an effusive account of the event, full of praise for the young monarch's "affability and condescension."[6] He proudly accompanied it with a diagram of the seating arrangement, just as a year earlier he had sent Polly Stevenson a sketch of the dining table at Versailles where he had been allowed to stand between the queen and one of Louis XV's numerous spinster sisters.

For all his fame, Franklin thirsted for recognition as self-made men often do. William who, one would think, stood in far greater need of reassurance, played up almost obsequiously to his father's vanity by reporting every tribute paid to him, great or small. The favor was not always returned. When William was elected to the Anglican Society for the Propagation of the Gospel, it took his father two years to congratulate him, and then William's modest achievement triggered a countercatalogue of far higher honors that had meanwhile come *his* way: the Batavian Society for Experimental Science, the French Academy of Sciences, and so forth. He was more prompt in reporting a conversation with Hillsborough's successor, Lord Dartmouth, during which the new secretary praised William as a "good Governor . . . who has kept his Province in good order in times of difficulty,"[7] but the main point of this letter was not so much the compliment to the son as the fact that the father was on very good terms with the colonial secretary.

Well aware of this facet of Franklin's character, British officials periodically floated rumors that he was about to be made a baronet, a colonial undersecretary, a provincial governor. But they never delivered, and any hopes they may have entertained of winning him over by dangling such flattering prospects were dashed by a series of dramatic events set in motion by Franklin himself in the closing days of 1772.

On December 2 of that year, he sent Thomas Cushing, speaker of the Massachusetts House of Representatives, a packet of eighteen letters written between 1767 and 1769 by several high officials in Boston. The most prominent of these officials was Thomas Hutchinson, lieutenant-governor of Massachusetts at the time of their writing, and now governor. Addressed to a former undersecretary of the Treasury in England, Thomas Whately, the letters underscored the seditious temper of the colony and suggested that the British government take harsher measures to restore order, including, if needed, "an abridgement of what are called English liberties."[8]

How had such documents found their way into Franklin's hands? He never revealed his source beyond saying that they came from a "gentleman of character and distinction." Upon sending the letters back to Massachusetts he warned Cushing that they should not be printed but seen only "by some men of worth in the province."[9] Yet he listed so many names of authorized readers that one cannot help wondering whether he really minded the possibility of a leak. Had not Poor Richard (1735) cautioned, "Three may keep a secret if two of them are dead?" And had he not emphasized, "If you would keep your secret from an enemy, tell it not to a friend?" (1741).

The Hutchinson letters were bruited about for a time, not very long. In June 1773, they appeared in the *Boston Gazette* under the indignant heading "Born and Educated among Us." Although they contained no opinion that had not been previously expressed, their publication had an immediate and incendiary effect. Hutchinson, whom Jane Mecom had compared to "Our Saviour"[10] at the time of the Stamp Act riots, was now vilified as the Judas of his people, branded as that "dark, intriguing, insinuating, haughty and ambitious" politician, as a "damn'd arch traitor," as a "tool of tyrants."[11] A reserved, wealthy man, basically honest but contemptuous of courting popular favor, he was virtually hounded out of the country. He moved to England and soon became an advisor to the ministry.

When William first heard of the affair, his sympathies instinctively went out to Hutchinson who, he wrote his father, was "made very unhappy by the Publication of his Letters."[12] What Franklin had viewed as little less than treason was to William little more than an excess of zeal intended to keep Massachusetts from total anarchy. Indeed Hutchinson and William shared the same paternalistic, law-and-order outlook. Rumors were already flying that it was Franklin who had forwarded the letters but William could not bring himself to believe them. Franklin, in his reply, avoided the subject of the letters themselves but denied the charges that he had incited unrest by his own dispatches to the Massachusetts leaders: Why should anyone resort to violence when the colonies were sure eventually to carry their point through their growing population and prosperity? He knew that William would agree so far. But when he added that in his opinion Parliament had "no right to make any law whatever binding on the colonies," he was prepared to hear that his son would differ. "You are a thorough government man," he pursued, "nor do I aim at converting you. I only wish you to act uprightly and steadily. . . . If you can promote the prosperity of your people, and leave them happier than you found them, whatever your political principles are, your memory will be honored."[13]

On October 6, 1773, when he wrote those lines, Franklin could still afford to take such an Olympian attitude: The storm had not yet broken over his head. Before long it did. John Temple, an American-born official in the British customs service, was accused of having been the party who had stolen the letters from the now deceased original addressee, Thomas Whately. As a correspondent of the latter, an enemy of Hutchinson, a friend of Franklin and William—and as a man of less than sterling reputation—he was indeed open to suspicion if not to conviction. After an exchange of verbal and printed insults, he fought a duel with William Whately, Thomas's brother and executor. Whately was wounded but asked for a second round. Franklin decided that the moment had come to speak up. On Christmas Day 1773, he published a statement in the *Public Advertiser,* claiming total responsibility. Self-righteously—for the duel could have taken the life of an innocent man —he remarked to William a few days later that he did not mind drawing some censure upon himself since his main concern was to be satisfied that he had acted rightly.

Throughout the affair, Franklin maintained that he had never intended to increase the strain between Britain and the colonies; on the contrary, he claimed that showing how the British government had been tragically misled by the counsel of irresponsible Americans such as Hutchinson was the best way to reconciliation. An honest miscalculation of this kind is fully credible. Not so his statement to Cushing, that Hutchinson and his friends, "if they are good men," would be willing to accept the idea of serving peace, be it "at the small expense of their reputation for sincerity and public spirit among their compatriots."[14] After two decades in political strife, after a lifetime spent in observing human nature, could Franklin really believe that?

His enemies in England had only been waiting their chance. Now they had it. On January 29, 1774, he was summoned before the Privy Council, ostensibly to present a petition from the Massachusetts Assembly asking the removal of Hutchinson as governor, actually to be pilloried for his recent actions. The news of the Boston Tea Party had reached England only a few days earlier and an enraged ministry could ask for no better scapegoat.

It was a hostile crowd, composed mostly of lords and ladies of the realm, gathered in the appropriately named Cockpit, an adjunct of Whitehall Palace, to see the Christian fed to the lion. The lion was the solicitor-general, Alexander Wedderburn, a brilliant, ambitious, and totally unprincipled lawyer, so damaging when in the opposition that he had been bought off with a place in the government. For an hour he abused Franklin, loading him with "all the licensed scurrility of the bar and deck[ing] his harangue with the choicest flowers of Billingsgate."[15] Franklin was a common thief and his motive in sending the letters, Wedderburn charged, was simply to become governor in Hutchinson's stead.* For an hour Franklin stood in his old-fashioned wig and suit of figured Manchester velvet, enduring in silence the insolent attack: "The Doctor seemed to receive the thunder of [Wedderburn's] eloquence with philosophic tranquillity and sovereign contempt." No defense was possible, he had already admitted transmitting the letters: "I made no justification of myself, but held a cool, sullen silence, reserving myself to some future opportunity."[18] The Massachusetts charges against Hutchinson were dismissed by the Privy Council as "vexatious, scandalous and seditious."[19]

The next day Franklin was fired from his postmastership. His immediate reaction was that William's fate was of course linked to his. While still in a state of shock three days after the event, he sent him a thinly veiled directive to resign: "This Line is just to acquaint you that I am well, and that my Office of Deputy-Postmaster is taken from me. As there is no Prospect of your being ever promoted to a better Govern-

---

* Wedderburn's attack was picked up by an anonymous poet:

> Thou base, ungrateful, cunning, upstart thing!
> False to thy country first, then to thy King;
> To gain thy selfish and ambitious ends,
> Betraying secret letters writ to friends:
> May no more letters through thy hands be past,
> But may thy last year's office be thy last.[16]

Franklin's defenders countered that the French saw him as "much more impudent and audacious in his Thefts" than his detractors had ever ventured to insinuate:

> Il a ravi le feu des cieux,
> Il fait fleurir les arts en des climats sauvages.
> L'Amérique le place à la tête des sages.
> La Grèce l'auroit mis au nombre de ses Dieux.

> [To steal from Heaven its sacred Fire he taught,
> The Arts to thrive in savage Climes he brought:
> In the New World the first of Men esteem'd;
> Among the Greeks a God he had been deem'd.][17]

ment, and that your hold has never defrayed its Expences, I wish you were well settled in your Farm. 'Tis an honester and a more honourable because a more independent Employment. You will hear from others the Treatment I have receiv'd. I leave you to your own Reflections and Determinations upon it."[20]

A few days later, however, he had second thoughts. He had heard that William might be pressured into resigning as part of his father's disgrace: "They may expect that your Resentment of their Treatment of me, may induce you to resign and save them the shame of depriving you when they ought to promote." But stand firm, he advised, "Let them take your place if they want it. . . . One may make something of an Injury, nothing of a Resignation."[21]

He kept vacillating over the next few months but did not relent in his painful reminders that William had never been able to live within his salary and constantly had to borrow from him. There was something ignoble about being an officeholder, especially an underpaid one: "I think Independence more honorable now than any Service."[22] In May he pushed brusquely for William's resignation, predicting "you will find yourself in no comfortable Situation and perhaps wish you had sooner disengaged yourself."[23]

In answering him, William showed his usual concern for his father's self-esteem. "It seems your Popularity in this Country, whatever it may be on the other Side, is greatly beyond whatever it was."[24] Having soothed the paternal ego, he equivocated about his own intentions. In fact, he had long since made up his mind to take Strahan's advice and dissociate himself from Franklin. On good terms from the start with Lord Dartmouth, William now pledged that "no attachments or connexions shall ever make me swerve from the duty of my station."[25] In turn, he was assured that he was not under his father's cloud and that for the moment at least his office was safe. While continuing to perform his duties faithfully, William supplied Dartmouth with secret intelligence about the mood of the colonies, especially when the first Continental Congress met in Philadelphia in September 1774. The Congress, he insisted, was far from representative; the bulk of the colonists remained loyal to the crown but were afraid to speak out because of intimidation on the part of the superpatriots.

To Dartmouth William was reporting the temper of his fellow Americans, filtered through the mind of a conservative; to Strahan and Strahan alone, as far as one can tell, he was confiding his innermost thoughts. In May 1774 he described to his friend the abyss that already separated him from Franklin's political thinking. Few letters remained private in those years. The contents of William's became known to his enemies, and he found himself a mini-Hutchinson, all the more odious because he appeared to be betraying his own father.

Deeply shocked, Jane Mecom told Franklin she could not believe the "horrid lie told and published here"[26] about his son. William himself, frantically wondering how much of his correspondence had been disclosed, rushed to Philadelphia, enlisted the aid of his brother-in-law Richard Bache, and demanded to see the letter reporting his views. A measure of relief: Since his criticisms of the ministry had not been publicized, his job was safe. But a lingering discomfort: His announced decision to remain loyal to the administration would henceforth make him an object of suspicion in the colonies.

As William was taking the irreversible steps down the road that would lead him to disaster, Franklin was wavering in London about the course to follow. The British administration was also wavering: repressive at one moment, conciliatory at another, governing "from hand to mouth."[27] Everybody claimed to be in favor of peace and reconciliation, of course, from British tory to American patriot. But what were the obstacles to peace? The king, his ministers, his treacherous advisors, as Franklin thought? Or the American hotheads, the kind who dumped tea into Boston harbor and then were outraged when asked to pay, as William and Strahan thought? When William suggested that the Bostonians should "do justice before they ask it,"[28] Franklin turned on him savagely, "You who are a thorough Courtier, see everything with Government Eyes."[29] Yet he himself had suggested earlier and would suggest again that reparation, though not owed, would be a wise gesture.

William could not understand why his father had stayed in England after the humiliation of the Cockpit. By his own admission Franklin had been stripped of all influence and had not been in touch with a single minister during virtually the entire year. Disgraced and impotent he could do nothing more for the Ohio land grant, nothing for the Pennsylvania petition to oust the Penns in favor of the crown—an exchange that had lost its appeal in any case ever since 1767. True, he still had friends, even in Parliament, but they were, he ruefully admitted, "in Disgrace at Court as well as myself."[30]

Obnoxious as he might be in England, his presence was very much desired in America. "You may depend, when you return here, on being received with every Mark of Regard and Affection,"[31] wrote William. Debbie was near death, her only wish to live long enough to see her husband again. After she had died, William pointed out with more bluntness than he had ever dared show before that it was high time, indeed almost too late, to come home: "If there was any Prospect of your being able to bring People in Power to your Way of Thinking, or of those of your Way of Thinking's being brought into Power, I should not think so much of your Stay. But as you have had by this time pretty strong Proofs that neither can be reasonably expected and that you are looked upon with an evil Eye in that Country, and are in no small Danger of being brought into Trouble for your political Conduct, you had certainly better return, while you are able to bear the Fatigues of the Voyage."[32]

The "no small Danger" William referred to was twofold. A civil suit had been brought against Franklin by William Whately over the misuse of his brother's private papers. Also, many believed that in the heat of the parliamentary elections in the fall of 1774, Franklin might be arrested for sedition. Before the House of Lords, Hillsborough referred unmistakably to him when he declared that there were men walking the streets of London who ought to be in Newgate or Tyburn jail.

Franklin must have been surprised by his son's new tone of authority, perhaps stung by the insinuations of his ineffectiveness and the futility of his prolonged absence. William had concluded the letter with a peremptory request that his son Temple be sent over for a year or two to study law at New York College: "I hope to see you and him in the spring."[33]

Franklin's reply, his self-justification, was ninety-six pages long. He had plenty of time to compose it in the course of his six-week crossing on the *Philadelphia Packet* (March–April 1775). Addressed to the world as much as to his son, it was a day-to-day, move-by-move account of the secret negotiations that had filled his last months in England.

Once the dust had settled after the Hutchinson letters and the Boston Tea Party, there were many Englishmen who were sorely troubled. Several of them tried desperately and in their separate and different ways to avert what they foresaw as ruin for both countries: William Pitt, who had led Great Britain to victory in the Seven Years' War, Franklin's Quaker friends, the merchant David Barclay and John Pringle, physician to the British aristocracy, who had the ear of Lord Dartmouth; Mrs. Howe, the sister of Lord Howe (admiral and M.P.), who invited Franklin to play chess and discuss mathematics at her house so that her brother could sound him out discreetly about the prospects for reconciliation. The only thing all these people had in common was their faith that Franklin could somehow produce a magic formula for patching up the quarrel. Flattered if never very sanguine, he drafted document after document to serve as a basis for discussion, but there always were points the British government could not swallow, concessions demanded of the colonies which they would never accept. Having received no authority to speak for the colonies as a whole nor any instructions from the Continental Congress, Franklin could only do his best to interpret the position of his countrymen as he understood it. His sense of humor, luckily had not deserted him. To a questioner who wanted to know what would satisfy the Americans, he replied that the answer could easily be comprised in a few "Re's":

Re {
   call your Forces,
   store Castle William [in Boston Harbor],
   pair the Damage done to Boston,
   peal your unconstitutional Acts,
   nounce your pretentions to Taxes,
   fund the duties you have extorted; after this
   quire payment for the destroyed Tea with the
      voluntary grants of the Colonies, And then
   joice in a happy
   conciliation.[34]

When Parliament reopened in mid-January 1775, the petition from the Continental Congress was introduced in the House of Commons, only to be ignored. In the Lords, Chatham determined to present a comprehensive plan for peace based on his discussions with Franklin (who had reassured him that there was absolutely no sentiment for independence in America). Chatham, who for so many years had not condescended to receive Franklin, now came to Craven Street and went over the proposal with his new-found ally. This visit, as Franklin admitted, "flattered not a little my vanity, and gave me the more pleasure as it happened on the very day twelvemonth that the Ministry had taken so many pains to disgrace me before the Privy Council."[35] The plan, however, was a total failure.

It was the end. A few more weeks of half-hearted attempts to salvage the unsalvageable, even some feelers to see if Franklin might be susceptible to bribery, then the recognition that all was in vain. And now, in his long account to William of these dramatic events, Franklin set out to prove that he had not given up while there was the least hope for peace, that nothing more could have been done to "preserve from breaking that fine and noble China vase, the British Empire."[36] The message for William: All efforts had come to nothing because of the blindness and corruption of the British government—a "herd of worthless parasites" in Fothergill's words.[37] Such a government no longer deserved William's loyalty.

The emotional strain of those last few weeks had been almost more than Franklin could bear. On his final day in London he went over the recently arrived American newspapers with his friend Priestley to cull from them material for propaganda; when they came to the addresses sent by the neighboring towns to the shut-down port of Boston, he lost control and "the tears trickled down his cheeks."[38]

Once on shipboard his composure returned and he enlisted Temple to help him with his observations of the Gulf Stream. While grandfather and grandson were on the high seas, Massachusetts militiamen and British regulars had started killing one another at Lexington and Concord.

XVII

Tug of War

Neighbor was against neighbor, father against the son and the son against the father, and he that would not thrust his own blade through his brother's heart was called an infamous villain.

—Stephen Gorham, petition of July 22, 1777

"I BROUGHT OVER A GRANDSON with me, a fine Lad of about 15. . . . You will be pleas'd with him when you see him."[1] Written to Jane Mecom a few weeks after his landing in Philadelphia on May 5, 1775, these words from her brother were probably the first intimation she had of Temple's existence. Elizabeth Franklin, too, may have been kept in the dark many years. Once it had become poignantly clear, however, that the governor and his wife would remain childless, there was no more talk of passing Temple off as the offspring of an indigent relation: He was coming home to be acknowledged finally as William's son and the last male Franklin of the American line. It took very little time for this London adolescent to become an unquestioned, essential member of the Philadelphia family. Before long he would be the only bridge between Benjamin and William, his love and loyalty fiercely contended for by both.

The leave from England had been a hasty one. Temple had been pulled out of school so precipitously that he had had no chance to say goodby to his comrades. But the headmaster and his wife, Mrs. Stevenson and Polly, the Strahans, and some other friends had been assured that the pair would be back by winter. Perhaps Franklin really believed that they would return as soon as his affairs were straightened out, perhaps he merely wanted to make the parting easier, perhaps it was a stratagem to elude those who planned to arrest him, using as a pretext the chancery suit brought by William Whately over the Hutchinson letters. Several years later a friend recalled that Franklin told him "a plan was laid for stopping him in England. . . . He gave out he should sail in a fortnight by the packet, but went off suddenly by another opportunity."[2] (A somewhat inaccurate recollection: Franklin did sail by the packet.)

Strahan had promised to write by every ship "till your return." He hoped Franklin would pour oil on the troubled American waters and strengthen the hand of the moderates. "I expect to see you quickly return to us with the Olive Branch in your Hand," he wrote confidently, "invested with full Powers to terminate all Differences upon reasonable and solid Terms."[3] The alternative would be a war which England was sure to win but which he feared would lead to "the immediate Destruction of half, and the ultimate Ruin of the whole of the most glorious Fabric of Civil and Religious Government that ever existed on this Globe."[4]

When he set sail, Franklin himself may not have known what course he would follow. All indecision vanished as soon as he set foot on American soil. Lexington and Concord had marked a watershed. Within a few weeks a bloody battle would be fought at Bunker Hill, Charlestown would be burned, and a British blockade thrown up along the coast. In Franklin's eyes Britain had begun a civil war from which there could be no retreat. True, Congress would make a last, futile gesture with the Olive Branch Petition, but nobody expected it to change anything. "Words and Arguments are now of no use,"[5] he told Strahan on July 7, 1775, the day before the Petition was sent. Two days earlier he had penned a far stronger letter to his old friend: "You are a member of Parliament and one of the majority which has doomed my country to destruction. You have begun to burn our towns and murder our people. Look upon your hands! They are stained with the blood of your relations. You and I were long friends. You are now my Enemy and I am Yours. B. Franklin."[6] This letter was never sent, but it shows the white heat of his passion. Well might he describe the prevailing temper as "little short of Madness."[7] His letters to England that summer were ferocious in their denunciation of British barbarity, enraptured with the new martial spirit of the Americans.

Rejuvenated, Franklin plunged into the heady work of revolution. If he had been apprehensive about his reception after ten years abroad, the tumultuous welcome given him by his fellow citizens removed his fears just as rapidly as it dispelled any illusions he might have had about retirement from public service. Twenty-four hours after landing he had been made a delegate to the Second Continental Congress—its oldest member. As soon as he had finished drawing up plans for a new postal service, he was appointed postmaster-general, at a salary of one thousand dollars which he donated to wounded soldiers. He busied himself with procuring lead and gunpowder. So great was the shortage of lead that a requisition was carried out from house to house for curtain weights and clock pendulums. Gunsmiths were so rare that he pro-

posed going back to pikes, much simpler to manufacture and often as
effective as the muskets of the time. Entrusted with an issue of paper
money, he drew on his botanical knowledge to suggest for each
denomination an intricate leaf design that would be hard to counterfeit.
His own family was not forgotten, of course: Richard Bache was one of
the three men chosen to supervise the currency printing and he became
comptroller of the postal service.

Such a warlike climate did not bode well for a rapprochement between Franklin and his son. When William had come to Philadelphia
in May to greet him, they had agreed that Temple would spend the
summer with his new family in Perth Amboy where the governor had
moved the previous autumn, then enter the College of Philadelphia—
not New York College as previously planned. Better, felt Franklin, to
have him in the institution run by his inveterate enemy, the Reverend
Mr. William Smith, than to let him out of his sight in that hotbed of
toryism, New York.

Politics must have been much on both men's minds but they avoided
a full discussion for several weeks. Franklin was extremely anxious to
meet with his old friend Joseph Galloway first. Galloway had been his
closest collaborator in Pennsylvania campaigns and particularly in the
struggle against the Penns. He had also been William's teacher in the
law. Although he had lost much of his political influence in recent
years, he still managed to hold onto his post as speaker of the Assembly.
Rejected by his constituents, he had made peace with the Penns, but
then so had William, and this no longer seemed such a cardinal sin;
there were far worse rascals to deal with now. During his ten years in
England, Franklin had never stopped confiding in Galloway; William,
too, had drawn closer to him than to any other American political
leader.

The three men came together at Galloway's estate in Bucks County
sometime in the late spring. They talked into the night, "the glass having gone about freely." Hitherto Franklin had been circumspect about
expressing his views to anyone in America; now "he opened himself
and declared in favour of measures for attaining to Independence, exclaimed against the corruption and dissipation of the Kingdom and
signified his opinion that from the strength of Opposition, the want of
union of the Ministry, the great resources in the Colonies,"[8] the Americans would finally prevail.* He urged Galloway to come back into
Congress and desist from the sulking stance he had adopted since the

* It is an irony of history that the only account of this meeting occurs in the diary of Thomas Hutchinson, of all people. He was reporting on a conversation held
with Galloway in England some three years later.

narrow defeat of his plan for British-American union. (Rejected by
only one vote, this plan—which owed much to Franklin's own Albany
proposals of 1754—called for a president-general appointed by the king
and a colonial legislature with "like Rights, Liberties and privileges as
are held and exercised by and in the House of Commons."[9]

Hoping to reach his son through Galloway, like William a man of
the younger generation, Franklin staked everything on this meeting.
For years, those two had been his closest collaborators, accustomed to
follow his lead almost unquestioningly. Now they were pulling away.
Hour after hour he mustered every argument he could think of to sway
their minds, but he failed. William would not be budged. England had
given him his wife and his first chance to wean himself from his father.
To England he would remain loyal. Or rather, as he put it, he was not
taking sides at all nor passing judgment on the "Merits of the Dispute,"
but simply insisting that only legitimate avenues of redress should be
used for colonial grievances. A few months earlier he had cautioned his
Assembly that there were only two possible paths open, "one leading to
Peace, Happiness, and a Restoration of the Public Tranquility—the
other inevitably conducting you to Anarchy, Misery and all the Horrors
of Civil War."[10] And he also made his position clear to his father,
warning him that if he, Franklin, "designed to set the Colonies in a
flame,"[11] he had better run away by the light of it. When Franklin realized that all his efforts were in vain, he tried no more. For the next few
months, communication between father and son was minimal.

Most of his time was devoted to Congress. True, John Adams, who
liked oratory and hated being upstaged, contemptuously described a
Franklin "from day to day sitting in silence, a great part of the time
fast asleep in his chair" and sighed that he was likely nevertheless to
get credit for everything achieved by the Congress, just as in England
he was regarded as the prime agent of American opposition. Indeed
Franklin's tendency to be silent in groups had often struck less biased
observers; but he was merely putting into practice his youthful resolution to avoid garrulousness, having long since found that words were
far more effective if saved for decisive moments, when a calm pronouncement or a bit of humor could break deadlocks or defuse passions.

The lot of the delegates was not all work. While the Congress was in
session, Philadelphia outdid itself in the brilliance and gaiety of its social life. Its population had grown rapidly in the almost two decades
since Franklin had first gone to England. It boasted fine public buildings and stately, beautifully furnished houses belonging to rich merchants who lived so sumptuously that John Adams called them "the no-

bles" of Philadelphia. To these homes the weary delegates repaired for what the same Adams labeled "most sinfull Feasts. . . . Everything which could delight the Eye or allure the Taste":[12] turtles, tarts, whipped sillabubs (a frothy mixture of cream and wine), curds, jellies, wines, porters, punches, and beer. Balls were considered inappropriate to the serious work at hand, but good eating was almost a matter of patriotic pride.

The journals of the delegates rarely mention Franklin as taking part in these Lucullan delights. Of course he was a recent widower—Debbie had not been dead six months when he arrived home. Did it seem strange and lonely to be in a Philadelphia without her, in a house they had labored together to build? If he felt grief and emptiness it remained unspoken. Not a single surviving letter of his mentions her in the year following her death. Just as surprising in that age of stylized politeness, no one, after the initial messages from William and Bache informing him of his loss, wrote a word of comfort or even alluded to his widowed state: not Jane Mecom, not Caty Greene, not Polly Hewson, not Mrs. Stevenson.

Mrs. Stevenson would have been abnormally selfless if his new status had not brought thoughts of a happier ending to her mind: After all, he was free now, free to marry her if he chose. About her own inclinations there is little doubt. Her letters to Franklin are full of anticipation of the "hapey day" when they would see each other again, mixed with forebodings that it might never be. Should the message from her and from Polly not be clear enough, an intimate friend of the threesome, Dolly Blunt, wrote that Mrs. Stevenson "gives frequent proof of weak spirits, which I am sure will be still weaker if your letter whenever it comes does not contain the strongest assurances of your return; for I am firmly persuaded that without the animating hope of spending the remainder of Life with you she would be very wretched indeed, for tho' many of your friends are also her friends, yet all of us are less to her than you."[13] When it became evident that he would not return, Mrs. Stevenson revived her old plan of coming to America, seconded this time by Polly who was an ardent champion of the colonies and wanted nothing more than to "transplant" her "young shoots to that soil."[14]

Franklin addressed Mrs. Stevenson as "my dear, dear Friend," offered advice on her financial affairs, and sent tidbits of news about Temple, but gave no hint whatever that he missed her company any more than he was grieving for his lost mate in Philadelphia. The one happy prospect he held out was that of dancing with her at the marriage of his grandson Benny Bache with her granddaughter Elizabeth Hewson, respectively six and not quite two at the time.

Though he did not join in most of the gay social doings of early Revolutionary Philadelphia, Franklin found diversion in one of his most
constant loves: music. "We have here a little musical Club at which
Catches are sometimes sung and heard with great Pleasure." Catches
were jocose, sometimes bawdy rounds sung by unaccompanied voices.
He may have enjoyed them enough to attend the Catch and Glee Club
founded in London in 1761; now he asked an English friend to send
"half a Dozen of those you think best among the modern,"[15] since his
comrades had only a few of the old ones.

Late in August 1775, Franklin went to Perth Amboy to bring Temple home for the fall term. He no longer cared to have William come to
Philadelphia; his loyalist son was an embarrassment to him. Temple
settled into the house on Market Street with his grandfather, his Uncle
Bache, his Aunt Sally, and two little cousins, Benny, six, and Willy,
two. He was a pleasant, polished youth, sociable and amusing. Sally's
later letters abound in nostalgic reminiscences of the good times they all
had together. Reading the undeliverable messages that wound up in
the dead-letter office, for instance, proved a particularly rich source of
amusement. Already something of a ladies' man, Temple toasted his favorite, Peggy Shippen, and long treasured her dried nosegay. (This
same Peggy would become the wife of the "more than wretched"[16] general, Benedict Arnold.) He was also as disorganized as boys are apt to
be at fifteen: His shoes, his socks, his linen always seemed to remain in
the last place he visited, and the correspondence between Perth Amboy
and Philadelphia in those historic days was devoted in large measure to
bringing him and his belongings together. As Elizabeth Franklin finally
remarked with tactful understatement, "You are extremely unlucky in
your Clothes."[17]

A young man of great expectations, Temple was accordingly subjected to much edifying advice. From long years as Poor Richard, his
grandfather knew how to temper his admonitions with literary digres-
sions and anecdotes. But William, overzealous in the unaccustomed
role of father, wrote stiffly and bluntly. His letters have something of
the sternness though little of the art of his addresses to the New Jersey
Assembly. Rigid in his ideas of filial duty, he demanded that his son report regularly and fully about his studies, that he put every minute to
good account and that he live within his allowance. "I am very anxious
to have you a good scholar, and particularly you should make yourself
Master of the Latin, Greek and French languages, and be well versed
in Mathematicks. Without you should possess a competent Knowledge
of these, my Intentions for your future Advantage will be entirely

frustrated."[18] As if this "useful and ornamental"[19] knowledge were not enough, Temple was also instructed to take night classes in German.

Dutifully he sent an outline of his schedule as soon as classes began. The roll was called at eight in the morning, followed by prayers. Being in the college he escaped the grim choice given the lower-school students who were absent: ferruling or a two-copper fine. Mornings were taken up with Latin and Greek or geography, afternoons with mathematics "of which I begin to understand something"—a tribute to his teacher, the Reverend Mr. William Smith. Classes ended at five, the students reassembled, prayed, and went home to do translations and write compositions in Latin or themes in English on such topics as Virtue and Honor. Suspecting that his father would notice there was an unaccounted-for gap between eleven and three, Temple hastened to assure him that it was devoted to "learning my tasks in Euclid." Somewhat wearily he added, "I will now leave it to you to judge whether you think there is any time left unoccupied [in] the Days either for Dancing or Fencing."[20]

More good advice came from England. A Mrs. Woolford urged him, now that he had found an "indulgent Father," to do "all in your power to merit his affection and look upon Dr. Franklin as the Second Parent that laid the foundation for so kind a reception."[21] And in a letter brimming with affection, his former schoolmaster, James Elphinston, insisted that Temple could best serve his new country by returning to England to finish his education. But this was out of the question. His parents, anyway, thought his writing style already "rather too *Elphinstonic*," meaning too artificial. William cautioned him to avoid "all Attempts at the Sublime, all Quaint Words and Phrases . . . in Letters as in Conversation," and was glad to see that his son was evolving towards "an easy Epistolary Style."[22]

Early in October, as Temple was embarking on his scholarly career, his grandfather departed for Cambridge to confer with General Washington, recently appointed commander in chief of the Continental forces. Twelve years had elapsed since Franklin had last set foot in New England, on his long visit to Boston with Sally. He would never again walk the streets of his native city. Now he could only glimpse at Boston, on the other side of the Charles, a Boston occupied by the British regulars, from which many inhabitants had fled, expecting it to become a battlefield any day.

Jane Mecom was among those who had packed—indeed she had packed very well, managing to hide some salable merchandise among her wearing apparel and bedding—bolted the door, and prepared to go forth with one of her granddaughters, "intending to seek my fortune

with hundred others and not knowing whither."[23] At the very last minute a providential invitation had arrived to join Catharine Ray Greene
in Warwick, Rhode Island. The refugees had made their way there to
the kindly welcome of Caty and her equally hospitable husband. On
the very day of her arrival at the Greenes, Jane heard of Franklin's
landing in Philadelphia and promptly dispatched him a note to reassure
him about her own safety. Thanking God for his mercy to both of
them, she described the horrors of Boston at war and the relief of living
among friends, albeit in crowded conditions: To the Greenes' already
numerous household a dozen relatives and friends had been added, and
more were expected. Caty's postscript shows her as ebullient as ever,
her style as breathless, her emotions as lively: "Welcome, a hundred
times welcome to our once happy land. . . . Allow me to ask you the
old question once again if you are the same good good soul you used to
be . . . your arrival gives a new spring to all that have heard mention
it. . . . [I] don't know but your good Sister and self shall mount our
old nags and come and see you."[24]

Though relieved about Jane, Franklin worried that she might prove
tiresome; better than anybody he knew the belligerence of her faith,
her touchiness, her quirks. His sister, he felt, was *his* responsibility: "I
think so many People must be a great Burden to that hospitable House;
and I wish you to be other wise provided for as soon as possible, and I
wish for the Pleasure of your Company."[25] Strangely enough, however,
Jane and Caty, a generation apart in age, a world apart in circumstances and temperament, had a marvelous rapport. They "entertained
each other charmingly," had, in Caty's words, "a nice dish of chat,"[26]
and played at being mother and daughter ("Would to God I had such
a one!"[27] exclaimed Jane).* Caty proclaimed she would spare Jane to no
one but Franklin. He stopped in Warwick on his way back from Cambridge, embraced his friends there, and promptly took off again for
Pennsylvania, accompanied by Jane and the ten-year-old Ray Greene,
about whom he was to decide whether the boy's intelligence warranted
an education at the Academy of Philadelphia.

War or no war, revolution or no revolution, the trip with her
brother, in a carriage and horses bought by him for the purpose, was an
enchantment to Jane: "My dear brother's conversation was more than
an equivalent to all the fine weather imaginable."[29] The only hitch

* Even though she hastened to add in the following sentence that her
own daughter was a good woman but that Providence did not permit them to be
together, Jane did not get along well with Jenny. She admitted it some years later:
"I [appear] indifferent about going to live with you. . . . Little vexatious incidents
would so often accrue that it would keep my mind perpetually uneasy."[28]

(she called it a "mortification") was that going through Connecticut they were so busily engaged in conversation they went beyond their destination for the day and missed a visit with the Hancocks. Franklin, at sixty-nine, had lost little of his charismatic appeal to women. In Cambridge he had charmed both the future historian of the Revolution, Mercy Warren, and Abigail Adams, who wrote rapturously, "I found him social but not talkative, and when he spoke something useful dropped from his tongue. He was grave, yet pleasant and affable. You know I make some pretension to physiognomy and I thought I could read in his countenance the virtues of his heart, among which patriotism shone in its full lustre, and with that is blended every virtue of a Christian: for a true patriot must be a religious man."[30]

The travelers stopped overnight at Perth Amboy on November 7. This was the last time that Franklin and William would meet face to face until after the Revolution. One would expect some echo of the drama that was taking place, the irreparable breach between two who had been so close. But there is none. The men remained tight-lipped, the women kept their comments on the mundane level. Jane simply remarked that the governor's new mansion was "very magnificient"[31] (and well it might be, he had spent more than a year supervising its renovation down to the last detail, as if there were not a cloud on the horizon). Elizabeth glossed over the moment's poignancy: She merely informed Temple that "we had the happiness of my father's and Aunt Mecom's company last Tuesday night; we would willingly have detained them longer, but Pappa was anxious to get home."[32] Like so many other hours of crisis in Franklin's life, this one went unrecorded.

Their journey behind them, with its interlude of coziness and privacy, brother and sister went back to the realities of life. Jane was soon meeting with her usual quota of tribulations. She heard of the death of her son Josiah "but by what means I am not informed."[33]* And her last two surviving sons were, as she said, "distracted." Peter was still vegetating near Boston in a state of complete imbecility; Benny, having drifted hopelessly from job to job in and around Burlington was now given to fits of violence. At the request of Benny's long-suffering wife, Franklin was asked by two Burlington citizens to find a place for him in the Philadelphia Hospital "or any other way of confining," for he was at times "very dangerous . . . and likely to become very troublesome to the inhabitants."[35] Jane derived what comfort she could from taking

---

* It is believed that he disappeared in the battle of Bunker Hill, fighting perhaps against a British officer named Turner, the man who had married the widow of his brother John. "O how horrible is our situation that relations seek the destruction of each other."[34]

care of little Ray Greene who had a mild case of smallpox (so light, she remarked with grim humor, that he would not have a single pit as a receipt), and from going to church: "I am so happy to have my choice of places of worship so near that the weather need not hinder me from going."[36]

The New Jersey Franklins and the Philadelphia Franklins settled into a pattern of uneasy formality, corresponding with each other only through Temple. Elizabeth would continue to send duty to "Papa," but William dropped even this convention, closing his letters to his son with a vague "love to the family."

William's political skills were never more in evidence than during that stormy year of 1775. He managed to keep both the Assembly and the Council from open defiance, though he could not always command their assent. The king had declared all the colonies in rebellion, but New Jersey was less rebellious than most. William even profited from something of a counter-revolutionary backlash in the fall, as the province began to resent the onerous taxes and conscription imposed by the patriot provincial Congress. He could claim it as a personal triumph, too, that the crown had at long last approved an issue of paper money credit. So conspicuous were his accomplishments at a time when many royal governors had already fled that the new colonial secretary sent him a letter of commendation.

Still, there were moments when William wondered if he was being foolhardy. Rumor had it that the Continental Congress was planning to take direct charge of the provincial governments and hold their appointed officials hostage. Unfortunately the solution adopted by his New York colleague, Governor Tryon—settling on a man-of-war sent by England and governing safely and legally from offshore—was not available to William. "I am loth to desert my Station," he declared, "as my continuation in it is a Means of Keeping up some Appearance of Government, and Matters may take such a Turn as to put it in my Power to do some Service. On the other Hand it would mortify me extremely to be seized upon and led like a Bear through the Country to some Place of Confinement in New England."[37]

Mortification was not long in coming. On January 2, 1776, Congress passed a resolution directing local authorities to "frustrate the mischievous machinations and restrain the wicked practices"[38] of the supporters of royal government. Three days later, William Alexander (Lord Stirling), the Scottish-American commander of eastern New Jersey's militia, seized the governor's outgoing mail in which he found William's voluminous report to the colonial secretary. While it did not contain anything that could be properly called treasonable, the report described the November Assembly and stated that though the majority of the population in Pennsylvania and New Jersey opposed independence, the radical minority might well make reconciliation with England impossible. A radical himself, and a personal enemy of the governor, Alexander immediately sent an armed detachment under a colonel to surround William's residence in Perth Amboy. At two o'clock in the morning on the night of January 5, the governor and his wife were awakened "with a violent Knocking at the Door." The colonel demanded from William a pledge that he would not leave town until Congress decided what to do with him. William retorted that he had "not the least intention to quit the Province . . . unless compelled by Violence," but refused to give any promise to men trespassing on his property with guns and bayonets.

Congress took no action against the governor—he had committed no crime—and Franklin apparently related nothing to Temple who on January 15 sent his father a letter making no mention of the incident. There had been as yet no declaration of independence and some members of Congress thought that Alexander had acted highhandedly; others were fearful of the turmoil that might result from proceeding any further against an official who still commanded respect among many of his people. In William's opinion, the patriots were hoping that the royal governors who, with the exception of Governor Trumbull of Connecticut, were loyalists to a man, would leave of their own free will. This would make it easier to set up independent republican administrations as had already happened in New Hampshire. William was not about to play into the radicals' hands but he feared the worst, for his wife even more than for himself. Two weeks after the attack on their residence, Elizabeth was still so shaken "that the least sudden Noise almost throws her into Hysterics. . . . Another Alarm of the like Nature will put an End to her Life." Repeatedly he had urged her to go back to London or home to Barbados, but she refused to leave him. In his humiliation and anguish, William turned bitterly on his family: "She has no Relations of her own in this Country to whom she can resort or from whom she can receive any Comfort in Time of Distress; and she cannot but take notice that mine do not at present seem disposed to give themselves any Concern about her, omitting even those Enquiries and outward Forms of Complaisance and Civility which she daily receives from Strangers."[39]

Not everyone in the family had abandoned Elizabeth. Sally, who had given birth to a baby in December after a difficult pregnancy, wrote reassuringly to her sister-in-law and asked her to be the little girl's godmother. She accepted. Unable, it seems, to comprehend how portentous were the events they were living through, Elizabeth chiefly lamented the way of life she had lost: "Amboy has been a very agreeable place till within these four weeks; but everything is now changed; instead of those joyous, social evenings we used to pass with each other, we only meet now to condole together over our wretched situation. But I will stop my pen lest I should infest you with vapours and dejection of spirits."[40] The whole tale of her grief would have to wait for Sally's proposed visit when she would be accompanied, Elizabeth hoped, by Franklin and Richard Bache.

None of them came to Perth Amboy. For months, William lived there in limbo, neither governor nor private citizen, neither captive nor free, confined to his capital but allowed to move about as he wished within its bounds, wondering how it would all end. He kept sending secret reports to England whenever he found a safe messenger, but performed no official functions after that January night.

In March, Franklin set out for Canada through ice and snow, as part of a last, hopeless attempt to bring this vast region into the struggle on the side of the colonies. While deploring that his father would undertake "such a Journey at his Time of Life and at this Season of the Year,"[41] William dutifully prayed God to take him under His protection. What he really wished was for his father "to quit all public Business."[42] He echoed in this the tireless attempts Strahan had been making throughout the summer and fall to dissuade his friend from embarking "in the most arduous, most dangerous and most uncertain Task that ever Man engaged in. . . . I wish your great Talents had found other Employment."[43] But Franklin, "now in the evening of life,"[44] as everybody kept reminding him, had thrown all caution to the winds and was exhibiting the revolutionary fervor of a young man.

Ironically, the genuine young man in the family was being admonished on all sides not to be a hothead. In this period of turmoil, Temple was unrealistically advised to stick to his studies and not concern himself with politics. In this moment of family disintegration, he was told by his father to honor his grandfather, by his grandfather to love his father, and by both generations to be grateful to his aunt and uncle. Alluding probably to the Baches, perhaps to the outside world, Temple confided to his father that he feared his position would be difficult during Franklin's absence. "However others may behave to you, be careful that your Conduct to them is as polite, affectionate and respectful as possible" was the high-minded reply.[45]

Strains there certainly were. William was cavalier about expecting Richard Bache to advance Temple whatever money was needed. Bache finally balked. Besides, he had his own problems. An official of the postal system of the United Colonies, he had not only a loyalist governor for a brother-in-law, but also one of the most prominent tory businessmen in New York for a brother. The brother was his beloved Theophylact who had first brought him to America, bailed him out when he had met financial disasters, and written him a moving letter begging him not to let political differences estrange them—a letter sent on the very day Franklin was beginning his long shipboard account of negotiations meant to win William to his own views. To add to his anguish, Richard was cut off from his mother and sisters in Yorkshire.

Tensions were mounting all over Philadelphia in the spring of 1776. It was a foretaste of Paris in the summer of 1789, a mixture of exhilaration and dread, daring and timidity, a moment of thinking the unthinkable. A year earlier independence had been spoken of—and then only in whispers—by a few men of advanced opinions. When Franklin, during his final months in England, had reassured Lord Chatham that separation was the last thing reasonable Americans wanted, he probably still believed it. But words and ideas lose their terror with time. Early in 1776 Tom Paine, recently arrived from England at Franklin's urging, carried the bolder ideas of the colonists to their boldest conclusions in his *Common Sense*. Challenging the legitimacy not just of the English monarchy but of monarchy itself, he argued that it was only a matter of time before the continent would break loose from the island; better to do it now while American society was still uncorrupted, natural, and democratic. The pamphlet was an instant sensation: Paine claimed that it sold 120,000 copies in the first three months.

Within days of its publication William was asking Temple to send it to him. Soon he was clamoring for the replies to *Common Sense*. Trapped in the isolation of provincial Perth Amboy, William was desperate to find out what was happening and bombarded his son with requests for newspapers and political literature. The other errands Temple was plied with seem incredibly trivial. Why, for instance, William's preoccupation with Germantown brown thread stockings on the eve of his downfall? Why the irritated insistence on bottled mustard? Elizabeth's commissions, reflecting her personality, were divided between the dressmaker and the pharmacist: ruffles, edgings for the ruffles, lace borders, indigo, asthmatic elixir (a continuous supply), pearl dentifrice, snuff.

As anxiety and inactivity began to take their toll, the requests did not become any fewer but the tone became more petulant: "If you are not more punctual in obeying my Orders, I must find some Person that will."[46] Temple's allowance was as sore a subject as his procrastination in running errands. It disappeared with intolerable rapidity. As fathers are wont to do, William pointed out that Temple received a larger allowance than he had been given as a boy and that more money would be the "Ruin of your Constitution."[47] When Temple attempted to defend himself, he was given a scathing rebuke. His thoughts on these matters great and small have disappeared along with all his letters for that period. The only extant document in his hand is a long and laboriously argued essay, dated May 16, 1776, on "Whether Space is a Real Being." It concludes that "Space is a mere abstract Idea and does not signify anything which has a Real and Positive Existence without us." It was in vain that Franklin many years earlier had fought to make the curriculum more relevant to contemporary life.

At the time Temple was thus absorbed in metaphysical speculation, his father's fate was being sealed. In mid-May, Congress, urged on by John Adams, determined to assert its supreme authority and remove all vestiges of royal government in the individual colonies. The provincial congresses created some months earlier were now directed to assume power and supplant the traditional assemblies. William refused to recognize this new order of things. When he received word from England that a peace commission was on its way, he convoked not the new provincial Congress but the old Assembly, to meet on June 20. On June 15, the provincial Congress found him in contempt and declared that he had "discovered himself to be an enemy of the liberties of this country." The order went out for his arrest and to halt his salary. As an afterthought, the members stipulated that the arrest be carried out "with all the delicacy and tenderness which the nature of the business can possibly admit."[48] Whatever delicacy may have been used was wasted on William who flew into a rage. For the few days between his notification and the hearing in Burlington he remained under house arrest, was allowed no visitors, not even Elizabeth's beloved doctor or the "ladies of the place"[49] who flocked to comfort her. He spent the time writing his own defense, no doubt aware that nothing he could say would help him now but hopeful that his testimony would stand him in good stead when the revolution was finally put down, as he had not the least doubt it would be.

On June 21 he was led to Burlington, like the bear he had once evoked. The hearing was a mere formality and his arrogant behavior only made the outcome more certain. So enraged was President Witherspoon of the College of New Jersey at Princeton, one of the examiners, that he exclaimed caustically, "[The governor] has made a speech every way worthy his exalted birth."[50] William was found guilty, of course, but the place and manner of his imprisonment were left to the Continental Congress in Philadelphia.

What about Franklin? How did he react to his son's humiliation? He had come back from Canada three weeks earlier, empty-handed and more dead than alive. On the day of William's examination he wrote Washington that he was just "recovering from a severe Fit of the Gout, which has kept me from Congress and Company almost since you left us so that I know little of what has pass'd here."[51] He made no mention of William but it is inconceivable he did not know what was happening, unless he chose not to know. Congress took up the matter three days later (June 24) and resolved that "William Franklin be sent under guard to Governor Trumbull (Connecticut),"[52] who was instructed to take the prisoner's word that he would not escape. There is no record of the vote, no indication whether Franklin took part in it or had already left to spend a few days in the country. It was a foregone conclusion, anyway, that he would make no move to help his son.

William's last words before going off into captivity were for his own son:

> Dear Billy,   *Burlington June 25, 1776*
>   I was ordered this Day to set out on a Guard to Princeton, on my Way, I hear, to Connecticut; but, as I had a pretty high Fever on me, their Low Mightinesses with great Difficulty were persuaded by some Friends of mine to postpone my Departure till Tomorrow Morning, when I must go (I suppose) dead or alive. Two of their Members, who are Doctors, came to examine me to see if my Sickness was not feigned. Hypocrites always suspect Hypocrisy in others.
>   God bless you, my dear Boy; be dutiful and attentive to your Grand-father to whom you owe great Obligations. Love Mrs. Franklin, for she loves you, and will do all she can for you if I should never return more. If we survive the present Storm, we may all meet and enjoy the Sweets of Peace with the greater Relish.
>   *I am ever Your truely affectionate Father*   WM. FRANKLIN[53]

The former governor and his captors reached Lebanon, Connecticut, on the day the Declaration of Independence was signed: July 4, 1776.*

Late that month, Temple went to Perth Amboy for the holidays, joining his afflicted stepmother who had feared that he, "like the rest of the world," had forsaken her in her adversity. She had warned him that this time he would find the town unpleasant. It was swarming "with unruly Soldiers. . . . They have been extremely rude, insolent, and abusive to me and have terrified me almost out of my Senses."[54] Mixing as she often did the inconsequential with the serious, she told a sad tale

---

* The Declaration of Independence was primarily the work of Jefferson, the youngest man in the Congress (born the same year as Sally Bache), with Franklin merely offering a few suggestions. Years later, Jefferson would remember how Franklin had soothed him with a humorous anecdote as he watched his masterpiece being amended by Congress.

of green apples thrown about the orchard and of a plot to steal his dog. Temple provided a modicum of normality by losing his clothes somewhere en route ("There seems to be a kind of Fatality attending the Conveyance of your Things between Amboy and Philadelphia,"[55] sighed his grandfather). Franklin had given him sixty dollars for Elizabeth which she, at least, chose to consider as a loan.

It may have been this token of good will from her father-in-law that emboldened her to intercede for her husband: "I will not distress you by enumerating all my Afflictions, but allow me, dear Sir, to mention that it is greatly in your Power to relieve them. Suppose that Mr. Franklin would sign a Parole not dishonorable to himself and satisfactory to Governor Trumbull, why may he not be permitted to return into this Province and to his Family? . . . His private Affairs are unsettled, his Family distressed, and he is living very uncomfortably and at great Expense, which he can very ill afford at present." Then, fearful lest she had overstepped herself, she added, "If I have said or done anything wrong, I beg to be forgiven."[56] Franklin continued to send his love to her via Temple and to ask for news of William but apparently remained unmoved by her plea.

As August passed, he became increasingly uneasy at the thought of Temple so far from him and so close to the British, who were just across the water in New York. He worried that the sixteen-year-old youth might all too gallantly embrace the role of protector of a lady in distress, especially when the lady was his unhappy and coquettish stepmother. Indeed, when Temple saw Elizabeth's misery over the impossibility of getting letters through to her husband, he proposed to go in person to his father in Connecticut. As soon as Franklin heard of this plan, he objected vigorously. But Temple persisted. Suspecting his grandfather was really afraid he would take intelligence to his father, he assured him he was the last person to know any secrets. This provoked an angry reply: "You would have been more in the right if you would have suspected me of a little tender Concern for your Welfare, on Account of the Length of the Journey, your Youth and Inexperience, the Number of Sick returning on that Road with the Infectious Camp Distemper, which makes the Beds unsafe, together with the Loss of Time in your Studies, of which I fear you begin to grow tired. . . . I rather think the Project takes its rise from your own Inclination to a Ramble and Disinclination for returning to College, join'd with a Desire I do not blame of seeing a Father you have so much Reason to love."[57] Franklin was surprised that Elizabeth should have approved such a piece of knight errantry so out of keeping with her "usual Prudence." Not totally unsympathetic to her plight, he sent her some franked covers directed to Governor Trumbull. Much better than Temple, Franklin knew how precarious the boy's position was, his vulnerability to the spy hysteria prevailing on both sides. He may not have been entirely in jest when he told Temple why he was not enclosing a message from his little cousin Benny: "It was thought to be too full of Pothooks and Hangers and so unintelligible by the dividing Words in the Middle, and joining Ends of some to Beginnings of others, that if it had fallen into the Hands of some Committee it might have given them too much Trouble to decypher it, on a Suspicion of its containing Treason, especially as directed to a Tory House."[58]

Franklin, as always, had his way. Temple did not go to Connecticut. But he did not go back to college either. Six days after the scolding, he received a hurried note from his grandfather, "I hope you will return hither immediately and that your Mother will make no Objections to it, something offering here that will be much to your Advantage if you are not out of the Way."[59]

The something that offered was a journey infinitely riskier than the one that had just been vetoed, a mission to France. It had been clear for months that if the colonies were to make good their claim to independence they would need outside help. They had little money, no system of taxation, scarcely any credit, no munitions industry, no fleet, few trained officers. France was the logical ally against England and there had been cautious feelers since late in 1775. France was prepared to ship arms secretly to the West Indies for American use but not ready to recognize the new state until it gave signs of strength. Such signs were dismally lacking in the fall of 1776: Benedict Arnold had been driven from Canada, George Washington from Long Island, the British were in possession of New York, their well-equipped forces outnumbering Washington's tattered army two to one. Franklin himself was more reluctant than his fellow members of the Committee for Secret Correspondence to seek foreign alliances, feeling that "a virgin state should preserve the virgin character and not go about suitoring for alliances, but wait with decent dignity for the application of others."[60] The war was going so badly, however, that there seemed no choice but to accept the appointment as one of three commissioners to the Court of Versailles. To an old friend in Boston he quipped that the public having, as it were, eaten his flesh seemed resolved now to pick his bones. His friend replied that the nearer the bone the sweeter the meat.

There is no indication that Franklin ever consulted William about taking Temple to Paris. William accepted the *fait accompli* with a show of good grace: "If the old gentleman has taken the boy with him, I hope it is only to put him in some foreign university."[61] As for

Elizabeth, her assent was taken for granted. At that moment, anyway, she was exasperated with Temple who had forgotten to mail a most important letter, the one she was trying to get through to William under Franklin's cover. Her stepson, she moaned, was utterly unreliable and she herself "truly miserable indeed to be here in a strange country without a Friend or Protector."[62]

Elizabeth has come through so far as an insubstantial, one-dimensional person, amiable to be sure, well-educated (she wrote a beautiful hand), devoted to her husband, kind to his motherless son, but essentially frivolous, a little Marie-Antoinette in her little Perth Amboy, delighting in quadrilles and horse races, overwhelmingly preoccupied with her own adornment and her own health. One is tempted to brush aside her endless laments about her weak frame, drooping spirits, and broken heart as so many attention-getting devices. But they were not. Just over a year after William had been led away, Elizabeth died. She died in New York where she had been taken to safety by the retreating British, never allowed to see her "poor dear persecuted prisoner" whose pleas for leave to visit her in her final days were turned down. "A happy release"[63] was all Richard Bache said when he relayed the news to Paris. "Temple will mourn for her,"[64] added Jane. Did he?

Far from her own people in Barbados, far from her husband's grave in London, far from the Franklin family tombstone in Philadelphia, she lies buried in St. Paul's church in New York—all by herself in a strange land, just as she had feared.

XVIII

No Watch for Benny, No Feathers for Sally

It is now the Season for you to acquire that, at the Expence of your Friends, which may be of Use to you when they are dead and gone, and qualify you to fill some Station in Life that will afford you a decent Subsistance.

—BF to Benny Bache, September 25, 1780

Je ferai toujours mes efforts pour vous contenter, et pour répondre aux bontés que vous avez pour moi.

—Benny Bache to BF, March 26, 1781

NOBODY KNOWS WHAT THOUGHTS were going through the little boy's head. He had been, at first, the center of all attention, surrounded by an adoring grandmother, proud parents, a childless uncle and aunt always eager to have him visit their mansion across the Delaware, fawning visitors on the lookout for charming stories to tell the faraway grandfather. He had been a little prince. Then a brother was born to share the spotlight with. Grandmother died and nobody would ever call him Kingbird again. The famous grandfather had suddenly popped in from England with a lanky cousin called Temple, whereupon visits with the uncle and aunt had stopped abruptly, indeed they were hardly ever mentioned anymore. A baby sister appeared and disappeared in the space of a few months, leaving the family in tears. Boys started playing war games, his brother toddled up and down the street carrying a toy gun; an old Aunt Mecom arrived from Boston, her house taken by the enemy, and settled in their home; Cousin Temple spent a whole summer in New Jersey, the subject of many whispered conferences. One day the little boy was told he was a fortunate child, just about to sail off across the ocean to learn a new language, receive a European education. Benny Bache had just turned seven.

Franklin, Temple, and Benny left Philadelphia in late October 1776.

Their departure was as surreptitious as his previous one, twelve years earlier, had been triumphal. The penalty for treason was hanging and the man who supposedly had quipped "If we don't hang together we shall all hang separately" was in real danger, if caught by the British, of doing just that. Fortune was on his side, however. Two men-of-war sent from England to block the mouth of the Delaware arrived a few days too late to intercept the travelers. Buffeted between gray skies and rough autumn waves, the *Reprisal* rushed toward France at record speed—it would sight land in just over thirty days. Franklin generally adored sea voyages, but this one, he would long remember, "almost demolished"[1] him. Quarters aboard the hastily converted merchantman were cramped, most of the food too tough for his aging teeth. "Boils continued to vex me, and the scurff extending to all the small of my back, on my sides, my legs, and my arms, besides what continued under my hair."[2]

Just off the coast of France, the *Reprisal* seized two prizes in rapid succession. The gales were so fierce that they could not make the mouth of the Loire, their intended destination, but had to lay to for several days in Quiberon Bay. Exasperated by the delay, Franklin had himself rowed ashore at Auray, "a wretched place."[3] Nobody was on hand to greet the forlorn trio; no one had even known they were coming. They had to send to the neighboring town of Vannes for a chaise, and a miserable one at that. Their route lay through bandit-infested woods where some travelers had recently been murdered. Yet the old philosopher soon recovered his spirits sufficiently to take notice of the splendid complexion of the local women, all pink and fair. Temple, who also had an eye for women, reported from a ball he attended in Nantes that the ladies' coiffures were from five to seven times the height of their faces.

They arrived in Paris just before Christmas on the very day that Washington was routing the Hessians at Trenton. Temple, a sophisticated young traveler with a smattering of French, was of great use during the early hustle and bustle, the first onrush of admiring visitors, the choice of a residence. Benny kept quiet. He was a grave child, his mother had said, one that might prove easy to govern because "he will do a great deal out of affection."[4] Not being troublesome was one of the chief virtues expected from children, and Benny was endowed with it to a high degree.

"A special good boy" is how Franklin described him to Polly Hewson a few days after their arrival. His intention, he joked, was to give Benny "a little French and Address and then send him over to pay his Respects to Miss [Eliza] Hewson."[5] Eliza was all of two and a half at the time, but amid the uprooting and anxiety, it was comforting for Franklin to cling to the old dream of merging his blood with the Stevensons'. Busy as he was during the first month, he found time to write to Polly twice, worrying about her still unsettled inheritance, wondering if his godson remembered his "Doctor Papa," expressing once again his wish to get her out of that "wicked Country" and over to America. Overwhelmed as he was with the complexities of his new work, he could still pause long enough to send Polly the kind of self-portrait that would make her smile: "Figure to yourself an old Man with grey Hair appearing under a Martin Fur Cap among the Powder'd Heads of Paris."[6]

After two months in the rue Jacob, Franklin and the boys moved out of Paris and settled in Passy, then a lovely cluster of villas overlooking the Seine from among woods and vineyards. Passy was an ideal spot, far enough from the lionizing crowds of Paris not to embarrass the French government (which had not yet recognized the United States), yet close enough to Versailles, the center of power, to hold fruitful though discreet conferences with the minister for foreign affairs. The Franklins took up residence in a wing of the Hôtel de Valentinois which had been bought a few months previously by a wealthy and dynamic businessman called Jacques Leray de Chaumont (the Chaumont part of his name coming from his earlier purchase of the château of Chaumont-sur-Loire).

Chaumont, whose ardor for the American or "insurgent" cause was matched only by his hatred for England, offered spacious quarters and meals, if desired, to what became in effect the first American embassy in Europe, his idea being that he would enter into commercial contracts of such magnitude that they would more than compensate him for his hospitality. "He would grasp, if he could, the commerce of the thirteen colonies for himself alone,"[7] snickered his enemies.* With modifications as time went by (such as paying some rent), this arrangement subsisted through Franklin's entire stay in France, eight and a half years. It provided him once again with a "family." One of the Chaumont daughters, the bookkeeping one, was soon dubbed his "wife," another his "friend," still another his "child." Their brother gave Temple his first entry into French society and invited him to glorious hunts and parties at the family's country estate. With its terraces, gardens, sweeps of steps, and numerous servants, the Valentinois offered living on a much grander scale than Craven Street. But Mad-

---

* As things turned out, Chaumont wound up bankrupt. His son went to America to recover his debts but, in spite of Franklin's best efforts, failed in that enterprise.

ame de Chaumont, though quite amiable, was no Mrs. Stevenson and none of the Chaumont girls, for all the atmosphere of cordiality, ever equaled Polly in Franklin's admiration.

Benny was placed in a nearby boarding school. Along with the few other English-speaking boys, he dined with Franklin every Sunday. Within a year he had progressed enough in French to send his parents a letter, all of his own composition, vouched his grandfather, except for the closing flourishes.

The Baches had led an eventful life since Benny's departure. First there had been the flight to Goshen, in Chester County, as the British Army, victorious in its sweep across New Jersey, threatened Philadelphia. In relative comfort but extreme boredom, Sally and her aunt Jane Mecom spent the winter and spring of 1777 in the country, Jane pining for New England, Sally for her husband who had gone back to Philadelphia once it was clear the city was not in immediate danger. Lulled by a false sense of security, the women returned to town in the summer. The day before the disastrous battle of Brandywine, September 11, Sally was delivered of a little Betsy. Less than one week after her lying-in she found herself forced to flee again, barely escaping before the enemy occupied Philadelphia. The Baches wandered from place to place, then settled in Manheim near Lancaster.

Their life there was materially very difficult—with one possible element of relief: Aunt Jane had gone back to Rhode Island. One jump ahead of the British, she settled in the house of a granddaughter who had married a relative of Catharine Greene.* Jane found her granddaughter's babies a little noisy, her grandson-in-law a little taciturn, the enemy too close for comfort (less than one mile at times), the neighbors too far away for "suitable conversation,"8 but she enjoyed occasional visits with Caty Greene and her husband, now governor of Rhode Island, and she coped with life as it came.

It is a stark comment on Jane's fate that the best thing to happen to her in those years was the death of her two mad sons. Benny disappeared first: During the confusion of the battle of Trenton—the very day Franklin reached Paris—he escaped from the house where he was confined, never to be heard from again. Meanwhile, Peter had become a source of particular worry because the woman who took care of him demanded more money than Jane could afford, and the Boston almshouse would not take him in. Providentially, however, Peter died. Reaching his last hour, he recovered his wits, committed himself to God, and "sank into eternity without a groan." Announcing both

* He was the brother of General Nathanael Greene.

deaths to her "dear dear brother" in a single letter, Jane commented that "it has pleased God to diminish us fast and thereby your Expense and care of us."⁹ Franklin, too, gave a realistic assessment of the situation when he replied that the news had given him a "melancholy satisfaction,"¹⁰ for he could not help thinking of the greater ease Jane would now enjoy.

Someone else's hardships are always difficult to empathize with, especially when they occur three thousand miles away. Having written "I pity my poor old Sister to be so harass'd and driven about by the Enemy," Franklin added "for I feel a little myself the Inconvenience of being driven about by my Friends"¹¹—a flippant comparison that did not fail to elicit a pained outcry from Jane.

He probably did not feel as lighthearted as he sounded. To keep an appearance of detachment, professing indifference about British successes, was an important part of his role as America's propagandist in France. Now was the time to put in practice the virtues inculcated by playing chess—a game he adored—such as "the habit of not being discouraged by present bad appearances in the state of our Affairs, the habit of hoping for a favourable change, and that of persevering in the search of resources."¹² Thus it was that, when told Howe had taken Philadelphia, he quipped, "Philadelphia has taken Howe!"¹³ as if he felt no anguish at all about the fate of his daughter, his friends, his house. In truth, he knew very little about their fate. In a letter introducing to the Baches France's first diplomatic envoy to the United States, he had remarked wistfully, "I know not whether even if Philadelphia is recovered you have a House left to entertain in."¹⁴

The house had been taken over by General Charles Grey and his aide, that dashing Captain John André who later, as Major André, would be hanged for his part in Benedict Arnold's attempted betrayal of West Point. An amateur musician, artist, and actor, André organized thirteen theatricals in five months to entertain the British officers and the local Tory gentry. They culminated in the greatest spectacle Philadelphia had ever seen, the so-called "Meschianza," a mock tourney and costume ball in honor of the departing British commander in chief, General William Howe. Taking part in the feast, exotically attired in a Turkish outfit, was André's sweetheart, the sixteen-year-old daughter of the Reverend Mr. William Smith. To compound the irony, she was the godchild of Elizabeth Graeme, William's ex-fiancée.

Joyous days for the Tories, evil days for Franklin's kin and his most treasured belongings. When Richard Bache returned to the city on the heels of the retiring British in July 1778, he found that André had purloined the Doctor's portrait.* Worse yet, the "rapacious crew"[15] (in fact André himself) had made off with many of his father-in-law's most valuable books and musical instruments. Gone were his Welsh harp, his bell harp, a set of tuned bells, a viola da gamba, and all his spare armonica glasses. As for his personal manuscripts, deposited for safekeeping at Galloway's house in the country, Bache found them scattered inside and out, some lost forever. Galloway himself had fled to England, leaving his wife to face the patriots' wrath. His previous vacillations had led him to espouse William's cause first, then the insurgents', then the British once again.

Communication with Europe was all but cut off during that troubled period. Six months after Benny had set sail, Sally did not know whether he had arrived safely. Her boy, she hoped, was behaving "so as to make you love him,"[16] it being the unquestioned notion that love had to be earned, not freely given, even to a grandchild. Franklin's terse replies were not the kind an anxious mother thirsts for: Benny, he said, was in good health and minded his learning. Never a chatty description of his sayings and doings. The school's itemized bills reveal a little more: One is relieved to find that in addition to the predictable clothes, milk, tips, and educational supplies, there is an entry for broken windowpanes. The Frenchification of Benny can be followed through the purchase of silk stockings, black silk breeches, the fees for both wigmaker and dancing master.

That was the hitch. Much as he proclaimed his unconditional love for France and his admiration for all things French, Franklin, when it came to his grandson, wanted him raised "a Presbyterian and a Republican," not exactly what Paris had to offer.** Hence Benny, not quite ten, was suddenly packed off to the Pension Marignac in Geneva: "Some of the Nobility here send their Sons to the same School thinking the Education there better, as well as safer with regards to morals than at Paris."[17] In Geneva Benny would remain for the following four and a half years, never once brought back to France for a holiday, never visited by Franklin or Temple, never supplied with Paris news and gossip, never complaining. A short while before Benny went off to

---

* André gave the portrait to General Grey and it remained in the latter's family until 1906, when it was returned by Earl Grey, governor-general of Canada, for the bicentennial celebration of Franklin's birth. Fifty years later, and only for three months, it hung once again side by side with the portrait of Deborah in an exhibition at the American Philosophical Society. It is now stored in the White House.

** Jefferson would follow the opposite course: he could not bear to be separated from his daughter Martha and sent her to a Parisian convent at thirteen. A few years later, when she announced her intention of taking the veil, he promptly withdrew her.

Switzerland, another boy, born on the same day as he, also left home to cross the water and study in a distant school: Napoleon Bonaparte.

Sally, though worried about her son ("when I consider the distance he is removed from you"), professed herself satisfied that her father was doing "everything for the best."[18] Richard ventured to express the hope Franklin would pay a visit to Geneva since traveling had always been beneficial to his health. Jane Mecom was the only one who dared to express some doubts: "Poor Ben, how will he support the loss of you both? Was he willing to go?"[19]

Willing or unwilling, he was entrusted to Philibert Cramer, a Swiss printer, publisher of Voltaire and admirer of Rousseau, who was going back home from Paris. On the way to Geneva, Benny did what he knew best: He became enormously fond of Mr. Cramer who, in turn, began looking upon him as a member of the family. This was in the spring of 1779. By August, Cramer was dead and Benny plunged into such depths of grief that his Swiss mentors were alarmed. As the late Cramer's sister-in-law explained, it was thought best that Benny should sleep in the widow's house so as to be of some comfort to her and her son. Whether this arrangement would be of any comfort to Benny does not seem to have been a consideration, but it worked. As soon as she recovered a little from her sorrow, Mrs. Cramer took a genuine interest in the young American. If anything at all is known about his burgeoning personality, it is thanks to her perceptive insights.

Benny pulled himself together. To his grandfather's unflagging admonitions that he learn those things that would be "reputable and useful"[20] when he grew up, that he make his parents proud and happy, be dutiful to his masters, and for goodness sake date his letters, he answered just as unflaggingly that he would do his best to oblige, that he would strive "to be the first of the class,"[21] that he was duly appreciative of everyone's kindness and of his own good luck, that he would henceforth remember to date his letters*—an unreliable pledge if ever there was one—and could he please be sent a portrait of Franklin and occasionally some news? He was sent the portrait and one news item: Four of his former schoolmates in the Passy pension had died of smallpox and wasn't he fortunate to have been inoculated as a baby? For decades, Voltaire and the *Encyclopédistes* had been waging a campaign in favor of inoculation, but France was particularly backward in accepting the procedure: Providence, said its opponents, should be allowed its ways.

Written first in an endearingly Gallicized English, eventually in

* It may have given Benny a flicker of mischievous pleasure to notice that the first letter in which his grandfather aired that complaint was misdated by one year, a common mistake in January.

Just IMPORTED from *LONDON*,
And to be SOLD by

JANE MECOM,

Near the *ORANGE TREE* :

A SMALL Affortment of MILLINARY, confifting of black, blue, crimfon, and rofe coloured white plains and figured fattins ; black, blue and crimfon farfenetts; black and white cat-gut; flowering thread : black, white, plain and figured gauze ; blond lace, black blond lace, book muflin, cap wire, patches, fans, and court plaifter ; necklaces and ear-rings; kid and lamb gloves and mitts ; black filk ditto. Womens fhoes ; black plumes ; pafte combs and broaches, &c. &c. Ready made hats, bonnets, caps, handkerchiefs, ruffs and terifas. At the fame place, Ladies may have all forts of Millinary work done from the neweft fafhioned patterns, with the greateft care and expedition.

Advertisement in the *Boston Chronicle,* May 30, 1768, for Jane Mecom's millinery business. With the help of Franklin and Mrs. Stevenson, Jane got off to a promising start embellishing the heads and bosoms of Boston's best ladies, only to run aground on the shoals of the Townshend Act and the boycott it inspired. Yale University, Franklin Collection.

Dinner with the king of Denmark. Franklin enclosed this sketch in a letter to his son, October 5, 1768. Some years later he commented in his *Autobiography,* "I did not think that I should ever literally stand before Kings, which however has since happened.—for I have stood before five and even had the honour of sitting down with one . . . to dinner." Yale University, Franklin Collection.

Benny Bache sketched this profile of his grandfather in the margin of a notebook, probably early in January 1790.   American Philosophical Society.

---

62   THOUGHTS

advantages which they enjoy as Englishmen by virtue of their British descent, but from a much more solid and rational principle,—their being faithful subjects of Great Britain; since the same advantages are by law expressly communicated to such of them as were born in Westphalia and the Palatinate, and who never let foot upon British ground till they meet with it on the other side of the Atlantic. In these and in many other respects they are widely different from either Greek or Roman colonies; so that whoever is really acquainted with the affairs of those ancient nations, must without difficulty perceive, that the Americans have preferred the word *Colony*, for the sake of assuming along with it a degree of independency, which from the words *plantation* or *province*, could not be so easily derived.

The plain truth is, that those countries, let them be called *plantations*, *settlements*, *colonies*, or by what other name they will, are, from their nature and situation, only subordinate parts in the empire of Britain.

ON GOVERNMENT.   63

and such they would necessarily continue, though perhaps in a much lower degree, in under some other powerful European state, in case their more safe and honourable tie, with what they are still pleased to call, their *Mother Country*, should happen to be dissolved.

I shall therefore conclude with saying, that the separation of Great Britain from her American appurtenencies would be destructive of the prosperity and liberty of both. If so, it seems to follow that till such time as New England is strong enough to protect Old England, and the feat of the British empire is transferred from London to Boston, there is an absolute necessity that the right of giving law to America, should continue to be vested in Great Britain. That it is the interest of Great Britain to protect and cherish her American provinces instead of oppressing them, is an undeniable truth, and it is, perhaps, no less true, that some farther attention, and some farther means of communication,

5

Presumed sketch of Franklin and a lady friend by Charles Willson Peale. This may or may not represent the scene of dalliance witnessed by the young artist when he called at Craven Street in 1767. American Philosophical Society.

An Indian Squaw King Wampum spies
Which makes his lustful passions rise
But while he doth a friendly Jobb
She dives her Hand into his Fob.
And thence conveys as we are told
His Watch whose Cases were of Gold

When Danger is threaten'd us mere Nonsense
To talk of such a thing as Conscience
To Arms to Arms with one Accord
The Sword of Quakers and the Lord
Fill Bumpers then of Rum or Arrack
We'll drink Success to the new Barrack.

Fight Dog, fight Bear! you're all my Friends
By you I shall attain my Ends.
For I can never be content
Till I have got the Government
But if from this Attempt I fall
Then let the Devil take you all.

The March of the Paxton Men, 1764. Franklin is shown on the right, scheming to get control of the government. On the left, Israel Pemberton's sympathy for the Indians is caricatured, while in the center panel the Quakers are depicted, ready to drop their pacifism whenever it suits their interest. Cartoon, 1764. Library Company of Philadelphia.

The balloon ascension of Pilâtre de Rosier and the Marquis d'Arlandes carried out on September 21, 1783, and viewed from Franklin's terrace in Passy. Engraving by Ch. de Lorimier. Frontispiece to Faujas de Saint-Fond, *Première Suite de la Description des Expériences Aërostatiques de M. Montgolfier* (Paris, 1784). Yale University, Franklin Collection.

Premier Voyage Aërien   En présence de M.{le Dauphin,
Experience faite   dans le Jardin de la Muette,
Sous la Direction   de M.{ Montgolfier,
Par M.{ le Marquis d'Arlandes   et M.{Pilatre du Rosier, le 21.9.{bre 1783
Vue de la Terrasse de M.{ Franklin à Passi.

Dessiné par le Ch.{ de Lorimier.   Gravé par N. De Launay.

In *Le Magnétisme dévoilé,* Franklin is shown exorcising the demons of ignorance and fraud with the report of his commission appointed to look into the
theories and practice of Mesmer and his disciples.   Engraving, 1784–85. Yale
University, Franklin Collection.

French, Benny's messages soon fell into a series of bland, repetitive formulas, as empty of substance as they were stilted in form. The most Benny ever allowed himself—or was allowed?—to say was that he had not heard from Paris for a long time "et je suis très en peine."[22] He also kept reiterating, always in vain, the wish that his brother Willy might be sent to join him, or his former schoolmate John Quincy Adams, or just any fellow American. While praising him for his reasonableness and kind heart, Mrs. Cramer worried about an excessive shyness in Benny which often made him appear uncouth, she said, and about the "indolence" that kept him from doing as well as he could in his studies. *Introvert* and *underachiever* are the words she would have used today. The good lady felt that the remedy lay in more frequent letters from home.

Little was heard from home and that little none too happy. The Baches were having their own problems, coping with a house that had been damaged and heavily looted by the enemy, hampered by congressional reluctance to pay its officials (anyway, Bache lamented, his salary as postmaster-general would scarcely pay for the salt on his porridge), plagued by various shortages, appalled by soaring prices. Sally begged her father to send her some finery from France, anything he fancied— she would be proud to show off his taste. Had she but stopped her letter at that point! But she committed the error of remarking, no doubt to justify her fling of frivolity, that "there never was so much dressing and pleasure going on, old friends meeting again, the Whigs in high spirit, and strangers of distinction among us."[23]

Franklin replied with a scolding more suited to a naughty child than to a woman in her mid-thirties: "I was charmed with the account you give me of your industry, the table-cloths of your own spinning, etc. But the latter part of the paragraph, that you had sent for linen from France because weaving and flax were grown dear, alas! that dissolved the charm; and your sending for long black pins, and lace, and *feathers!* disgusted me as much as if you had put salt into my strawberries. The spinning, I see, is laid aside, and you are to be dressed for the ball! You seem not to know, my dear daughter, that of all the dear things in this world, idleness is the dearest, except mischief."

To Sally's relief, he then moved on to a more pleasant topic, his expectation that both Temple and Benny would be "a comfort" to him. But those pernicious black pins and feathers could not be laid to rest. A few lines down, he upbraided her again, and through her all those Philadelphians whose behavior did not match the highly idealized picture of them he was painting for the edification of their French allies·

When I began to read your account of the high prices of goods, *"a pair of gloves seven dollars, a yard of common gauze twenty-four dollars, and*

that it now required a fortune to maintain a family in a very plain way,"
I expected you would conclude with telling me that every body as well as
yourself was grown frugal and industrious; and I could scarce believe my
eyes in reading forward, that *"there never was so much dressing and pleasure
going on;"* and that you yourself wanted *black pins and feathers from
France,* to appear, I suppose in the mode! . . . I therefore send all the articles you desire that are useful and necessary and omit the rest, for as you
say you should *"have great pride in wearing anything I send and showing it
as your father's taste,"* I must avoid giving you an opportunity of doing that
with either lace or feathers. If you wear your cambric ruffles as I do, and
take care not to mend the holes, they will come in time to be lace; and feathers, my girl, may be had in America from every cock's tail.[24]

To self-indulgence back home, a flat NO; but to Polly Hewson in
England he penned some sweet pleasantries about a pair of diamond
earrings that were to be hers if a certain lottery ticket he had left
behind turned out to be the winning one; and to the French ladies
flocking around him he addressed delightful little notes from which
such plebeian notions as industry and frugality were completely
banished. No wonder these ladies called him *mon cher papa* while his
daughter hardly ever deviated from a dutiful *dear and honoured Sir*.

Sally's answer was not angry, it was sad. Her father would never
have sent her such a reprimand, she said, if he had known how much
it would hurt. She should have explained that the preceding winter
had been a season of triumph for the Whigs and they had spent it
gaily: "You would not have had me, I am sure, stay away from the
Ambassador's or the General's entertainments, nor when I was invited
to spend the day with General Washington and his Lady, and you
would have been the last person, I am sure, to have wished to see me
dressed with singularity. Though I never loved dress so much as to
wish to be particularly fine, yet I never will go out when I cannot appear so as to do credit to my Family and Husband."*

She had never meant that feathers and pins are the necessaries of
life, only that since the necessaries were so dear she could not afford
any luxury. Mixing with the world on occasion had been her way of
keeping up her spirits—and indeed she had kept them up better than
most other people, even when driven from place to place and obliged to
get up and go five days after her baby's birth. Anyway, the season of rejoicing had come and gone. The coming winter (1779–80) "approaches
with so many horrors that I shall not want anything to go abroad in if I
can be comfortable at home. . . . Home will be the place for me this

* Washington professed to be as appalled as Franklin by the goings on in Philadelphia: "If I was to be called upon to draw a picture of the times and men . . .
I should in one word say that idleness, dissipation and extravagance seem to have
laid fast hold of most of them."[25]

winter as I cannot get a common winter cloak and hat but just decent under two hundred pounds. As to gauze, it is now fifty dollars a yard and I should think it not only a shame but a sin to buy it if I had Millions."[26]

Coupled with this profession of frugality was a profession of industry. Spinning was going on under the Baches' roof with great alacrity, and knitting too. They always had. The bottleneck occurred at the weaving stage where one had to send out. The weavers had raised their prices and become totally unreliable. They did not want to work for townspeople anymore, they had to be bribed and cajoled. Interspersed with the narrative of Sally's harrowing pursuit of cloth were frequent hints to Mr. Bache's old-fashioned integrity: not for him the "monopolizing and forestalling" through which some entrepreneurs were making quick fortunes out of the war. Sally's husband had principles.

Did so much homely virtue touch Franklin's heart? Up to a point. After remarking, with complete disregard for her hardships, that he was glad to hear "weaving work is so hard to get done: 'tis a sign there is much spinning," he announced the shipment of all the things she "had ordered." But with the condescending comment that her request was granted "as you continue to be a good Girl, and spin and knit your Family Stockings."[27]

The expression "all the things you ordered" comes as a surprise: Sally in her self-defense had not hinted at any wishes. But in a separate letter to Temple she had pleaded for his intercession at the psychologically opportune moment and had sent her nephew a list of pressing needs.[28] These covered a wide range: writing supplies "from paper down to sand" (to dry the ink), scissors, needles, some of that excellent French thread, material for caps now that she had grown too old to go without them; all of this packed, if possible, in a trunk or basket that would replace her own, worn out by too much traveling. Worn out, too were their beds and pillows, and no ticking was to be found. As for dishes, the household had been so badly plundered that she had to borrow whenever a friend came to visit—not that such visits were at all frequent, she hastened to add. In return, she pledged to send Temple any squirrel skin she could bribe little boys to procure.

In her letters to Temple, Sally never failed to give him news of his father. Though she refrained from any comment on William's political activities, she was unflinching in her affection for him. Upset because under one pretext or another Temple hardly ever sent her a line, she reminded him that when his own father was a "gay young gentleman" in England, he still found time to write "very long entertaining letters" to his sister in Philadelphia. "I should hope the Son had as much affection for me; I feel no less for him than I did and now do for the Father. I care not into what hands this letter falls, nor who sees it, for I should despise the Person who could not make a distinction between a Political difference and a Family one; the latter I . . . hope and believe will never happen in ours. I ever held those People cheap, who were at variance with their near connections."[29] Refusing to ingratiate herself with her father by carping on William's defection, trying to narrow the gap in the family rather than widen it to her own advantage, such was the firm and loyal side of Sally's character. Franklin made no comment on her attitude toward her brother, but—perhaps because he wanted her loyalty all to himself—he was often brusque toward her in that period, as if she were forever committing some *faux pas*.

The story of the silk is typical. Craving a spot, no matter how small, on the French scene, Sally conceived the plan of sending the queen of France a piece of American homespun silk: "It will make me happy if she condescends to wear it."[30] Monsieur Gérard, France's envoy to Congress thought Sally's idea a good one. But she needed her father's help to carry it out: "I could not presume to ask her acceptance from myself but from you it may be agreeable, it will show what can be sent from America to the looms of France."[31] She packed the silk with some of the squirrel skins for Temple and sent it. Franklin had for years been an ardent promoter of silkworm culture in America; he had often proclaimed his devotion to the French royal family. Surely this could not fail to please him. But it did. He found fault with both intention and execution. "You mention the Silk being in a Box with Squirrel Skins, but it is come to Hand without them or the Box. Perhaps they were spoilt by the Salt Water and thrown away; for the Silk is much damag'd and not at all fit to be presented as you propose. Indeed I wonder how having yourself scarce Shoes to your Feet it would come into your Head to give Clothes to a Queen. I shall see if the Stains can be cover'd by dyeing it and make Summer Suits of it for myself, Temple and Benny."[32]

Sally had still another ambition, to have "the little stranger who is hourly expected" named after one of the French sovereigns. The queen had so many names, any one of them would be "honor enough":[33] Could her father choose the most pleasing to him? No suggestion came. When the stranger turned out to be a boy, Sally went ahead anyway and had him christened Louis, a name evidently so uncommon in America that Jane Mecom was long in a quandary about whether the baby was a boy or a girl. Sally's husband approved this political choice;

her brother, when informed through a common friend, "merely smiled"; her father did not bother to comment.

Franklin was far more favorably impressed with another initiative of Sally's soon after the silk fiasco. The war was not going well in the early months of 1780. American soldiers were in rags, there was little money forthcoming from Congress, the British were gaining the upper hand in the south and at sea. A determined band of Philadelphia women with Sally in the vanguard organized a subscription to raise money for the demoralized troops, hounding their fellow citizens until they contributed. Much of the money was used to buy cloth which the ladies sewed into shirts. By December 26, Sally could inform Washington that 2,005 shirts were being sent to the army at Trenton. This time Franklin wrote warmly to his daughter: She and her friends had "confuted the assertion of the Scotch Writer who says that Women have not the amor Patriae."[34] An account of Sally's "patriotic activity" sent him by a French visitor to Philadelphia was promptly translated and published in France under his care.

Stories about his grandchildren were another sure-fire way of pleasing him, and Sally told them with great charm. Willy had a nightmare about death, jumped out of bed in his long gown, went down on his knees with uplifted hands, and, addressing Hercules, recited the Lord's Prayer. Should one hasten to instruct him further in religion or let him "pray a little longer to Herculas [sic],"[35] she wondered. "*Hercules* is now quite out of fashion,"[36] answered Grandfather. Somewhat older but still immersed in classical tradition, the same Willy was later depicted as having memorized Anthony's speech over Caesar's body "which he can scarcely speak without tears." Little Betty had sparkling black eyes, sang like a bird, and was fond of kissing. She gave "such old-fashioned smacks General [Benedict] Arnold says he would give a good deal to have her for a school Mistress to teach the young Ladies to kiss" (a comment made two years before Arnold's treason). Looking at her grandfather's picture Betty would try to tempt him "to walk out of the frame to play with her, with a piece of apple pie, the thing of all others she likes best."[37] As for Louis, he was so fat (following the example of his august namesake) that when the need arose to bleed him, the doctor could not find a vein. On their grandfather's birthday, January 6, 1782, the children gave a dance hugely enjoyed by their sixty guests and most of all by their baby sister, Deborah, now fifteen months old and "called after her dear Grand Mamma. . . . I have not a wish for her to be a better Woman than she was."[38]

All by himself in faraway Switzerland, Benny never quite managed to keep up with this avalanche of babies (four new ones by the time he came home and a fifth later). With great tenderness his mother tried to keep him part of the family circle:

> Little Debby is one year old this day. Betsy was quite distressed that you did not send your love to your little sister. I told her that you lived so far away that you had not heard of her. "Do then, Mama, write him word how beautiful she is," say Betsy and Louis, for Louis is always Betsy's echo. She is indeed very beautiful and very sweet; she cannot walk but goes along the floor in a most curious manner, her head held up, her hands before her; she does not put her leg under her but puts the soles of her feet together and glides along very cleverly, makes everybody laugh that sees her. . . . Betsy is hemming me a pocket handkerchief, and I make no doubt will be able to make your shirts when you return. Her Mistress begg'd me to give her work for she talked so much she did not know what to do. Your Papa loves you dearly, we often look at your Picture. If he is not too busy he will write to you. Accept the love of your Brothers and Sisters with that of an affectionate Mother.

Still, the gap between them was widening, made worse by the language barrier. Unlike modern parents who would praise their child for his fluency in a foreign language, the Baches worried: "I hope you will endeavour to regain your English or how will you be able to converse with me when you see me, as I am too old and too much engaged with your little brothers and sisters to learn French?"[39] Benny's feeble attempts at writing English only alarmed his relatives further. Franklin asked Polly Hewson to buy some English books of her own choosing, one set for Benny, a duplicate for his godson. Polly applied herself diligently and came up with one book at least that she felt would be perfect because it mentioned Franklin's name frequently: Whenever her own young folks came upon it, "that passage was sure to be read with delight."[40]

As the object of all this concern, Benny kept blandly reassuring one and all that everything would work out all right. Yes, he would relearn his mother tongue as soon as he was given a chance to practice it; yes, he would apply himself to this and other pursuits. Benny at thirteen wanted most of all to be left in peace. Russian-born Mrs. Cramer, his landlady, felt keenly the lack of Slavic passion, or of any passion in this boy: "He is cold. He has few needs, no whims. Even though I had offered to ask you to give him a somewhat larger allowance (all his friends receive more than he does) he showed no great interest in the suggestion." While reiterating that Benny was in excellent physical health, except for chilblains which denoted a sluggish circulation, Mrs. Cramer lamented that he was still very taciturn and showed no inclination to partake in youthful pastimes such as playing cards or fighting. "To sum up, Sir, I believe that unless he has one of those temperaments that mature quite late, he will never display the kind of fire that leads young men into such trouble, much to their parents' chagrin, but then he won't develop those great talents either that are sometimes associated with excess but gratify the parents' pride."[41]*

And yet this same Benny had lived some glorious moments the previous year when he had won first prize for a translation from Latin. No small matter, this prize. It was handed to the recipient by the chief magistrates of the city, right in Geneva's Cathédrale St. Pierre, amid pomp and circumstance. An ecstatic Benny had requested his grandfather's permission to offer his schoolmates the traditional goûter. The headmaster had added a postscript to the effect that foreigners were not expected to follow tradition but that if Franklin accepted the extra expense of the goûter (four louis), the school would be grateful and delighted. Permission was granted, the goûter's cost was added to such items on Benny's bill as skates, a dozen night caps, and hair ribbons. The prize, a silver medal, was sent to Paris, then forwarded to Philadelphia. In the excitement of the hour Benny had pledged to do even better the following year but had then fallen into his puzzling slump. "When reminded of his Latin prize," mused Mrs. Cramer, "he answered coldly that it had been sheer luck."[42] That Benny might have first been a lonesome child, later a depressed adolescent does not seem to have occurred to anyone.

To get him back on the right track, Franklin sent his grandson one of those admonitions so dear to his age, its uplifting message somewhat diminished by an intensely utilitarian bias:

> You see everywhere two Sorts of People. One who are well dress'd, live comfortably in good Homes, whose Conversation is sensible and instructive, and who are respected for their Virtue. The other Sort are poor and dirty, and ragged and ignorant, and vicious, and live in miserable Cabbins or Garrets, on coarse Provisions, which they must work hard to obtain, or which if they are idle, they must go without and starve. The first had a good Education given them by their Friends and they took Pains when at School to improve their Time and increase their Knowledge; the others either had no Friend to pay for their Schooling and so were never taught, or else when they were at School they neglected their Studies, were idle and wicked and disobedient to their Masters, and would not be instructed, and now they suffer.[43]

So pleased was he with this piece that he sent a copy of it to Sally. Sally, in turn, was enraptured: "Willy shall get it by heart and I hope they will neither of them ever forget it."[44] But Benny's reaction was

---

* Unless she read the Philadelphia newspapers of the 1790s, Mrs. Cramer never knew how wide of the mark she was and what a firebrand the apathetic Benny would become.

one of such indifference that he did not even mention having received it. Whereupon he was sent a fresh copy and directed henceforth to translate into French and send back to Paris all of his grandfather's communications, to make sure he had understood every word. He promised to comply. He was also instructed to improve his penmanship, far inferior to Willy's who was almost four years younger. He promised to do that, too. And to keep an account book. And to date his letters.

Excitement finally came into Benny's life in the shape of Samuel Cooper Johonnot, a grandson of Franklin's old friend, the Reverend Samuel Cooper whose sermons in Boston's Brattle Street Church had done so much to soothe Jane Mecom's sorrows. As one grandfather to another, the Reverend Cooper recommended the youth to Franklin's care: "I send him as a dear Pledge of my own Esteem and Gratitude for a Nation to whom my Country is so much indebted and . . . in the true Spirit of the Alliance."[45] France does not seem to have appreciated the honor. Just as Colonel Johonnot, the boy's father, left behind him a trail of irate creditors, young Johonnot left a trail of exasperated schoolmasters. Franklin first put him in the Passy school which the sons of John Adams attended. In March 1780, after a Sunday dinner the Doctor predicted enthusiastically, "If God spares his Life, he may make a very serviceable Man to his Country."[46] By December the situation was no longer quite so idyllic. Though still telling the Reverend Cooper that his grandson was a "fine Boy," Franklin added ominously, "The Master and Mistress complain of his being turbulent and factious, and having in him too much of the Insurgent. I give him occasionally my best Advice and I hope those little Unpleasantnesses will by degrees wear off."[47] One week later, Franklin was wondering whether he should put the Cooper family to the extra expense of the private room and fire Johonnot was demanding. After a few months in a military academy in Lyons, the young insurgent was dispatched to the Pension Marignac in Geneva.

M. de Marignac was quick to sense that this new student was no Benny; whereas young Bache could be called "un excellent enfant," Johonnot, he felt, had been in bad company and picked up some deplorable habits such as talking off the top of his head and squandering his money. Nothing that a stay in the well-run Marignac establishment would not cure, however. But Johonnot did not see it that way and was promptly agitating to get himself and Benny removed to a French school more to his liking. This so alarmed Franklin that he took time off to send the two adolescents a stern warning that might still be posted in many a dean's office: "I hope you will . . . not indulge any Fancies of Change. It is time for you to think of establishing a Character for manly Steadiness which you will find of great Use to you in Life. The Proverb says wisely, *A rolling Stone gathers no Moss.* So in frequent changing of Schools much Time is lost, before the Scholar can be well acquainted with new Rules and get into the Use of them; and Loss of Time will to you be a Loss of Learning. If I had not a great Regard for you I should not take the Trouble of advising you."[48]

Though this quashed all dreams of leaving the pension, Benny perked up remarkably in the following months. The expression "I am having fun" ("je m'amuse") is used with increasing frequency. He has, all of a sudden, things to talk about: He loves harvesting and grape picking, he collects butterflies, his English flows back as he acts as interpreter for Johonnot and another American boy who has miraculously appeared at the school, he enjoys drawing and, tiring of shepherdesses and pretty sheep, tries his hand at a portrait of his grandfather. More extraordinary still, Benny has some wishes! He hints that Johonnot and himself could use a raise in their allowances, asks insistently for permission to invest three and a half louis in *Le Voyageur Français,* a "very educational" work in twenty-eight volumes: Franklin's lack of response was interpreted by M. de Marignac as consent and the set purchased. But when, some months later, Benny made bold to mention a watch ("I beg you to permit Mr. Marignac to procure me a good golden one I shall have particular care of it"),[49] Franklin felt he had to draw the line: "I cannot afford to give Gold Watches to Children. When you are a Man, perhaps, if you behave well, I may give you one or something that is better. You should remember that I am at a great Expence for your Education . . . and you should not tease me for expensive things that can be of little or no Service to you."[50]

Benny did not insist. He and Johonnot were caught up in a new excitement: the civil disorders sweeping Geneva. It was in some respects a preview of the French Revolution. Theoretically a democratic republic, the fatherland of Rousseau was in fact ruled by a two-tiered oligarchy of birth and wealth, the *représentants* and the *négatifs,* the latter so called because they had veto power over the *représentants.* Although Rousseau's works were officially banned, his ideas had made such headway among the *représentants,* that they ordered the enfranchisement of the mass of the population in the "Beneficent Edict" of February 10, 1781. This provoked the vehement opposition of the *négatifs* which in turn touched off open insurrection and fighting in the streets. The leaders of the aristocracy were deported and in April 1782 a Committee of Safety with dictatorial powers took over the government of the city, to the distress of France, Piedmont, and the Republic of Bern which had long exercised a joint protectorate over

Geneva. Much as the three powers disliked and distrusted each other, they feared the spread of radical ideas even more. All three sent sizable contingents to undo the revolution. After a short resistance, the insurgents surrendered, the city was occupied by the foreign troops, and the old rulers restored.

In spite of repeated assurances from Mrs. Cramer and the headmaster that the situation was under control, the school virtually stopped functioning during these tumultuous times, and the students, who were taken out of town every night for safety, seem to have spent many of their daylight hours roaming the streets in search of interesting incidents. On command or of his own volition, Benny started keeping a diary in the summer of 1782. His original manuscript in French has disappeared but an English translation made by one of his grandsons is still in existence. Obviously the work of a child, the diary is candid, often tough, good-humored but detached.

Benny, the future journalist, describes a scene from the occupation: "I went to see a Piedmontese soldier shot, who had stolen some coppers. This was the mode of procedure. The regiment surrounded the criminal who marched accompanied by a priest. Arrived at the place of execution, he was seated on a bank of turf and was tied to a picket. The priest continues to speak as he retires, the officer gives the sign, the soldiers fire, the regiment marches around the dead body and they carry it away" (October 9, 1782). And a *fait divers:* "A house opposite ours fell down about 8 o'clock this morning. No one was hurt. An old woman was dressing at the moment unfortunately; she turned her back to those looking and only suffered from fright and mortification" (August 31, 1782).

He records the wonders and pastimes that delight a young boy, such as seeing a giant, seven feet tall, whose arms were as thick as Benny's own body but who was so dirty one had to flee, or the famous magician Pinetti whose tricks he describes, or a huge wolf that had destroyed everything on its way including two large dogs. He tells of the birth of three guinea pigs in his room, and the theft, two days later, of one of them by a cat. He and Johonnot resolved to kill some cat, "innocent or guilty," the following Sunday and indeed they did, soothing their consciences with some circumstantial evidence that it really was the guilty cat.

Benny the adolescent was beginning to emerge: his first dance filled him with horror and he was relieved when a fire across the street gave him a chance to escape early. At the second he amused himself somewhat. At the third, he was not bored "from beginning to end."[51]

It all sounds gay enough. The boys' letters to Franklin through 1782 and the opening months of 1783 were reassuringly full of school chatter, a first prize for Johonnot, a third prize for Benny. Their only complaint was the almost total blackout of news from Paris, due no doubt to Franklin and Temple's absorption in the intensive peace negotiations. Yet all was not well at the Pension Marignac. Had it not been for his old acquaintance, Robert Pigott, a rich Englishman established near Geneva, Franklin might never have known how much was amiss. This Mr. Pigott had become fond of both boys. "I consider them as two young Plants which will produce good Fruit when transplanted into their native soil."[52] After several pleasant reports about their welfare, he suddenly sent Franklin a most alarming message in late June 1783. Benny's health, he declared, was in danger; he had a persistent fever, "the cause of which may be reasonably attributed to his unhealthy dwelling, improper diet, and ignorance on the part of his tutors. His apartment is in no respects better than that of a Prisoner, it is so confined with Walls, included in a little Alley and crowded with other Contemporaries who sleep in the same Chamber that it would be almost a Miracle that he should escape some Pestilential Disorder."[53] Things were so bad that Mr. Pigott was prepared—by force if need be—to get Benny out of a school that seemed to be disintegrating.

Within two weeks, Johonnot was on his way to Boston* and Benny on his way to Paris.

---

* Johonnot dawdled so much en route, however, that it took him from July to January to reach his destination, in spite of Franklin's urging him to make haste because the Reverend Cooper was gravely ill and in anguish at the thought that he might not live to see his cherished grandson again. He died two weeks before the boy's return. Johonnot used his inheritance to go to Harvard.

XIX

"Temple Is My Right Hand"

Thus while Governor Franklin is planning our destruction in London, his father and son are entrusted with all our secrets in Paris.
—Arthur Lee to John Adams, December 12, 1782

WHEN BENNY CAME BACK TO PARIS in the summer of 1783, his grandfather, mission accomplished, peace treaty all but signed, was at the pinnacle of his fame and glory. But the road had been long and rough, and his apparent neglect of Benny is somewhat more understandable when one takes a closer look at the battles the old man had been fighting.

The problems were not on the French side. Exactly five days off the boat in 1776 and still far from Paris, Franklin was already telling Jane Mecom how much respect he was shown "by the first People"[1] although still in his private capacity. Two years later, his tongue-lashing of Sally for desiring feathers and lace had started with a description of his own popularity as witnessed by the number and variety of his portraits made and distributed in France, "some to be set in the lids of snuff-boxes, and some so small as to be worn in rings. . . . These, with the pictures, busts and prints (of which copies upon copies are spread everywhere), have made your father's face as well known as that of the moon."[2] He was not exaggerating. Even John Adams, when he came to Paris, grudgingly admitted the tremendous impact Franklin had on the French: "His name was familiar to government and people, to kings, courtiers, nobility, clergy and philosophers, as well as plebeians, to such a degree that there was scarcely a peasant or a citizen, a *valet de chambre*, coachman or footman, a lady's chambermaid or a scullion in the kitchen who was not familiar with it and who did not consider him a friend to human kind."[3]

In French eyes, the old Doctor in his fur cap was much more than the lobbyist of an insurgent colonial nation struggling for survival. He was the embodiment of their ideals—backwoods philosopher à la Rousseau, urbane wit à la Voltaire, the hero who had, in Turgot's words, "snatched the lightning from the heavens, the scepter from tyrants."

The attacks came from his own countrymen and they were vicious. While Franklin romantically depicted the hoped-for alliance as a blissful union between innocent, dutiful, maidenly America and honorable, loving France, the virgin's bridal party was rent with suspicion, dissent, and backbiting.

The American commission in Paris was an impossible trio from the start. Aside from Franklin, Congress had appointed Arthur Lee and Silas Deane, both nearing forty, at the height of their energy and ambition. Deane, a well-to-do lawyer and merchant from Connecticut, had been in Paris since the summer of 1776, a few months before Franklin's arrival. Entrusted with procuring arms and uniforms on credit if possible, for cash if absolutely necessary, he had joined forces with the playwright Beaumarchais who, between *The Barber of Seville* and *The Marriage of Figaro*, was in the gunrunning business, the secret service business, and some other ventures on the side. It has not been possible so far to prove or disprove the charges of bungling and embezzlement hurled against the two of them in the following years—Deane's accounts defy all attempts at unraveling—but they both paid a heavy price for their involvement. Beaumarchais was to lose a fortune in the enterprise and Deane, recalled by Congress for an audit, eventually sank into despair, dishonor, exile, and a mysterious death in utter poverty. Still, it should be said that eight shiploads of supplies sent by Deane and Beaumarchais had arrived in time for the Saratoga campaign.

Coming straight from London, Arthur Lee arrived in Paris shortly after Franklin and proceeded immediately to find fault with everything his colleagues were doing—and not doing. A highly intelligent man, trained in law and medicine, but afflicted with a fair degree of paranoia, Lee was a Franklin-hater of long standing. Back in the London days they had been connected with rival land companies and had competed for the post of agent from Massachusetts. Arthur belonged to the influential Lee family of Virginia, one of four brothers consumed with a passion for politics and fanatically devoted to the cause of American independence. The brothers worked as a team, two at home, in and out of Congress (Richard Henry and Francis Lightfoot), and two in Europe (Arthur and William, the only American ever elected alderman in London). Arthur had remained in England through the early stages of the Revolution, sending information to the Secret Committee of Correspondence, and forwarding malicious reports about Franklin to his brother who wasted no time in spreading them through Congress. Indeed, Franklin was barely back on American soil in 1775 when Richard Henry Lee had accused him of returning "rather as a spy than as a friend. . . . He means to discover our weak side and make his peace with the minister by discovering it to him."[4]

And now Franklin found himself in harness with Arthur Lee. Libel first, prove later, such was Lee's method. To his brother in Congress he wrote, "I am more and more satisfied that the old doctor is concerned in the plunder, and that in time we shall collect the proofs."[5] To make matters worse, William Lee also appeared in Paris within months. He had been appointed commercial agent in Nantes to replace the incumbent, Thomas Morris, who was busily drinking himself to death. But Franklin had already replaced Morris—albeit unofficially—with his own grandnephew Jonathan Williams, Jr. This was the very Jonathan who had lived under Mrs. Stevenson's roof with his blind brother Josiah, had later returned to England from Boston, and had now hastily crossed over to France to be of use in the American cause.

Sensing his chance to deal a blow to that Franklin family forever blocking the path of the Lees, William Lee suggested to Franklin that he appoint Jonathan formally to the position previously held by Morris, with the responsibility of inspecting supplies for the colonies and selling prizes taken by American privateers. When he made this apparently kind proposal, Lee knew full well that his brother Arthur was about to spring an accusation of embezzlement against Jonathan Williams and that if Franklin had made the appointment official he, too, would be implicated in the scandal.

Franklin was too shrewd to fall into the trap. He ordered a thorough investigation of his relative's books by a commission of prominent merchants who exonerated him. Still, Franklin insisted that the coveted post of commercial agent should go to a third party, a Swiss merchant who was in the good graces of Arthur Lee. Thus Jonathan fell victim to the principle that Franklin's kinfolk must be above suspicion. He turned over his books to the new man as he was bid, settled for being a private merchant, remained diligent and devoted, but never recovered from this setback, though Franklin always gave him whatever business he could.

William Lee, in the meantime, had been appointed commissioner to Berlin and Vienna, but those courts would have nothing to do with the representative of a rebellious state they did not care to recognize. After some futile journeys about Europe, he came back to Paris and joined in the bitterness and frustration of another would-be commissioner who had likewise been snubbed by the court of Tuscany: Ralph Izard. A wealthy South Carolina planter who had befriended the Lee brothers while in London, Izard considered himself entitled to sit on the commission, a claim Franklin never recognized.

These two disgruntled "commissioners" added their poison to that of Arthur Lee who was sincerely convinced that he was the only virtuous patriot around, what with Deane a profiteer, Jonathan Williams an embezzler, the French merchants all crooks, the commission staff made up of spies, and Franklin dishonest, or, to say the least, woefully remiss, "more devoted to pleasure than would become even a young man in his station, and neglectful of the public business."[6]

All this criticism did not go unchallenged. When Lee's constant carping drove him to exasperation, Franklin would lash back that he was not going to bear those "magisterial snubbings" any longer and that he felt sorry for Lee's "sick mind . . . forever tormenting itself with its jealousies, suspicions and fancies."[7] But then, more often than not, when his outbursts had been put down on paper, he would not mail them. To a third party, however, he exploded, "That Genius must either find or make a Quarrel wherever he is. . . . I am persuaded that if some of the many Enemies he provokes do not kill him sooner, he will die in a Madhouse."[8] Or else, to defuse his anger, he would turn to sarcasm, as in his "Petition of the Letter Z." Frustrated Z, which in those days was called zed, ezzard, or izard, protests its humble position at the tail of the alphabet and insists on replacing the "hissing, crooked, serpentine, venomous Letter called S" in the word WISE. It is briskly told by the Censor-General to be content with its station and to remember its own small usefulness.[9] This piece, too, remained in the drawer for several years before being shown to Jane Mecom who had heard of Izard's anti-Franklin campaign, and even then she was pledged to secrecy.

Another type of charge against Franklin was to be formulated later by John Adams: indolence. "I found out that the Business of our Commission would never be done unless I did it."[10]

Was there any basis in fact for such accusations? Since they cover a broad spectrum, there was bound to be some basis. A prey to the infirmities of age, frequent and painful attacks of gout, a chronic skin disease, swollen joints, eye fatigue, and lowered resistance, Franklin was only too glad to leave commercial transactions to Deane, professing his ignorance in that field. Deane, in turn, was in the hands of an unscrupulous band of merchants bent on making a quick profit by selling inferior merchandise. In the end everybody fleeced everybody else, for Congress never paid anyone; it was simply part of the pattern of swindling and bungling that has its parallel in every war.

Even the well-disposed French foreign minister, Comte de Vergennes, was sometimes out of patience with Franklin's apathy which he ascribed to "age and love of tranquillity."[11] Struggling as he was with a foreign language and unfamiliar social customs, Franklin did not show enough firmness in many matters that came before him. The question of volunteers, for instance. Entrusted by Congress to send over a few qualified technicians, he let himself be swamped by thousands of requests from unemployed veterans, ambitious lieutenants, arrogant colonels, and brazen adventurers. Eager to please, susceptible to the flattery he was subjected to in more massive doses than at any other time in his life, he allowed many undesirable people, along with a few highly desirable ones, to cross the ocean and become a serious problem to those who had to clothe, feed, place, and pay them.

In the matter of spies, too, he was strangely lax. To a friend warning him about that danger, he answered flippantly that he knew full well he was surrounded by spies, indeed that his butler was probably one, but that he did not care because he had nothing to hide—a very inappropriate answer since morality is one thing, intelligence another. The American cause certainly suffered grave damage at the hands of that spying genius, the double-agent Edward Bancroft, Franklin's protégé and the commission's secretary, whose dispatches from Passy, hidden in a hollow trunk in the Tuileries, sometimes reached Whitehall before their duplicates were in Versailles. Lee raved and ranted about Bancroft but never suspected that two of his own secretaries also were on the British payroll.

And yet, under these tensions and disabilities, the commissioners, a little over a year after their arrival, scored a great diplomatic victory: the conclusion of a Treaty of Amity and Commerce and a Treaty of Alliance, both signed in February 1778. France's craving for revenge against England after her defeat in the Seven Years' War, coupled with the stunning American triumph at Saratoga prepared the way for the treaties. Franklin's personal prestige, tact, and sense of timing also played a major role. A master diplomat, he knew when to apply pressure and when to bide his time, always without making himself obnoxious. He also knew that the best way to endear oneself to a foreign nation is to embrace its people and its ways. What Lee and Adams branded as Franklin's love of pleasure and neglect of public business were in large measure a concession to the French style. In colonial America it was sinful to look idle, in France it was vulgar to look busy. The way Franklin budgeted his time filled a young Frenchman with admiration: "He would eat, sleep, work whenever he saw fit . . . so that there never was a more leisurely man though he handled a tremendous amount of business. No matter when one asked for him, he was always available."[12]

Six weeks after the signing of the two treaties came the hour of official recognition. On the first day of spring, 1778, Franklin, clad in a russet velvet coat (tradition has it that it was the very one he wore on his day of humiliation at the Cockpit), stunned the French court by the republican simplicity of his appearance: no wig, no ceremonial sword. Flanked by Silas Deane and Arthur Lee, he was admitted into the royal presence, formally introduced by Vergennes, graciously told by the king that His Majesty hoped the alliance would be of benefit to both nations, condescendingly allowed by Marie-Antoinette to watch her at the gaming table. Here was one final king to add to the list of those before whom he stood.

Was Arthur Lee satisfied? His brother William had been invited to take part in the ceremony and so had Ralph Izard. No, Arthur Lee was not placated in the least. Louis XVI, he grumbled, "had his hair undressed, hanging down on his shoulders; no appearance of preparation to receive us, nor any ceremony in doing it."[13] And William Lee noted acidly that the king of France was famous for being as shifty as his colleague George III. Though largely brought about by their relentless campaign, Deane's departure a few days later, to face the congressional audit, did not disarm the Lee brothers. On the contrary, they raged at Franklin for having allowed Deane to sneak away before his accounts could be thoroughly examined.

John Adams had hardly set foot in Paris as Deane's successor before he was caught up in the "infernal quarrels" of his colleagues. The Lees and Adamses had made common cause in the Congress, but Adams ended up heartily despising Arthur Lee. Toward Franklin he had deeply ambivalent feelings: bursts of admiration in a general climate of aversion. Adams could never bear to be in the shadow of men greater than himself. "On Dr Franklin the eyes of all Europe are fixed. . . . Neither Lee nor myself are looked upon of much consequence."[14] He may have thought that he was keeping his wounded pride to himself by confiding such remarks only to his diary, but to outsiders it was clear that he was "jealous of Franklin in the extreme."[15]

Franklin was puzzled by Adams. As he later told Jefferson, he found him "always an honest man, often a great one, but sometimes absolutely mad."[16] While Franklin believed that "a true American patriot must be a friend of France,"[17] Adams thought the old doctor downright servile and had nothing but contempt for his attendance at court and his paeans to French generosity. "Every American minister in Europe, except Dr. Franklin," he wrote in disgust, "has discovered a judgement, a conscience, and a resolution of his own, and, of consequence . . . has been frowned upon. On the contrary, Dr. Franklin, who has been pliant and submissive in everything, has been constantly cried up to the stars."[18]

The difference in temperament between the two men shows up in their approach to learning the French language. Franklin, if he did not literally follow the dictum that a foreign language is best learned on the pillow, made his study of French a sociable affair. He enlisted his friends, both male and female, to do what comes naturally to the French—instruct him in the fine points and correct his awkward literary efforts until at last he was able to print his charming *Bagatelles* partly in French, partly in English, on his own little press at Passy. Adams, who had been putting himself through laborious exercises in grammar and doggedly reading such grim models as Bossuet's *Funeral Orations,* grumbled that his colleague's "ungrammatical" French did not deserve all the praise it received.

The only point on which Franklin, Lee, and Adams agreed was that they could no longer function together and that the Paris mission should be entrusted to a single man. Lee felt sure he should be that man. But Congress, well aware of Franklin's enormous popularity in France, voted 12 to 1 to appoint him minister plenipotentiary. It took more than five months, from September 1778 to February 1779, for this news to reach him, and when it did, a new campaign was on, the most vicious as far as he was concerned: the campaign against Temple.

When it came to Temple, Franklin was another person. Nobody, not even William, had ever gripped his emotions as this youth did, this abandoned boy whose only family he had been for ten years and whom he had made his own again by wrenching him from his father. Temple, the only link with all his worlds, the Craven Street world of London, the Market Street world of Philadelphia, now his emotional anchor in an alien land. This good-looking adolescent who delighted him with his flashes of playful humor, with his incipient roguishness, and the hope that through him, and him alone, the family name would survive. Franklin, who had always put a screen of detachment between himself and passion, a veil of irony between himself and suffering, lay unprotected and vulnerable when it came to Temple, blind to his own weakness, blind also to the omens that the object of so much devotion would eventually prove disappointing.

The Lee faction knew where to strike. There had been some initial grumbling when Temple was entrusted with copying the Treaty of Alliance. Now the complaints became more serious. In a letter congratulating his father-in-law on his appointment as minister plenipotentiary, Richard Bache felt compelled to offer a warning: "I am informed they [the Lees and Izard] lay some stress upon your employing as a private secretary your Grandson whom they hold out as unfit to be trusted because of his father's principles." The same insinuations, said Bache, had been used to influence the Pennsylvania delegation to cast the only vote against Franklin's appointment as minister plenipotentiary and to determine Congress against the prompt exchange of Governor Franklin. One of the delegates had said that since William had a son living with Franklin "much evil might ensue to the United States."[19]

Franklin professed to be unruffled by these attacks: "I know those gentlemen have plenty of ill-will to me, though I have never done to either of them the smallest injury or given the least just cause of offence. But my too great reputation and the general good-will this people have for me, the respect they show me . . . all grieve those unhappy gentlemen, unhappy in their tempers, and in the dark uncomfortable passions of jealousy, anger, suspicion, envy and malice." He was surprised, he said, that there could be any objection to Temple being with him or a cabal for removing him: "Methinks it is rather some merit that I have rescued a valuable young man from the danger of being a tory and fixed him in honest republican whig principles." He went on to praise his grandson for the "integrity of his disposition, his industry, his early sagacity and uncommon abilities for business" and predicted that he might in time "become of great service to his country." At the end, suddenly, a note poignantly different from the complacent beginning: "It is enough that I have lost my *son,* would they add my *grandson?* An old man of seventy, I undertook a winter voyage at the command of the Congress, and for the public service, with no other attendant to take care of me. I am continued here in a foreign country, where, if I am sick, his filial attention comforts me, and, if I die, I have a child to close my eyes and take care of my remains. His dutiful behaviour towards me and his diligence and fidelity in business are both pleasing and useful to me. . . . I am confident the Congress will never think of separating us."[20]

In a letter to Sally written at the same time, Franklin was briefer and more categorical. If his enemies tried to deprive him of his grandson, he declared, "I should not part with the child but with the employment." Temple, then, was dearer than his country's service. But he reiterated his conviction that it would never come to a choice since "the Congress is too wise and too good to think of treating me in that manner."[21]

The tie with William was a trump Franklin's adversaries would not lightly discard. (Yet Izard had his own skeleton in the closet: His wife's brother and uncle were leading tories in New York.) Conversely, Franklin's prominence in the revolutionary cause was a constant thorn in William's side. "His Father is and has been every way his Misfortune,"[22] wrote a British observer.

The captive governor had spent the first months of his parole in private homes in several Connecticut towns, attended by his servant, free to ride around in his carriage. In spite of worries about Elizabeth and about lack of money—he had made no contingency plans before his arrest—his captivity was not so stringent that it did not allow for occasional good times. One night in Middletown the watch had to be called out to break up a riotous party in William's quarters: The guests were all very drunk, very profane, and very tory.

William seems to have been supremely confident that he would soon be exchanged and in fact Congress approved his exchange in November 1776. But before it could be put into effect there were second thoughts and the order was rescinded. Furious, he violated his parole brazenly by intensifying his contacts with the British commander, General Howe, and his brother Lord Admiral Howe (Franklin's acquaintance from London days), both of whom were in New York. Fully appreciating the propaganda value of the Franklin name, the Howes authorized William (who would continue to use his title of governor for the rest of his life) to issue clandestine pardons in the king's name to loyalists in Connecticut and New Jersey, a quixotic scheme if there ever was one.

In due time Washington got wind of these contacts and had William jailed in Litchfield, deprived of all writing materials, forbidden to leave his cell (located over a noisy tavern), or receive visitors alone. Harsh as his treatment sounds, it was a good deal preferable to the Simsbury copper mines where other loyalists were held.

When the news reached him that Elizabeth was seriously ill in New York, William sent Washington an urgent plea to be allowed to see her. He insisted on his innocence of the charges that had brought about his jailing and swore he could submit evidence to prove it. Washington was caught between his friendly memories (he had enjoyed the hospitality of the governor's mansion) and his anger at William's dishonorable behavior. It was a decision for Congress, in any case, and by the time Congress got around to turning down the request, Elizabeth was dead. William, for the first time, was plunged into depression: "My Life has become quite a Burthen to me."[23] He would soon die, he declared, if he were not released.

But there were more people pleading his case than he knew. His old friend Strahan, for one. "Whatever his Demerits may be in the Opinion of the reigning Powers of America," he argued to a deaf Franklin, "the Son of Dr. Franklin ought not to receive such Usage."[24] His brother-in-law Richard Bache, for another. Bache carried his campaign to Congress and it was grudgingly agreed that William could leave the jail and move to a private house in East Windsor, Connecticut. Finally, in October 1778, Congress arranged for his exchange. He headed straight for British-occupied New York and threw himself into the loyalist struggle with a burst of energy born of his years of pent-up anger.

Before long he had organized both propaganda and intelligence-gathering units. He quickly discovered, to his chagrin, that he would have to do battle not only with the rebels but with the British command in America which was indifferent—when not openly hostile—to its loyalist allies, irritated with their penchant for giving advice, scornful of their value as a fighting force.*

Yet he was taken notice of across the ocean. Lord Germain, secretary for the colonies, was impressed enough with William's proposals, to make him an initial grant and provide an annual salary to be kept in trust in England by William Strahan. After two years of haggling with authorities at all levels, permission was finally granted for the establishment of the Board of Associated Loyalists. William became its first (and last) president and as such the most influential loyalist in America.

Under his direction the board planned and executed innumerable commando-type raids against the rebel coasts; it also fed to a mildly interested British command endless amounts of intelligence, some of it disastrously misleading. The military impact of all this activity was hardly significant; the promiscuous killings and burnings may even have pushed some apathetic citizens into the rebel camp. To Franklin, however, it was a tremendous blow. He might perhaps have ended by forgiving William his views. He never forgave these actions.

There was no communication between Franklin and his son as long as the war lasted, only what little news Sally passed on when she could. Knowing how pointless it would be, William never made any claims on Temple, and Temple continued to serve as his grandfather's secretary and constant companion, dubbed "Franklinet" because of the strong resemblance between the two and their great intimacy. Flattering

---

* By an irony of history, one of the few British officers sympathetic to William's grand designs was that Captain John André who had occupied Franklin's house on Market Street and stolen the Doctor's portrait. When André was hanged for his part in the Benedict Arnold affair, William raged more than ever at the bungling indecisiveness of the British commander in New York who had failed to get him exchanged.

Franklinet became a way of life with those who wanted to get through to Franklin.

The family pattern repeated itself in a still more devastating way. William may have been dwarfed by his father, but at least he had a law degree, some sense of his own worth and separateness, the courage, finally, to make his own choices even if they were the wrong ones. Temple was not only dwarfed, he was eaten up, spoiled, annihilated. "Virtue and a Trade are a Child's best Portion," said Poor Richard (1753), but Temple, brought to France ostensibly to complete his education, never took another course or learned any trade. The College of Philadelphia did grant him a degree *in absentia* in 1780, but it was a meaningless gesture, for he had no field of competence, nothing but the polish given him by residing in Paris and a sense of his own importance that was sheer delusion.

For a brief moment it looked as if, at nineteen, he might fulfill himself in the world of military action. He was invited to take part as an aide-de-camp to Lafayette in the projected invasion of England to be carried out in the summer of 1779 by the joint forces of France and Spain. Already back from his first triumphs in America, Lafayette (only three years older than Temple) was anxious to have Franklin's grandson at his side. As status-conscious as he was clothes-conscious, Temple fretted over his rank, his uniform, his epaulettes, but Lafayette strongly advised him to settle for the title of volunteer. He added, however, that if Temple really desired it, Franklin could bestow on him a commission of captain in the Continental Army and Washington would certainly ratify it. Just as the great day seemed imminent and Franklin was being congratulated on his fortitude in letting the beloved grandson go, the scheme was called off, a preview of Temple's whole life which was to be a succession of false starts. Though he may have been secretly relieved, Franklin expressed only disappointment: "It would have been of infinite Advantage to him," he wrote Lafayette, "to have been present with you so early in Life at Transactions of such vast Importance. . . . I flattered myself too that he might possibly catch from you some Tincture of those engaging Manners that make you so much the Delight of all that know you."[25]

His dreams of glory indefinitely postponed, Temple went on with his secretarial duties which had grown much heavier once Franklin became minister plenipotentiary. "Temple is my right hand,"[26] the old man insisted. "Temple and I are perfect drudges,"[27] he said. It could be argued, of course, that the variety of problems that crossed the ambassador's desk was an education in itself. Franklin acted as a kind of secretary of the treasury in Europe, a treasury perpetually in deficit that caused him to be bombarded with bills from Congress before he had time to finish negotiating the loan that would, he hoped, pay them. And he served as mediator between the French merchants and their American counterparts. And as adviser to the hundreds of Frenchmen who wanted to fight for liberty or find a sinecure in the New World or submit their latest brain child or tell their tale of woe. And, more time-consuming than all the other concerns, he was head of naval operations, supervised the selling of prizes, arbitrated between crews and captains,* spent countless hours arranging for the exchange of men captured at sea.

No captain was captured at sea more often than his own nephew Peter Collas, some seven times in the first few years of the Revolution. With the deaths of Peter and Benjamin Mecom, Franklin may have thought that his obligations toward Sister Jane's flock had come to an end, but the last surviving daughter, Jenny, had married a man whose incredible bad luck seemed to have predestined him to join the family. "Wretched" and "unfortunate" are the epithets that sprang from his mother-in-law's pen whenever she took up the narrative of his adventures. Collas was soon looked upon with superstitious horror by his fellow seamen. Needless to say, less and less business came his way with each succeeding capture. "I think there was hardly ever so unfortunate a family," brooded Jane. "I am not willing to think it is all owing to misconduct."[29]

Jane was now bearing the brunt of every misfortune that struck the Collas household because she had become a part of it. The "tender and sensible and dutiful" granddaughter with whom she had made her home for five years, Jenny Flagg Greene, had suddenly died, carried away by consumption like so many other Mecoms. On her deathbed the young mother had tried to exact from Jane a promise that she would raise her three small children, but Jane, seventy, asthmatic, grief-stricken all over again by the death of one of those children, unable to draw close to the desperate widower, fled Rhode Island and went to live in Cambridge with her daughter Jenny Collas, an arrangement she had rejected previously. Apprised of Collas's continuing bad luck at sea, Franklin suggested a different line of work and offered to finance him in the soapmaking business, an enterprise Jane could help with, thanks to her knowledge of the family recipes. But she demurred: new, inferior soaps had made their way onto the market and, she felt, it would

---

* "You can have no Conception of the Vexations the Maritime affairs occasion me," he sputtered to a friend. "It is hard that I who give others no Trouble with my Quarrels should be plagu'd with all the Perversities of those who think fit to wrangle with one another."[28]

take more acumen, more energy, more intelligence than Collas or his wife possessed to re-establish the pre-eminence of the crown brand. Left to his own dark destiny, Collas tumbled from mishap to mishap until Jane, unable to support him any further, prevailed on him to ship out as mate and no longer as master, a gloomy parallel to her own Benny's downfall from printer to journeyman. Toward her daughter who was giving in to fatigue and depression, "a poor low-spirited creature when anything befalls her,"[30] Jane felt more contempt than compassion.

Her brother Benjamin was now the undisputed center of her life. She shook with indignation when she heard that Ralph Izard had begun denouncing him the minute he reached America in late 1779. "Izard was very laborious at Newport to make people believe you had done something criminal in money matters . . . pretending he had strong vouchers he was carrying with him to Congress." Jane was worried that, however baseless, some of the "dirt will stick." Mrs. Greene, wife of General Nathanael Greene, warned Izard to stop spreading such tales lest he be stoned by Franklin's supporters, but he declared his intention to keep at it "till he got to Congress." Jane hoped that by then he would have "sunk into oblivion."[31]

Far from sinking into oblivion, Izard was, as Richard Bache reported, "pretty open mouthed"[32] against Franklin. Abetted by the Lee brothers, he carried on such a vigorous campaign that on December 15, 1780, the French minister at Philadelphia informed Vergennes that Franklin's support was at rock bottom. A motion for his recall was introduced into Congress. Only Massachusetts and South Carolina voted in favor, but the erosion of confidence in his abilities showed itself in the appointment of Colonel John Laurens as special envoy to Versailles to negotiate a new loan. It was, in fact, a desperate moment for the United States: The British had retaken Charleston and routed Gates at Camden, South Carolina, the treasury was empty, the army mutinying for lack of food. But unknown to Congress at the time, Franklin, less indolent and ineffectual than his enemies would have it, had wheedled a gift of six million livres from the French, who were not far from being as bankrupt as the Americans.

Deeply hurt by what he heard of the congressional debates, Franklin offered his resignation—on grounds of age and health—adding that he would remain in France, "among a People that love me and whom I love"[33] until peace. Congress turned down the resignation and immediately appointed him one of the five commissioners to negotiate peace when the time was ripe. Even this reparation was scant balm for his wounds: His was the last of the five names and it had been included only because of intense behind-the-scenes pressure applied by the representative of Vergennes. Still, he had emerged victorious if not unscarred.

This time it was Richard Bache who paid the price. In late 1781 he wrote apprehensively that a shuffle in the American post office, which he had headed for five years, was in the offing, pushed by the New England states who had a candidate of their own. Nobody had accused him of mismanagement; he simply was no "favorite with the Eastern Delegates." He had intended to bear it all with "philosophic fortitude"[34] but when the blow came, he was incensed and could not help revealing his true reading of the matter: "These Eastern Men, I am informed, have aimed at your recall, but finding themselves failed in that attempt, have struck at me, thinking thereby, I suppose, to hurt *your* feelings."[35] This setback could not have come at a worse time, oppressed as Bache was with the cares and expenses of a growing family, all the harder to meet since his import business was not going well because of the effectiveness of the British blockade.

Would the younger generations ever stop needing help? Franklin had done all he could to favor the commercial expansion of the newly created firm of Bache and Shee. He circulated their broadside to the merchants he knew in France, Germany, and the Lowlands. He got Jonathan Williams to serve as one of their representatives—but Jonathan was soon to fall on hard days himself. Hopelessly entangled in the trans-Atlantic commercial anarchy of wartime, he had to declare bankruptcy in the summer of 1783. When some merchants implied ominously that his failure to pay their bills would reflect unfavorably on Bache and Shee's credit, Franklin quietly took care of the matter.

Still, much as he felt responsible for Jonathan's difficulties, much as he worried about Richard Bache and his Philadelphia grandchildren, his chief concern was always Temple. He was determined to impose Temple as secretary of the peace commission, a steppingstone, he hoped, to future diplomatic posts. Even Silas Deane, his old ally in the early days of the Paris mission, remarked acidly that "in certain matters the Doctor is no more of a Philosopher than the rest of the world. He has a Grandson on whom he dotes and whom he wishes to fix as Secretary in France."[36] The proposal aroused little enthusiasm. Temple appeared to most observers as a man about town and not much else. His friends were often fops with whom he sought out the company of the demimondaines that Paris provided in such lavish abundance, those "elegant nymphs of the boulevards,"[37] as Adams awkwardly put it.* In

---

* Jefferson may have had Temple in mind when, a few years later, he advised a young friend against coming to Europe for his education because of the irresistible "spirit for female intrigue"[38] and the low premium set on marital fidelity.

their letters to him, his correspondents dwell on luxuries: gold watch chains, silver buckles, modish outfits for the carnival, brocade vests, balls, intimate suppers with easy women, handsome equipages, and fine horses—he had his own favorite mount painted by the horse portraitist Carle Vernet.

Nevertheless Franklin had his way. Congress went along with the appointment of Temple. None of Franklin's four fellow commissioners was in a position to quibble anyway since they were not yet in Paris at the opening of negotiations in April 1782. Jefferson had again declined to serve because his wife was dying. Henry Laurens had been captured at sea, imprisoned in the Tower of London, and was now recovering in England; John Adams was in Holland negotiating a commercial treaty with the Dutch; John Jay was in Madrid where he had spent a frustrating two years trying unsuccessfully to bring the Spaniards into an alliance with the colonies. He reached Paris in June 1782, stuffed full of Adams's warnings against Franklin. In fact, though the wealthy and reserved Huguenot lawyer from New York held views often very different from those of the tallow chandler's son from Boston, they worked together remarkably well and a real affection sprang up between Franklin and the Jays. After their return to America in 1784, Franklin wrote how much he missed "your, I may almost say *our*, dear little Family."[39]

Cornwallis's surrender at Yorktown, on October 19, 1781, had brought in its wake the collapse of the North ministry in England after more than a decade in power. Now those who had spent the war in opposition were at the helm. Foremost among them was Lord Shelburne, first as secretary for the colonies, then as prime minister, a man Franklin had known and found sympathetic in the past but of course no partisan of independence.

A primary stumbling block was semantic but critical. Who was England dealing with? Agents of rebellious colonies or emissaries of a sovereign nation? Jay eventually found an acceptable formula which implied American independence without actually stating it, and the negotiations could begin. Weeks were spent in shadowboxing, in exploring the weak points of the alliances involved, the differences of opinion within the individual governments. Many sessions after that were devoted to haggling over the boundaries of the new state, but even thornier was the question of American rights to the fisheries off Newfoundland and Nova Scotia. John Adams lived some of his finest hours arguing the case for New England fishermen.

Another sore point was the compensation for American loyalists. To his colleagues' amazement, Franklin held out bitterly against any indemnification for them. Using the fine art of blackmail, he threatened to match any list of tory claims with a demand to compensate the patriots, item by item, for all the lootings, burnings, and scalpings carried out by the British and their Indian allies during the war. They could then strike a balance, declared the quondam shopkeeper, and see who owed whom. Adams who would have expected him to give in on this particular point because of his son marveled that the old man stood "very staunch against the Tories, more decided a great deal on this point than Mr. Jay or myself."[40]

The Treaty of Alliance with France forbade either party to conclude a separate peace and the American commissioners were bound by their instructions to make no moves contrary to the advice of the French king. Jay soon began to suspect, however, that Vergennes was deliberately stalling and that American independence was far less important to him than the interests of France and her Spanish allies in other parts of the world. Franklin was loath to believe Vergennes capable of double-dealing and felt uneasy about discussing a separate peace. This distrust between the allies played into the hands of England, eager to conclude a peace with the United States in order to be free to deal with her other enemies.

At the crucial period in the negotiations, during September 1782, Franklin was laid up with such a severe attack of both stone and gout that the field was left to Jay. He decided to bypass France.

The preliminary treaty was signed between England and the United States on November 30, 1782, to take effect as soon as a general peace was concluded among all the powers—which took place on September 3 of the following year. The cod and the mackerel had not been surrendered nor had the American government agreed to a penny of reparations for the loyalists, leaving the matter entirely up to the states—and knowing full well they would do nothing either. The treaty was a *tour de force* for the trio of American negotiators. Franklin was fond of repeating that "there never was a good war or a bad peace,"[41] but this peace was far better than the young nation might have expected. So much did it seem to favor the United States that it provoked a storm of protest in England. The Shelburne government was soon hounded out of office, its principal peacemakers abused and disgraced.

Vergennes of course was furious but not a little impressed by how well the Americans had done for themselves. Franklin hastened to apologize profusely for the oversight in not including the French. "We have been guilty of neglecting a point of *bienséance*."[42] He even sweet-talked the minister into some more financial aid: The ship that bore the preliminary treaty to Philadelphia also carried assurance of a new French loan of six million livres.

As secretary of the peace commission, Temple put his signature to the treaty, but his role, that of a scribe, stopped there. If he appears as one of the prominent figures in the painting that immortalizes the occasion, it is not because he attended it, which he did not, but because the painter, Benjamin West, was an old friend of Franklin's and had known Temple since he was a little boy. Once again, Temple was promoted to the center of the stage not on the strength of his own accomplishments but out of deference to his grandfather, once again he was the beneficiary of glory by proxy.

XX

"Nothing Has Ever Hurt Me So Much"

We are commanded to forgive our enemies, but we are nowhere commanded to forgive our friends.

—Franklin to Alexander Small, November 5, 1789

ARTICLE X OF THE CAPITULATION signed at Yorktown in October 1781 decreed that all loyalists would be dealt with according to the laws of their respective states. Since the British command in New York had made no provision to evacuate the loyalists to safety, there was widespread panic as soon as the magnitude of the defeat became known. William, if taken in New Jersey, could expect to be hanged for treason.

Almost alone except for George III, he refused to believe that the war was lost. And for a moment, in the spring of 1782, Admiral Rodney's smashing victory over de Grasse's French fleet in the West Indies seemed to justify William's pugnaciousness against the fainthearted. "There never was a more glorious opportunity for striking a decisive stroke against Washington,"[1] he exulted. If only the House of Commons would not tie the hands of Cornwallis's successor, victory could still be won and the "honor of Great Britain" would no longer be prostrated "at the feet of Banditti." Possessed by a kind of suicidal energy, William and his die-hard band continued to harry the rebel-held coasts. In a particularly vindictive raid into New Jersey, a Captain Lippincott hanged a captured soldier as retaliation for executed loyalists, pinning a note to his body with a threat "to hang man for man while there is a Refugee existing."[2] This infuriated the British commander in chief every bit as much as it did Washington, and Lippincott was brought to trial on criminal charges. The loyalist bitterness welled over. "By a strange Fatality," declared a petition in defense of Lippincott, "the Loyalists are the only People that have been treated as Rebels during this unhappy War."[3] Since he was only carrying out the orders of his superiors, the Board of Directors of the Associated Loyalists, Lippincott was found not guilty. In many British eyes it was the Board who should have stood trial—and its chief was William Franklin.

The Lippincott affair was abruptly pushed into the background by the news (premature as it turned out) that the king had granted the colonies unconditional independence. William, his life's work more unappreciated than ever, harked back to the dream that had long haunted him: the governorship of Barbados. But he had little time for regrets. With everything lost on the American side of the Atlantic, the only hope lay on the other. He was chosen by his fellow loyalists to go to England and press their cause with all the urgency and eloquence he could muster. Twenty years to the month after he had been appointed governor, on August 18, 1782, he sailed off on a British man-of-war. By a curious coincidence, three of the four functioning American peace commissioners in Paris had defecting members of their family in England: For Henry Laurens and Benjamin Franklin it was their sons, for John Jay it was his brother.

William reached England in a miserable state. He had lost his wife, his family, his land, most of his possessions (burned in a British warehouse in New York)—and his country. His near-neighbor and friend from happier days, Patience Wright, the expatriate American artist who did portraits in wax, was moved by his woebegone appearance: "His health is bad, [he] looks old and excites in me the old feelings of Friendship."[4]

He soon found out that he had not lost his son as irretrievably as he had feared. Apparently on his own initiative and without consulting his grandfather, Temple had tried to alleviate the governor's plight even before William had sailed from America. He had talked to Benjamin Vaughan, Franklin's old friend and editor, now one of Lord Shelburne's many agents in and out of Paris during the peace negotiations. Vaughan reported to Shelburne that "young Mr. Franklin has intimated hopes to see something done for his *father* as he was the only governor who gave his court plain and wholesome advice before the war."[5] What Temple had hinted at was, it seems, some post in the diplomatic corps, and Vaughan felt the matter should be "kept in mind."

Temple was experienced enough in the ways of office-seekers to keep up the pressure. Vaughan broached the subject to his patron again in the fall and winter of 1782 after the preliminary peace treaty had been signed. He sensed that Temple was not exactly disinterested in his exertions: "If his father is provided for, he knows that he has more chance of being the *sole* heir to the Doctor, which I assure your

Lordship would not displease him and would much forward his views."
Vaughan then expressed an opinion shared by many during this period,
friend and foe alike: *"Any one* who is near an easy man like Dr.
Franklin has great means of influencing him, and as Dr. Franklin is
still likely, in some shape or other, to be an important character, I cannot but feel attention to these little minutiae important, in order the
better to have access to him, through his son, and through his grandson
and secretary."[6] Much as Vaughan misread Franklin's current attitude
toward his son, he was not far off the mark in his evaluation of the
grandson's importance.

When Shelburne had received William soon after the latter's arrival
in England, he had promised to do all he could for the suffering
loyalists. In reality he abandoned them in the peace treaty. Whether he
intended to be more generous toward William personally is impossible
to tell: In the storm of indignation aroused by the recognition of American independence and the alleged sell-out to the colonists, Shelburne
was soon to be so absorbed by the fight for his own political life that he
had no margin to spare for the problems of the loyalists.

As often happens with refugees, the loyalists who had fled to England found themselves highly unpopular. They were blamed in many
quarters for having led the British government astray by exaggerating
their own strength and minimizing that of the revolutionaries. Now
they expected compensation from the British just when the country was
deep in debt after an inglorious war. Even the king was quoted in
loyalist circles as having allowed that "he wished the Nation rid of
their Importunities."[7] Still, William, Galloway, and their other spokes-
men would not be ignored.

Finally, in June 1783, Parliament appointed a commission to look
into their grievances. Intended to sit for nine months, it dragged on for
seven weary years until the last of the more than three thousand claims
was settled. William's own case was not terminated until 1788. He discovered to his amazement that from the very start complaints had come
to the ears of the commissioners to the effect that he and his father had
been in collusion all along. They were accused of having followed the
precedent of the English Civil Wars a century earlier and chosen opposite sides of the Revolution so that one of them would be sure to come
out on top and be able to help the other! After all his efforts on behalf
of fellow loyalists, William now found himself on the defensive,
obliged to marshal every witness and scrap of evidence to clear his own
name.

He had submitted claims for £48,245 4s 7d, covering confiscated
lands, rents, salary, and £1,500 in debts to his father that never

would have been pressed, he argued, if he had joined the rebels. In the end he was given only £1,800, the estimated value of his goods lost in the New York fire—much less than many other claimants—while his pension was increased to £800 for life. Shameful treatment, he contended, for one whose loyalty had cost him so dear.

The signing of the final peace treaty in September 1783 presented him with something of a dilemma. Now the time had surely come to patch up his differences with his father. But how to do this without jeopardizing his claims for compensation, claims which he of course expected to be settled much sooner than they actually were? If he delayed too long his father would have gone home and there would be no further chance to meet. Almost a year passed. Finally, on July 22, 1784, William penned a circumspect letter. "Dear and Honoured Father," he began his first communication in nine years,

> Ever since the Termination of the unhappy Contest between Great Britain and America, I have been anxious to write to you, and to endeavour to revive that affectionate Intercourse and Connexion which till the Commencement of the late Troubles had been the Pride and Happiness of my Life. Uncertain, however, whether the decided and active Part I took in Opposition to the Measures you thought proper to adopt, might not have left some unfavourable Impressions on your Mind, or, if that should not be the Case, whether you might not have some political Reasons for avoiding such Correspondence while you retained your present Employ under Congress, I was induced to postpone my Intention of writing till I could by some Means or other learn whether your Inclinations were likely to meet my Wishes in that respect.

He had delayed writing, too, because so many of their London friends expected Franklin would soon be stopping off in England on his way home to America and because "narrow illiberal Minds" on both sides might make political capital of any contact between them. The charges of collusion had already caused him much pain although they both knew how false they were: "I can with Confidence appeal not only to you but to my God, that I have uniformly acted from a strong Sense of what I conceived my Duty to my King, and Regard to my Country, required. If I have been mistaken, I cannot help it. It is an Error of Judgment that the maturest Reflection I am capable of cannot rectify; and I verily believe were the same Circumstances to occur again Tomorrow, my Conduct would be exactly similar to what it was heretofore." Having stated his case with pride and dignity, William unwisely tried to stir Franklin's pity by referring to "the cruel Sufferings, scandalous Neglects, and Ill-treatment which we poor unfortunate Loyalists have in general experienced."

These disagreeable but necessary matters out of the way, he ventured to express the hope that his father too would be happy to resume their earlier intimacy, a hope nurtured by certain favorable signs. He also made a point of mentioning the flattering reports he had lately heard about Temple, "who owes so much to you for his Education and other Advantages." Should Franklin not come to England, William proposed to meet him in Passy, for there were many family affairs and other subjects that "cannot well be adjusted without a personal interview."[8]

A dutiful letter but an unyielding one: William was asking for reconciliation, not forgiveness; there was nothing to forgive, no wrong on either side. He did not comprehend the violence of his father's resentment against the loyalists in general and himself in particular. He could not have seen the essay his father had sent Sally only a few months before, denouncing those who wanted to make hereditary the newly created honorific Order of Cincinnatus (occasionally rendered as Saint Cinnatus by the French). No doubt thinking of the disgrace his son had brought upon him, Franklin had no desire to make him the beneficiary of his own achievements. How little his views had softened is underscored by the lumping of royalists with rogues, fools, scoundrels, and prostitutes in his mathematical demonstration of where the Cincinnati would end up in a few generations.

Even after the conclusion of peace, Franklin was not willing to make distinctions between "good" and "bad" loyalists. As usual he defused some of his rage by composing a satire, this time in the form of an animal story. It concerned a lion who ruled over a forest inhabited by faithful dogs. Under the influence of evil counselors, the lion turned against the devoted dogs and, deaf to their humble petitions, called in fierce beasts to destroy them. A few mongrels, "corrupted by royal promises of great reward,"[9] deserted the honest dogs and joined their enemies. When they found themselves on the losing side, the mongrels claimed their reward from the king and his council. The wolves and the foxes supported their demands, but the noble horse pointed out that the mongrels had been the trouble makers all along and the king would be ill-advised to encourage such fratricides.

Franklin's answer to William was not as inexorably black-and-white as this allegory, but it bore no trace of a paternal blessing on a prodigal son. For each small step toward a rapprochement, he took a giant step backward. Yes, of course, he desired peace between them: "I received your Letter of the 22d past, and am glad to find that you desire to revive the affectionate Intercourse that formerly existed between us. It will be very agreeable to me." But there were wounds William should not forget: "Indeed nothing has ever hurt me so much and affected me with such keen Sensations, as to find my self deserted in my old Age by my only Son; and not only deserted, but to find him taking up Arms against me, in a Cause wherein my good Fame, Fortune and Life were all at Stake." Did his son not recognize the hierarchy of human duties? "You conceived, you say, that your Duty to your King and Regard for your Country required this. I ought not to blame you for differing in Sentiments with me in Public Affairs. We are Men, all subject to Errors. Our Opinions are not in our own Power; they are formed and governed much by Circumstances, that are often as inexplicable as they are irresistible. Your Situation was such that few would have censored your remaining Neuter, tho' *there are Natural Duties which precede political Ones, and cannot be extinguished by them.*" Let us try to ignore the past: "This is a disagreeable Subject. I drop it. And we will endeavour as you propose mutually to forget what has happened relating to it, as well as we can."

This far he would extend the olive branch; no further. Though he expected to stay another year in France on congressional business, he definitely did not want William to come to Paris. Instead he proposed sending Temple to England to discuss the family affairs that both were eager to attend to. Franklin hoped William would turn out to have some of the papers and books left with Galloway in 1776. Temple was discreet and William could confide their most private business to him, but, he added, "I trust that you will prudently avoid introducing him to Company that it may be improper to be seen with"—a reference presumably to politics rather than to morals.

Temple himself, the grandfather declared, was "much improved. He is greatly esteemed and beloved in this Country and will make his Way any where." Once again, as a decade earlier, he proposed that the young man study law "as a necessary Part of Knowledge for a public Man"[10] and asked William to lend him his law books. This blandly optimistic appraisal of Temple and his future masked the real situation which was a good deal bleaker. Now that the work of the peace commission was over, Temple had no official employment. The diplomatic assignment that Franklin had desired for him was not forthcoming and not likely to be. Richard Henry Lee had become president of Congress and, as Bache put it with nice understatement, "He is no friend to us or our connection."[11]

A mysterious letter to Temple dated New York, November 1, 1784, and signed only with the initials "F.H." suggests the spirit of faction and intrigue that prevailed. F.H. alluded to "an intimacy with your father" which gave him the right to offer advice and claimed an "Interest in the Welfare of your Family" as his sole motive in writing. He went

right to the point, declaring that Temple's prospects were dim indeed
unless he charted a more independent course:

> You must have already observed that the Influence of your Grandfather
> is very small, from several Circumstances that have lately happened and it
> is thought that there will be a Motion to recall him as it is assured that he is
> unfit to discharge the duties of his Appointment from bodily Infirmities.
> Some Private letters from public people in Europe mention this.
>
> If you want to ruin the Career you have already commenced you must
> make friends for yourself. At present you have but few. Those you have
> most seen in France are your greatest enemies and will lay every obstacle in
> the way of your preferment. This is unfortunate as I think you might have
> attached them to you. . . .
>
> Marquis de Lafayette's unwearied exertions for your Grandfather have
> injured him as they led people to suspect that he meant only to retain a man
> that was perfectly subservient to his Court.[12]

Did Temple take to heart this all-too-accurate assessment of his predicament, this painful reminder of his total identification with his
grandfather and the ultra-Francophiles? Did he put it down as the
work of a crank? He was twenty-four now, feeling his oats, becoming
restless in the role of Franklinet, the Doctor's shadow. In the Mesmer
affair, for example, Temple took an independent tack, refusing to be
ruled by his grandfather's opinions.

Mesmerism was the rage during the waning years of the *ancien
régime*, overshadowing in the salons, the newspapers, and even the
academies and universities such important issues as the financial crisis,
the economy of free trade, the ideology of the social contract, the new
criminology, the new physics. A fashionable and diverting parlor game?
The medical breakthrough of the age? A dangerous pack of scientific
rubbish? Opinions diverged and, to some extent, they still do.

An Austrian physician, Friedrich-Anton Mesmer tried to combine
concepts borrowed from Paracelsus and Newton with his own hazy
metaphysics to produce and explain phenomena that would now be
called psychosomatic. He postulated that the heavenly bodies emit a
planetary fluid which has the power to penetrate all living and nonliv-
ing matter, and that if the path of that fluid is obstructed the human
body falls prey to disease. This theory was by no means uncongenial to
the scientific thought of the eighteenth century, which tended to link
to the action of fluids or vital spirits such key phenomena as electricity,
gravity, light, even fire. The heart of the controversy, however, was the
remedy Mesmer advocated in case of obstruction: replacing the
planetary fluid with what he called "animal magnetism," a fluid
derived from human beings, and doing this with a technique known to him
alone and revealed by him only to his disciples. Actually some cases

seemed to respond dramatically to his cures, others little or not at all. Mesmer admitted gradually that his system worked only for certain types of ailments and modified the theory to fit the experience. His "cures" had something in common with the future hypnotic experiments of Charcot and Freud, but his behavior smacked of quackery and magic.

In Vienna the medical profession reacted with hostility to Mesmer's ideas, but the general public proved more receptive. Wolfgang Mozart and his father were among his prominent friends, and *Così fan tutte* alludes to mesmerism. There was much disenchantment, however, after the relapse of one of the physician's most celebrated patients, a blind young pianist (for whom Mozart had written a concerto) whose sight he claimed to have restored. Hounded out of Vienna, Mesmer found his way to Paris, arriving there in 1778.

Not endowed with a French medical license, he associated himself with Charles Deslon, a well-known Paris doctor, and proceeded with increasing success to break down the initial skepticism of the populace. His partisans, who included Marie-Antoinette, the Comte d'Artois (the future Charles X), and Lafayette, were as vocal in their praise as his detractors, Lavoisier and most of the medical establishment, were rabid in their denunciation. By 1783 his séances had grown extremely popular. In the center of the room stood a tub (the famous *baquet*), filled with powdered glass, iron filings, symmetrically disposed bottles. Around the *baquet* and connected with it by iron rods sat the patients, arranged in concentric circles and joined to each other by a cord. Walking all around them, Mesmer, a tall, handsome man dressed in lavender silk, carrying an iron wand with which he touched the diseased parts of the patients' bodies. As soon as one of the patients was seized with convulsions, a sign that animal magnetism was at work, he or she would be carried to the mattress-lined "crisis room." Crucial to the whole procedure was the soft background music of wind instruments, piano, or the glass armonica.

When Franklin, accompanied by his musical friend Madame Brillon, paid a visit to Mesmer in 1779 he wanted to discuss his beloved armonica just as fervently as Mesmer wanted to promote his medical views. The resulting conversation was so unsatisfactory that Madame Brillon later exclaimed she hoped that once they were all in heaven "M. Mesmer will content himself with playing the armonica and will not bother us with his electrical fluid!"[13]

Before long, Mesmer came under fire from a number of directions. One of the charges was that when he provoked a trance by placing himself *en rapport* with a subject, knee against knee, foot against foot,

he just put older women to sleep but treated the younger ones to *titilla-
tions délicieuses*. What was whispered about the erotic aspects of the
séances was enough for the king to appoint two independent commissions to investigate the matter. Franklin agreed to serve on one of them,
along with some of the most eminent members of the Academy of Sciences and the Faculty of Medicine.

During the spring and summer of 1784 the commission often met in
Passy because the ailing Franklin was confined at home. Since Mesmer
was a nonperson to the French medical establishment, they cross-
examined his disciple Deslon instead; but this was considered a gross injustice by the orthodox mesmerists, for Deslon had been feuding with
Mesmer for some time. Lafayette sent Franklin an urgent plea to bypass the treacherous Deslon and go straight to the source, Mesmer himself (whose theories, he enticingly suggested, owed much to
Franklin's). But the committee, unmoved, went ahead to the climactic
test: Deslon magnetizing the trees in Franklin's own garden. Benny
Bache was on hand with his diary:

> Mr. Deslon . . . made several passes with his cane close to a tree. After-
> wards a young man blindfolded was introduced, who had been brought by
> Mr. Deslon and whom he had cured in three months of a paralysis which
> had extended over half of his body, by means of Animal Magnetism. He
> was made to embrace several trees. . . . He felt, said he, a giddiness which
> redoubled at each tree. At last, at the fourth, he stood without answering
> and afterwards he fell and they laid him on the grass where he made several
> singular contortions, then suddenly got up.[14]

The test was impressive, but according to the official report the blind-
folded young man had fainted at the wrong, unmesmerized tree.

Benny also met Mesmer's protégée, Mlle. Paradies, the blind and
exquisitely neurotic pianist who had been at the center of the scandal
that had provoked his departure from Vienna. She came to Passy to
perform. The assembly applauded her, but Benny thought her playing
loud and devoid of expression. Blind she certainly was, and Mesmer
had long since given up hope of curing her a second time, especially
since she seemed much more comfortable and gifted in the world of
darkness—and more certain of her court pension.

The commissioners then impersonated Deslon and found that they,
too, could magnetize people while wearing his clothes. They concluded
that magnetic fluid as such did not exist and that the observed
phenomena must be due to physiological causes as yet unknown. Their
report was published in August 1784, with Franklin's signature at the
head. It became an overnight sensation and sold out the first twenty
thousand copies in short order. Now that the sages had spoken, animal

magnetism quickly became a subject for ridicule on the stage and in the press. That was the end of Mesmer's personal ascendancy but not of mesmerism which continued to thrive until the Revolution in the *Sociétés de l'Harmonie* founded throughout France by his followers as a sort of magnetic freemasonry.

Years later, when Temple got around to writing the life of his grandfather, he airily dismissed magnetism as pure humbug, Deslon and Mesmer as charlatans making their fame and fortune from human gullibility. But that was not the way he had seen it at the time. He was known among his friends as a *"mesmériste"* and had in fact paid 100 louis to become a full-fledged member of the Paris *Société de l'Harmonie,* as Lafayette pointedly reminded Franklin. A note from Mesmer, dated April 1785, invited him to a meeting to discuss the society's bylaws. He may have enjoyed the suggestive ambiance of the reunions at the Hôtel de Coigny as much as the chance to tease his grandfather.

Temple left for England just at the time the report was due. In his first letter he could not resist poking a little—well justified—fun at traditional medicine. Talking about the poor health of a friend, he commented, "Tho' I have not much faith in *Magnétisme,* I have more than in bleeding him as they do."[15] And after he had been miserably sick himself during the Channel crossing, he bravely suggested that it might prove a *"crise salutaire,* as Mesmer styles it."[16] His grandfather, in turn, did not fail to send him a copy of the report, along with the observation that there were people who feared this fresh triumph of reason might weaken faith in some of the miracles of the New Testament. But Franklin saw little danger of that, in fact little chance that the report would even damage mesmerism itself: "There is a wonderful deal of Credulity in the World and Deceptions as absurd have supported themselves for Ages."[17] Temple's friends kept him jokingly abreast of Mesmer's declining fortunes and his cousin Jonathan Williams even passed on a sarcastic poem Franklin had just received.*

Temple had long been champing at the bit to visit England. He had once written a former neighbor in Craven Street how much he longed to see old friends and "embrace my Father," adding, "He cannot regret

---

* Le magnétisme est aux abois,
  La Faculté, l'académie,
  L'ont condamné tous d'une voix,
  et l'ont couvert d'ignominie.

  Après ce Judgment bien Sage et bien légal,
  Si quelque Esprit original
  Persiste encore dans son délire,
  Il sera permis de lui dire,

  Crois au magnétisme—Animal![18]

more than I do our long Separation and the interruption of our Correspondence."[19] Undoubtedly it was Franklin who held him back until the trip could be made with no great political risk.

His journey got off to an unauspicious start: The rented carriage barely held together as far as Calais, then contrary winds delayed the passage. Temple had no sooner recovered from his seasickness and "renewed his acquaintance with beefsteaks and potatoes"[20] than he came down with a violent fever and ague. He dragged himself on to London where he was soon nursed back to health by his father and his father's attentive landlady (probably the Mrs. D'Evelin who four years later became William's wife). He asked for an extension of his leave to make up for time lost, and Franklin, in an expansive mood, agreed that he might accompany William to the seaside and need not return to Paris until mid-October; he even sent love to his son.

But three weeks later the philosopher sounded as querulous and sorry for himself as any parent who feels forgotten: "I have not received a Line from you . . . now near a Month. I have waited with impatience the Arrival of every Post. But not a Word. All your Acquaintances are continually enquiring what News from you. I have none. Judge what I must feel, what they must think, and tell me what I am to think of such Neglect."[21]* Jonathan Williams tried to cheer him up but without success. He had not been separated from Temple since they had come to France. Finding himself once again his son's rival for the young man's affection, he was in a panic at the thought of losing him.

Temple was having a splendid time indeed. All of Franklin's English friends lionized him and wrote glowingly about him, praising his polished manners, his quick mind and intelligence. The English publisher Benjamin Vaughan drew on Temple's firsthand knowledge of mesmerism for help with a translation of the commission's report, and pressed him on Shelburne's behalf to come down to his lordship's country seat in Wiltshire. Ladies begged his presence at tea, the lord mayor invited him to a formal reception at Guildhall. He dined with members of the Royal Society and with one of the philosophical clubs at the George and Vulture. At William's insistence he had his portrait painted by Gilbert Stuart. It was quite a turn of fortune for the unknown boy who had left England less than ten years earlier not even graced with the Franklin name. Now he came armed with introductions not only to his grandfather's "ingenious acquaintance" but also with a list of the best tailors, bootmakers, and hatters, all provided by his foppish friend Henry Grand, son of the Paris banker for the United States; a note was

---

* Temple had not been remiss about writing; his letters had merely been slow in coming.

thoughtfully appended to this directory, "And when lewd, go to the following safe Girls who I think are very handsome."[22]

There is no telling how far Temple progressed in the delicate task of mediation between his father and his grandfather nor in the less arduous one of re-establishing complete harmony between Franklin and his old friend William Strahan. As long as the war continued, relations with Strahan had been cool, indeed frigid on Franklin's part, but neither was quite ready to bury the long comradeship. Though he had had the best tutor there was, Strahan, the king's printer and a member of Parliament, had never understood the American position. So obsessed was he with the glories of the British constitution and the blood ties of the Anglo-American family that he found it incomprehensible that the colonists should ever want to sever those ties. Franklin, on his side, took every criticism of America, every slur on the character of its people as a personal affront. Almost ten years after the fact he still bristled at Strahan's readiness to believe all the silly stories told early in the war about American cowardice and lack of purpose. And he probably resented Strahan's loyalty to William.

The conflict within Franklin between personal fondness and political exasperation is revealed by the way he ended successive drafts of a single letter to Strahan, going from a harsh "your formerly affectionate Friend" in his first to an ambiguous "your long affectionate humble Servant"[23] in the version he finally sent. With the return of peace he went back to warmer greetings, even the assurance of "unchangeable Esteem." Whenever the tension between them became too great (for they still disagreed on most major issues) he would lapse into printer's jargon, a way of stressing their common bond while turning the debate into some kind of joke: "I remember your observing once to me, as we sat together in the House of Commons, that no two journeymen printers within your knowledge had met with such success in the world as ourselves. . . . But we have risen by different modes. I as a Republican printer, always liked a form well *planed down,* being averse to those *overbearing* letters that hold their heads so *high* as to hinder their neighbours from appearing. You, as a monarchist, chose to work upon *crown* paper, and found it profitable; while I worked upon *pro patria* (often indeed called *foolscap*) with no less advantage."[24]

In answer to Strahan's urgent and repeated entreaties that he establish himself in England where he would find devoted friends, the best doctors in the world, and all possible comforts and amusements, Franklin (who gave the idea some thought before rejecting it) sent a message via Temple inviting Strahan to visit him in Passy. But Strahan, desperate as he was to have one more talk with his friend—one talk that would dispel all their misunderstandings—was no longer able to take such a trip, even in Temple's company. Wistfully he commented on Franklin's vigor of mind and body "which enables you to write as clearly, distinctly, sensibly and accurately as you did almost half a century ago."[25] As for himself, though a few years younger, he could hardly see anymore, he could hardly write.

Temple had also been commissioned to bring back Polly Hewson. She admitted that "to have such a young man ready to run off with me, and yet to stay behind, argues great virtue or great stupidity," but yet she wavered. She wrote Franklin of her delight in seeing "our old Friend Temple changed into young Franklin. . . . I believe you may have been handsomer than your Grandson is," she teased, "but then you never were so genteel; and if he has a little less philosophy he has more polish." She could not resist twitting Franklin about his earlier deception which had not fooled them at all: "We see strong resemblance of you, and indeed saw it when we did not think ourselves at liberty to say we did, as we pretended to be as ignorant as you supposed we were, or chose that we should be."[26]

Was it simply inertia that held her back or was Polly fearful that the old intimacy could not be recaptured in the alien world of Passy? Finally her spirits rallied, she gathered up her children, and announced to Temple, who had been secretly delighted with the delay her vacillations had caused, that she would come.

On December 2, 1784, they all arrived in Passy.

XXI

Indian Summer

May I govern my passions with an absolute sway,
Grow wiser and better as my strength wears away,
Without gout or stone, by a gentle decay.
But what signifies our wishing? Things happen, after all, as they will happen. I
have sung that wishing song a thousand times when I was young, and now find,
at fourscore, that the three contraries have befallen me, being subject to the gout
and the stone, and not being yet master of all my passions.
—Franklin to George Whatley, May 23, 1785

THE GIRL THAT FRANKLIN had first met when she was eighteen was
now a matron of forty-five, widowed for more than a decade after four
brief but happy years of marriage. His confident assertion that she
would come into "easy Circumstances"[1] thanks to her wealthy aunt's
death had proved premature. Polly saw not a penny of the inheritance
for a long time, as litigation, claims, and counterclaims dragged on.
Mrs. Stevenson's finances fared no better. Mother and daughter had to
leave the cosmopolitan atmosphere and comfort of Craven Street, then
quit London altogether for the quiet village of Cheam, near Epsom,
where they could live frugally, with little diversion besides Polly's three
children. She suckled her youngest for a whole year and devoted herself completely to their education, often wishing that Franklin's
phonetic alphabet had been adopted. Of all this he highly approved:
"Your Delight and Duty go together by employing your Time in the
Education of your offspring. This is following Nature and Reason instead of Fashion."[2]

It was also following Rousseau. Ever since his *Emile,* children were
no longer unfashionable in Western Europe. Pedagogy was the rage
and Franklin sent to Polly—though not to Sally—the latest literature on
the subject, including Mme. de Genlis's *Adèle et Théodore,* the most
popular work on both sides of the Channel in the early 1780s. Using
the epistolary form so dear to the age, the author had her hero and her-
oine retire from the artificial life of Paris to a remote corner of Lan-

guedoc and devote themselves entirely to the upbringing of their two children in conformity with the dictates of nature, simplicity, and good sense. The family in question, baronial in rank of course, turned their whole castle into a schoolroom. It was not quite Cheam, and Polly, while generally agreeing with the book, detected in it "sophistry . . . particularly with regard to suckling and stays":[3] Mme. de Genlis countenanced both wet nurses and the barbarous custom of incarcerating little girls in stays and stiff collars to make them stand up straight. Young Eliza Hewson wondered aloud to her mother at the inconsistency of mankind: How could her grandmama endorse stays when Franklin, "her best friend, the one she thinks most of, says you do right to keep me without?"[4]

The exasperating tangle of her affairs, her mother's precarious health, "these dreadful hostilities," conspired at times to dampen Polly's usually bright spirits. She had unhesitatingly supported the American cause but eventually came to feel that she could not rejoice at the success of either America or England "for all the evil that the war produces."[5] Her mother saw the war in more personal terms. "Many say you blew up all this mischief," she blurted to Franklin. The worst of the mischief, to her, was that it kept them apart. She was unhappy at Cheam; not that the place was too quiet—"the children are noise enough"[6]—but it was so dull, and when not dull, dangerous. She almost lost her life trying to keep the cow out of the cabbage patch. Born and bred a city woman, Mrs. Stevenson became so depressed that Polly had to take her back to live in Kensington, sadly leaving her boys in the famous boarding school at Cheam.

War or no war, bad leg, dropsy, or whatever else might ail her, Mrs. Stevenson was determined to go to France. Franklin was more than willing to reconstruct the Craven Street ménage on Gallic soil: "Do you think your good Mother is still able to go thro' the Trouble of being as formerly my Oeconome?" he asked Polly. True, she spoke no French, "but that Want, if we made one Family, you could supply."[7]* To Mrs. Stevenson he spoke of their "long continu'd Friendship" and how happy he would be "to experience again your faithful tender Care and Attention to my Interests, Health and Comfortable Living, which so long and steadily attach'd one to you."[8] The good lady might have preferred a more conjugal title to that of "oeconome," but she did not let it diminish her enthusiasm. It was Polly who held back. At first she worried about her shaky financial situation; then, when her inheritance was settled and she was assured of a "competent income,"[9] she pleaded

* Polly had a good reading knowledge of French. She had translated a philosophical tract by one of Franklin's friends, Dr. Jacques Barbeu-Dubourg.

her obligations to her children and the sheer difficulty of the journey in wartime.

Well, then, Mrs. Stevenson would come with somebody else; friends were frequently crossing the Channel. "Don't be surprised if I pack myself up . . . and pipe upon you."[10] But something always happened to frustrate this dearest scheme of her life, and on January 13, 1783, Polly wrote Franklin, "I know you will pay the tribute of a sigh for the loss of one who loved you with the most ardent affection."[11] Her mother had died on New Year's Day after weeks of painful illness. On the bottom of the last letter he had received from Mrs. Stevenson, sent the preceding July when she had high hopes of coming to Paris, Franklin penned her simple epitaph: "This good Woman my dear Friend died the first of January following. She was about my Age."[12] He reflected somberly that the previous year had carried away many of his closest friends in England: "this has begun to take away the rest and strikes the hardest. Thus the ties I had to that country and indeed to the World in general are loosen'd one by one and I shall soon have no Attachment left to make me unwilling to follow."[13]

But with the return of spring and the advent of peace he had cheered up again and redoubled his reminders to Polly of that quarter-century during which their friendship had been "all clear Sunshine without the least Cloud in its Hemisphere."[14] Comparing himself to a building in need of "so many Repairs that in a little time the Owner will find it cheaper to pull it down and build a new one,"[15] he had urged once more that she come.

And now she was there. Almost ten years had elapsed since they had last seen one another. The embattled, vigorous man of the London years was quite old now, a few days away from his seventy-ninth birthday, and laid low with an attack of the stone. He wanted to go home, agreeing with Jane that he had "done enough for the Public" and that it was time "to sit down and spend the evening with friends."[16] But Congress was not yet ready to release him: A series of commercial treaties with the various European nations had still to be negotiated, and he had accepted to do this, along with Jefferson and Adams, working at a slower pace, enjoying his first interlude of serenity in twenty years, savoring reunions with friends from the past now pouring into Paris.

Whatever shock Polly may have felt at the change in her friend has remained unrecorded, but in her first report from France, even though she insisted that the Doctor's conversation was as "amusing and instructive" as ever, she sounded disheartened, even disgruntled. Asked by her sister-in-law whether she was "frenchified," she replied indignantly, "Indeed I am not." She could see, of course, that all the French ladies wore rouge but she did not feel "horribly pale" without it and, with splendid insularity, refused to change her style. What did it matter, anyway? Except for one evening at the *Comédie*, she had not gone into public company. Temple was monopolizing the Doctor's carriage and in French eyes a lady of her rank was not supposed to send for a hackney coach as she would have done in London. Unwilling to trouble Franklin, she limited her outings to walks to the village of Passy where her boys were in boarding school.

The truth of the matter was that Polly, after her initial enthusiasm, felt a growing aversion toward Temple, a young man who did not improve upon near acquaintance, as she put it. While conceding that he was rather intelligent and not bad-tempered, she noted with asperity, "He has such a love of dress and is so absorbed in self-importance and so engaged in the pursuit of pleasure that he is not an amiable nor a respectable character; he is just fit to be employed in a court and to be the galant of the French ladies, nothing else."

Benny, on the contrary, met with her wholehearted approval. Without reviving the old fantasy of calling him the fiancé of her little Eliza, she stressed the extraordinary physical resemblance between the two youngsters. Temple, she thought, had inherited Franklin's looks but Benny had his grandfather's mind. "He is sensible and manly in his manner without the slightest tincture of the coxcomb." And the straitlaced visitor remarked that although Benny was already of an age when "the youths of Paris are initiated into all the foppery, the gaiety and the licentiousness of the place," he still wore his hair just as English boys did and had retained, with the simplicity of his dress, "a lovely simplicity of character."[17]

Franklin himself was seeing to it that Benny's character be formed in a down-to-earth, realistic way. His disenchantment with the ups and downs of political life, his fears for Temple's future led him to feel that this grandson at least should be equipped with some sound craft. He naturally thought of his own fondly remembered trade. Benny, he decided, would become not only a skilled printer but a good typecaster. He had installed a private press on his premises several years earlier for the purpose of printing passports and other official American documents, and he now added a foundry and procured the services of a master founder. Benny threw himself into his apprenticeship with great zeal, working, said Polly, from dawn till seven in the evening. So anxious was he to do well that on one occasion he woke up in the middle of the night and thinking the time had come, proceeded to light the furnace in order to melt the metal and cast types. Another sign of stress in Benny's diary is his mention of sleepwalking. He must have been terrified at the thought of being sent away to school again: Shortly after his return from Geneva, Franklin had spoken of having him join the Hewson boys at Cheam but Benny had been so upset and Temple had pleaded his cause so eloquently that he had been kept at home.

Even though he must have felt some curiosity about young William Hewson, the godson who had always been his rival in his grandfather's affection, Benny made only a terse entry on the long-awaited arrival of the English guests: Willy, he wrote, was about thirteen and a half, Tom was eleven (though "from his height one would say he was six, by his mind fifteen"). And Eliza?—"The last is a girl of ten years."[18] His only comment was that all three appeared good-natured.

Life could be interesting without leaving Passy. At a time when America was "the hope of the human race," Franklin was the most famous, the most popular American in Europe, and Europe beat a path to the Hôtel de Valentinois. Lafayette paid one of his many calls that winter, bringing fresh news from the Baches in Philadelphia. Jefferson, who had settled in Paris the previous summer with his twelve-year-old daughter, was a frequent visitor. His wife had died two years earlier; now he and Franklin revived the warm affection that had sprung up between them at the Continental Congress. John Adams often stopped by, more on business than pleasure. Royalty came: Feeling improperly dressed for the occasion, Benny tried hard to avoid being introduced to Prince Henry, brother of Prussia's Frederic the Great, but the prince sought him out and Benny was disappointed to find him "ugly, very short," and wearing "but one pin to fasten his shirt frill."[19]

The Chevalier d'Eon, that celebrated transvestite and secret agent, was residing in Paris in the early months of 1785 and called to pay Franklin his respects—or rather *her* respects for he was under court orders at the time to wear only women's clothes and to refer to himself as "la Chevalière." Brothers from the Lodge of the Nine Sisters (the lodge of Voltaire and Helvétius) came to discuss masonic affairs and whatever new idea was in the air. Neighbors dropped in to chat and make music: Madame Brillon—to whom Boccherini dedicated some pieces—played the piano well enough to win Charles Burney's praise. The physicist Jean-Baptiste Le Roy came to play chess, the chemist Lavoisier to discuss how best to protect the Paris Arsenal from lightning, the liberal economist Abbé Morellet to sing drinking songs of his and Franklin's composition (either Temple or Benny illustrated a piece written by their grandfather in honor of the perfect location Providence had given the human elbow, neither too near the hand nor too near the shoulder, but perfectly placed to carry wine to mortal lips).

Some of the friends of the early years had already died: The bumbling physician Barbeu-Dubourg, Franklin's first French champion and translator of his scientific work. Turgot, fallen from power because of his enlightened views on commerce and taxation. But new names, new faces were clamoring for one minute of the Doctor's time, one brief answer to their queries. They were the names that the French Revolution would make forever famous. Guillotin who sat with Franklin on the Mesmer commission. Robespierre who wanted information on the lightning rod. Marat who desired Franklin's support of his views on air and fire. Mirabeau who requested his opinion on the Society of the Cincinnati. A roster of others, all eager for communication with the man they considered their spiritual father.

One of the most glamorous visitors during Polly's stay was Dr. John Jeffries who came to dinner on January 15, 1785, exactly one week after making history's first crossing of the Channel by balloon. He hand-delivered to Temple a letter from William, part of the very first batch of international airmail—and the only document from that batch to have survived until today. England had finally joined what was being hailed as the new age of space exploration, an age Franklin had applauded ever since its beginning, eighteen months previously. As a stupendous succession of feats captured the imagination of France and Europe, his privileged grandsons had been given front seats at every performance and a sense of personal involvement with the participants.

Benny had returned from Geneva just in time. True, he had missed the very first launching by the Montgolfier brothers in the sky of Lyons, but he was on hand to watch the second, by Jacques Charles, at the Champ de Mars in Paris, on August 27, 1783. A friend and admirer of the inventor, Franklin was there too, in the downpour, cheering as the balloon took off, wet and shiny, on an adventure that had a surprise conclusion forty-five minutes later when the terror-stricken inhabitants of a small village destroyed the fallen monster with their pitchforks. Within weeks it would be the turn of the Montgolfiers again, whose new balloon ascended from the Faubourg Saint-Antoine in the presence of the royal family and carried to the upper regions a sheep, a duck, and a rooster.

After the animals, the humans. In late November two aeronauts, wearing frock coats and duly equipped with champagne, were launched from the Château de la Muette in that heady eighteenth-century style, a mixture of daring, nonchalance, and splendor. As they hovered above the Seine, they noticed that the water gave off an echo and regretted not having brought along their flutes. The following evening, one of the heroes of the day paid a call on Franklin, along with

Joseph Montgolfier, and Benny watched his grandfather sign the official report of the ascension.

The climax came ten days later, December 1, with Charles as the principal actor. Riding in a chariot-shaped gondola suspended from the most sophisticated balloon yet devised—it had been financed by private subscription, with Franklin among the contributors—Charles and a companion took off from the Tuileries and demonstrated that henceforth the aeronauts would be able to some extent to regulate their flight. They landed late in the afternoon, still thirsty for action, and Charles took off once more by himself, the first man ever to witness two sunsets on the same day, an experience, as he related it, of mystical happiness.

Little else was discussed around the dinner tables of France during that fall and winter of 1783–84. The technical aspects of the rival experiments were hotly debated. What was the best shape for a balloon? Which had more lifting power, the "rarefied air" produced by the Montgolfiers through the burning of straw and wool, or the "inflammable air" (hydrogen) that Charles obtained by pouring oil of vitriol over iron filings?* Who was the real father of the balloon, Montgolfier or Charles? (Montgolfier could be called the father, Franklin suggested, and Charles the wet nurse.) The moral implications of the new accomplishment were pondered: Was mankind ready for such a momentous discovery? Would it be put to peaceful use or inflict death and destruction? There were those who dwelt on the poetic aspects of the venture and those who were thrilled by its endless line of frivolous by-products: hairdos, snuffboxes, tableware, fans, gloves, hats, clocks, jewels, walking sticks, swords, birdcages, wallpaper, a new liquor, and a new dance. Everybody who could afford them bought little hydrogen-filled contraptions in the shape of nymphs, animals, and mythological beasts. "Come for tea and balloons" became a fashionable invitation. Temple and Benny launched their own small one: It cleared the roof but fell on the other side of the house, "having several little holes in it."[21]

Science in Paris was as gregarious and joyful as it had been in Philadelphia during the early days of electricity. "A few Months ago, the Idea of Witches riding thro' the Air upon a Broomstick, and that of Philosophers upon a Bag of Smoke would have appear'd equally impossible and ridiculous,"[22] Franklin joked. To an American lady (who promptly forwarded his words to his mother), Benny confided that "he

* A third proposal for high quality, inexpensive, and plentiful hot air was sent to the *Journal de Paris* by an anonymous "lady correspondent" (Franklin in a playful mood): "the promises of lovers and of courtiers, . . . the sighs of widowers, . . . the good resolutions taken during a storm at sea or on land [or] during an illness, and especially the praises to be found in letters of recommendation."[20]

found his Grand Papa very different from other Old Persons, for they were fretting and complaining, and dissatisfy'd, and my Grand Papa is laughing, and chearful, like a young Person."[23] The Grandpapa could not resist twitting the English over the French headstart, "Your Philosophy seems to be too bashful,"[24] he chided Sir Joseph Banks, president of the Royal Society. The English attitude, shared by some skeptics in France, that balloons were an amusing but useless and expensive toy, provoked his famous retort, "What is the use of a new-born baby?" The bon mot quickly made the rounds of Paris.

There were bound to be setbacks, of course, just as there had been with electricity. Benny, who had become a balloon aficionado, tells how the subscribers to the largest airship yet devised gathered in the gardens of the Luxembourg Palace, with the king of Sweden among the spectators, only to see it catch fire one hour before take-off: "The people were furious and threw themselves upon the Balloon and tore it to pieces, each one carrying off a sample, some large enough to make a mattress. And I believe that the authors would have been subjected to the same fate if they had not been escorted by a detachment of French Guards. They have not yet rendered any account to the public of the money expended."[25]

All this was educational as well as fun. Benny attended lectures on "natural philosophy" given by Charles. He kept track of flights outside the Parisian region and wrote down the measurements of the most important airships. He learned to set up a telescope on the roof and stay on the lookout so that his grandfather could play chess indoors until the last moment. He became interested in the problems of air and combustion and was full of admiration for the experiments Temple performed in his *cabinet philosophique:* "The other day he killed a mouse with an air that is called fix'd air; and after everybody saw it stretched out, he brought it to life again by means of some stuff in a bottle. After it had run about for some time, he killed it again with an electric spark. I am sure he would pass for a conjurer in America!"[26] On the practical side, Benny foresaw the day when he could fly back to his family by balloon but fondly added he was unwilling to wait that long.

Each new balloon venture reserved a surprise. When he came to dinner, for instance, Boston-born Dr. Jeffries related how close he and his colleague had come to falling into the sea a few miles short of Calais on their crossing from Dover. In a frantic effort to regain height lost through escaping air, they had jettisoned first the printed cloth and garlands which ornamented their car, then their food, brandy, books, finally their coats and pants. Clad in no more than their shirts, they had awaited rescue twenty-eight minutes in the top of a tree—all details reverently noted down by Benny, while Polly wrote home rather disapprovingly that the aeronauts had been more fortunate than prudent. Jeffries may have lost all but his shirt but he kept his ardor. His thank-you note to Temple for all "civilities" shown him during his stay in Paris expresses his frustration at not having been able to communicate properly, for lack of French, with the charming Madame C. and the equally charming Mademoiselle de V. but ends on the gloating evocation of a long evening spent at Lucienne's, "where the smiles of good humour of the lovely priestess of that hallowed place banished any restraint."[27] As a cicerone of Paris-by-night, Temple had no peer.

For Polly, when winter lost its grip, the more respectable sights of Paris by day. The first volumes of Sébastien Mercier's famous *Tableau de Paris* had just come out, and now she could see for herself the splendid *hôtels* of the Marais and the aristocratic Faubourg St. Germain rising almost cheek by jowl beside the chaotic, crumbling slums of the Cité and St. Michel; the fine new boulevards of the northern fringe contrasting with the cramped and crooked streets of the center. The "eternal smoke rising from innumerable chimneys"[28] blackened the once gleaming white limestone of the houses, but Paris was less industrialized and altogether less polluted than London. Right in the middle of the huge agglomeration whose more than 700,000 inhabitants filled the enlarged space then being enclosed within the new fortifications, the Seine flowed graciously, a vital thoroughfare pumping in food and firewood.

The Seine which, said Mercier, was supposed to spring from the flanks of an angel, was Benny's closest friend in Paris, his constant companion. His diary is a hymn to the river. In winter he skated on it by the hour, in spring he watched it swell and flood, by mid-May he was bathing and recording in his own cool way how many people drowned in a certain hole—twelve in the course of six weeks, including a child Benny felt sure he could have saved if he had been on the spot a few minutes earlier. In the summer he flew kites of his own devising on its banks, swimming back and forth to retrieve them when they fell, dodging the *galiotte* that plied the river, balancing his bundle of clothes on his head, glorying in his strength and skill as the other Benjamin had gloried in the waters of Boston Bay sixty years previously. As a child enamored of swimming, the other Benjamin had once rigged himself to a kite and been borne swiftly across a wide pond "without the least fatigue and with the greatest pleasure imaginable."[29]

Once Benny had completed his five-month marathon of typecasting, he squired Polly and her children on their jaunts. Franklin did not accompany them, for the jolts of the carriage would have been too excruciating to bear. During Holy Week they joined the throngs making their way to Longchamps, just outside the city in the Bois de Boulogne. No longer the center of devotion which over the years had attracted growing crowds with its fine liturgical music, Longchamps had become the worldly goal of elegant outings: as Benny put it, "a parade of carriages and horses, where some come to exhibit their equipages, some to exhibit themselves, others, among whom I was one, to see."[30]

Upon a visit to the Invalides, that behemoth of a military hospital, Benny marveled as much at the technology of the gigantic cooking pots as at the statuary and paintings. He catalogued conscientiously the saints and angels of a Notre Dame not yet tidied up by Viollet-le-Duc and stood in awe before the graves of the "most illustrious families of France."[31]

The most exciting spectacle Benny recorded in his diary was the illumination celebrating Marie-Antoinette's recovery from her recent confinement. He had seen many fireworks before, but none so grand as this. "Imagine a heavy rain of fire which covered one quarter at least of the Place Louis XV, which is immense."[32] A few years later the Place Louis XV, renamed Place de la Concorde, would be splashed with the blood of this same queen, but for the moment all Paris rejoiced in her maternity.

Of all experiences, the most moving was their visit to the Foundling Hospital. "We entered a room in which were the youngest. Some ugly, others pretty, laughing, crying, dying. From the numbers rescued annually, we calculated it was about 15 daily. They numbered about 15,000. We did not desire to penetrate further." Benny sounds rather detached, as usual, but his grandfather was quite concerned about the problem of unwanted children. The practice of leaving them at the hospital, he noted, had grown from one out of ten early in the century to one out of three in 1770, and perhaps up to one out of every two babies born in Paris at the time of Polly's visit, in 1785. The government, he felt, was taking a step in the right direction by subsidizing mothers to nurse their babies, but it met with great resistance. A surgeon of his acquaintance "excused the Women of Paris by saying seriously that they *could not* give Suck, *car, dit il, ils* [sic] *n'ont point des Tetons*. He assur'd me it was a Fact, and had me look at them, and observe how flat they were in the Breast; they have nothing more there, says he, than I have upon the Back of my Hand. I have since thought that there might be some Truth in his Observation, and that possibly Nature finding they made no use of Bubbies, has left off giving them any." His heart went out to the abandoned babies, nine-tenths of whom died "pretty soon" in the institution and to those other, somewhat luckier ones, sent out to nurse in the country. On a given day of the week, he would observe batches of nurses on the road, "returning to the neighbouring Village with each a Child in Arms."[33]

All this was discussed in the evening with Polly, over a cup of tea and a game of cribbage. Wracked by pain though he was, he would remember that winter as the shortest he ever passed, he told her after she had gone back to England in the spring. For a fragile moment, his various "families" were almost in perfect poise, drawing closer in a network of good will of which he was the center. His French women friends selected the dolls and mittens that would delight his little granddaughters in Philadelphia. Jane Mecom sent from Boston the cases of crown soap he was proud to distribute among his Parisian acquaintances. Polly was by his side, catering to him, meeting his French circle—"une bien digne dame," they said. Had Temple but married the daughter of his special friend, Madame Brillon, his bliss would have been complete.

Nobody had been closer to him in the first years of his Parisian stay than Madame Brillon, his neighbor in one of the lovely Passy villas. She had been the one to dub him "mon cher papa," a term of endearment soon adopted by most of his good friends including the men. She had wooed him with Scottish music, innumerable cups of tea, games of chess, outpourings of the soul. When he pressed her for more tangible evidence of her devotion, she had played coy and managed to stabilize the relationship on a level delicately balanced between the erotic and the familial, with her husband and two daughters more in evidence than they had previously been. By the time Temple turned twenty-one, Franklin felt that his grandson, "who has no vices," would make a good husband to the amiable Cunégonde. To parry the objection that the Brillons would suffer when their daughter went off to America or that Temple would suffer if he stayed behind when his grandfather departed for home, Franklin pledged to remain in France till the end of his days, should the happy event take place. He would also see to it that Temple be given some diplomatic post: "He is still young and perhaps paternal bias leads me to form too flattering an opinion of him, but it seems to me that he has what it takes to become, in time, a distinguished man."[34]

The Brillons tactfully declined the offer on the ground that Temple was not a Catholic. Franklin countered that all religions are basically the same except for the wrapping: "The divergencies are only the paper and the string."[35] But it was to no avail. The Brillons now stressed that any prospective son-in-law should be well versed in French custom and law in order to inherit Monsieur Brillon's high administrative post. The discussion went no further. Much as they worshipped Franklin, the Brillons felt about Temple the way Polly would feel some four years later: that he was a playboy and no more.

Did Polly find out that, true to family tradition, Temple had sired an illegitimate son in Paris? The mother in this case is known. She was Blanchette Caillot, wife of the famous actor Joseph Caillot who lived in nearby Saint Germain on an estate given him by the king's brother. Blanchette's passion for Temple, whom she called her "little Excellency," was turbulent, effusively expressed and lasted much longer than his for her.

As long as Temple lived in France the child was never mentioned, at least not in any surviving letter, and his existence must have been a well-kept secret. But the young man's blatant love affairs were much discussed and the John Adamses looked upon him as the perfect example of what they did not want their John Quincy to become. Like father, like son, they muttered. Like grandfather, like father, like son. What else could one expect? Look at the way the old Doctor had taken to these French women. Abigail Adams could not believe her own eyes when she saw on what terms of easy familiarity the man she had been taught to venerate now was with the aging widow, Madame Helvétius. Why, this fading—nay, this faded—beauty dared throw her arm around the Doctor's neck in the course of a dinner party. She dared throw all of herself on a settee and show "more than her feet!" And how did the Doctor react to this vulgar display? He proclaimed that Madame Helvétius was one of the best women in the world. He praised her for being free from affectation, he ate dinner with her once a week. And Abigail concluded, "I own I was highly disgusted."[36] Her language grew stronger still when she referred to Franklin, Deane, Temple, *et alia* as a junto that would soon be known in America as "wicked unprincipled debauched wretches, from the old Deceiver to the young Cockatrice."[37]

Her husband, of course, could have told her so all along. He had never cared for Franklin, not even in the days of their political partnership on the eve of the Declaration of Independence. But now this distaste deepened as his hatred of all things French deepened. He could not disentangle what he saw as Franklin's repulsive servility toward France from what he saw as Franklin's repulsive attachment to women: "The moment an American minister gives a loose to his passion for women, that moment he is undone; he is instantly at the mercy of the spies of the court, and the tool of the most profligate of the human race."[38] The fact that he was dealing with a man well into his seventies did not make him feel that his charges might be sadly unrealistic. On the contrary. Those French women, he sneered, had "an unaccountable passion for old age" whereas his own countrywomen, if he remembered right, "had rather a complaisance for youth."[39]

It never seemed to cross his irate mind that Franklin's immense popularity in France was an asset to their country, that in spite of tremendous odds, this Protestant envoy swayed public opinion in a Catholic nation, this delegate of a republic obtained gifts and loans from an absolute monarchy, this son of a candlemaker was treated with respect in the most snobbish court in the world, that what Adams saw as a life of "continual dissipation" was in truth a life of diplomatic triumph.

Stripped of the moralistic rage Adams and Lee brought to them, turned indeed into charming capers by the winking tolerance of a modern world geared to the sexual, those charges have been endorsed by posterity to the point of becoming part of the national heritage. The myth of an amusingly debauched Franklin, Franklin the roué, Franklin the rogue, kissing, flirting, fondling, dallying, seducing, responds to a need for comic relief, the reassuring notion that here at least was one American completely at ease on the depraved European scene, one old man whose powers remained unimpaired. Such a view, held more by his compatriots than by Europeans, robs Franklin of the essential dignity the French never ceased to grant him,* much to his satisfaction, since "being treated with respect" was extremely important to him. Such a view also deprives him of a rich and complex humanity from which the tragic facets—the defection of his son, the full awareness of advancing age—were never absent. But this has never bothered the authors of musicals and facile plays who may believe they praise him when they are in fact echoing his sharpest critics and diminishing him forever.

Did he really have affairs with French women? There is no shred of evidence. In that age of diaries and memoirs not a single Parisienne ever boasted that she had captured the famous *philosophe*. Never at a loss for an innuendo, Adams and Lee named no names. There are numerous, overt allusions in the Franklin papers to kissing and embracing. Beyond that, nothing. He tried to dispel any notion that he spent his time cavorting and when writing to women back home (Jane, Catharine Greene, his stepniece Elizabeth Partridge), he stressed that

---

* Two generations later, George Sand, forerunner of the liberated woman, revered him as the symbol of her lost innocence: "I should have stuck to Franklin who was my delight until the age of twenty-five and whose picture above my bed always makes me want to cry, as would that of some friend I had betrayed."[40]

his fascination with the women of Paris stemmed from the charm of their presence, not from hope of their favors. "This is the civilest Nation upon Earth. Your first Acquaintances endeavour to find out what you like, and they tell others. If 'tis understood that you like Mutton, dine where you will find Mutton. Somebody, it seems, gave it out that I lov'd Ladies; and then everybody presented me their Ladies (or the Ladies presented themselves)—to be *embrac'd*, that is to have their Necks kiss'd. For as to kissing of Lips or Cheeks it is not the Mode here, the first is reckon'd rude and the other may rub off the Paint. The French Ladies have however 1000 other ways of rendering themselves agreeable, by their various Attentions and Civilities and their sensible Conversation. 'Tis a delightful People to live with."[41]

When two of his most "lov'd" lady friends, first Madame Brillon, then Madame Le Roy (whom he affectionately called "my pocket wife"), came all in tears to tell him of their husbands' infidelities, he did not try to take advantage of their distress but said the soothing words an older person is expected to say to help patch up the marriages. It was an echo of the faraway pattern with Catharine Ray: the excitement of pursuit, the thrill of flirtation, the retreat before the emotions can be in real turmoil.

The texture of his life in Paris, as it emerges from his letters, his journal, his portraits drawn by French contemporaries, is infinitely less glamorous than in legend, but infinitely more human and vulnerable. It shows a man resilient enough to become adept in his seventies at the game of *amitié amoureuse*—so adept indeed that he took his place among the best in the very city where the game has always been played with the greatest skill. It shows a courageous man who fights off with wit the humiliations and terrors of age, writing an amusing dialogue between himself and the gout rather than complaining about his aches and pains, a gregarious man who soon understands that going out in Paris means going to women's salons, not to men's clubs as in London. Above all, it shows a lonely man, anguished at times, struggling to surround himself with warmth. When the Brillons turned down the idea of a marriage between their daughter and Temple, Franklin's *cri du coeur*—"Who will close my eyes if I die in a foreign land?"[42]—was immediately answered by Madame Brillon's: "I will."[43] None of their hundreds of other exchanges matched this one in intensity. Aging along with one's friends, sometimes playing with them at being young, sometimes joking with them about common ailments, making the most of the moment's short-lived mellowness, lingering around the table for one last song, one last discussion, straightening up with difficulty to embrace one another, this was but another stage of a life whose every stage had been joyfully accepted and lived to the full.

Jefferson understood this perfectly: "I remember in France when his friends were taking leave of Dr. Franklin, the ladies smothered him with embraces and on his introducing me to them as his successor, I told him I wished he would transfer these privileges to me, but he answered, 'You are too young a man.' "[44] On the day Jefferson thus wistfully reminisced, at Madison's inaugural ball, he also had become too old to follow the ladies: The ladies were following him. As he had learned, it did not mean a thing.

XXII

From Seine to Schuylkill

Another Paradise was waiting for you in America. Providence could not, without you, make that country free and happy; we respect its designs too much to complain that it has given happiness to others at our expense.
—Abbé de la Roche to Franklin, July 27, 1787

THEY HAD ARRIVED in France on a windswept December day, unheralded, exhausted, forlorn. They left at the height of summer, kissed and hugged by a whole crowd. Until the last minute, Franklin's friends had hoped he would yield to their entreaties and remain among them. At times the pain of leaving had been almost too much: "Many honorable tears were shed on both sides."[1] On that July 12, 1785, Benny recorded, "My grandfather mounted his litter among a great number of people of Passy. A solemn silence reigned around him, only interrupted by sobs." And Jefferson commented that it looked as if Passy had lost its patriarch.

Nine years earlier, making his way up from Brittany, Franklin had had trouble procuring even a miserable chaise. Now he was lent the queen's own litter and Spanish mules; he was presented with a miniature of the king encircled by more than four hundred diamonds. Packed under Benny's supervision, their not so frugal 128 crates of luggage went by barge down the Seine.

Franklin's French friends had wanted him to live out his days in France. Strahan had kept begging him to settle in England. Jane Mecom entertained her private fantasy that he would buy an estate in New England and allow her to stay under his roof away from the world except for a few interesting friends, but he had called it a project of the heart rather than the head. It was too late in life, he said, they would both be dead before that new house was ready. As a solace he gave her an appointment in a rather sober hereafter ("a House more lasting and I hope more agreeable than any this World can afford us"[2]), a far cry from the jolly paradises he was forever tantalizing his Parisian lady friends with, replete with angels, good music, roasted apples, and a convenient absence of husbands.

The one person who might have made him stay in France by marrying him, Madame Helvétius, was overcome with worry and grief after he left. She sent one last message to him on the road: "I picture you in the litter, farther from us at every step, already lost to me and to those who loved you so much and regret you so. I fear you are in pain. . . . If you are, come back, mon cher ami, come back to us!"[3] But there was no turning back. He was determined to spend his last years with Sally and her children. The journey, his first in almost nine years, was soon having its miraculous effect: He was feeling better by the minute.

His friends would have to settle for the souvenirs he had left them, his armchair, his tea table, his magic wand—that hollow cane containing the drops of oil with which he would perform his conjurer's trick of calming turbulent waters. Better still, he had left them the *Bagatelles*, written in French and printed on his own press, some of them pieces of mere whimsy, others meant to provide them with the answers that only an American well attuned to Europe's curiosities and aspirations could give. To those who wondered what kind of people the Indians were (noble savages? ferocious savages?), he pointed out—drawing from his long personal experience—how decent, dignified, and sensitive they could be ("Remarks on the Politeness of the Savages"). To the countless Frenchmen eager to emigrate to America, hoping to find there a new Eden, he stressed that his country was no Eldorado, that Americans worked hard, and that a nation where the first question put to a newcomer was not "Who are you?" but "What can you do?" might prove disappointing to a French aristocrat in search of fortune ("Advice to those who would remove to America").

Franklin's Indian summer was also the Indian summer of the *ancien régime*. The topics that had seemed all-important were on the wane: mesmerism discredited and rent with dissension in its ranks, the balloons out of favor after the crash in June 1785 of the pioneer Pilâtre de Rozier as he was trying to fly from France to England (with favorable winds, he had boasted, it would take him only two days from Calais to Philadelphia!). New ideas, new attitudes were on the horizon. Soon Vergennes would die and with him the pro-American orientation of France's foreign policy. That policy had already brought to the brink of bankruptcy the richest nation in Europe, and bankruptcy was the first step on the path to revolution.

When Franklin bade farewell to his French friends, he knew he would never see them again, but nobody could have guessed that so many of them would die so soon and in so brutal a fashion. Lavoisier

and Bailly, his fellow members on the Mesmer commission, were to end
on the scaffold. So would Condorcet who never tired of querying him
about America's black population and the country's natural wonders.
And Paulze, the farmer-general, who had helped cut through red tape
and expedite the saltpeter Washington's army needed so badly. And his
neighbor in Passy, Le Veillard, who now accompanied him as far as
England and saw to it that his ship was well stocked with the famous
mineral waters of his own company. And the colonies' gentle
propagandist, the Duc de la Rochefoucauld who had translated the constitutions of the thirteen states: He would be stoned to death.

Graciously entertained all along the way, Franklin and his grandsons
pursued their royal progress, reaching Le Havre in a week, well ahead
of those 128 crates coming down the Seine—which eventually missed
the ship and had to be rerouted. As he addressed a last farewell to Madame Helvétius, his "dear Helvetia," a brief moment of sadness and
doubt overtook him: "Je ne suis *sur d'être heureux* in Amerique; mais
il faut que je m'y rende. Il me semble que les choses sont mal arrangées
dans ce bas monde, quand je vois que les êtres si faits pour être heureux
ensemble sont obligés à se séparer."[4]*

The whole expedition loomed terrifying. He had tried in vain to find
a ship that would take him home directly from a French port but none
was to be had before the storms of the equinox. Contingency plans
were made for his return to Paris, should the crossing of the Channel
prove unbearably painful. As it turned out, he was the only member of
his party not to be violently sick during the forty-five hours it took
them to reach Southampton against rough winds; the discovery that the
motions of the sea were easier on his stone than those of a carriage gave
him the courage to face the Atlantic. The Passy neighbor who was
prepared to escort him back to Paris, if necessary, now took his leave;
the litter standing by in Le Havre turned around and left.

In the course of four bittersweet days in Southampton, Franklin
plunged back into his past, pain and pleasure mixing intensely. Pain
because Strahan did not make it to their rendezvous: He had died two
weeks too soon. Disappointment because Polly Hewson and her children were not there to make the crossing with him in the spacious
cabin he had engaged; they would join him later, she promised. (He
could have chartered the whole boat to accommodate the French appli-
cants, male and female, asking to be taken along, but he had discouraged them.) Pleasure in embracing the several friends who rushed over

* "I am not sure to find happiness in America, but I must go back. It seems
that things are poorly arranged in this world when I see that people so obviously
meant to be happy together are forced to separate."

at the news of his arrival, foremost among them the Bishop of St. Asaph, Jonathan Shipley, at whose country house not many miles away he had begun his *Autobiography*. Shipley's loyalty had never faltered: his uncompromising support of the American cause may have cost him the archbishopric of Canterbury. Kitty was there, too, his old fellow traveler as she styled herself, remembering the happy hours spent in the carriage when he had escorted her back to school. There was hardly time to talk in the bustle of visitors, but she managed to snip a lock of his hair and extract a promise that he would put his crossing to good use by writing another installment of the story of his life.

More pain than pleasure in seeing William again. The reunion with his son is dealt with tersely, even by the laconic standards of his journal: "Met my son who had arrived from London the evening before."[5] No hint of his feelings, of how William looked, of the temperature of their greeting. Benny's diary is just as unrevealing. Even Temple, describing many years later what must have been a momentous occasion in his life, could offer no more than that Franklin "had the satisfaction of seeing his son, the former Governor of New Jersey."[6]

What had happened to the promised reconciliation? No one has yet offered an explanation. Whether destroyed or lost, not a single letter between father and son has survived for the seven months after Temple's return from England, but communication of some sort there must have been. On May 19, 1785, for instance, a deed was executed transferring William's property on the Upper Susquehanna to Temple, for the sum of £1,500, paid by Franklin.

Some hitherto overlooked documents give a possible clue. They concern the Williamos affair. Charles Williamos (originally Vullyamoz) was a Swiss soldier of fortune who had served in the British army and administration in America for a quarter of a century before the Revolution. A quick-witted man with a gift for languages and engaging manners, he soon gathered a remarkable store of information about North America (in particular about the Indians) and laid claim to vast tracts of land. Back in England on half-pay in 1772, he hedged his bets during the war but maintained close ties with American loyalists, among them the ferocious New York tory, John Wetherhead.

With the coming of peace, Williamos lost no time in switching sides. In Paris by late 1783, he finessed a passport from Franklin and took off for America. He was soon back in France, armed with glowing letters of recommendation to both Jefferson and Franklin from General Horatio Gates, the hero of Saratoga. So taken was Jefferson with Williamos that he made him his confidant and Abigail Adams, favorably impressed, noted that they were constant dinner companions. He seems also to have been on easy terms with Franklin.

But the smooth and insinuating adventurer had made the mistake, six years earlier, of sending his friend Wetherhead a letter in which he not only acknowledged a debt of £220 but openly expressed pro-British sentiments. By February 1785, the debt had still not been paid. Wetherhead, now one of the impoverished band of refugees in England, turned to William Franklin for help. Their scheme was to have Temple call on Williamos and threaten to disclose his duplicity to the Doctor unless the bill was promptly paid—in which case Franklin was to be kept in the dark about the whole transaction. Temple was furnished with the letters that had passed between Wetherhead and Williamos but instructed to send them back if he was successful. What followed is a mystery: Temple did not return the dossier, neither does he seem to have communicated its contents immediately to his grandfather since cordial relations were maintained with Williamos through the spring of 1785.

The bubble burst in late June, shortly before Franklin's departure. A secret report to the French government described Williamos as a possible double agent and expressed concern about his intimacy with the American commissioners. A few days later, Jefferson sent Williamos one of the angriest letters he ever wrote, ostensibly about a tailor's bill, but accusing him in substance of passing himself off as an official of the United States when he was not even a citizen. How much did Franklin know about all this? There is no direct evidence, but a cringing letter from Williamos about procuring him a ship home indicates the relationship had suddenly cooled. The most likely guess is that Franklin had found out the whole story and deeply resented his son's involving Temple behind his back in loyalist affairs and with unsavory characters. The failure of their promised reconciliation would then become more understandable.*

Still, there was important business to transact with William during the brief stopover in Southampton, and Franklin made sure that all the legal niceties were attended to before they weighed anchor. Protected by the Franklin name, William's land in New Jersey had not been confiscated. Franklin was willing to buy all of it, partly for cash, partly in return for canceling some of William's debts. The farm on Rancocas Creek, New Jersey, would be just the thing for Temple, the grandfather thought. He drove a hard bargain, offering a price far below the

---

* Williamos died destitute in Paris the following November, many of his possessions in the pawnshop. During his last illness he was subsidized anonymously by Jefferson.[7]

current value of the properties: William, ever in need of cash and knowing he had no choice, acquiesced. At the end of those four days, he no longer had clear title to a square foot of American soil. On the other hand, he was empowered to recover what he could of the money still owed to his father by the British government and to look into the Nova Scotia claims made many years earlier. Small compensation, and there were strings attached: Whatever William recuperated should be split equally with Sally.

It was all very businesslike and final. Writing to his sister four days later, William could not bring himself to talk about the meeting; instead he chatted inconsequentially about her children and the troubles he was having in sending her his portrait. Only at the close did he let a note of poignancy creep in. Picturing the happy reunion that awaited the returning travelers, he sighed, "My fate has thrown me on a different side of the globe."[8] Never again would Franklin and William write to each other. Rarely would Franklin mention his son and then only with unforgiving coldness.

Exhausted by so many farewells, somberly aware that he would never set foot in Europe again, the guest of honor slipped away in the midst of the gala party on shipboard the night before sailing and went to sleep. When he awoke the following morning, the English friends had quietly vanished and the *London Packet* was on her way to America.

While she sailed pleasantly on, rumors were flying around London and Paris: Franklin had died at sea . . . Franklin had been captured by Barbary pirates and sold into slavery . . . he was submitting to his fate with philosophic fortitude but Temple had to be warned that Muslim husbands were not as accommodating as the French. . . . Actually the travelers were busily engaged each in his own pursuit.

The sculptor Jean-Antoine Houdon, on his way to America to carve the statue of Washington that now stands in Richmond, was coping as best he could with the loss of his luggage.* Benny was drawing dolphins, observing their change of color in and out of the water. And Temple? He kept a brief, desultory journal. What lay ahead for him? There was no more hope of ever seeing his father and his grandfather reconciled, only the knowledge that if he pleased one he was bound to displease the other. He had no family to come home to, no circle of friends, no roots, only his memories of London and Paris, some longing for Blanchette and little Theophile, some nebulous plans for going

---

* His tools and clay were part of the 128 cases, bales, boxes, hampers, casks, and baskets that missed the Southampton connection by one day and did not reach America until after he had gone home.

back to Europe—if his grandfather succeeded in obtaining a ministerial post for him. Indeed his rakish friend Henry Grand was convinced that this was Franklin's sole reason for undertaking the voyage, and Bishop Shipley confidently expected to hear that Temple had been appointed minister to Denmark.

Franklin, in one of his most concentrated bouts of writing, composed three scientific pieces in the course of the crossing: on smoky chimneys, on the burning of pit coal, and on navigation. Jonathan Williams, who had come on board at Southampton, supplied him with daily readings of wind direction, air and water temperature, latitude and longitude. These not only found their way into Franklin's *Maritime Observations* but formed the germ of Williams's own scientific treatise, *Thermometrical Navigation,* presented to the American Philosophical Society in 1790 and published a few years later.

Jonathan was, of all Franklin's family, the one who most resembled him in interests and character, a resemblance that did not escape the observant Jefferson. Failure had dogged Jonathan, however, as much as success had smiled on Franklin. His efforts to collect long-overdue debts up and down the British Isles had not yielded enough to satisfy his French creditors. Now he was returning to America in search of the solvency that had eluded him in France, temporarily leaving behind his wife and two daughters but bringing with him his eight-year-old illegitimate son Josiah (fondly called after the blind brother who had first accompanied him to England). True to the Franklin tradition, he was not remiss in shouldering his responsibilities and when the boy was only five had requested Franklin to enter his name in the lists of future midshipmen in the United States Navy as the steppingstone to a later career.

On September 13, 1785, the *London Packet* entered the Delaware with "water smooth, air cool, day fair and fine."[9] The following day "dear Philadelphia" appeared in full sight. The first greeting was delivered by Richard Bache, who had come out in a boat to bring the travelers ashore. Aware of their imminent arrival, a crowd had gathered on Market Street Wharf and its cheers punctuated their every move. Bells rang. Cannon boomed. Temple was moved to tears. On the doorstep of Franklin Court stood Sally: "The joy that I received . . . in seeing father, mother, brothers and sisters can be felt, not described."[10] End of Benny's diary.

They were all there, the little brothers and sisters to whom he had sent love in his stilted French or his shaky English. Here was Willy, a toddler when they left, now a sturdy boy of twelve with much more mischief in him than the sober Benny ever had. And here were four new faces, two girls (Betsy, eight, and Deborah, four) and two boys (Louis, six, and Richard, eighteen months). Curtsies and bows from all the "little Prattlers."[11] Had any one of them inherited some facet of the grandfather's genius?* He did not live to find out but did live long enough to be at home, for once, when the youngest of his grandchildren, Sarah Bache, was born in 1788.

Benny was enrolled without delay at the University of Pennsylvania, Temple promptly packed off to his farm in Rancocas. As to Franklin, he had no sooner settled down with the Baches than he realized that his house, so grand when he had planned it with Debbie, was now bursting at the seams. To a man just back from Paris it also looked shabby and not adequately fireproof. He would have liked to duplicate France's stone staircases, tile floors, and slate roofs, but he had to compromise with local possibilities and was satisfied in the end with a substantial three-story wing that ran along the whole east side of the house, adding half again to its size. It provided a new dining room, large enough to seat twenty-four (regularly used for the meetings of the American Philosophical Society), and above it a library "lin'd with Books to the Ceiling,"[12] a chance to use the arm-extender he had invented to reach the top volumes. "I hardly know how to justify building a Library at an Age that will so soon oblige me to quit it," he confessed to Jane, "but we are apt to forget that we are grown old, and building is an Amusement."[13]

For profit as well as amusement he tore down the three old tenant houses that screened him from the bustle of Market Street and put up two modern, fireproof dwellings in their place with the entrance to Franklin Court through an arch between them, wide enough for a carriage. Did he feel a moment of nostalgia when those old buildings were demolished? He had courted Debbie in one of them during his first six months in Philadelphia. In another he had found work, teased his master, reveled in his own powers of disputation, and met the governor who had changed his life by sending him on his fool's errand to England. But Franklin was more geared to the future than to the past. And the future meant providing for his grandchildren, taking advantage of the rise in real estate values now that the public market had extended up to his property.

These domestic enterprises did not mean that Franklin was carrying

* As it turned out, the brilliance if not the genius took one more generation to reappear. The notable Franklins of the nineteenth century were a son of the current baby Richard (Alexander Dallas Bache, physicist at the Franklin Institute, first president of Girard College) and Benny's oldest son (Franklin Bache, professor of chemistry at Jefferson Medical College).

out his long-heralded plan of withdrawing from the public arena and quietly "going to bed"[14] in the evening of life. On the contrary. He had been pleasantly surprised by the tumultuous welcome given him upon landing, "far beyond my Expectations,"[15] for he had feared the Adams-Lee-Izard faction might have badly hurt his reputation. Within six weeks he found himself chosen chief executive of Pennsylvania, a post to which he was re-elected without opposition for three consecutive one-year terms. He also continued to be regularly designated as president of the American Philosophical Society as he had been ever since 1769, to the abiding displeasure of the Reverend Mr. William Smith, now somewhat under a cloud because of his lack of enthusiasm for the Revolution. When the Society for Political Enquiries was founded in 1787 to apply to problems of government the rigorous study accorded the natural sciences, Franklin was made its head.

That same year, the Constitutional Convention met in Philadelphia to frame a charter that would both preserve hard-won liberties and prevent the new nation from drifting into anarchy. As one of the Pennsylvania delegates, Franklin, at eighty-one the oldest man on the floor, rarely missed a session but he seldom spoke. He left the drafting of the Constitution to younger, more ambitious men. Still, he knew his assets and how to use them best. Power might be slipping from him but not prestige. To that bitterly divided assembly he brought what was expected from him: a measure of calm and a note of humor. No other man in America could have blandly told his overheated, self-righteous colleagues about that French lady who in a dispute with her sister had said, "I don't know how it happens, sister, but I meet with nobody but myself that's always in the right."[16] Not for a minute did he forget that it was more important for the union to survive than for the government to be perfect. By July 4, 1788, the Constitution had been adopted by ten of the states, more than the necessary majority, and the day was celebrated in Philadelphia with a glorious "federal procession." At the head of the parade rode Richard Bache, his surrogate, attended by a herald and proclaiming the dawn of a new era.

Much as he told his French friends how reluctant he had been about reentering public life, Franklin admitted to Jane that "this universal and unbroken confidence of a whole people flatters my vanity."[17] His sister was disappointed. She had looked forward, she said, "to a little familiar domestic chitchat like common folks,"[18] but now felt she should not intrude upon his time. He talked for a while of visiting her in Boston, she talked of coming to Philadelphia, then they both realized they were too old to travel and would have to settle for occasional messages of serene good cheer on his part, frequent messages of edgy cheer on hers.

Jane had finally found a measure of peace. Her depressing daughter was off in the country most of the time, the daughter's ever-failing husband trading in the West Indies. Jane spent her days frugally in a cozy house put at her disposal by Franklin, well supplied by him with wood and flour, her only anxiety that she would outlive her brother.* She enjoyed the company of a granddaughter—still another orphaned granddaughter, still another Jenny, this one a child of her insane son Benny. After Benny's final breakdown the little girl had been cared for by strangers who gave her no other training than that of a maid. In her teens she turned up in Boston, settled in with her grandmother, and defied heredity by living almost to a hundred, robust, intelligent, good-humored, a tribute to the resiliency of the human race.

Still very much the patriarch, Franklin tried to pick up the reins of the family as soon as he returned. Where were all the New England relatives? What about his mother's people, the Folgers of Nantucket? They seemed "wonderfully shy"[20] when the time came to pay him a visit. (Cousin Kezia Coffin and her husband, he was informed, were in jail for collaboration with the British and other shady dealings.)

Franklin now took pleasure in reminiscing with Jane. He who had run away from the vats and candles of his childhood kept promoting plans to restore the crown soap to its former glory. Several younger relatives were pressed to learn from Jane the secret of its fabrication but nobody persisted. Judging by the number of exchanges devoted to the vagaries of the soap cakes (too green, too crumbly, too dry, or too pale), Jane's recipe must have left a good deal to be desired.

At the very time Franklin's obligations toward the Mecoms seemed amply fulfilled, another of Jane's descendants, a crippled grandson named Josiah Flagg, made his appearance in Philadelphia and begged to be employed as a clerk. Jane's anger when she heard of this "audacity"[21] pushed her to forward to her brother a letter in which this grandson had asked her not to reveal to the Franklin family that he had worked three years as a cobbler. Whether she did this, as she maintained, out of horror at his vanity or because she was peeved at having been bypassed, the incident illustrates the strange dichotomy that had been developing in Jane: her fawning love for her brother in contrast to her harshness toward her own brood. Once Josiah had been granted

---

* She did by four years. Her last days were spent evoking the pleasures he had given her ("they passed like little streams from a beautiful fountain") and recalling the sad refrain of a song they had sung in Philadelphia: "But now they are withered and waned away."[19]

the post, however, and Franklin seemed to like him, she relented and expressed the hope her grandson would be the beneficiary of liberal quantities of good advice. But Franklin had lost some of his early belief in that direction. Quoting Ariosto's idea that all things lost on earth are treasured on the moon, he commented with more skepticism than was his wont that there must be plenty of good advice on the moon.

The only one quite impervious to guidance and good advice was Temple.

Temple, at the outset, had been enthusiastic about his farm: Rancocas Creek, he allowed, was a "charming spot."[22] The creek flowed into the Delaware and would be ideal for shipping his produce. Still, all hopes of a diplomatic post for him had not been given up. Within a month of their return, Franklin dispatched him to New York, ostensibly to settle accounts with Congress, actually to make himself visible and ready for possible offers. Richard Bache, still smarting from the loss of his postmastership, went along. They found out to their dismay that the old Doctor might be covered with honors in Philadelphia but did not enjoy much regard in Congress. They obtained nothing.

Franklin complained bitterly of the niggardly treatment Temple was receiving. His grandson, he stressed, had sacrificed all chances to study law in order to serve him as secretary when Congress refused to supply any other. By the time the mission to France was completed, many years had been lost and Temple's "habits of life become so different" that a career in law was no longer practicable. On the other hand, the young man had gained such valuable experience in the diplomatic line that he was ideally suited, Franklin maintained, for a post in some foreign embassy. Nor did the grandfather feel that he was biased in his opinion of Temple's qualifications since "three of my colleagues, without the smallest sollicitation from me, chose him Secretary of the Commission for Treaties." But what good had this done? "I took the liberty of recommending him to Congress for their protection. This was the only favor I ever asked of them; and the only answer I received was a Resolution superseding him and appointing Col. Humphrey in his place."[23] (Actually Franklin's request was not unreasonable: John Quincy Adams, much younger than Temple, had been made secretary to Francis Dana, minister to St. Petersburg.) The Pennsylvania delegation nominated Temple for secretary to the Constitutional Convention, but he was bypassed. From undeserved adulation to an undeserved series of rebuffs, it was quite a tumble, and Temple was understandably bitter. Don't believe Grandfather's pronouncements, he cautioned his intimates in France: The country, in his now jaundiced view, was sorely divided, in fact on the verge of anarchy, and Franklin too old and inactive to stop the disintegration.

Back in Rancocas, he played at gentleman-farmer, much more gentleman than farmer. It was very well for his grandfather who had never lived anywhere but in towns to extol agriculture as "the most honourable of all our Employments,"[24] but Temple was restless. He wanted to turn his land into a show place in the French style. Letter after letter was fired off to his long-suffering friends in Paris to supply him with the necessary vines, fruit trees, wooden shoes for his laborers, hunting dogs, and deer for the dogs to hunt. The native American species of deer was unthinkable, he declared, for anyone with a taste for venison. After several deer had died in transit and the problem proved insurmountable, he lost interest in the whole enterprise and concentrated on the social life of Philadelphia—much livelier than he had imagined it would be—leaving the management of his domain to a steward he had imported from England. Whereupon he quarreled with the steward who departed and left the farm untended. Franklin admitted ruefully to Lafayette that "Temple hankers a little after Paris or some other of the polished cities of Europe, thinking these preferable to what he meets in the woods of Rancocas."[25]

Perhaps, as Jane suggested, he needed a helpmate to make rural life more palatable. "How happy I would be to live here with my Blanchette!"[26] he once exclaimed, not meaning it seriously. Blanchette —certainly not the kind of helpmate Jane had in mind—replied indignantly that much as she adored him, no self-respecting Parisian woman would ever dream of burying herself in the American countryside. When, oh when was he coming back? He pressed her for news of their friends and of the "petit Monsieur," gave her a glimpse of the Philadelphia social whirl, and announced coolly that he would not be back in France as soon as he had hoped. The endless pages of tender nothings she deluged him with became more frantic as she sensed that his ardor was dimming. The cruelest blow came when their little Theophile died and Temple reproached her for not having taken proper care of him.

Eventually he spent much more time in Philadelphia than on his estate. Franklin knew all this, of course, but closed his eyes. The extent to which he denied reality when it came to Temple is sharply revealed by an exclamation from Polly Hewson. As good as her word, Polly had moved her family to Philadelphia in 1786. Her sons had studied at the college and the older one, William, after a moment of glory as valedictorian, decided on farming as his vocation. Upon Franklin's suggestion that he settle with Temple and profit from his experience, Polly's reaction was such a "Not with a bachelor!"[27] (read, Not with *that* bachelor!) that no doubt is left as to the low opinion she entertained of the favorite grandson.

She still thought well of Benny. A spring outing, open wagon and all, which she described to her sister-in-law back in England, involved a goodly amount of Baches and Hewsons frolicking together. Franklin may have basked in the thought that his London "daughter" and his Philadelphia daughter had finally met and that his two families were thriving side by side, but Sally and Polly, while perfectly polite, do not seem to have become friends. The gap between a woman who had grown up in London and one who had never left Philadelphia was too wide to bridge, or was it the unspoken rivalry between them?

After a brief interlude at the University of Pennsylvania, Benny took up printing in earnest under his grandfather's eye. In Paris he had been apprenticed to François-Ambroise Didot, "the best printer of this Century or that ever has been,"[28] but only for the few weeks that preceded their departure. Some of the finest equipment in the world, including a variety of fonts to be found nowhere else in America at the time, had been shipped in those 128 crates that went down the Seine. One of the little houses Franklin built on Market Street was now destined to serve as Benny's printing office, with rooms for type founding, printing, and binding.

Franklin had preordained that Benny would carry on his craft and Franklin made most of the decisions on how Benny should go about it. First he had him concentrate on type-casting but the market was glutted and that had to be given up. Then Benny was told to publish books: Mrs. Barbauld's *Lessons for Children* in graduated series, Latin texts, Greek and Latin grammars. None of them sold. Franklin defended his choices, moaned about the abysmal state of contemporary schools, feuded with booksellers and customers. Altogether, it was an inauspicious start for Benny in a trade not really of his own choosing.

Still pliant, though, he spent long hours as his grandfather's secretary, drafting letters and copying the last installment of the *Autobiography*. Much as he adored his grandfather—and he did, he admired everything about him, even the way he could write with a scratchy pen!—Benny was beginning to chafe under the old man's domination, to feel unsettled and melancholy. Just like Temple, he had been indelibly marked by his nine years abroad. The cousins wrote to each other in French and Benny's hints about the amorous escapades of Temple's cat have an unmistakably Gallic flavor. France would remain their obsession.

Franklin, too, would write to his Parisian friends that "in his most pleasant dreams"[29] he saw France, the gardens of Madame Helvétius, and her thousand sofas. Sally, of course, did the best she could: She entertained the stream of his visitors, served them tea in the garden under a mulberry tree, and let her children play as they wished around Grandpapa. A visitor commented acidly that she could not keep discipline and that she looked "very gross and rather homely." But Franklin was not so critical. He described his daughter as "the Comfort of my declining Years," "a kind, attentive nurse to me when I am at any time indisposed," and stressed that the grandchildren amused him.[30] His only complaint was that he had grown so old as to have buried most of the friends of his youth: "I seem to have intruded myself into the company of posterity when I ought to have been abed and asleep."[31] Early in 1787, he suffered a severe fit of the stone from which he never fully recovered; by late 1788, having come to the end of his third term as president of Pennsylvania, he quit public service at long last.

His mind was as alert as ever, his will almost as strong, but the final stretch was a test of his stoicism and his principles: "No repining, no peevish expression ever escaped him during a confinement of two years in which, I believe, if every moment of ease could be added together the sum would not allow to two whole months. When the pain was not too violent to be amused, he employed himself with his books, his pen, or in conversation with friends."[32]

The French, when he was in Paris, had sent him enough bizarre recipes to flush out a heap of stones but nothing had worked. Only laudanum, in ever-increasing doses, would alleviate the pain, while preying upon his enormous energy. He lost his appetite, he was reduced to skin and bones. At times he would rally, as when Polly came to read poetry or Jefferson to give him news of Paris and ask him about the boundaries of the expanded American frontier. At times he overcame his suffering, as when he wrote Washington that it had been worth living those extra years in torment, to watch in the end the blossoming of their nation, or when he conceived a plan for insuring farmers' crops. At times he seemed to lose interest, as when he failed to recognize the immense advantages of steam power, the other new force that, with electricity, would soon revolutionize the world, or when he limited his comments on the outbreak of the French Revolution to a wish that all would end well.

He tried to concentrate on the unfinished task his admirers were urging him to complete: bringing the *Autobiography* to its conclusion. In the respites that his disease gave him, he carried the narrative beyond the fiftieth year of his life, dictating to Benny when it became too painful to sit up. But he was not sure anymore of saying the right thing with the right touch. He feared that only the account of his earlier years would be "of . . . use to young readers as exemplifying strongly the effects of prudent and imprudent conduct in the commencement of a life in business."[33] When he shipped the new parts of the manuscript to England, he left it up to his friends to decide, "I am now grown so old and feeble in mind as well as body that I cannot place any confidence in my own judgment."[34]

In his literary judgment, perhaps. But on all the basic issues he was still perfectly sure of himself. His faith in the dignity of men, his hatred of arbitrary power, his combativeness tinted with humor were all brought to bear on one final issue: slavery. In France he had lived for the first time in a nation where slavery had been legally abolished.* Once back in America, he had to face the problem that haunted all the founding fathers: How could slavery be tolerated in a country that had just fought a bitter war in defense of human liberties? He accepted in 1787 the presidency of the Pennsylvania Society for the Abolition of Slavery and the Relief of Free Negroes. His last energies would be turned against the "peculiar institution" which had taken such deep root in American life that slaves had become essential, if often unrecorded, members of countless American families, northern as well as southern.

"Life," he had once said, "like a dramatic Piece, should not only be conducted with Regularity, but methinks it should finish handsomely. Being now in the last Act, I begin to cast about for something fit to end with. Or if mine be more properly compar'd to an Epigram, as some of its few lines are but barely tolerable, I am very desirous of concluding with a bright Point."[35]

* This was not exactly the case in England. The landmark decision of Lord Mansfield in 1772 had declared that a slave might not be taken out of the country against his will, but it had not ruled categorically on the legality of slavery itself.

XXIII

Slaves

The Smallpox has now quite left this City. The Number of those that died here of that Distemper, is exactly 288. . . . 64 of the Number were Negroes; if these be valued one with another at £30 per head, the Loss to the City in that Article is near £2000.

—*Pennsylvania Gazette*, July 8, 1731

Slavery is . . . an atrocious debasement of human nature. . . . The unhappy man, who has long been treated as a brute animal, too frequently sinks beneath the common standard of the human species. The galling chains that bind his body do also fetter his intellectual faculties and impair the social affections of his heart . . . reflection is suspended, he has not the power of choice.

"Address to the Public from the Pennsylvania Society for Promoting the Abolition of Slavery," November 9, 1789

BETWEEN THE INSENSITIVITY of the first quotation (when Franklin was twenty-five) and the humanity of the second (when he was eighty-four) lies more than a half-century of evolution in his mind, from narrow provincialism and strict functionalism to a commitment embracing the whole of mankind. Change, of course, was in the air: Slavery, once an institution hardly anybody questioned, was troubling a growing number of men of good will. A revulsion had set in, but powerful forces were still exerting their pull in the traditional direction.

When young, Franklin had often run ads for slaves in his newspaper: "A likely Wench about fifteen Years old, has had the Smallpox, been in the Country above a Year and talks English. Inquire of the Printer hereof."[1] Or, "A very likely Negro Woman aged about thirty Years who has lived in this City from her Childhood and can wash and iron very well, cook Victuals, sew, spin on the Linen Wheel. She has a Boy of about Two Years old, which is to go with her. . . . And also another Boy aged about Six Years, who is the Son of the abovesaid Woman. He will be sold with his Mother, or by Himself, as the Buyer pleases."[2]*

---

* Franklin's father Josiah (or perhaps his seafaring brother of the same name) sold slaves at his house on at least one occasion (*Boston News Letter*, Aug. 3, 1713).

Why should the buyer not please himself? Like molasses, chocolate, and rum the Negro was an exotic tropical import. When revenues were needed, he too was subject to duties. True, some Quaker merchants who traded with the West Indies complained about having to accept slaves as part of the package. This protest, however, was not on grounds of conscience but because the slaves they received were generally the rejects of the plantation economy. Unlike rum and molasses, they were distressingly mortal, prone to arrive in poor shape, and prey to the un-fathomable visitations of Providence.

Of course, a printer carried advertisements for slaves and notices of runaways in the normal line of business, regardless of whether he was in sympathy with what he printed. (One exception was the German-language printer, Christopher Sauer, who refused to carry any adver-tisements for slaves in his paper.) Late in life, Franklin recalled with pride that he had published two of the earliest abolishionist tracts to ap-pear in the colonies, one by Ralph Sandiford (1729) and the other by Benjamin Lay (1732), both arguing primarily from the unimpeachable ground of Scripture. But the fact that the printer's name did not appear on the pamphlets indicates that at the time of publication Franklin was not eager to take any credit.

Lay was also given to dramatic gestures in Old Testament style. In the midst of a Quaker meeting, he ripped open a sheep's bladder filled with blood, shouting, "Thus shall God shed the blood of those persons who enslave their fellow creatures!"[3] Women swooned. Another time, he kidnapped the son of a slaveholder, so that the father might realize from his own experience how Negro fathers suffered. For such conduct he was expelled from the Society of Friends; but from the seclusion of a cave in which he lived for nine years he went on writing against slav-ery and his former fellow Quakers. He entrusted the product of those years to Franklin, asking him to improve its organization. The work was an enormous mass of undigested material, not all relevant but, as Franklin later recalled, containing "just thoughts and good sense . . . in bad order."[4] The title alone was twice the length of the Lord's Prayer, far in excess of the generous standards of the time. Deborah was impressed enough to acquire, during Franklin's absence, a full-length portrait of Lay. Since he was a tiny hunchback, it must not have taken up too much space on the wall.

The fact is that Franklin himself kept slaves for over thirty years. The last did not die until 1781. His son and daughter were also slave owners; indeed, Richard Bache's black "boy" Bob was a fixture of the Market Street ménage during Franklin's last years. Like most masters, Franklin complained about their shortcomings: He wrote to his mother in 1750 that he intended to sell his man and woman "for we do not like Negro Servants [slaves]."[5] And yet seven years later he still owned a couple (the same or another), though in the will drawn up on the eve of his departure for England in 1757 he included instructions for the manumission of "my Negro Man Peter and his wife Jemima"[6] in the event of his death.

Peter had traveled with him to Virginia the previous year and come down with a serious fever in Maryland but recovered thanks to or in spite of a good bleeding and a dose of camomile tea. He accompanied Franklin to England along with William's own slave, King, and was bid to scrub the moss-covered gravestones of the Franklin ancestors. To replace him, Debbie bought a "Negrow boy"[7] for £41.10, a rather steep price, it would seem, which probably reflected the shortage during the French and Indian War. He may be the "Othello" she writes about enrolling in a school for black children; he is almost certainly the one whose death a few years later caused much grief. "I am sorry for the Death of your black Boy," her husband wrote with mild concern, "as you seem to have had a regard for him. You must have suffered a good deal in the Fatigue of Nursing him in such a Distemper."[8]

Franklin never allowed himself to become so attached. When Debbie inquired how Peter and King were getting on in England, he replied somewhat irascibly, "Peter continues with me and behaves as well as I can expect in a Country where there are many Occasions of spoiling Servants, if they are ever so good. He has a few Faults as most of them, and I see with only one Eye and hear only with one Ear, so we rub on pretty comfortably." King, however, had run off two years earlier to Suffolk where he had been taken into the "Service of a Lady that was very fond of the Merit of making him a Christian and contributing to his Education and Improvement." She had taught him to read and write, to play the violin and French horn, "with some other Accomplishments more Useful in a Servant." Franklin, by then an advisor and member of an association to catechize and instruct black children, concluded with the sober comment that "in the meantime he is no Expense to us."[9]

King apparently remained in his Suffolk paradise, and Peter dropped out of sight. Back in Philadelphia, in the short interval between his two London missions, Franklin acquired a new slave, George, as part payment for a debt. "Gorge," as he invariably appears in Debbie's letters, was put to work in the hurly-burly of readying the new house and continued with her in sickness and in health (his and hers), in harmony and discord, after Franklin had gone back to England. He became a widower and was much afflicted—"a dredfull Creyer"[10]—Debbie reported, but his wife's name is not even known. After Deborah's death he passed to the Baches and Sally described his own long illness and death to her father in France. But never so much as a passing comment on any of this from Franklin.

Philadelphians had kept slaves since the city was founded. William Penn himself, though a humanitarian Quaker and apostle of religious liberty, was a slave owner. True, he exhorted masters to treat them kindly and ordered that his own be freed on his death (which his heirs neglected to do). The first settlers in the city exhausted most of their hard currency in purchasing slaves to lighten their burdens in the wilderness. Only the Moravian Germans consistently opposed slavery and lived up to their principles. A Swedish traveler who visited Philadelphia in 1750 observed that the Quakers had as many slaves as anybody else.

In the years immediately following his visit, the French and Indian War (1754–63) increased the dependence on black labor by reducing the stream of free Scotch-Irish and German immigrants to a trickle. It also made it uneconomic to pay for indentured servants to come over from Europe since they were liable to be drafted by the British after they had arrived, while slaves were exempt from conscription. Hitherto most slaves had been brought to Philadelphia from the West Indies after a period of acculturation in the New World—often as second-generation captives. But by the later years of the war the demand was so insatiable that many "parcels" of blacks were being transported directly from Africa. This had its drawbacks, not the least of which was their susceptibility to the cold. By the mid-1760s the proportion of slaves in the population of the city had probably reached its peak, amounting to as many as one in twelve, employed not only in the fields but in a variety of urban occupations, from house servants to sailors, dockworkers, and artisans.

The growth in the slave population filled Franklin with alarm. Even before the war intensified their import, he had attacked the dependence on slaves in his *Observations concerning the Increase of Mankind* (1751). The attack was not in the name of humanity, however, but of American self-sufficiency and the well-being of her white population: "The Whites who have Slaves, not labouring, are enfeebled," he argued, "and therefore not so generally prolific; the Slaves being worked too hard, and ill-fed, their Constitutions are broken, and the Deaths among them are more than the Births, so that a continual Supply is needed from Africa." With a touch of superiority over his white fellow countrymen of the southern colonies, he added, "The northern Colonies, having few Slaves, increase in Whites," thanks to the abundance of land and employment which encourage early marriage. Further, he warned that "Slaves . . . pejorate the Families that use them; the white Children become proud, disgusted with Labour, and being educated in Idleness, are rendered unfit to get a living by Industry."[11] And he insisted that free labor is always cheaper in the long run. In other words, slavery is bad because it threatens America's fertility, industry, and frugality—the public and private virtues Franklin never tired of extolling, the combined assets of Polly Baker and Poor Richard.

Buried deep under these pragmatic arguments one can also detect something instinctive: a fear and loathing of a people of different color, a repulsion Franklin overcame little by little, perhaps never entirely. The prospect of an ever-blacker America worried him profoundly at this period. All the other continents, he maintained, were already swarming with black or tawny people—among which he included, curiously, Swedes and Russians—and it was time to protect America before it was too late, to preserve the "lovely White and Red Complexion of the Country," the ruddy cheeks of the fair Anglo-Saxon settlers. He eliminated these politically explosive lines from subsequent editions of the essay, but his taste did not change: When he went to France in 1776 one of his first pleasing impressions was the "fair white and red Complexion"[12] of the women of Normandy.

Franklin was not alone in his apprehensions. Earlier in the century, William Byrd had lamented that so many slaves were being brought into Virginia that it "will some time or other be confirmed in the name of New Guinea."[13] To discourage the slave trade, Franklin had proposed high duties on slaves and an end to the conscription of indentured servants; in fact, the Pennsylvania Assembly imposed a duty of £10 per head in 1761, raised a few years later to a prohibitive £20. The Virginia legislature went even farther and tried to ban the importation of new slaves altogether but was overruled by the British Board of Trade under pressure from English commercial interests. Fear of slave insurrection was widespread and well-founded, both in the south and the north, as a bloody outbreak in New York and its even bloodier suppression had shown early in the century. Then, too, there was the constant danger that slaves would desert in time of war: The French during the French and Indian War and the British during the Revolution made a policy of attracting slaves to their cause and sending them against their masters.

In the early eighteenth century, abolitionists had been no more than a lunatic fringe in colonial America, but by the 1750s the movement began to gain ground. In Philadelphia its leader was Anthony Benezet, Quaker teacher and publicist who, with others sympathetic to his views, pressured the Society of Friends until virtually all Quaker merchants extricated themselves from direct involvement with the trade and Quaker families gradually began to give up their own slaves.

Little had been done hitherto in the North American colonies to educate or even to convert blacks, whether slave or free. The Catholic Church had baptized shiploads before they left Africa, but Protestants were more cautious. Equal access to heaven might make it harder to maintain inferior status on earth. Then, too, converted slaves were often reported to be uppity and smug about their hallowed condition. Educating slaves was still less in favor; at best it was useless, at worst dangerous. But there were exceptions: Cotton Mather was one, George Whitefield another. Whitefield, the apostle of the "Great Awakening," preached a nonsegregated brand of salvation; he even purchased an enormous tract of land on the Delaware for a Negro School and solicited contributions in the *Pennsylvania Gazette* (1740), but the school never opened. The Quakers had made desultory gestures toward including black children in their schools and black worshippers in their meetings (in areas set aside for them), but on the whole had taken less initiative than the Anglicans. In England the Associates of the late Dr. Bray (an offshoot of the Anglican Society for the Propagation of the Gospel) gradually shifted their emphasis from charity schools at home to Negro children in the British colonies.

In 1757, the secretary of the Bray Associates in London asked Franklin for advice on starting a school for black children in Philadelphia, "to imbue the minds of [the] young Slaves with good principles."[14] The project was a little like the German charity schools he and others had been pushing during these years to assimilate German immigrants into the English-speaking culture of the colony, and Franklin immediately saw the importance of extending the idea to blacks. For many years he served on the governing board of the Bray Associates and became their leading American member.* A school was opened the following year with thirty pupils. The boys were taught to read, "the girls to sow [sic], and knit, read and work."[15] Twice a week they were all taken to Christ Church to be catechized by the Reverend Mr. Sturgeon. Debbie went to hear them and found they answered "so prettily" and behaved "so decently"[16] that she enrolled her own boy Othello in the school, while her husband entered her letter as a testimonial in the Minute Book of the Bray Associates.

---

* It may have been at a dinner of the Bray Associates in 1760 that Franklin met Dr. Johnson for the first and probably only time. Although Strahan was Johnson's publisher and close friend, he kept them apart perhaps because of Johnson's well-known antipathy to Americans.

The Philadelphia venture was so successful that additional schools were opened, with Franklin's help and advice, in Williamsburg, New York, and Newport. Once back in America, Franklin made a point of visiting them while on his post-office tours. What he saw had a profound effect on his attitude toward the Negro and his view of slavery itself. "I then conceived," he wrote the Bray Associates back in London, "a higher Opinion of the Natural Capacities of the black Race, than I have ever before entertained. Their Apprehension [is] as quick, their Memory as Strong, and their Docility in every Respect equal to that of the White Children."[17] This was not exactly the prevailing view—it was certainly not shared by Jefferson who always suspected that blacks were of lower intelligence—and Franklin seems a little surprised himself. It was, however, what men like Anthony Benezet had been insisting to the few who cared to listen. Since 1750 the saintly Benezet had been instructing slave children in whatever time he could spare from his regular teaching. "I have found amongst the negroes," he declared, "as great a variety of talents as amongst a like number of whites; and I am bold to assert that the notion entertained by some that the blacks are inferior in their capacities is a vulgar prejudice, founded on the pride or ignorance of their lordly masters, who have kept their slaves at such a distance as to be unable to form a right judgment of them."[18*] Unlike the Bray Associates or George Whitefield, Benezet was totally committed to the eradication of slavery. He wanted not only to save black souls but to free black bodies, and to that end wrote a steady stream of tracts, pressured the legislature, and prodded his friends.

Franklin was not yet ready to follow Benezet all the way, but he was beginning to look at blacks as human beings, not simply as unsatisfactory units of labor, procreation, and pigmentation. Then, too, the sight of his fellow whites' reprisals against innocent Indians in 1764 had jolted him into rethinking the complacent distinction between "civilized" and "uncivilized" peoples. He compared the behavior of the Paxton boys to the account he had read of an African chief who, in his own country, saved the life of a white man by reminding his subjects that one ought to distinguish between evil and innocent whites. "Some among these dark People have a strong Sense of Justice and Honor . . . and even the most brutal among them are capable of feeling the Force of Reason and of being influenced by a Fear of God."[19]

Nevertheless, in the decade leading up to the Revolution, Franklin was so preoccupied with the defense of American liberties that he

* Benezet was also a pioneer in the education of girls, as was that other early abolitionist, the Puritan Samuel Sewall who spoke out in defense of women as vigorously as he opposed the slave trade.

rarely discussed slavery for itself, only as it related to the larger struggle. Thus the essay "Concerning Sweets" (1765), promoted by the
Sugar Act of 1764 (the first in the series of British measures restricting
North American trade) is as much a paean to the honey bee and the
homely virtues as an excoriation of slavery. Franklin contrasted the
"voluntary Labour of Bees" with the "forced Labour of Slaves," the
"extreme Slovenliness of the West-India Slaves in making Molasses,
and the Filth and Nastiness suffered to enter it or wantonly thrown
into it,"[20] with the tidiness of bees and the superiority of honey to sugar
and molasses. The bee embodied the virtue of self-reliance, the repudia-
tion of luxury. To the end of his days, Franklin objected to the fact
that the "greatest part of the Trade of the World was carried on for
Luxuries, most of which were really injurious to health or society, such
as *tea, tobacco, rum, sugar* and *negro slaves*."[21]

As spokesman for America, Franklin found himself obliged before
long to answer the growing chorus of English critics who charged the
colonists with hypocrisy in denying so large a portion of their countrymen the liberties which they were demanding so loudly for themselves. He counterattacked with the *Conversation on Slavery* (1770), a
dialogue meant to expose the British role in the "enormities" of slavery
as far worse than anything the Americans were guilty of. Hadn't the
British brought the slave trade to its present magnitude and efficiency
and grown immensely rich in the traffic of human bodies? Hadn't the
British government said no whenever the colonists tried to stem the
flood of slave imports with high duties? And what about the working
poor in England or the miners in Scotland who were slaves in all but
name, perhaps even worse off since they had no kind masters to look
after them when they were old and ill? In his polemical ardor, here and
elsewhere, Franklin tended to minimize the harshness of slavery just as
he minimized its extent. Not one family in a hundred kept slaves, he
declared at a time when the number was closer to one family in five
even in Philadelphia (including his own).

Two years after this rather ambivalent piece, the first known correspondence with Anthony Benezet began, though it is impossible to believe they had not become acquainted well before this. Benezet's name
appears in the pages of Franklin's Shop Book, 1735–39, and the
families may have been linked by some sort of kinship ties: Debbie
once wrote her husband of the impending marriage of "cousin Sally
Bennyset,"[22] Anthony's niece. Then, too, there was their common sympathy for the Indians, which may have brought them together at the
time of the Paxton massacres in late 1763. In any case, Benezet was determined to push Franklin into a more strenuous role in the struggle for

abolition of the slave trade and by the early 1770s Franklin was ready to be pushed.

"Now as thy prospect is clear, with respect to the previous iniquity practised by our nation towards the Negro," Benezet wrote him in London during the spring of 1772, "I venture to take up a little more of thy time . . . earnestly to request thou woulds't deeply consider whether something may not be in thy power towards an effectual step and a kind of basis lay'd for the removal in time (if not at present) of that terrible evil [the slave trade]."[23] He reminded Franklin that the slave trade corrupted those who engaged in it every bit as much as it scarred those who were its victims. Through Benezet, Franklin met leading British abolitionists and even his language soon took on the sonorities of the Philadelphia Quaker: "I hope in time," Franklin wrote home to Dr. Benjamin Rush, "that the Friends to Liberty and Humanity will get the better of a Practice that has so long disgraced our Nation and Religion."[24]

Benezet's influence was also apparent in an unsigned article by Franklin in the *London Chronicle* in 1772, "The Somerset Case and the Slave Trade," a commentary on the reaction to the decision by Lord Mansfield that slavery was contrary to the laws of England. After paraphrasing Benezet's figures of numbers involved in the slave trade, the high mortality rate among slaves, and the growing tide of antislavery sentiment in the colonies, Franklin lashed out on his own: "Can sweetening our tea with sugar be a circumstance of such absolute necessity? Can the petty pleasure thence arising to the taste compensate for so much misery produced among our fellow creatures, and such a constant butchery of the human species by this pestilential, detestable traffic in the bodies and souls of men?—*Pharisaical Britain!* to pride thyself in setting free a single slave [Somerset] that happens to land on thy coasts while thy Merchants in all thy ports are encouraged to continue a commerce whereby so many *hundreds of thousands* are dragged into a slavery that can scarce be said to end with their lives, since it is entailed on their posterity!"[25] Familiar themes, but a new tone of compassion. Not since the pamphlet on the Indian massacre in 1764 had Franklin given vent to such eloquence on behalf of an oppressed people.

There was unanimity among abolitionists that the slave trade should be ended as quickly as possible, but what was to be done about the slaves already in the colonies? Franklin's views in the commentary of the Somerset case are vague, but he seems to be advocating "if not liberty for those that remain in our Colonies," at least a law "declaring the children of present slaves free after they come of age."[26] By this time

Philadelphia Quakers had passed a resolution to manumit their slaves, but they no longer owned very many. The difficulty for Franklin (as for Washington, Jefferson, and others) was that he feared the immediate effects of emancipation; he did not believe that most blacks were prepared for freedom and anticipated a serious problem in assimilating them.

In truth, a great deal of ambiguity still beclouded Franklin's feelings. He believed black children could be educated: To Condorcet, he wrote in 1774, "Negroes . . . are not deficient in natural Understanding, but they have not the Advantage of Education,"[27] a reaffirmation of his observations in the Bray Associates' schools. Grown blacks, on the other hand, were still a terrifying people to him. He hated slavery but unlike Benezet could not love the slave. This explains why he was able to condemn the trade so vigorously at the very time he was working as agent for Georgia to have the colony's slave code accepted by the British government. "Perhaps you imagine the Negroes to be a mild tempered, tractable Kind of People," he wrote in the *Conversation on Slavery*. "Some of them are so. But the Majority [are] of a plotting Disposition, dark, sullen, malicious, revengeful and cruel in the highest Degree." Look at the bloody mutinies on slave ships—all the more comprehensible when one remembers that slaves were often criminals whom their own countrymen were eager to dispose of. As long as Britain would not permit the colonists to keep slaves out, they must protect themselves "by such Laws as are thought necessary to govern them while they are in it."[28]

During the Revolution the question of slavery was tabled as far as Franklin was concerned. As minister to France, however, he was obliged to protect the interests of all Americans seeking compensation for losses to the British, including slave traders and slave owners. He even interceded with the French government on behalf of his kinsman Jonathan Williams, Jr., who was trying—unsuccessfully—to win permission to keep a slave in France after the royal edict abolishing slavery throughout the kingdom (1779). And when John Jay's slave woman Abbe ran away, Franklin had the French police track her down and put her in prison till she repented her ingratitude.

Franklin was over eighty when he was made president of the Pennsylvania Abolition Society on his return. His name rather than his active participation was expected to be his greatest contribution to the cause. And it was sufficient to attract honorary members as famous as Josiah Wedgwood who produced antislavery cameos, and to carry some clout when the Society petitioned the governors of the various states to close their ports to the slave trade and discourage their citizens from engaging in it. The Society had hoped to induce Franklin to present a petition against the slave trade to the Constitutional Convention, but he withheld it for fear that South Carolina and Georgia would turn their backs on any union that forbade the import of slaves.

Pennsylvania had been the first state to pass legislation providing for the gradual elimination of slavery; now it was time to give serious thought to the integration of the freed slave lest "freedom . . . prove a misfortune to himself and prejudicial to society."[29] Free Negroes had traditionally been considered troublesome: Early legal codes in the colony had insisted on bonds being given by anyone freeing a slave since they were expected to be "idle, slothful people and often prove burdensome to the neighborhood."[30] The Abolition Society proposed to remedy the situation by drawing up a comprehensive plan for advising free Negroes, for placing young people in trades, providing schools for children of promising intellect, and offering employment for adults. Whether or not Franklin personally drafted the plan to which he affixed his signature, it rings with his lifelong preoccupations. Its aim was to "instruct, to advise, to qualify those who have been restored to Freedom, for the Exercise and Enjoyment of Civil Liberty, to promote in them Habits of Industry, to furnish them with Employments suited to their Age, Sex, Talents, and other Circumstances, and to procure their Children an Education calculated for their future Situation in Life."[31]

A few months after the plan was published, Franklin signed a memorial to Congress asking for an end to slavery in the United States. Noting that Congress had been brought into being "to [promote] the welfare and [secure] the blessings of liberty to the People of the United States," he argued that this should be done "without distinction of color to all descriptions of people" since all are created by the "same Almighty Being, alike the objects of his care and equally designed for the enjoyment of happiness." Invoking both Christianity and the Constitution, the memorial pleaded for mercy and justice for "this distressed people."[32]

The response to this memorial—and to similar ones presented at the same time by Quakers from Philadelphia and New York—was predictably vociferous. Franklin was attacked, the Quakers were denounced, slavery was justified by Holy Writ, by necessity, by nature. Franklin summoned his fading energies for a last riposte. Appropriately it was in the form of a hoax, his literary medium par excellence, and as usual it was taken seriously by a good many readers. Signed simply "Historicus," it purported to reprint a speech of Sidi Mehemet Ibrahim to the Divan of Algiers defending the time-hallowed custom of enslaving Christians captured by Barbary pirates.

Parodying the arguments used by Representative James Jackson of Georgia to denounce the abolitionist petitions, Sidi Mehemet declared, "If we cease our Cruises against the Christians, how shall we be furnished with the Commodities their Countries produce, and which are so necessary for us? If we forbear to make Slaves of their People, who in this hot Climate are to cultivate our Lands? Who are to perform the common Labours of our City, and in our Families? Must we not then be our own Slaves? And is there not more Compassion and more Favour due to us as Musselmen, than to these Christian Dogs?" Similarly, the Koran could be just as convenient as the Bible for justifying slavery: "How grossly are they mistaken in imagining Slavery to be disallow'd by the Alcoran! Are not the two Precepts, to quote no more, *Masters, treat your Slaves with Kindness; Slaves, serve your Masters with Cheerfulness and Fidelity,*' clear Proofs to the contrary? . . . Let us then hear no more of this detestable Proposition, the Manumission of Christian Slaves, the Adoption of which would, by depreciating our Lands and Houses, and thereby depriving so many good Citizens of their Properties, create universal Discontent, and provoke Insurrections, to the endangering of Government and producing general Confusion."[33] Accordingly the Divan rejected the abolition petition, just as Franklin pessimistically expected the Congress and the British Parliament to do.

This was his swan song, written less than a month before he died. Fittingly it echoed the first courageous condemnation of slavery by Pastorius and the Germantown Friends a century earlier: "Now what is this better done as Turcks doe? Yea, rather is it worse for them which say they are Christians."[34]

XXIV

"Our Little Fleet of Barques"

Let us sit till the Evening of Life is spent; the last Hours were always the most joyous. When we can stay no longer 'tis Time enough then to bid each other good Night, separate, and go quietly to bed.

—Franklin to Hugh Roberts, July 7, 1763

WHEN THE DAY CAME, April 17, 1790, he was ready.

All his life he had been gingerly taming death, stripping it of its awe and power, clothing it in appealing metaphors of travel and bliss, humoring it, giving it a place in the family circle until finally, obsessively, longingly it became "going to bed."

In the Puritan Boston of his childhood, death was not all that grim an event. Those who attended funerals expected gifts of gloves, rings, scarves. Had it not been for burials, weddings, and executions people would have had little occasion to congregate. Children often attended and acted as honorary pallbearers for other children.

Franklin's first tentative approach was the facetious epitaph he composed for himself when still young enough to be flippant about the faraway end:

The Body of
B. Franklin,
Printer;
Like the Cover of an old Book,
Its Contents torn out,
And stript of its Lettering and Gilding,
Lies here, Food for Worms.
But the Work shall not be wholly lost:
For it will, as he believ'd, appear once more,
In a new & more perfect Edition,
Corrected and amended
By the Author.[1]

With the passing of years his outlook became more serious but remained resolutely optimistic, whether he was brooding on the afterlife or writing a letter of condolence. The deaths of his parents and of Deborah's mother had elicited no more than conventional words, but he was moved enough by his brother John's to set down some thoughts that the family admired, copied, and treasured: "We have lost a most dear and valuable relation, but it is the will of God and Nature that we mortal bodies be laid aside, when the soul is to enter into real life; 'tis rather an embrio state, a preparation for living; a man is not completely born until he be dead: Why then should we grieve that a new child is born among the immortals? . . . Our friend and we are invited abroad on a party of pleasure—that is to last for ever. His chair was first ready and he is gone before us. We could not all conveniently start together, and why should you and I be grieved at this, since we are soon to follow, and we know where to find him."[2]

His relationship with God was perfectly relaxed: "That Being who gave me Existence . . . and has been continually showering his Favours upon me . . . can I doubt that he loves me? And if he loves me, can I doubt that he will go on to take care of me not only here but hereafter? This to some may seem Presumption; to me it appears the best grounded Hope: Hope of the Future built on Experience of the Past."[3] Furthermore, he had some hope of not disappearing altogether. In complete agreement with Lavoisier's principle that nothing in the physical world is created or lost, he extended it to the spiritual realm and speculated that God—as thrifty as Poor Richard?—would not "suffer the daily Waste of Millions of Minds ready made that now exist, and put himself to the continual Trouble of making new ones."[4]

When he felt that the last hour was coming, this tranquility helped him to dismiss calmly Sally's suggestion that he might recover and live many years longer: "I hope not."[5] Polly, who hovered around, "the faithful witness of the closing scene," desperately anxious for him to make some commitment to formal religion, obtained no more than this highly individualized brand of piety which "could support pain without a murmur and meet death without terror."[6]

His loyal Benny was there, too, admiring "his Resolution unshaken, his Principles fixed even in Death"—the ultimate proof of that specific quality which in other days had made his grandfather so "unlike other old Persons." Now twenty-one and madly in love, Benny poured his sorrow in a letter to the young woman he wished to marry and wanted to associate with this, the most tragic event he had yet experienced. Her name was Margaret Markoe; her family, originally Danish, had recently come from St. Croix to Philadelphia. Neither the Baches nor the Markoes were well disposed toward the match and Margaret still hesitated. "I have spent a Spring of great Uneasiness, Fatigue, Anxiety and Fear, Trouble and Fear," moaned Benny. "'Tis time Summer should come to restore my Spirits and Strength."

Margaret, he presumed, would be interested in the provisions of the will; he emphatically assured her that it was "a great Man's Will . . . of a piece with his Life."[7] In fact it was a testament that left him, Benny, much less than he might have expected and gave Temple much more than anybody would have thought. The greatest surprise of all was its treatment of William. William received the worthless claims to the Nova Scotia lands, whatever books and papers of his father he already held in his possession, and the cancellation of his still outstanding debts to Franklin's estate. In other words, nothing. Nothing, wrapped in a final reproof: "The part he acted against me in the late war, which is of public notoriety, will account for my leaving him no more of an estate he endeavored to deprive me of."[8]

Such an unforgiving farewell drove William, for the only time on record, to express anger, real anger at his father. He spoke of the "shameful injustice" of this will and bitterly remarked that it dissolved forever all his connections, public and private, with his native land. Indeed, he never set foot in America again but devoted his last twenty-five years to his old obsession, land schemes in the American wilderness. Year after year, like a caricature out of Dickens or Balzac, he pushed through the legal maze. He badgered his relations and friends to help in collecting what he felt was his due deriving from the colonization projects of the Burlington Company and the Indiana Company. But in vain. He wound up empty-handed, his pockets drained by lawyers' fees.

All the hope William had ever conceived ended in frustration. In his young days he had dreamed that he would wind up his life as the husband of Elizabeth Graeme and the master of Graeme Park. Instead he spent it in straitened circumstances in London, and Graeme Park fell into the hands of none other than his old enemy, the Reverend Mr. William Smith. The pattern of Elizabeth Graeme's life had been a strange one, somewhat parallel to William's own: a period of splendor followed by a fatal political choice. Sent to London in her early twenties to recover from the depression triggered by William's marriage, she had gained fame there as a poet. Back in Philadelphia, she became the first lady of belles-lettres, translated French works into English verse, and married a Scot ten years younger than herself. Her husband fought on the British side in the Revolution. She separated from him but did not quite cast her lot with the patriots. She played an ambiguous role as messenger from the tories, fell into disgrace, and would have seen all her property confiscated after the war had it not been for the exertions of her influential friends, Smith among them. It was to him that she sold Graeme Park, shortly after Franklin's death. Not unlike William, she considered herself to the end of her days "an injured person."[9]

Irony piled upon bitter irony. Who, of all people, would be asked by the American Philosophical Society to pronounce Franklin's eulogy? The same William Smith. In March 1791, in front of the state and federal authorities, in the presence of Washington and the whole Philadelphia intelligentsia, Smith, who was famous for his eloquence, delivered a magnificent oration, studded with rhetorical questions and laudatory exclamations carefully confined to Franklin's scientific and philanthropic achievements. When the preacher's young daughter asked him that afternoon if he believed more than one-tenth of what he had said about "old Ben Lightning-rod,"[10] he laughed instead of answering. The subject of the eulogy might have appreciated the humor of the situation.

The lion's share of Franklin's heritage that had been earmarked for William in all preceding wills now went to Richard and Sally Bache: Franklin Court, the new houses built on Market Street, the printing office, a goodly number of lots and buildings here and there in Philadelphia, all the silver plate, pictures, and household goods.

Specifically for Richard, the lands near the Ohio and some recently purchased lots in the center of Philadelphia, the cancellation of the more than two thousand pounds he still owed his father-in-law, with the stipulation that he immediately "manumit and set free his negro man Bob."* A slave at Franklin Court must have been an acute embarrassment to the president of the Pennsylvania Abolition Society. Also for Richard, all of Franklin's musical instruments, his gold watch, the never-worn gold watch chain "of the Thirteen United States," and the right to collect a number of debts.

Specifically for Sally, one-half of whatever funds were deposited with Franklin's bankers in Paris and London, the income of some shares in the Bank of North America, to be put at her disposal *as her private money* (Franklin made clear in a codicil that this separate provision for his daughter did not reflect "any disrespect . . . for her husband"). Also for her, the miniature of Louis XVI, and with it a special request, an ultimate lesson in frugality: The 408 diamonds that surrounded it were not to be made into ornaments either for herself or her

---

* "Daddy Bob" was set free but, according to Sally's granddaughter, could not cope with freedom and was more often drunk than sober. He asked Sally to restore him to slavery. She did not but kept him in her house until he died, much lamented by the entire family.

daughters, in order not to introduce the "expensive, vain, and useless fashion of wearing jewels in this country."

Ignoring the spirit if not the letter of Franklin's will, the Baches promptly sold the outer circle of diamonds and took off for Europe with their oldest daughter. Thus Sally, almost fifty, finally fulfilled the dream of her youth: She saw England. They settled in the capital, close to William and his second wife, his former landlady Mary D'Evelin. William, who had so often entertained them in the governor's mansion, observed sadly that his present house was not large enough to offer hospitality, but introduced them to the circle of his father's friends. The only surviving portrait of Sally was painted that winter by the well-known portraitist John Hoppner (son-in-law of Franklin's old friend, the waxwork artist Patience Wright). Clad in a *fichu Marie-Antoinette* and the kind of Phrygian cap fashionable during the French Revolution, Sally appears plump and pink, fair and curly, somewhat like a good-natured milkmaid, very much the kind of woman one imagines from her correspondence. Her husband, too, sat for his portrait: He looks stern, smug, and very affluent. Did William ever think back on the day when he had warned his father against Richard Bache and called him a fortune hunter? If such he had been, Richard had certainly succeeded beyond his wildest imagination.

After their return home—they did not go to France as planned because of the turbulent situation—Richard retired from his altogether unsuccessful career in business and moved his family to a country estate on the Delaware. He had always wanted to be a gentleman-farmer, and, disgruntled with the government's failure to recognize his merits, he did not care to remain in Philadelphia, now the federal capital. But Sally, for the fourteen years she was still to live, never stopped missing the city. She found the atmosphere depressing and lonely in those primly Quaker surroundings where the family's chief recreation, music, was darkly looked upon as too much of a sensuous pleasure. Still, she had long been accustomed to let others have their way. There was the river, nobody could object to swimming, and the Baches outdid one another in endurance and skill in the water.

Next to the Baches, the biggest chunk of the estate went to Temple, but with strings attached. This was Franklin's last chance to prod his wayward favorite, guide his life, give him a professional goal and an emotional mooring. "Temple's Portion," Benny explained to Margaret, "is [grandfather's] Library and all his Manuscripts and Papers, a very valuable Legacy by itself. His Estates in Jersey which he is to be completely Master of on the Day of his Marriage . . . will be a Spur to

his Batchelor Spirit and may effect a happy Change in it."[11] Appointed
his grandfather's literary heir, Temple could easily gain fame by editing
and annotating the manuscripts in his possession. Nobody had better
knowledge than he did of the background of those eight crucial years
in France. The coveted manuscript of the *Autobiography* was a potential gold mine.* But Temple was not to be manipulated. He could not
wait to say goodby to farming, to leave a country he scarcely knew and
had scant cause to be grateful to. Within a year he sold the library and
sailed back to England, taking along only a few thousand among the
most interesting documents of the enormous collection of manuscripts.

For the first time in his life William had his son to himself, but
whatever happiness he may have anticipated did not materialize. Temple was in his thirties now, and not about to submit meekly to another
paternal hand. William's oft-repeated good advice about getting married, doing something useful with his life, settling down to the editing
of those papers, left him unmoved. Settling down as a married man?
Not until he had found a rich heiress, snapped Temple. Irritated as he
was with his father's will, William was still anxious to honor his memory. Nor was he alone in nagging Temple. Several of Franklin's
friends, deeply upset because a pirated edition of his memoirs had appeared in Paris a few months after his death, kept urging him to hurry.
Temple countered their efforts not only by his own inertia but by the
absolute veto on publication he imposed on the two men (Benjamin
Vaughan in London, Louis-Guillaume Le Veillard in Paris) who had
genuine copies of the *Autobiography* in their hands. Nobody had been
more instrumental in pushing Franklin to complete the history of his
life than his former neighbor in Passy, that very Le Veillard who had
accompanied him as far as Southampton and had never stopped regret-
ting he had not moved his whole family to the New World. In spite of
repeated promises to join him any day and start working with him,
Temple tarried in England from 1791 until 1798. By that time Le
Veillard had long before perished on the scaffold.

The only tangible result of Temple's activity during those seven
years in England was a baby girl. Born in 1798—a few months before
he decamped for Paris—to Ellen Johnson D'Evelin, the unmarried sister
of William's wife, the child was baptized Ellen Franklin. Aside from
making some provisions in his will, Temple never took the slightest interest in her. But William raised this girl, who was his niece as well as
his granddaughter, and soon came to adore her. Never able, even late

* Other legacies to Temple included a timepiece, a Chinese gong, and an option
to take up three thousand acres of undeveloped land granted to Franklin by the
state of Georgia.

in life, to banish his father from his mind, he would write to Jonathan Williams that nine-year-old Ellen was "very like my father and has every promise of making a fine, sensible woman."[12] In fact Ellen took care of him when he was widowed, and inherited what little fortune he had.

Could Temple have run back to Blanchette in Paris? There was no more Blanchette. At just about the time he settled in London in 1791, she had died under mysterious circumstances, her end variously ascribed to consumption, poison, or jumping out of a window. What Temple did with his life once he got back to Paris has never been traced. Bitterly estranged from his father, he sent no news for fourteen years. The words in which William expressed his anguish ("more trouble of mind than I had ever before experienced")[13] sadly echo the words Franklin had used in assessing their own break ("Nothing has ever hurt me so much"). To the end, William's life was to be a harrowing caricature of his father's.

Suddenly, in March 1812, Temple broke the long silence and announced to his father that he was eager at last to publish Franklin's works, would soon come to England to consult him, and might even settle there. William, now well over eighty, received the news joyfully, "not being able to bear the thought of dying at enmity with one so nearly connected."[14] But Temple delayed once again and William died the following year without having seen him.

Twenty-seven years after coming into possession of Franklin's manuscripts and papers, Temple finally brought out in 1817 the first volume (to be followed by two others) of the *Memoirs of the Life and Writings of Benjamin Franklin.* Not in the least apologetic about having "so long withheld from public view . . . such interesting documents," he proclaimed it had been a wise and deliberate act of self-restraint on his part: "There are *times* and *seasons* when prudence imposes the restriction of silence in the gratification even of the most laudable curiosity."[15] For his belated effort he won praise from an unexpected quarter. John Adams, *mirabile dictu,* sent Temple a cordial note: "The volume of Dr. Franklin's Correspondence has seemed to make me live over again my Life at Passy. I rejoice that the Publick are to have a compleat Edition of his Works, for there is scarce a scratch of his Pen that is not worth preserving.—I am pleased to see you at length appearing on the stage of human Affairs."[16] Thus does the passing of years mellow one's memories! Actually what Temple had published was only a small selection of already selected papers. The bulk of the material had remained in Philadelphia, stored in a stable belonging to a friend who kept it first as a deposit and eventually received full title through Temple's will.*

He lived only six years more, all of them apparently in Paris where he was buried in 1823. A few days before his death, he married his longtime companion, the English-born Hannah Collyer, who had been going by his name. (The widow apparently brought the precious manuscripts back to London where she abandoned them. They were discovered accidentally about 1840 in the shop of a tailor who was using them as paper patterns.)

Thus ended the handsome and witty Temple and with him the Franklin name. Torn between two men and three cultures, idolized at one moment and used as a pawn the next, told successively that he ought to become a lawyer, a diplomat, a farmer, an editor, Temple turned cynical, self-indulgent, self-righteous, too passive for any other form of rebellion than forever disappointing everybody's expectations.

Benny was exactly the other way around. To enhance his grandfather's reputation and glory, to fulfill the old man's wishes (as he interpreted them), to use the press as "the Bulwark of Liberty" and the means to "enlighten the People," such would be the mission of his brief and passionate life.

Franklin left him about one thousand pounds' worth of printing equipment (though not the little house where the shop was located), some books, his share in the Library Company, one-fourth of the cash on hand in Paris and London. That his portion, though much larger than his brothers' and sisters', should be so much smaller than Temple's had surprised some of his "good Friends and well-wishers"[17] but not Benny himself. The legacy, he commented bravely to Margaret, squared perfectly with his expectations.

Within six months of his grandfather's death, Benny-the-pliant had become Benny-the-bold. In spite of some cautionary advice because of his youth and lack of official patronage, he launched his own newspaper. The *Philadelphia General Advertiser*, later to be rechristened with the more stirring name of *Aurora*, came to the light exactly seventy years after James and Benjamin Franklin had shaken staid Boston with the equally combative but less scurrilous *New-England Courant*. The moment seemed propitious. Parties were beginning to jell: on the one hand the conservative Federalists, led by Adams, Hamilton, and Jay,

* The friend and his descendants (the Fox family) had no great appreciation of this gift, used some of the letters as souvenirs for their guests, and took no special care of the others. Recovered piecemeal through the second half of the nineteenth century, some thirteen thousand of them made their way to the American Philosophical Society.

pro-English, advocating a strong centralized government, supported mostly by the upper class; on the other hand the anti-Federalists, soon to be organized by Jefferson under the name of "Democratic-Republican party," leaning toward France, state autonomy, the defense of agrarian interests, and cheap money. Philadelphia was an anti-Federalist strong-hold, and Jefferson's ideas fairly close to Franklin's; Benny was natu-rally attracted to that side, though Jefferson's support remained more verbal than real. The program announced in the *Advertiser*'s first issue did not stress internal politics as much as thorough coverage of interna-tional news and the diffusion of both scientific and practical informa-tion among those who could not afford expensive books—a goal that had always been close to the Doctor's heart.

Among the first to send congratulations was Jane Mecom. She remembered a little grimly that her brother had called the debts a pub-lisher tries to collect "an estate in the clouds"; but she praised Benny's paper for appearing "very respectable."[18] Respectable hardly turned out to be the right word. After a slow, stately, and somewhat dull start under the placid motto of "Truth, Decency, Utility," Benny was soon caught up in the vituperative style of journalism prevailing in the 1790s. "Ben who was the flower of the family has engaged so much in the Democratic party and so violently, that he has lost the esteem of all others. What a pity that a few years should alter a man so much."[19] Thus commented Polly Hewson's daughter Eliza, Benny's childhood "fiancée," with the distaste of one whose affiliations were with the op-posite side. Displaying all the zeal and intolerance of a crusader, Benny worked as hard as his grandfather had ever worked, writing editorials, translating lengthy articles, keeping abreast of developments in Paris, at-tending to the printing and sale of the paper, distributing free copies to those who claimed they could not pay. Margaret Markoe, whom he had married in 1791, stood squarely behind him: "Poor woman," said Eliza, "her old acquaintance have almost all deserted her. She is luckily of opinion that her husband is quite in the right."[20]

Benny had a scoop: In 1795 an anti-Federalist senator gave him a copy of the rather disadvantageous treaty Jay had negotiated with Eng-land, a treaty Washington wanted to keep secret until the Senate had approved it. Published in the *Aurora*, it sent Philadelphia into an up-roar. Benny traveled all the way to Boston selling copies at every stop and collecting applause at rallies of the "Friends of Equal Liberty," as the militant anti-Federalists then called themselves. The paper's circula-tion increased, but so did the number of his enemies. Most vitriolic among them was William Cobbett, a recently emigrated Englishman, a royalist, a hater of France, and a master of invective and satire. He dubbed Benny "Lightning Rod jr.," baited him by exhibiting in his window a portrait of Franklin side by side with one of Marat, declared the young publisher should be treated "as a Turk, a Jew, a Jacobin, or a Dog."[21]

Benny in turn became more reckless. He accused Washington, who had drawn close to the Federalist position, of having violated the Constitution and overdrawn his salary. At its peak in 1797, the *Aurora,* with a circulation of more than seventeen hundred copies, was the most widely read paper of its day and no longer a negligible opposition force.

When the authoritarian John Adams became president and led America to the brink of war against France, Benny redoubled his attacks and suffered the consequences. His readership dropped dramatically. Were it not for the French envoy, Citizen Genet, who was rumored to be buying an "amazing number"[22] of copies, the *Aurora* might have folded. Physical violence soon erupted. A few steps from the spot where Deborah had once stood firm in the face of a threatening riot, her Kingbird saw his windows smashed three times. On June 26, 1798, he was arrested on the charge of libeling the president and exciting sedition, then released on bail, the trial date being set for the October term.

But he never went on trial. He was so enmeshed in battle that he omitted the customary precaution of moving out of Philadelphia during the summer. Exhausted by tension and overwork, he caught the yellow fever and succumbed on September 10, 1798, at the age of twenty-nine, exactly one week after his wife had given birth to their fourth son. Benny was so estranged from his parents at the time of his final illness that his sister Betsy had to sneak away from their country place in the middle of the night to come to town and help Margaret nurse him through his last days.

Margaret was a tiny woman of immense determination. Right after her husband's death she circulated a handbill announcing that very soon the *Aurora* would appear again under her direction. And it did. She pooled forces with her husband's right-hand man, a talented, belligerent Irishman by the name of William Duane. Together they kept the paper going until Jefferson's coming to power created the political climate that would make it thrive. They were married in 1800 (Duane's first wife had died the same summer as Benny) and in 1808, ten years ahead of Temple, Duane published the first of a six-volume selection of Franklin's papers. Thus, vicariously absorbed into Franklin's "family," he took over both the political mission Benny had been unable to carry out and the literary task Temple was still reluctant to begin.

Benny's widow deeply shocked the Baches when she married Duane. Some years later their own daughter Debbie would shock them still more when she married Duane's son by his first wife. Indeed, Richard Bache, a highly conventional man, was in for a number of shocks from his children who had inherited their grandfather's drive toward self-fulfillment, but not his extraordinary intelligence. Before bringing about his own death through excess of ardor, Benny had antagonized all his former circle. Willy, the second Bache son, went off to study medicine in England but soon was lured to revolutionary France. When funds from home dried up to force his return, he embarked on a French privateer, lived adventurously, came back to Philadelphia full of "new" ideas, and eventually moved to Virginia to be closer to Jefferson. Betsy, the third child, did not please her parents either when she fell in love with an actor, went into a serious depression because she was prevented from marrying him, and after some years of misery married him anyway—just as her mother had married her father.

The Baches had been on bad terms with Jonathan Williams, too, ever since their financial affairs had become entangled during the war. Jonathan had won a lawsuit against Richard's firm which only reinforced their hostility. Franklin's affection had remained undiminished, however, and Jonathan had spent many hours working with him in his library, never once "exchanging a word with Mr. or Mrs. Bache or even being by them invited to view the inside of an apartment or to wet my lips."[23] He suffered a second bankruptcy in 1788 and it was not until the following year that he was able, at last, to fetch from England his wife and their surviving daughter. In spite of all his business troubles, Jonathan continued the scientific and military studies that would lead to his appointment as the first superintendent of West Point when Jefferson became president, in 1801, studies that ranged from resuscitation techniques to better soap and candles to the latest in fortification.

Through all his tribulations, Jonathan was sustained by the steady friendship of Polly Hewson, a friendship that spanned more than twenty years and three countries. Possibly because of her loyalty to him, she too was on rather cool terms with the Baches, though the farm she had bought for her oldest son on the banks of the Delaware was less than five miles from theirs. Polly, to whom Franklin surprisingly bequeathed nothing more than a silver tankard, was overwhelmed after his death with the homesickness she had been repressing as long as she thought her transplantation was of benefit to her children. When her second son, Tom, sailed for England, along with Willy Bache, to study medicine, she opened her heart to him and poured out her disenchantment and growing melancholia in a series of possessive, querulous, and desperately unhappy letters.

She told him of her longing for home (how much better London's rain and beggars than Pennsylvania's heat and slaves!), of her disillusionment with the system of government (total anarchy, she predicted, as soon as Washington died), of her low opinion of the fate of American women ("Nothing but insignificance or slavery awaits a woman here"),[24] of the boredom she and Eliza endured living in isolation in the country. She finally came to the sad awareness that by heeding Franklin's urgings she had made a terrible mistake: "Indeed I do repent I ever brought you to this country."[25]

Reproached for having fallen too much under the influence of Willy Bache, reproached for frequenting Temple in London while neglecting his own English relatives and friends, reproached for just about everything he wrote, Tom fell into long periods of silence. When Polly died suddenly, in 1795, only five years after Franklin, William and Eliza Hewson felt sure their brother would remain in England. But a letter arrived, its message sharp and clear: "I look to America as the promised land. The people [in England] enjoy some portion of liberty but it is not that full and perfect liberty that I have been taught to desire. It contains a great deal of the old leaven. I caught from Dr. Franklin my enthusiasm for America. He was able to paint the blessings of that country in glowing colours. I burnt with a desire of visiting it. . . . It answered the expectations a heated imagination had formed. Since then I have seen nothing to lessen my attachment."[26]

Tom came back to become one of the most distinguished doctors of his day. Eliza married an American. Poor Mrs. Stevenson never fulfilled her dream, but all her descendants took root in Pennsylvania, producing at least one doctor in every generation.

So many lives touched by Franklin. Some he put his stamp on more than he would ever realize; others resisted his efforts to direct them. Like most young men, he had believed fervently in the ability of one generation to mold the next; like most old men, he came to doubt it profoundly.

To his dear friend Bishop Shipley, who could not help brooding over the disastrous marriage of his most promising daughter, he quoted from his favorite poet, Isaac Watts: "He that raises a large Family does indeed, while he lives to observe them, *stand a broader Mark for Sorrow.*" But his own irrepressible optimism caused him to add, "but then he stands a broader Mark for Pleasure too." An optimism tempered by life, however: "When we launch our little Fleet of Barques into the Ocean, bound to different Ports, we hope for each a prosperous Voyage; but contrary Winds, hidden Shoals, Storms, and Enemies come in for a Share in the Disposition of Events; and though these occasion a Mixture of Disappointment, yet, considering the Risque where we can make no Insurance, we should think ourselves happy if some return with Success."[27]

Notes

Unless otherwise specified, all references are to the Yale edition of *The Papers of Benjamin Franklin*. Since this is complete only through 1771, subsequent references are given to other published sources or, in the case of unpublished manuscripts, to the dates under which they are filed in the Franklin Collection at Yale.

Abbreviations:

BF	Benjamin Franklin
DF	Deborah Franklin
WF	William Franklin
SF	Sally Franklin
SB	Sally Franklin Bache (after 1767)
RB	Richard Bache
BFB	Benjamin Franklin Bache
WTF	William Temple Franklin
JM	Jane Mecom
WS	William Strahan
PS	Polly Stevenson
PH	Polly Stevenson Hewson (after 1770)
MS	Margaret Stevenson
APS	American Philosophical Society
PMHB	*Pennsylvania Magazine of History and Biography*

Prologue

1. *The Autobiography of Benjamin Franklin*, ed. Leonard Labaree et al (New Haven, 1964), p. 44. (Hereafter cited as *Autobiography*.)

I: Son and Sibling

1. G. B. Warden, *Boston, 1689–1776* (Boston, 1970), p. 19.
2. Ralph L. Ketcham, ed., *The Political Thought of Benjamin Franklin* (Indianapolis, 1965), p. xxviii.
3. Carl Bridenbaugh, *Cities in the Wilderness* (New York, 1960), p. 388.
4. *Autobiography*, p. 113.
5. Ibid., p. 52.
6. BF to JM, July 17, 1771, *The Papers of Benjamin Franklin*, ed. Leonard Labaree, William Willcox, et al 18 vols. (New Haven, 1959–   ), 18: 185. (Hereafter cited by volume and page numbers only.)
7. *Autobiography*, p. 54.
8. Ibid., p. 144; epitaph, p. 56.
9. Ibid., p. 81.

10. Ibid., p. 169.
11. W. C. Ford, "Franklin's *New England Courant*," *Proc. Mass. Hist. Soc.* 57 (April 1924): 347–48.
12. Cotton Mather, "Diary," *Coll. Mass. Hist. Soc.* 7–8, 7th Ser., pt. 2: 639.
13. *Autobiography*, p. 113.
14. Samuel Johnson, "Addison," *Lives of the Poets, Works,* 2 vols. (London, 1854), 1: 175.
15. *Autobiography*, p. 68.
16. Ibid., p. 69.
17. Ibid., p. 70.
18. BF to JM [June ? 1748], 3: 303.
19. *Autobiography*, p. 71.
20. *Peter Kalm's Travels in North America,* rev. and ed. Adolph B. Benson, 2 vols. (New York, 1937), 1: 33.

II: Errata Committed, Errata Corrected

1. Ellis P. Oberholzer, *Philadelphia: A History of the City and Its People,* 2 vols. (Philadelphia, [1912]), 1: 235.
2. *Autobiography*, p. 89.
3. Ibid.
4. Ibid., p. 92.
5. Ibid., p. 90.
6. Ibid., p. 95.
7. Ibid., p. 96.
8. BF to Benjamin Vaughan, Nov. 9, 1779, Albert Henry Smyth, ed., *The Writings of Benjamin Franklin,* 10 vols. (New York, 1905–7), 7: 412. (Hereafter cited as Smyth.)
9. BF to DF, Nov. 22, 1757, 7: 274.
10. BF to Catharine Ray, Sept. 11, 1755, 6: 184.
11. *Autobiography*, p. 112.
12. Ibid., p. 107.
13. Ibid., p. 128.
14. Ibid.
15. Bridenbaugh, *Cities,* p. 226.
16. *Autobiography*, p. 129.
17. 11: 370–71n.
18. *Autobiography*, p. 129.
19. BF to Jonathan Williams, Jr., Apr. 8, 1779, Smyth, 7: 282.
20. Jonathan Williams, Jr., to BF, Apr. 13, 1779.
21. *Autobiography*, p. 129.
22. Ibid.
23. Ibid., p. 148.
24. Claude-Anne Lopez, *Mon Cher Papa: Franklin and the Ladies of Paris* (New Haven, 1966), p. 277.
25. Ibid.
26. The virtues are listed and discussed in the *Autobiography*, pp. 148–60.
27. J. G. de R. Hamilton, ed., *The Best Letters of Thomas Jefferson* (Boston, 1926), p. 157: Jefferson to Thos. Jefferson Randolph, Nov. 24, 1808.

28. D. H. Lawrence, *Studies in Classic American Literature* (paperback ed., New York, 1955), p. 28.

29. Charles Coleman Sellers, *Benjamin Franklin in Portraiture* (New Haven, 1962), p. 81.

30. John Adams, *The Adams Papers, Diary and Autobiography*, ed. L. H. Butterfield, 4 vols. (Cambridge, Mass., 1961), 4: 87.

31. *Autobiography*, p. 160.

32. Ibid., p. 156.

33. Lawrence, p. 23.

34. *Autobiography*, pp. 87–88.

III: Industry, Frugality, Fertility

1. *Autobiography*, p. 129.

2. 1: 219.

3. 2: 128.

4. BF to J. and T. Leverett, Mar. 11, 1755, 5: 514.

5. *Autobiography*, pp. 125–26.

6. Ibid., pp. 144–45.

7. BF to JM, May 27, 1757, 7: 216.

8. Carl Bridenbaugh, ed., *Gentleman's Progress: The Itinerarium of Dr. Alexander Hamilton, 1744* (Chapel Hill, 1948), pp. 22–23.

9. BF to Miss Alexander, June 24, 1782, Smyth, 8: 459.

10. "Reply to a Piece of Advice," Mar. 4, 1734/35, 2: 23.

11. *Autobiography*, p. 145.

12. BF to Jonathan Williams, Sr., Nov. 25, 1762, 10: 156.

13. BF to DF, June 27, 1760, 9: 175.

14. BF to Jos. Priestley, June 7, 1782, Smyth, 8: 451–52.

15. 2: 23.

16. *The Speech of Miss Polly Baker*, 3: 123–25.

17. 3: 122.

18. Max Hall, *Benjamin Franklin and Polly Baker* (Chapel Hill, 1960), p. 112.

19. BF to John Alleyne, [Aug. 9, 1768], 15: 184.

20. 3: 30.

21. BF to Mme. Brillon, Nov. 23, 1780; Lopez, *Mon Cher Papa*, p. 82.

22. BF to John Alleyne, [Aug. 9, 1768], 15: 184–85.

23. BF to James Read, Aug. 17, 1745, 3: 40.

24. Daniel Fisher, "Extracts from the Diary of Daniel Fisher 1755," ed. C. R. Howard, *PMHB* 17 (1893): 277.

25. Sarah Broughton to BF, July 3, 1766, 13: 329.

26. 13: 330.

27. "A Scolding Wife," July 5, 1733, 1: 325.

28. BF to SB, Jan. 26, 1784, Smyth, 9: 161.

29. BF to DF, Feb. 19, 1758, 7: 383.

30. 4: 72–73.

31. BF to William Dunlap, Apr. 4, 1757, 7: 169.

32. *Poor Richard*, 1747, 3: 100.

33. "An Account of the New Invented Pennsylvania FirePlaces," 2: 425.

34. *Autobiography*, p. 116.

35. "I Sing My Plain Country Joan," 2: 353–54.

IV: Out of the Home and into the World

1. *Autobiography*, p. 196.
2. Ibid., p. 240.
3. BF to Collinson, Mar. 28, 1747, 3: 118–19.
4. BF to Collinson, July 28, 1747, 3: 157, 158.
5. BF to Cadwallader Colden, Oct. 31, 1751, 4: 202.
6. BF to Collinson, Apr. 29, 1749, 3: 364–65.
7. BF to [John Franklin], Dec. 25, 1750, 4: 82–83.
8. I. Bernard Cohen, ed., *Benjamin Franklin's Experiments* (Cambridge, Mass., 1941), p. 45.
9. BF to Collinson, Aug. 14, 1747, 3: 171.
10. D'Alibard Report, 4: 303–10.
11. Collinson to BF, July 7, 1752, 4: 333.
12. Collinson to BF, Sept. 27, 1752, 4: 358.
13. *Autobiography*, p. 209.
14. 4: 368.
15. 4: 408.
16. Eleanor M. Tilton, "Lightning-Rods and the Earthquake of 1755," *New Eng. Quar.* 13 (1940): 87.
17. BF to Colden, Apr. 12, 1753, 4: 463.
18. Report to the Committee of the Royal Society, Aug. 27, 1772, Smyth, 5: 421–22.
19. BF to DF, June 10, 1758, 8: 94.
20. [Cadwallader Evans], report in *Medical Observations and Inquiries*, 2 vols. (London, 1757), 1: 84–85.
21. BF to JM, June 19, 1731, 1: 201.
22. BF to Josiah and Abiah Franklin, Sept. 6, 1744, 2: 413.
23. BF to Abiah Franklin, Apr. 12, 1750, 3: 474.
24. BF to Abiah Franklin, Oct. 16, 1747, 3: 179.
25. Josiah Franklin to BF, May 26, 1739, 2: 231.
26. Abiah Franklin to BF, Oct. 14, 1751, 4: 199.
27. BF to JM, May 21, 1752, 4: 318.
28. BF to Colden, Oct. 11, 1750, 4: 68.
29. 4: 68n.
30. Lopez, *Mon Cher Papa*, p. 210.
31. Penn to Richard Peters, June 9, 1748, 3: 186.
32. 2: 380.
33. 7: 73.
34. Dunlap to BF, [Oct. ? 1764], 11: 420.
35. BF and John Foxcroft to Dunlap, [Oct. ? 1764], 11: 421.
36. BF to Peter Franklin [before 1765], 11: 539.
37. BF to John Franklin, Sept. 27, 1750, 4: 65.
38. BF to John Franklin, Mar. 16, 1755, 5: 520.
39. BF to C. Ray, Sept. 11, 1755, 6: 183.
40. BF to C. Ray, Oct. 16, 1755, 6: 225.
41. BF to C. Ray, Sept. 11, 1755, 6: 183–84.
42. BF to C. Ray, Mar. 4, 1755, 5: 502–3.
43. Ibid.

44. BF to C. Ray, Sept. 11, 1755, 6: 184.
45. C. Ray to BF, June 28 [1755], 6: 96.
46. BF to C. Ray, [Mar.–Apr. 1755], 5: 537.
47. BF to C. Ray, Sept. 11, 1755, 6: 183.
48. BF to C. Ray, [Mar.–Apr. 1755], 5: 536.
49. BF to C. Ray, Oct. 16, 1755, 6: 225.

V: "Much of a Beau"

1. Elizabeth Duane Gillespie, *A Book of Remembrance* (Philadelphia, 1901), p. 17.
2. Fisher, "Diary," *PMHB* 17 (1893): 276–77.
3. WF to BF, May 10, 1768, 15: 123.
4. BF to JM, [June ?] 1748, 3: 303.
5. William M. Mariboe, "The Life of William Franklin, 1730(1)–1813, 'Pro Rege et Patria'" (Ph.D. diss., University of Pennsylvania, 1962), p. 37.
6. BF to Colden, June 5, 1747, 3: 142.
7. BF to WS, Oct. 19, 1748, 3: 321.
8. Mariboe, p. 42.
9. Charles Moore, ed., *George Washington's Rules of Civility and Decent Behavior* (Cambridge, Mass., 1926).
10. BF to Abiah Franklin, Apr. 12, 1750, 3: 474–75.
11. BF to JM, Oct. 24, 1751, 4: 200.
12. DF to Collinson, Apr. 30, 1755, 6: 24.
13. *Autobiography*, p. 224.
14. BF to DF, Jan. 25, 1756, 6: 364–65.
15. BF to DF, Jan. 30, 1756, 6: 379.
16. BF to DF, Nov. 13, 1756, 7: 17–18.
17. BF to Collinson, June 26, 1755, 6: 87.
18. 6: 409.
19. 7: 13n.
20. 7: 73.
21. 7: 74.
22. BF to Collinson, Nov. 5, 1756, 7: 13–15.
23. BF to Richard Partridge, Nov. 27, 1755, 6: 273.
24. William Smith to Thos. Penn, [Sept. ? 1755], 6: 211.
25. BF to PS, Mar. 25, 1763, 10: 234.
26. BF to Collinson, Nov. 5, 1756, 7: 12.
27. WF to WS, Feb. 18, 1765, Charles Henry Hart, "Letters from William Franklin to William Strahan," *PMHB* 35 (1911): 441.
28. *Pa. Journal*, May 20, 1756, Ralph Ketcham, "Benjamin Franklin and William Smith: New Light on an Old Philadelphia Quarrel," *PMHB* 88 (1964): 150n.
29. Peters to Th. Penn, Feb. 14, 1757, 7: 133n.
30. BF to C. Ray, Sept. 11, 1755, 6: 182.
31. WF to Elizabeth Graeme, Apr. 7, 1757, 7: 177–78.
32. DF to Susannah Wright, July 14, 1757.

VI: "The Seeds of Every Female Virtue"

1. *Autobiography*, p. 60.
2. 1: 20.

3. *Autobiography*, p. 166.
4. BF to DF, Feb. 19, 1758, 7: 384.
5. BF to WS, Nov. 4, 1754, 5: 440.
6. BF to PS, June 11, 1760, 11: 121.
7. Carl Holliday, *Woman's Life in Colonial Days* (Boston, 1922), p. 145.
8. BF to Abiah Franklin, Oct. 16, 1747, 3: 179–80.
9. Alice Morse Earle, *Colonial Dames and Good Wives* (Boston, 1895), p. 234.
10. PH to SB, Aug. 16, 1771.
11. Earle, p. 75.
12. Ibid., p. 65.
13. Ibid., p. 66.
14. BF to DF, Feb. 19, 1758, 7: 384.
15. [Richard Allestree], *The Whole Duty of Man* (London, 1730), Preface.
16. Lady Mary Wray, *The Lady's Library*, ed. Richard Steele, 3 vols. 3d ed. (London, 1722), 1: 36.
17. Ibid., 1: 1.
18. Ibid., 1: "Employment."
19. *The World* 1 (1753): 9.
20. Wray, 1: 96.
21. BF to WS, June 2, 1750, 3: 479–80.

VII: London

1. BF to WS, Jan. 31, 1757, 7: 116.
2. WS to DF, Dec. 13, 1757, 7: 295–98.
3. BF to DF, Jan. 14, 1758, 7: 359–60.
4. BF to DF, June 10, 1754, 8: 93.
5. 8: 93*n*.
6. Anne H. Wharton, *Colonial Days and Dames* (Philadelphia, 1908), p. 115.
7. BF to DF, [July 17, 1757], 7: 243.
8. WF to Eliz. Graeme, July 17, 1757, 7: 244.
9. WF to Eliz. Graeme, Dec. 9, 1757, 7: 288–92.
10. Reprinted in Simon Gratz, "Some Material for a Biography of Mrs. Elizabeth Ferguson née Graeme," *PMHB* 39 (1915): 263–67.
11. BF to DF, Mar. 5, 1760, 9: 32–33.
12. MS to BF, [1763?], 10: 427.
13. BF to PH, Jan. 27, 1783, Smyth, 9: 13.
14. BF to PH, May 13, 1782.
15. BF to PS, Sept. 13, 1760, 9: 216.
16. BF to DF, Feb. 19, 1758, 7: 382.
17. Ibid.
18. BF to DF, June 10, 1758, 8: 94.
19. BF to DF, Apr. 7, 1759, 8: 307.
20. BF to DF, Feb. 19, 1758, 7: 381.
21. BF to DF, Apr. 7, 1757, 8: 307.
22. BF to DF, Feb. 27, 1760, 9: 27.
23. BF to PS, Oct. 29, 1761, 9: 377.
24. BF to DF, Feb. 19, 1758, 7: 382.
25. BF to DF, June 27, 1760, 9: 175.
26. 9: 174.

27. BF to [Isaac Norris], Jan. 14, 7: 360–62.
28. BF to Jos. Galloway, Feb. 17, 1758, 7: 374.
29. BF to DF, Feb. 19, 1758, 7: 380.
30. *Autobiography*, p. 207.
31. BF to DF, Feb. 19, 1758, 7: 380.
32. BF to DF, Sept. 6, 1758, 8: 137.
33. *Autobiography*, p. 48.
34. Mary Fisher to BF, Aug. 14, 1758, 8: 121.
35. BF to DF, Sept. 6, 1758, 7: 134, 144, 146.
36. BF to Lord Kames, Jan. 3, 1760, 9: 9.
37. David Hume to BF, May 10, 1762, 10: 81–82.
38. John Bartram to BF, July 29, 1757, 7: 246.
39. BF to DF, June 10, 1758, 8: 95.
40. Hugh Roberts to BF, May 15, 1760, 9: 113.
41. BF to DF, Nov. 22, 1757, 7: 278.
42. BF to DF, Jan. 21, 1758, 7: 364–65.

VIII: *Homecoming, Homesickness*

1. WS to DF, Dec. 13, 1757, 7: 297.
2. WF to BF, Sept. 3, 1758, 8: 132.
3. 10: 147.
4. John Adams, *Diary and Autobiography* 4: 151.
5. 10: 155n.
6. BF to PS, Aug. 11, 1762, 10: 142–43.
7. BF to Lord Kames, Aug. 17, 1762, 10: 147.
8. BF to WS, Aug. 23, 1762, 10: 149.
9. 7: 167–68; 10: 100–101.
10. BF to Richard Jackson, Dec. 2, 1762, 10: 160.
11. BF to WS, Dec. 2, 1762, 10: 161.
12. BF to Kames, June 2, 1765, 10: 159.
13. BF to WS, Dec. 7, 1762, 10: 169.
14. BF to WS, Aug. 8, 1763, 10: 320.
15. BF to PS, Mar. 25, 1763, 10: 232–33.
16. MS to BF, [1763?], 10: 427–28.
17. BF to Giambatista Beccaria, July 13, 1762, 10: 130.
18. 10: 425.
19. 7: 177n.
20. Gratz, "Elizabeth Graeme," *PMHB* 39: 271.
21. WF to WS, Hart, "Letters," *PMHB* 35: 421.
22. WS to Hall, Oct. 20, 1763, Mariboe, "William Franklin," p. 116; WS to Hall, Nov. 1, 1763, 10: 155n.
23. BF to JM, Nov. 25, 1762, 10: 154–55.
24. WF to WS, Apr. 25, 1763, Hart, "Letters," p. 425.
25. 10: 237n.
26. 10: 200–201n.
27. WF to WS, Apr. 25, 1763, 10: 236n.
28. J. H. Plumb, "The French Connection," *American Heritage* 26, No. 1 (Dec. 1974): 32.
29. BF to PS, June 10, 1763, 10: 287.
30. BF to DF, June 16, 1763, 10: 291.

31. Edmund S. Morgan, *The Gentle Puritan: A Life of Ezra Stiles, 1727–1795* (New Haven, 1962), p. 149.
32. BF to Sarah Davenport, [June ? 1730], 1: 171.
33. BF to JM, Apr. 19, 1757, 7: 190.
34. BF to JM, Jan. 9, 1760, 9: 18.
35. BF to JM, June 19, 1763, 10: 292.

IX: Faith or Deeds?

1. BF to JM, Jan. 6, 1726/27, 1: 100–101.
2. JM to BF, Apr. 22, 1786, Carl Van Doren, ed., *The Letters of Benjamin Franklin and Jane Mecom* (Princeton, 1950), p. 263.
3. JM to DF, Sept. 28, 1765, Van Doren, p. 84.
4. BF to Benjamin Vaughan, Oct. 24, 1788, Smyth, 9: 677.
5. BF to Abiah Franklin, Apr. 13, 1738, 2: 202.
6. William Robertson to WS, Feb. 18, 1765, 12: 69–70.
7. BF to John Franklin, [May ? 1745], 3: 26.
8. 3: 26n.
9. BF to Jared Ingersoll, Dec. 11, 1762, 10: 175–76.
10. BF to JM, July 28, 1743, 2: 385.
11. BF to Joseph Huey, June 6, 1753, 4: 505.
12. BF to JM, Sept. 16, 1758, 8: 154–55.
13. BF to JM, Jan. 9, 1760, 9: 17–18.
14. BF to JM, May 30, 1757, 7: 223.
15. BF to Edward and Jane Mecom, [1744–45], 2: 448.
16. BF to JM, [June ? 1748], 3: 302–3.
17. BF to WS, Oct. 19, 1748, 3: 322.
18. BF to Edward and Jane Mecom, Sept. 14, 1752, 4: 356.
19. BF to Edward and Jane Mecom, Nov. 30, 1752, 4: 385.
20. BF to JM, June 28, 1756, 6: 465.
21. BF to JM, May 30, 1757, 7: 223.
22. BF to DF, May 27, 1757, 7: 221.
23. Benj. Mecom to DF, Feb. 9, 1761.
24. BF to WS, June 2, 1763, 10: 271.
25. BF to Rev. John Lathrop, May 31, 1788, Smyth, 9: 651.
26. BF to Abiah Franklin, Apr. 12, 1750, 3: 475.
27. JM to DF, Jan. 29, 1758, Van Doren, *Letters*, p. 65.
28. BF to JM, Dec. 15, 1763, 10: 393.
29. Van Doren, p. 101.

X: The Dream and the Nightmare

1. PS to BF, May 24, 1764, 11: 203.
2. June 9, 1763.
3. BF to R. Jackson, Feb. 11, 1764, 11: 77.
4. Ibid.
5. BF to John Fothergill, Mar. 14, 1764, 11: 103.
6. BF to Jackson, Feb. 11, 1764, 11: 77.
7. BF to Fothergill, Mar. 14, 1764, 11: 103.
8. Ibid.
9. BF to Henry Bouquet, Sept. 30, 1764, 11: 367.

10. BF to Fothergill, Mar. 14, 1764, 11: 103.
11. 11: 173n.
12. BF to Jackson, June 25, 1764, 11: 239.
13. BF to Jackson, Sept. 1, 1764, 11: 329.
14. 11: 383.
15. 11: 387.
16. BF to WS, Sept. 1, 1764, 11: 332.
17. 11: 391.
18. 11: 402n.
19. BF to SF, Nov. 8, 1764, 11: 449–50.
20. DF to BF, Oct. 8, 1765, 12: 302.
21. DF to BF, Feb. 10, 1765, 12: 44.
22. 12: 82n.
23. DF to BF, Apr. 7, 1765, 12: 102.
24. BF to DF, Feb. 14, 1765, 12: 62.
25. BF to DF, June 4, 1765, 12: 167.
26. BF to DF, July 13, 1765, 12: 211.
27. DF to BF, Aug. 1–8, 1765, 12: 225.
28. BF to DF [Aug. 1765], 12: 251.
29. SF to BF, Oct. 14, 1765, 12: 318.
30. BF to Chas. Thomson, July 11, 1765, 12: 207–8.
31. JM to BF, Dec. 30, 1765, 12: 417.
32. WF to Grey Cooper, Jan. 15, 1766, Edmund S. Morgan and Helen M. Morgan, *The Stamp Act Crisis* (Chapel Hill, 1953), p. 190.
33. WF to BF, Nov. 13, 1765, 12: 369.
34. BF to John Hughes, Aug. 9, 1765, 12: 234.
35. BF to Samuel Rhoads, July 8, 1765, 12: 204.
36. BF to DF, Feb. 14, 1765, 12: 64.
37. Hall to BF, Sept. 6, 1765, 12: 659.
38. 12: 264.
39. 12: 266.
40. JM to DF, Feb. 27, 1766, Van Doren, *Letters*, p. 90.
41. DF to BF, Sept. 22, 1765, 12: 270–74.
42. BF to DF, Nov. 9, 1765, 12: 360.
43. DF to BF, [Oct. 6–13? 1765], 12: 294.
44. DF to BF, [Oct. 8, 1765], 12: 300.
45. DF to BF, [Oct. 6–13? 1765], 12: 294–98.
46. DF to BF, Apr. 20–25, 1767, 14: 138.
47. BF to DF, June 22, 1765, 14: 194–95.
48. DF to BF, [Oct. 6–13? 1765], 12: 297.
49. DF to BF, [Oct. 9, 1765], 12: 301.
50. Jos. Galloway to BF, Oct. 17, 1768, 15: 232.
51. DF to BF, Nov. 3, 1765, 12: 353.
52. DF to BF, [Oct. 9, 1765], 12: 301.
53. 12: 351.
54. DF to BF, [Oct. 9, 1765], 12: 303.
55. 12: 353n.
56. Morgan, *Stamp Act*, p. 198.
57. 12: 40.
58. BF to Daniel Wister, Sept. 27, 1766, 13: 429.

59. 13: 7–8.
60. "Examination," 13: 129–62.
61. BF to DF, Apr. 6, 1765, 13: 283.
62. 13: 165–66.
63. 13: 176.
64. SF to BF, Mar. 25, 1766, 13: 199.
65. Baynton, Wharton & Morgan Co. to BF, Aug. 28, 1766, 13: 397.
66. BF to JM, Mar. 1, 1766, 13: 188.
67. JM to BF, Nov. 8, 1766, 13: 489.
68. BF to Galloway, Nov. 8, 1766, 13: 488.
69. BF to DF, Apr. 6, 1766, 13: 233–34.
70. DF to BF, [Feb. 5–8? 1766], 13: 118.

XI: *Father of the Bride*

1. SF to BF, May 30, 1765, 12: 152.
2. DF to BF, Jan. 12, 1766, 13: 33.
3. *Pa. Gaz.*, Sept. 4, 1766.
4. Gillespie, *A Book of Remembrance*, p. 25.
5. Ibid.
6. "The Mount Regale Fishing Company of Philadelphia," *PMHB* 27 (1903): 89.
7. RB, "Day Book, 1761–1792," unpubl. ms., Philadelphia, Franklin Institute.
8. DF to BF, Apr. 20–25, 1767, 14: 136.
9. BF to DF, May 23, 1767, 14: 166–67.
10. BF to DF, June 22, 1767, 14: 193.
11. Ibid.
12. Ibid.
13. WF to BF, [May ? 1767], 14: 174.
14. RB, "Day Book," Mar. 28, 1767.
15. WF to BF, [May ? 1767], 14: 174–75.
16. SF to RB, May 14, 1767.
17. BF to RB, Aug. 5, 1767, 14: 220–21.
18. BF to DF, Aug. 5, 1767, 14: 225.
19. SF to RB, May 14, 1767.
20. DF to BF, May 16, 1767, 14: 157.
21. BF to DF, Dec. 3, 1757, 7: 278.
22. MS to DF, Sept. 18, 1767.
23. DF to BF, Oct. 13, 1767, 14: 280.
24. *Pa. Chron.*, Nov. 2, 1767.
25. JM to BF, Dec. 1, 1767, 14: 334.
26. BF to JM, Feb. 21, 1768, 15: 57.
27. BF to JM, Feb. 23, 1769, 16: 50.
28. WF to BF, May 10, 1768, 15: 123.
29. Ibid.
30. DF to S and RB, Aug. 16, 1768.
31. BF to RB, Aug. 13, 1768, 15: 186.
32. Gillespie, p. 20.
33. DF to S and RB, Aug. 23, 1768.
34. BF to DF, Dec. 2, 1768, 15: 292.
35. BF to DF, Mar. 1, 1769, 16: 57.

36. BF to DF, Mar. 21, 1769, 16: 68.
37. SB to BF, May [1770], 17: 153.
38. SB to RB, Dec. 2, 1771.
39. PS to BF, Sept. 1, 1769, 16: 191.
40. PH to BF, Oct. 31, 1771, 18: 236–37.
41. RB to DF, Dec. 3, 1771, 18: 258.
42. Mary Bache to BF, Feb. 5, 1772.
43. BF to JM, Jan. 13, 1772, Van Doren, *Letters*, p. 134.
44. BF to SB, Jan. 29, 1772, Smyth, 5: 376–77.
45. BF to WF, July 14, 1773, Smyth, 6: 97.
46. RB to BF, May 16, 1772.
47. RB to BF, Apr. 6, 1773.
48. BF to SB, Apr. 6, 1773, Smyth, 6: 32.
49. SB to BF, Oct. 30, 1773.

XII: *The Patriarch of Craven Street*

1. Quoted in L. H. Gipson, *Lewis Evans* (Hist. Soc. Pa., Philadelphia, 1939), p. 80.
2. Amelia Evans to BF, May 23, 1769, 16: 134–35.
3. BF to DF, Sept. 1, 1773.
4. BF to DF, July 22, 1774, Smyth, 6: 234.
5. Amelia Barry to BF, July 3, 1777.
6. Amelia Barry to BF, Dec. 31, 1779.
7. Amelia Barry to BF, Dec. 10, 1784.
8. Amelia Barry to BF, Feb. 9, 1789.
9. BF to Jonathan Williams, Sr., Oct. 4, 1769, 16: 212.
10. BF to Timothy Folger, Aug. 21, 1770, 17: 210.
11. Martha Johnson to BF, Nov. 15, 1777.
12. Martha Johnson to BF, Oct. 18, 1781.
13. Hannah Walker to BF, Oct. 26, 1765, 12: 338.
14. 16: 179*n*.
15. BF to DF, Oct. 11, 1766, 13: 446.
16. DF to BF, Oct. 13, 1767, 14: 280.
17. BF to DF, Aug. 5, 1767, 14: 225.
18. BF to Samuel Francis, June 8, 1770, 17: 165.
19. BF to DF, Dec. 1, 1772.
20. WF to BF, [ca. Jan. 2, 1769], 16: 5.
21. Quoted J. A. Cochrane, *Dr. Johnson's Printer: The Life of William Strahan* (Cambridge, Mass., 1964), p. 94.
22. PH to Barbara Hewson, Oct. 4, 1774.
23. BF to WF, Jan. 30, 1772, Smyth, 5: 381.
24. BF to WF, July 14, 1773.
25. BF to WF, Aug. 1, 1774.
26. Jonathan Williams, Sr., to BF, Aug. 27, 1770, 17: 213.
27. BF to JM, July 17, 1771, 18: 187.
28. BF to JM, Dec. 30, 1770, 17: 314.
29. Henry Marchant to BF, Nov. 21, 1772.
30. "Complaints of William Hunter against William Hewson," [July ? 1771], 18: 192–93.

31. BF to DF, June 10, 1770, 17: 167.
32. BF to MS, Nov. 3, 1772, 14: 299–300. This letter is misdated 1767 in the *Papers*.
33. BF to PS, Sept. 29, 1769, 16: 208.
34. William Trent to George Croghan, June 10, 1769, William E. Lingelbach, "William Trent Calls on Benjamin Franklin," *PMHB* 74 (1950): 49.

XIII: "Sorrows Roll upon Me Like the Waves of the Sea"

1. BF to WS, Dec. 19, 1763, 10: 406.
2. Parker to BF, Jan. 4–May 6, 1766, passim, and July 1, 1766, 13: 327.
3. Parker to BF, July 15, 1766, 13: 344.
4. Parker to BF, Feb. 23, 1767, 14: 61.
5. BF to DF, Dec. 21, 1768, 15: 292.
6. WF to BF, [ca. Jan. 2, 1769], 16: 5–6.
7. Van Doren, *Letters*, pp. 12–13.
8. JM to DF, Sept. 28, 1765, Van Doren, p. 83.
9. BF to JM, Mar. 2, 1767, 14: 73.
10. JM to BF, Nov. 8, 1767, 13: 489–90.
11. JM to BF, Dec. 1, 1767, 14: 334.
12. DF to BF, Oct. 14, 1770, 17: 251.
13. JM to BF, [Oct. 23, 1767], 14: 294.
14. JM to BF, Dec. 1, 1767, 14: 334.
15. Ibid.
16. BF to JM, Feb. 21, 1768, 15: 57.
17. BF to Samuel Cooper, Apr. 27, 1769, 16: 118.
18. BF to JM, Feb. 23, 1769, 16: 51.
19. BF to JM, Apr. 27, 1769, 16: 121.
20. JM to BF, Nov. 7, 1768, 15: 263.
21. Quoted in BF to JM, Sept. 29, 1769, 16: 210.
22. BF to JM, Dec. 30, 1770, 17: 316.
23. DF to BF, Dec. 13, 1769, 16: 262.
24. DF to BF, Nov. 20, 1769, 16: 231.
25. DF to BF, Oct. 14, 1770, 17: 251.
26. BF to JM, July 17, 1771, 18: 185.
27. BF to JM, Mar. 2, 1767, 14: 72.
28. BF to JM, Nov. 1, 1773, Van Doren, *Letters*, pp. 142–43.
29. BF to JM, Feb. 17, 1774, Van Doren, p. 144.
30. BF to JM, July 28, 1774, Van Doren, p. 145.
31. BF to JM, Sept. 26, 1774, Van Doren, p. 147.
32. JM to BF, Nov. 3, 1774, Van Doren, p. 149.
33. Ibid., p. 151.

XIV: "Your A Feck Shonet Wife"

1. DF to BF, [July 14–Aug. 15 ?], 1766, 13: 338–39.
2. JM to DF, Nov. 24, 1766, Van Doren, *Letters*, pp. 96–97.
3. DF to BF, Jan. 21–22, 1768, 15: 24.
4. DF to BF, May 20–23, 1768, 15: 138.
5. DF to BF, Jan. 21–22, 1768, 15: 24.

6. Thomas Bond to BF, June 7, 1769, 16: 153.

7. DF to BF, Nov. 20–27, 1769, 16: 230–31.

8. DF to BF, July 3, 1767, 14: 207.

9. BF to DF, June 10, 1770, 17: 166.

10. BF to DF, Oct. 3, 1770, 17: 239.

11. BF to PH, Nov. 25, 1771, 18: 253.

12. BF to DF, May 1, 1771, 18: 91.

13. DF to BF, June 30, 1772.

14. BF to DF, Jan. 6, 1773, Smyth, 6: 4.

15. DF to BF, Dec. 13, 1769, 16: 262.

16. BF to WF, Aug. 19, 1772, Smyth, 5: 414.

17. BF to DF, Sept. 1, 1773.

18. BF to DF, Apr. 28, 1774, Smyth, 6: 230.

19. BF to DF, May 7, 1774.

20. BF to DF, July 22, 1774, Smyth, 6: 234.

21. BF to DF, Sept. 10, 1774.

22. *Pa. Gaz.*, Dec. 28, 1774.

23. WF to BF, Dec. 24, 1774, William Duane, ed., *Letters to Benjamin Franklin from His Family and Friends, 1751–1790* (New York, 1859), pp. 59–60.

24. BF to Jan Ingenhousz, Feb. 12, 1777.

25. BF to Mme. Lavoisier, Oct. 23, 1788, Lopez, *Mon Cher Papa*, p. 210.

XV: *Steering through Storms*

1. William A. Whitehead, *Contributions to the Early History of Perth Amboy* (New York, 1856), p. 9.

2. WF to BF, Oct. 13, 1772.

3. WF to WS, Feb. 18, 1765, Hart, "Letters," *PMHB* 35: 443.

4. BF to Whitefield, July 2, 1756, 6: 468.

5. BF to Samuel Elbert, Dec. 16, 1787, Smyth, 9: 625.

6. BF to Whitefield, July 2, 1756, 6: 468.

7. BF to Thos. Pownall, [July 1754], 5: 401.

8. Samuel Wharton to BF, Dec. 2, 1768, 15: 279.

9. WS to WF, Apr. 3, 1771, 18: 65.

10. BF to Jos. Galloway, Apr. 6, 1773, Smyth, 6: 33.

11. Mariboe, "William Franklin," p. 148.

12. WF to BF, May 11, 1769, 16: 127.

13. WF to BF, Mar. 2, 1769, 16: 62.

14. 10: 155.

15. BF to WF, Mar. 13, 1768, 15: 74.

16. WF to BF, [July 3], 1766, 13: 334.

17. BF to Samuel Cooper, Feb. 5, 1771, 18: 24.

18. *Archives of the State of New Jersey*, 10, 1st ser. (Newark, 1886): 46.

19. Ibid., pp. 68, 70.

20. WF to BF, [Jan. 31, 1769], 16: 37.

21. BF to John Ross, May 14, 1768, 15: 129.

22. BF to Jos. Galloway, Jan. 29, 1769, 16: 31.

23. BF to WS, Nov. 29, 1769, 16: 246, 248–49.

24. WS to David Hall, Apr. 7, 1766, "Correspondence between William Strahan and David Hall, 1763–77," *PMHB* 10 (1886): 95.

25. WS to ?, Apr. 1769, WS to Hall, Aug. 24, 1770, "Correspondence," *PMHB* 11 (1887): 106, 351.
26. WS to Hall, Nov. 7, 1770, "Correspondence," *PMHB* 11: 357.
27. BF to Hall, Mar. 20, 1772.
28. WF to BF, [Sept. 3? 1771], 18: 218.
29. E.g., BF to ?, Nov. 28, 1768, 15: 273.
30. Arthur Lee to Samuel Adams, June 10, 1771, 18: 128.
31. BF, "Account of Audience with Hillsborough," Jan. 16, 1771, 18: 15-16.
32. BF to Samuel Cooper, Feb. 5, 1771, 18: 25.
33. WS to WF, Apr. 3, 1771, 18: 65.
34. WF to WS, June 18, 1771, Hart, "Letters," *PMHB*, 35: 448-49.
35. Elizabeth Empson to BF, Apr. 23, 1771, 18: 83.
36. BF to Georgiana Shipley, Sept. 26, 1772, Smyth, 5: 438.
37. BF to Anna Mordaunt Shipley, Aug. 12, 1771, 18: 202.

XVI: *"You Are a Thorough Courtier"*

1. Cohen, *Franklin's Experiments*, p. 135.
2. Ibid., p. 138.
3. BF to WS, Dec. 19, 1763, 10: 407.
4. BF to John Ross, May 14, 1768, 15: 129.
5. BF to WF, Oct. 6, 1773, Smyth, 6: 144.
6. BF to WF, Oct. 5, 1768, 15: 225.
7. BF to WF, Nov. 3-4, 1772, Smyth, 5: 445.
8. Carl Van Doren, *Benjamin Franklin*, paperback ed. (New York, 1964), p. 445.
9. BF to Thos. Cushing, Dec. 2, 1772, Smyth, 6: 262, 266.
10. JM to BF, Dec. 30, 1765, Van Doren, *Letters*, p. 89.
11. Bernard Bailyn, *The Ordeal of Thomas Hutchinson* (Cambridge, Mass., 1974), pp. 3-4.
12. WF to BF, July 29, 1773.
13. BF to WF, Oct. 6, 1773, Smyth, 6: 144-45.
14. BF to Cushing, Dec. 2, 1772, Smyth, 6: 266.
15. *Pa. Gaz.*, Apr. 20, 1774.
16. *Satirical Verses addressed to D——R F——N* [Jan. 11, 1774].
17. Letter to the *Public Advertiser*, Feb. 16, 1774.
18. BF to WF, Mar. 22, 1775, Smyth, 6: 319.
19. Van Doren, *Franklin*, p. 478.
20. BF to WF, Feb. 2, 1774, Smyth, 6: 176.
21. BF to WF, Feb. 18, 1774, Smyth, 6: 197.
22. BF to WF, May 7, 1774.
23. Ibid.
24. WF to BF, May 3, 1774.
25. *New Jersey Archives*, 10: 459.
26. JM to BF, Nov. 3, 1774, Van Doren, *Letters*, p. 151.
27. BF to WF, Apr. 6, 1773, Smyth, 6: 31.
28. WF to BF, July 3, 1774.
29. BF to WF, Sept. 7, 1774, Smyth, 6: 241.
30. BF to JM, Sept. 26, 1774, Van Doren, *Letters*, p. 147.
31. WF to BF, May 3, 1774.

32. WF to BF, Dec. 24, 1774.

33. Ibid.

34. BF, "Answer to a Nobleman's Question. . . . [1775]," Papers of Henley Smith, Lib. of Cong. 20857.

35. BF to WF, Mar. 22, 1775, Smyth, 6: 365.

36. BF to Lord Howe, July 30, 1776, Smyth, 6: 460.

37. BF to WF, Mar. 22, 1775, Smyth, 6: 399.

38. John T. Rutt, *The Life and Correspondence of Joseph Priestley*, 2 vols. (London, 1831), 1: 212.

XVII: *Tug of War*

1. BF to JM, June 17, 1775, Van Doren, *Letters*, p. 158.

2. P. O. Hutchinson, *The Diary and Letters of Thomas Hutchinson*, 2 vols. (Boston, 1883-86), 1: 238: Jan. 6, 1779.

3. WS to BF, June 7, 1775.

4. WS to BF, July 5, 1775.

5. BF to WS, July 7, 1775, quoted in WS to BF, Sept. 6, 1775.

6. BF to WS, July 5, 1775, Smyth, 6: 407.

7. BF to Jonathan Shipley, July 7, 1775.

8. Hutchinson, *Diary*, 1: 237-38.

9. Julian P. Boyd, *Anglo-American Union: Joseph Galloway's Plans to Preserve the British Empire* (Philadelphia, 1941), p. 114.

10. *New Jersey Archives*, 10: 540.

11. Hutchinson, *Diary*, 1: 237.

12. Adams, *Diary*, 2: 127.

13. Dorothy Blunt to BF, Apr. 19, 1775.

14. PH to Mlle. Biheron, Aug. 29, 1776.

15. BF to Lord Le Despencer, Sept. 3, 1775.

16. SB to WTF, Oct. 30, 1780.

17. Eliz. Franklin to WTF, July 16, 1776.

18. WF to WTF, Sept. 14, 1775.

19. WF to WTF, Oct. 26, 1775.

20. WTF to WF, Oct. 18, 1775.

21. Mrs. D. Woolford to WTF, July 29, 1775.

22. WF to WTF, Oct. 9, 1775.

23. JM to BF, May 14, 1775, Van Doren, *Letters*, p. 154.

24. Catharine Ray Greene to BF, postscript to JM, May 14, 1775, Van Doren, pp. 155-56.

25. BF to JM, June 17, 1775, Van Doren, p. 158.

26. Catharine Greene to JM, Feb. 20, 1776, William Greene Roelker, *Benjamin Franklin and Catharine Ray Greene: Their Correspondence, 1775-1790* (Philadelphia, 1949), p. 67.

27. JM to Catharine Greene, Nov. 24, 1775, Van Doren, p. 165.

28. JM to Jane Collas, Apr. 1778, Van Doren, pp. 174-75.

29. JM to Catharine Greene, Nov. 24, 1775, Van Doren, p. 165.

30. Abigail Adams to John Adams, Nov. 5, 1775, *Adams Family Correspondence*, 1: 320-21.

31. JM to C. Greene, Nov. 24, 1775, Van Doren, p. 165.

32. Eliz. Franklin to WTF, Nov. 9, 1775.

33. JM to C. Greene, Nov. 24, 1775, Van Doren, p. 165.
34. JM to BF, July 14, 1775, Van Doren, p. 159.
35. Van Doren, p. 13.
36. JM to C. Greene, Nov. 24, 1775, Van Doren, p. 165.
37. WF to Lord Dartmouth, Sept. 5, 1775, *New Jersey Archives*, 10: 658.
38. Mariboe, "William Franklin," p. 449.
39. WF to WTF, Jan. 22, 1776.
40. Eliz. Franklin to SB, Feb. 5, 1776.
41. WF to WTF, Mar. 14, 1776.
42. WF to WTF, June 3, 1776.
43. WS to BF, Oct. 4, 1775.
44. Ibid.
45. WF to WTF, Mar. 14, 1776.
46. WF to WTF, June 13, 1776.
47. WF to WTF, May 8, 1776.
48. Mariboe, p. 460.
49. Ibid., p. 461.
50. Ibid., p. 464.
51. BF to George Washington, June 21, 1776, Smyth, 6: 449–50.
52. Mariboe, p. 464.
53. WF to WTF, June 25, 1776.
54. Eliz. Franklin to WTF, July 16, 1776.
55. BF to WTF, Sept. 19, 1776, Smyth, 6: 467–68.
56. Eliz. Franklin to BF, Aug. 6, 1776, Duane, *Letters*, pp. 70–71.
57. BF to WTF, Sept. 22, 1776.
58. BF to WTF, Sept. 19, 1776, Smyth, 6: 468–69.
59. BF to WTF, Sept. 28, 1776.
60. BF to Arthur Lee, Mar. 21, 1777, Smyth, 7: 35.
61. WF to Eliz. Franklin, Nov. 25, 1776.
62. Eliz. Franklin to WTF, Oct. 11, 1776.
63. RB to BF, Jan. 31, 1778.
64. JM to BF, Aug. 18, 1777, Van Doren, *Letters*, p. 170.

XVIII: *No Watch for Benny, No Feathers for Sally*

1. BF to R and SB, May 10, 1785, Smyth, 9: 327.
2. William Bell Clark, *Lambert Wickes, Sea Raider and Diplomat* (New Haven, 1932), p. 96.
3. Ibid., p. 100.
4. SB to RB, Dec. 2, 1771.
5. BF to PH, Jan. 12, 1777, Smyth, 7: 10.
6. Ibid.
7. Claude-Anne Lopez, "Benjamin Franklin, Lafayette, and the *Lafayette*," *Proc. APS* 108, no. 3 (June 1964): 187.
8. JM to BF, July 27, 1779, Van Doren, *Letters*, p. 194.
9. JM to BF, Feb. 14, 1779, Van Doren, p. 188.
10. BF to JM, Oct. 25, 1779, Van Doren, p. 198.
11. BF to C. Greene, Feb. 28, 1778, Roelker, *Benjamin Franklin*, p. 87.
12. BF to Jacques Barbeu Dubourg, before June 28, 1779, Smyth, 7: 359.

13. "Excerpts from the Papers of Dr. Benjamin Rush," *PMHB* 29 (1905): 27–28.
14. BF to SB, Mar. 31, 1778, Smyth, 7: 126.
15. RB to BF, July 14, 1778.
16. SB to BF, Feb. 23, 1777, Duane, *Letters*, p. 75.
17. BF to Samuel Cooper, Dec. 9, 1780.
18. SB to BF, Sept. 14, 1779, Duane, p. 105.
19. JM to BF, Sept. 12, 1779, Van Doren, *Letters*, p. 197.
20. BF to BFB, May 3, 1779.
21. BFB to BF, May 30, 1779.
22. BFB to BF, Dec. 25, 1779.
23. SB to BF, Jan. 17, 1779, Duane, pp. 91–92.
24. BF to SB, June 3, 1779, Smyth, 7: 347–49.
25. George Washington to Benjamin Harrison, [late 1778], Oberholzer, *Philadelphia*, 1: 287.
26. SB to BF, Sept. 14, 1779, Duane, pp. 106–8.
27. BF to SB, Mar. 16, 1780.
28. SB to WTF, Sept. 16, 1779.
29. Ibid.
30. SB to BF, Jan. 17, 1779, Duane, p. 93.
31. SB to BF, Sept. 14, 1779, Duane, p. 105.
32. BF to SB, Mar. 16, 1780.
33. SB to BF, Sept. 25, 1779, Duane, p. 112.
34. BF to R and SB, Oct. 4, 1780.
35. SB to BF, Jan. 17, 1779, Duane, p. 93.
36. BF to SB, June 3, 1779.
37. SB to BF, Sept. 9, 1780.
38. SB to BFB, Oct. 19, 1781.
39. SB to BFB, Oct. 1, 1782.
40. PH to BF, May 1, 1782.
41. Mrs. Cramer to BF, May 15, 1781.
42. Ibid.
43. BF to BFB, Sept. 25, 1780.
44. SB to BF, Jan. 14, 1781.
45. Samuel Cooper to BF, Mar. 16, 1780.
46. BF to Samuel Cooper, Mar. 16, 1780, Smyth, 8: 38.
47. BF to Samuel Cooper, Dec. 2, 1780, Smyth, 8: 185.
48. BF to Johonnot, Jan. 26, 1782.
49. BFB to BF, Jan. 30, 1783.
50. BF to BFB, May 2, 1783.
51. BFB, "Diary," Mar. 20, 1783.
52. R. Pigott to BF, Nov. 26, 1782.
53. R. Pigott to BF, June 27, 1783.

XIX: *"Temple Is My Right Hand"*

1. BF to JM, Dec. 8, 1776, Van Doren, *Letters*, p. 168.
2. BF to SB, June 3, 1779, Smyth, 7: 347.
3. Charles Francis Adams, ed., *The Works of John Adams* (Boston, 1856), 1: 60.
4. Irving Brant, *James Madison: The Virginia Revolutionist* (Indianapolis, 1941), p. 169.

5. Arthur Lee to Richard Henry Lee, Sept. 12, 1778, quoted *Dictionary of American Biography*, 20 vols. (New York, 1928–37), 11: 97.

6. Arthur Lee to Congress, Dec. 7, 1780, Gerald Stourzh, *Benjamin Franklin and American Foreign Policy* (Chicago, 1954), p. 296.

7. BF to Arthur Lee, Apr. 3, 1778, Smyth, 7: 132.

8. BF to Samuel Wharton, June 17, 1780, Smyth, 8: 96.

9. BF to JM, Jan. 6, 1786, Van Doren, *Letters*, p. 256.

10. John Adams, *Autobiography*, 4: 118.

11. Stourzh, *Benjamin Franklin*, p. 153.

12. P.-G. Cabanis in Lopez, *Mon Cher Papa*, p. 9.

13. Lee in ibid., p. 180.

14. Adams, *Diary*, 3: 189.

15. Anne-Robert Turgot, quoted in Stourzh, p. 297.

16. Fawn Brodie, *Thomas Jefferson: An Intimate History* (New York, 1974), p. 258.

17. Lopez, "Benjamin Franklin," *Proc. APS* 108: 183*n*.

18. Stourzh, p. 297.

19. RB to BF, Oct. 22, 1778.

20. BF to RB, June 2, 1779, Smyth, 7: 344–45.

21. BF to SB, June 3, 1779, Smyth, 7: 348.

22. Mariboe, "William Franklin," p. 474.

23. Ibid., pp. 479–80.

24. WS to BF, July 14, 1778.

25. BF to Lafayette, Oct. 15, 1779.

26. BF to R and SB, Oct. 4, 1780.

27. BF to SB, June 27, 1780.

28. BF to Samuel Wharton, June 17, 1780, Smyth, 8: 97.

29. JM to BF, Aug. 18, 1777, Van Doren, *Letters*, p. 171.

30. JM to SB, Jan. 17, 1779, Van Doren, p. 188.

31. JM to BF, Dec. 29, 1780, Van Doren, p. 205.

32. RB to BF, Sept. 10, 1780.

33. BF to R and SB, May 14, 1781.

34. RB to BF, Dec. 2, 1781.

35. RB to BF, Feb. 9, 1782.

36. Silas Deane to John Jay, July 2, 1781, *Deane Papers*, N.Y. Hist. Soc., 4 vols. (New York, 1889), 4: 445.

37. John Adams to James Warren, Mar. 16, 1780, Richard Morris, *The Peacemakers* (New York, 1965), p. 192.

38. Thomas Jefferson to John Bannister, Oct. 1785, Brodie, *Thomas Jefferson*, p. 196.

39. BF to John Jay, Feb. 8, 1785, Smyth, 9: 287.

40. Adams, *Diary*, 3: 77.

41. BF to Josiah Quincy, Sept. 11, 1783, BF to F. Grand, Mar. 5, 1786, Smyth, 9: 96, 492–93.

42. BF to Vergennes, Dec. 17, 1782, Morris, *The Peacemakers*, p. 384.

XX: "Nothing Has Ever Hurt Me So Much"

1. WF to WS, May 12, 1782, Hart, "Letters," *PMHB* 35: 461–62.

2. Mariboe, "William Franklin," p. 537.

3. Ibid., p. 547.

4. Patience Wright to BF, Feb. 22, 1783.

5. Vaughan to Shelburne, July 31, 1782, Mariboe, p. 553.

6. Vaughan to Shelburne, Dec. 10, 1782, Mariboe, pp. 553–54.

7. Wallace Brown, *The Good Americans: The Loyalists in the American Revolution* (New York, 1969), p. 158.

8. WF to BF, July 22, 1784.

9. "The Claims of the American Loyalists; an Apologue," [1782], Smyth, 8: 650.

10. BF to WF, Aug. 16, 1784, Smyth, 9: 252–54.

11. RB to WTF, Dec. 14, 1784.

12. F.H. to WTF, Nov. 1, 1784.

13. Lopez, *Mon Cher Papa*, p. 170.

14. BFB, "Diary," May 22, 1784.

15. WTF to BF, Aug. 26, 1784.

16. WTF to BF, Aug. 27, 1784.

17. BF to WTF, Aug. 25, 1784, Smyth, 9: 268.

18. Jonathan Williams, Jr., to WTF, Oct. 20, 1784.

19. WTF to Caleb Whitefoord, Aug. 7, 1783.

20. WTF to BF, Aug. 28, 1784.

21. BF to WTF, Oct. 2, 1784, Smyth, 9: 274.

22. Henry Grand to WTF, Aug. 19, 1784.

23. BF to WS, Jan. 24, 1780.

24. BF to WS, Aug. 14, 1784.

25. WS to BF, Nov. 21, 1784.

26. PH to BF, Oct. 25, 1784, Whitfield J. Bell, Jr., " 'All clear Sunshine': New Letters of Franklin and Mary Stevenson," *Proc. APS* 100, no. 6 (Dec. 1956): 533.

XXI: *Indian Summer*

1. BF to JM, Sept. 26, 1774, Van Doren, *Letters*, p. 148.

2. BF to PH, June 13, 1782, Smyth, 8: 456.

3. PH to BF, July 19, 1784.

4. PH to BF, May 1, 1782.

5. PH to BF, Jan. 11, 1779.

6. MS to BF, Mar. 16, 1779.

7. BF to PH, ca. Dec. 1778.

8. BF to MS, Jan. 25, 1779, Smyth 7: 220–21.

9. PH to BF, Apr. 2, 1780.

10. MS to BF, Mar. 16, 1779.

11. PH to BF, Jan. 13, 1783.

12. July 24, 1782.

13. BF to PH, Jan. 27, 1783, Smyth, 9: 11–12.

14. Ibid.

15. BF to PH, Mar. 19, 1784, Smyth, 9: 181.

16. JM to BF, Apr. 29, 1783, Van Doren, *Letters*, p. 221.

17. PH to Barbara Hewson, Jan. 25, 1785.

18. BFB, "Diary," Dec. 5, 1784.

19. BFB, "Diary," Sept. 30, 1784.

20. Lopez, *Mon Cher Papa*, p. 222.

21. BFB, "Diary," July 12, 1784.
22. BF to Sir Joseph Banks, Nov. 21, 1783, Smyth, 9: 117.
23. Dorcas Montgomery to SB, July 26, 1783.
24. BF to Sir Joseph Banks, Nov. 21, 1783, 9: 117.
25. BFB, "Diary," July 11, 1784.
26. BFB, "Diary," Oct. 30, 1783.
27. John Jeffries to WTF, Feb. 18, 1785.
28. Louis-Sébastien Mercier, *Tableau de Paris*, 12 vols. (Amsterdam, 1783–88), 1: 16.
29. BF to Barbeu Dubourg, [1773], Smyth, 5: 545.
30. BFB, "Diary," Mar. 24, 1785.
31. BFB, "Diary," Apr. 2, 1785.
32. BFB, "Diary," May 23, 1785.
33. BF to George Whatley, May 23, 1785, Smyth, 9: 334–35.
34. BF to Mme. Brillon, no date [before Apr. 20, 1781], Lopez, *Mon Cher Papa*, pp. 92–93.
35. Ibid., p. 94.
36. Abigail Adams to Lucy Cranch, Sept. 5, 1784, C. F. Adams, ed., *Letters of Mrs. Adams*, 2 vols. (Boston, 1840), 2: 55–56.
37. Abigail Adams to John Adams, Oct. 21, 1781, *Adams Papers, Correspondence*, 4: 230.
38. Thomas Fleming, *The Man Who Dared the Lightning* (New York, 1971), p. 464.
39. Morris, *The Peacemakers*, p. 192.
40. G. Sand to Sainte-Beuve, Mar. 1835, A. Maurois, *Lélia* (New York, 1954), p. 194.
41. BF to Elizabeth Partridge, Oct. 11, 1779, Smyth, 7: 393–94.
42. BF to Mme. Brillon, [before Apr. 20, 1781], Lopez, *Mon Cher Papa*, p. 92.
43. Mme. Brillon to BF, Apr. 20, 1781, Lopez, p. 95.
44. Brodie, *Thomas Jefferson*, p. 425.

XXII: *From Seine to Schuylkill*

1. Lopez, *Mon Cher Papa*, p. 299.
2. BF to JM, Sept. 13, 1783, Van Doren, *Letters*, p. 224.
3. Mme. Helvétius to BF, n.d., Lopez, p. 299.
4. BF to Mme. Helvétius, July 19, 1785, Smyth, 9: 364.
5. July 24, 1785, Smyth, 10: 469.
6. WTF, ed., *Memoirs of the Life and Writings of Benjamin Franklin*, 6 vols. (Philadelphia, 1818), 2: 165.
7. Julian P. Boyd, ed., *The Papers of Thomas Jefferson*, 19 vols. (Princeton, 1950–74), 8: 269–73; 9: 267–70.
8. WF to SB, Aug. 1, 1785.
9. BF, "Journal," Smyth, 10: 471.
10. BFB, "Diary," Sept. 14, 1785.
11. BF to John Jay, Sept. 21, 1785, Smyth, 9: 466.
12. BF to JM, May 30, 1787, Van Doren, *Letters*, p. 295.
13. BF to JM, Sept. 21, 1786, Van Doren, p. 282.
14. BF to David Hartley, July 5, 1785, Smyth, 9: 359; cf. BF to JM, July 13, 1785, Van Doren, p. 236.

15. BF to John Jay, Sept. 21, 1785, Smyth, 9: 466.
16. Smyth, 9: 607.
17. BF to JM, Nov. 4, 1787, Van Doren, p. 300.
18. JM to BF, Oct. 1, 1785, Van Doren, p. 240.
19. JM to SB, Sept. 6, 1790, Van Doren, p. 342.
20. BF to JM, Aug. 3, 1789, Van Doren, p. 327.
21. JM to BF, Feb. 26, 1786, Van Doren, p. 259.
22. WTF to Blanchette Caillot, [Nov.], 1785.
23. BF to Charles Thomson, Dec. 29, 1788, Smyth, 9: 694.
24. BF to JM, May 2, 1786, Van Doren, p. 265.
25. BF to Lafayette, Apr. 17, 1787, Smyth, 9: 571.
26. WTF to Blanchette Caillot, [Nov.], 1785.
27. PH to Barbara Hewson, Apr. 6, 1787, Bell, " 'All Clear Sunshine,' " *Proc.
    APS* 100: 535.
28. BFB, "Diary," Apr. 5, 1785.
29. BF to Mme. Helvétius, Oct. 25, 1788, Smyth, 9: 678; cf. BF to Mme.
    Lavoisier, Oct. 23, 1788, Smyth, 9: 668.
30. BF to Alexander Small, Dec. 17, 1789, Smyth, 10: 2.
31. BF to George Whatley, May 18, 1787, Smyth, 9: 588–89.
32. PH to Thomas Viny, May 5, 1790, Bell, p. 535.
33. BF to La Rochefoucauld, Oct. 24, 1788, Smyth, 9: 665.
34. BF to Benjamin Vaughan, Nov. 1789, Smyth, 10: 50.
35. BF to George Whitefield, July 2, 1756, 6: 469.

XXIII: *Slaves*

1. Van Doren, *Franklin*, p. 129.
2. 1: 345.
3. George Brookes, *Friend Anthony Benezet* (Philadelphia, 1937), pp. 78–79.
4. "Excerpts from the Papers of Dr. Benjamin Rush," *PMHB* 29 (1905): 25.
5. BF to Abiah Franklin, Apr. 12, 1750, 3: 474.
6. 7: 203.
7. 8: 425*n*.
8. BF to DF, Mar. 18, 1760, 9: 38.
9. BF to DF, June 27, 1760, 9: 74–75.
10. DF to BF, June 30, 1772.
11. 4: 231.
12. W. T. Franklin, *Memoirs*, 1: 309.
13. Winthrop D. Jordan, *White over Black* (New York, 1969), p. 143.
14. BF to John Waring, Jan. 3, 1758, 7: 356.
15. Edgar L. Pennington, "The Work of the Bray Associates in Pennsylvania,"
    PMHB 58 (1934): 7.
16. DF to BF, Aug. 9, 1759, 8: 425.
17. BF to John Waring, Dec. 17, 1763, 10: 396.
18. Roberts Vaux, *Memoirs of the Life of Anthony Benezet* (Philadelphia, 1817),
    p. 30.
19. "Narrative of the Late Massacres," 11: 62.
20. 12: 9.
21. "Excerpts from the Papers of Dr. Benjamin Rush," *PMHB* 29: 26.
22. DF to BF, May 20 [–23], 1768, 15: 138. Cf. 18: 90*n*.

23. Anthony Benezet to BF, Apr. 27, 1772.
24. BF to Benjamin Rush, July 14, 1773.
25. *London Chronicle,* June 18-20, 1772.
26. Ibid.
27. BF to Condorcet, Mar. 20, 1774.
28. *A Conversation on Slavery,* Jan. 26, 1770, 17: 41.
29. "An Address to the Public from the Pennsylvania Society for Promoting the Abolition of Slavery," Nov. 9, 1789, Smyth, 10: 67.
30. Oberholzer, *Philadelphia,* 1: 120.
31. "Address," Smyth, 10: 67-68.
32. *Federal Gazette,* Feb. 17, 1790.
33. *On the Slave Trade,* Mar. 23, 1790, Smyth, 10: 86-91.
34. Oberholzer, 1: 61.

XXIV: *"Our Little Fleet of Barques"*

1. 1: 111.
2. BF to Elizabeth Hubbart, Feb. 22, 1756, 6: 406-7.
3. BF to George Whitefield, June 19, 1764, 11: 231-32.
4. BF to George Whatley, May 23, 1785, Smyth, 9: 334.
5. Van Doren, *Franklin,* p. 779.
6. PH to Thomas Viny, May 5, 1790, Bell, " 'All Clear Sunshine,' " *Proc. APS* 100: 535.
7. BFB to Margaret Markoe, May 2, 1790.
8. BF, "Last Will and Testament," Smyth, 10: 493-510.
9. Thomas Firth Jones, *A Pair of Lawn Sleeves* (Philadelphia, 1972), p. 173.
10. Ibid., p. 167.
11. BFB to Margaret Markoe, May 2, 1790.
12. Mariboe, "William Franklin," p. 583.
13. Ibid., p. 573.
14. Ibid., p. 574.
15. WTF, Preface to *Memoirs.*
16. John Adams to WTF, May 5, 1817.
17. BFB to Margaret Markoe, May 2, 1790.
18. JM to SB, Dec. 2, 1790, Van Doren, *Letters,* p. 344.
19. Eliza Hewson to Tom Hewson, Nov. 30, 1795, APS.
20. Eliza Hewson to Tom Hewson, Oct. 24, 1796, APS.
21. John D. R. Platt, *The Home and Office of Benjamin Franklin Bache* (Washington, Independence National Historical Park, 1970), p. 100.
22. Eliza Hewson to Tom Hewson, June 5, 1797, APS.
23. Jonathan Williams, Jr., to WF, Oct. 22, 1807, quoted in Dorothy Zuersher, "Benjamin Franklin, Jonathan Williams and the United States Military Academy," (Doctor of Ed. dissertation, University of North Carolina, Greensboro, 1974), p. 77.
24. PH to Tom Hewson, Nov. 3, 1794, APS.
25. Ibid.
26. Tom Hewson to Eliza Hewson, Jan. 15, 1799, APS.
27. BF to Jonathan Shipley, Feb. 24, 1786, Smyth, 9: 490.

Bibliography

Unpublished materials:

Franklin Collection. Yale University.

Richard Bache. "Day Book, 1761–1792." Philadelphia, Franklin Institute.

Hewson material in the possession of Mrs. Addinell Hewson, APS microfilm 103–103.1.

Mariboe, William Herbert. "The Life of William Franklin, 1730(1)–1813, 'Pro Rege et Patria.'" Ph.D. dissertation, University of Pennsylvania, 1962.

Zuersher, Dorothy. "Benjamin Franklin, Jonathan Williams and the United States Military Academy. Doctor of Ed. dissertation, University of North Carolina, Greensboro, 1974.

Published sources: A select list

Adams, Abigail. *Letters of Mrs. Adams.* Ed. Charles Francis Adams, 2 vols., 2d ed. Boston, 1840.

Adams, John. *The Adams Papers, Diary and Autobiography.* Ed. L. H. Butterfield. Series 1, 4 vols. and supplement. Cambridge, Mass., 1961–66.

———. *Adams Family Correspondence.* Ed. L. H. Butterfield. Series 2. Cambridge, Mass., 1963–.

———. *Familiar Letters of John Adams and His Wife Abigail Adams during the Revolution.* Ed. Charles Francis Adams. New York, 1876.

Aldridge, A. O., "Franklin's 'Shaftesburian' Dialogues not Franklin," *American Literature* 21, no. 2 (May 1949): 151–59.

[Allestree, Richard]. *The Whole Duty of Man.* London, 1730.

Archives of the State of New Jersey, 10. 1st series. Newark, 1886.

Bailyn, Bernard. *Education in the Forming of American Society.* Chapel Hill, 1960.

———. *The Ordeal of Thomas Hutchinson.* Cambridge, Mass., 1974.

Becker, Carl. *The Spirit of '76 and other Essays.* Albany, 1927.

Bell, Whitfield J., Jr. "'All Clear Sunshine': New Letters of Franklin and Mary Stevenson Hewson," *Proceedings of the American Philosophical Society* 100, no. 6 (December 1956): 521–36.

———. "Benjamin Franklin and the German Charity Schools," *Proceedings of the American Philosophical Society* 99 (1955): 381–87.

Benson, Mary S. *Women in Eighteenth-Century America.* New York, 1935.

Biddle, Gertrude, and Lowry, Sarah. *Notable Women of Pennsylvania.* Philadelphia, 1942.

Bowen, Catherine Drinker. *The Most Dangerous Man in America: Scenes from the Life of Benjamin Franklin.* Boston, 1974.

Boyd, Julian P. *Anglo-American Union: Joseph Galloway's Plans to Preserve the British Empire*. Philadelphia, 1941.

——. *The Papers of Thomas Jefferson*, 19 vols. Princeton, 1950–74.

Branscombe, Arthur. "The Cradle of the Franklins." *Munsey's*, July 1907.

Brant, Irving. *James Madison: The Virginia Revolutionist*. Indianapolis, 1941.

——. *James Madison: The Nationalist*. Indianapolis, 1948.

Bremner, Robert, ed. *Children and Youth in America*. 3 vols. Cambridge, Mass., 1970–71.

Bridenbaugh, Carl. *Cities in the Wilderness*. New York, 1960.

——. *The Colonial Craftsman*. New York, 1960.

——, and Bridenbaugh, Jessica. *Rebels and Gentlemen: Philadelphia in the Age of Franklin*. New York, 1942.

——, ed. *Gentleman's Progress: The Itinerarium of Dr. Alexander Hamilton, 1744*. Chapel Hill, 1948.

Brigham, Clarence S. "James Franklin and the Beginnings of Printing in Rhode Island." *Proceedings of the Massachusetts Historical Society* 65 (1936): 536–44.

Brodie, Fawn. *Thomas Jefferson: An Intimate History*. New York, 1974.

Brookes, George S. *Friend Anthony Benezet*. Philadelphia, 1937.

Brown, Wallace. *The Good Americans: The Loyalists in the American Revolution*. New York, 1969.

——. *The King's Friends: The Composition and Motives of the American Loyalist Claimants*. Providence, 1966.

Bruns, Roger A. "Anthony Benezet and the Natural Rights of the Negro." *Pennsylvania Magazine of History and Biography* 96, no. 1 (1972): 104–13.

Bushman, Richard L. *From Puritan to Yankee: Character and the Social Order in Connecticut, 1690–1765*. Cambridge, Mass., 1967.

——. "On the Uses of Psychology: Conflict and Conciliation in Benjamin Franklin." *History and Theory* 5, no. 3 (1966): 225–40.

Butler, Ruth L. *Doctor Franklin, Postmaster General*. New York, 1928.

Calhoon, Robert McCluer. *The Loyalists in Revolutionary America, 1760–1781*. New York, 1973.

Calhoun, Arthur W. *The Social History of the American Family*. 3 vols. New York, 1945.

Callahan, North. *Flight from the Republic: The Tories of the American Revolution*. Indianapolis, 1967.

Carey, Lewis J. *Franklin's Economic Views*. New York, 1928.

Clark, William Bell. *Lambert Wickes, Sea Raider and Diplomat*. New Haven, 1932.

Cochrane, J. A. *Dr. Johnson's Printer: The Life of William Strahan*. Cambridge, Mass., 1964.

Cohen, I. Bernard, ed. *Benjamin Franklin's Experiments*. Cambridge, Mass., 1941.

——. *Franklin and Newton*. Philadelphia, 1956.

——. "Benjamin Franklin and the Mysterious 'Dr. Spence.'" *Journal of the Franklin Institute* 235, no. 1 (January 1943): 1–25.

——. "The 200th Anniversary of Benjamin Franklin's two Lightning Experiments and the Introduction of the Lightning Rod." *Proceedings of the American Philosophical Society* 96 (1952): 331–66.

Compton, Arthur H. "The World of Science in the Late Eighteenth Century and Today." *Proceedings of the American Philosophical Society* 100 (1956): 296–303.

The Connoisseur. 6th ed. Oxford, 1774.

Cramer, Lucien. *Une Famille Genevoise, les Cramer. Leurs Relations avec Voltaire, Rousseau et Benjamin Franklin-Bache.* Geneva, 1952.

Crane, Verner. *Benjamin Franklin, Englishman and American.* Providence, 1936.

———. "Benjamin Franklin on Slavery and American Liberties." *Pennsylvania Magazine of History and Biography* 62 (1938): 1–11.

Darnton, Robert. *Mesmerism and the End of the Enlightenment in France.* Cambridge, Mass., 1968.

Deane, Silas. *Deane Papers, New York Historical Society.* 4 vols. New York, 1889.

De Cou, George. *Burlington: A Provincial Capital.* Philadelphia, 1945.

Drake, Thomas E. *Quakers and Slavery in America.* Gloucester, Mass., 1965.

Duane, William, ed. *Letters to Benjamin Franklin from his Family and Friends, 1751–1790.* New York, 1859.

Eames, Wilberforce. "The Antigua Press and Benjamin Mecom, 1748–1765." *Proceedings of the American Antiquarian Society* 38 (1928): 303–48.

Earle, Alice Morse. *Child Life in Colonial Days.* New York, 1899.

———. *Colonial Dames and Good Wives.* Boston, 1895.

———. *Customs and Fashions in Old New England.* London, 1893.

———. *Two Centuries of Costume in America.* London, 1903.

Faris, John T. *The Romance of Old Philadelphia.* Philadelphia, 1918.

Fäy, Bernard. *The Two Franklins.* Boston, 1933.

———. "A Democratic Leader of the Eighteenth Century: Benjamin Franklin Bache." *Proceedings of the American Philosophical Society* 40 (October 1930): 277–303.

———. "Early Party Machinery in the United States: Pennsylvania in the Elections of 1796." *Pennsylvania Magazine of History and Biography* 60 (1936): 357–90.

Fennelly, Catherine. "William Franklin of New Jersey." *William and Mary Quarterly,* 3d series 6 (1949): 361–82.

Fisher, Daniel. "Extracts from the Diary of Daniel Fisher 1755." Ed. C. R. Howard. *Pennsylvania Magazine of History and Biography* 17 (1893): 263–68.

Fisher, Sydney G. *The Making of Philadelphia.* Philadelphia, 1896.

Fleming, Thomas. *The Man Who Dared the Lightning.* New York, 1971.

Flexner, James Thomas. *The Traitor and the Spy.* New York, 1953.

Ford, P. L. *The Many-Sided Franklin.* New York, 1899.

Ford, W. C. "Franklin's *New England Courant.*" *Proceedings of the Massachusetts Historical Society* 57 (April 1924): 336–53.

Franklin, Benjamin. *The Autobiography of Benjamin Franklin.* Ed. Leonard Labaree et al. New Haven, 1964–.

———. *The Papers of Benjamin Franklin.* Ed. Leonard Labaree, William Willcox, et al. New Haven, 1959–.

Franklin, Phyllis. *Show Thyself a Man: A Comparison of Benjamin Franklin and Cotton Mather.* The Hague, 1969.

Franklin, W. T. *Memoirs of the Life and Writings of Benjamin Franklin.* 6 vols. Philadelphia, 1818.

Freehling, William W. "The Founding Fathers and Slavery." *American Historical Review* 77 (1972): 81–94.

Genlis, Mme. de. *Adèle et Théodore, ou Lettres sur l'Education* . . . 3 vols. Paris, 1782.

Gillespie, Elizabeth Duane. *A Book of Remembrance*. Philadelphia, 1901.

Gipson, L. H. *Lewis Evans*. Philadelphia, 1939.

Gleason, Philip. "A Scurrilous Colonial Election and Franklin's Reputation." *William and Mary Quarterly*, 3d series 18 (1961): 68–84.

Gratz, Simon. "Some Material for a Biography of Mrs. Elizabeth Ferguson, née Graeme," *Pennsylvania Magazine of History and Biography* 39 (1915): 257–321; 41 (1917): 385–98.

Greene, Lorenzo J. *The Negro in Colonial New England*. Port Washington, 1966.

Griswold, A. Whitney. "Three Puritans on Prosperity." *New England Quarterly* 7 (1934).

Hall, Max. *Benjamin Franklin and Polly Baker*. Chapel Hill, 1960.

Hamilton, J. G. de R., ed. *The Best Letters of Thomas Jefferson*. Boston, 1926.

Hart, Charles Henry. "Letters from William Franklin to William Strahan." *Pennsylvania Magazine of History and Biography* 35 (1911): 415–62.

———. "Who Was the Mother of Franklin's Son?" *Pennsylvania Magazine of History and Biography* 35 (1911): 308–14.

Hastings, G. E. *The Life and Works of Francis Hopkinson*. Chicago, 1926.

Hays, I. Minis. *Calendar of the Papers of Benjamin Franklin in the Library of the American Philosophical Society*. 5 vols. Philadelphia, 1908.

Hobart, Lois. *Patriot's Lady: The Life of Sarah Livingston Jay*. New York, 1960.

Holliday, Carl. *Woman's Life in Colonial Days*. Boston, 1922.

Howard, George Elliott. *A History of Matrimonial Institutions*. 3 vols. Chicago, 1904.

Hughes, M. M. "Benjamin Franklin, Lover." *Cornhill*, no. 149 (January 1934), pp. 101–6.

Jenkins, Charles F. "Franklin Returns from France, 1785." *Proceedings of the American Philosophical Society* 92, no. 6 (December 1948): 417–32.

Johnson, Samuel. "Addison," *Lives of the Poets, Works*. 2 vols. London, 1854.

Jones, Edward Alfred, ed. *The Loyalists of New Jersey*. Newark, 1927.

Jones, Thomas Firth. *A Pair of Lawn Sleeves*. Philadelphia, 1972.

Jordan, Winthrop D. *White over Black*. New York, 1969.

Jorgenson, C. E. "Sidelights on Benjamin Franklin's Principles of Rhetoric." *Revue Anglo-Américaine* 11, no. 3 (Février, 1934): 208–22.

Kalm, Peter. *Peter Kalm's Travels in North America*. English version of 1770, rev. and ed. Adolph B. Benson. 2 vols. New York, 1937.

Kammen, Michael. *A Rope of Sand*. Ithaca, 1968.

———. "Thomas Jefferson's America—and Ours." *The Occasional Review*, no. 2 (Autumn 1974), pp. 107–26.

Ketcham, Ralph L. "Benjamin Franklin and William Smith: New Light on an Old Philadelphia Quarrel." *Pennsylvania Magazine of History and Biography* 88 (1964): 142–63.

———, ed. *The Political Thought of Benjamin Franklin*. Indianapolis, 1965.

Larrabee, Harold A. "Poor Richard in an Age of Plenty." *Harper's Magazine* 212, no. 1268 (January 1956): 64–68.

Lawrence, D. H. *Studies in Classic American Literature.* Paperback ed. New York, 1955.

Levin, David, ed. *The Puritan in the Enlightenment: Franklin and Edwards.* Chicago, 1963.

Lingelbach, William E. "William Trent Calls on Benjamin Franklin." *Pennsylvania Magazine of History and Biography* 74 (1950): 43–50.

Lopez, Claude-Anne. *Mon Cher Papa: Franklin and the Ladies of Paris.* New Haven, 1966.

———. "Benjamin Franklin, Lafayette, and the *Lafayette.*" *Proceedings of the American Philosophical Society* 108, no. 3 (June 1964).

———. *A Good House Contrived to my Mind.* Washington, D.C., Independence National Historical Park, 1975.

Manceron, Claude. *Le Vent d'Amérique, 1778–1782.* Paris, 1974.

Mather, Cotton. *Essays to Do Good.* Lexington, Ky., 1822.

Mencken, H. L. *The Vintage Mencken.* New York, 1955.

Mercier, Louis-Sébastien. *Tableau de Paris.* 12 vols. Amsterdam, 1783–88.

Miller, Perry. *The New England Mind: From Colony to Province.* Cambridge, Mass., 1953.

Millikan, Robert A. "Benjamin Franklin as a Scientist." *Journal of the Franklin Institute* 232, no. 2 (November 1941): 407–21.

Monaghan, Frank. *John Jay.* Indianapolis, 1935.

Moore, Charles, ed. *George Washington's Rules of Civility and Decent Behavior.* Cambridge, Mass., 1926.

Moore, Charles. *Notes on the History of Slavery in Massachusetts.* New York, 1866.

Morgan, Edmund S. *The Gentle Puritan: A Life of Ezra Stiles, 1727–1795.* New Haven, 1962.

———. *The Puritan Family.* 2d ed. Boston, 1956.

———. *Virginians at Home: Family Life in the Eighteenth Century.* Williamsburg, 1952.

———. "Slavery and Freedom: The American Paradox." *Journal of American History* 59 (1972): 5–30.

———, and Morgan, Helen M. *The Stamp Act Crisis.* Chapel Hill, 1953.

Morison, Samuel Eliot. *The Intellectual Life of Colonial New England.* New York, 1956.

Morris, Richard. *The Peacemakers.* New York, 1965.

"The Mount Regale Fishing Company of Philadelphia." *Pennsylvania Magazine of History and Biography* 27 (1903): 88–90.

Nadelhaft, Jerome. "The Somerset Case and Slavery: Myth, Reality and Repercussions." *Journal of Negro History* 51 (1966): 193–201.

Nash, Gary B. "Slaves and Slaveowners in Colonial Philadelphia." *William and Mary Quarterly,* 3d series 30 (1973): 223–55.

Newcomb, Benjamin H. *Franklin and Galloway: A Political Partnership.* New York, 1972.

Norton, Mary Beth. *The British-Americans: The Loyalist Exiles in England, 1774–1789.* Boston, 1972.

Oberholzer, Ellis P. *Philadelphia: A History of the City and Its People.* 2 vols. Philadelphia, [1912].

Pennington, Edgar L. "The Work of the Bray Associates in Pennsylvania." *Pennsylvania Magazine of History and Biography* 58 (1934): 1–25.

Pitt, Arthur S. "Franklin and the Quaker Movement against Slavery." *Friends History Association Bulletin* 32 (1943): 13–31.

Platt, John D. R. *Franklin's House*. Washington, D.C., Independence National Historical Park, 1969.

———. *The Home and Office of Benjamin Franklin Bache*. Washington, D.C., Independence National Historical Park, 1970.

Plumb, J. H. "The French Connection." *American Heritage* 26, no. 1 (December 1974): 26–57.

Pomfret, J. E. "Some Further Letters of William Strahan, Printer." *Pennsylvania Magazine of History and Biography* 60 (1936): 455–89.

Priestley, Joseph. *The History and Present State of Electricity*. London, 1775.

Quincy, Josiah. *Memoir of the Life of Josiah Quincy of Massachusetts by His Son*. Boston, 1825.

Quinlan, Maurice J. "Dr. Franklin Meets Dr. Johnson." *Pennsylvania Magazine of History and Biography* 73 (1949): 34–44.

Roach, Hannah B. "Benjamin Franklin Slept Here." *Pennsylvania Magazine of History and Biography* 84 (1960): 127–74.

Roelker, William Greene. *Benjamin Franklin and Catharine Ray Greene: Their Correspondence, 1755–1790*. Philadelphia, 1949.

Rothman, David J. "A Note on the Study of the Colonial Family." *William and Mary Quarterly*, 3d series 23 (1966): 627–34.

[Rush, Benjamin]. "Excerpts from the Papers of Dr. Benjamin Rush." *Pennsylvania Magazine of History and Biography* 29 (1905): 23–30.

Rutt, John T. *The Life and Correspondence of Joseph Priestley*. 2 vols. London, 1831.

Saveth, Edward. "The Problem of American Family History." *American Quarterly* 21 (1969): 311–29.

Sayre, Robert F. *The Examined Self: Benjamin Franklin, Henry Adams, Henry James*. Princeton, 1964.

Schermerhorn, William E. *The History of Burlington, N.J.* Burlington, 1927.

Seegal, Rhoda. "Benjamin Franklin Fund Falls Short of His Goal." *Boston Globe*, October 15, 1974.

Sellers, Charles Coleman. *Benjamin Franklin in Portraiture*. New Haven, 1962.

Sewall, Samuel. *Diary*. 3 vols. *Collections of the Massachusetts Historical Society*, 5th series 5–7. Boston, 1932.

Shelling, Richard I. "Benjamin Franklin and the Dr. Bray Associates." *Pennsylvania Magazine of History and Biography* 63 (1939): 282–93.

Smyth, Albert Henry, ed. *The Writings of Benjamin Franklin*. 10 vols. New York, 1905–7.

Sparks, Jared. *The Works of Benjamin Franklin*. 10 vols. Boston, 1840.

Stannard, David E. "Death and Dying in Puritan New England." *American Historical Review* 78, no. 5 (December 1973): 1305–30.

Stourzh, Gerald. *Benjamin Franklin and American Foreign Policy*. Chicago, 1954.

[Strahan, William]. "Correspondence between William Strahan and David Hall, 1763–77." *Pennsylvania Magazine of History and Biography* 10 (1886): 86–99; 217–32; 322–33; 461–73; 11 (1887): 98–111; 223–34; 346–57; 482–90; 12 (1888): 116–22; 240–51.

Stevenson, Lloyd G. "William Hewson, the Hunters and Benjamin Franklin." *Journal of the History of Medicine and Allied Sciences* 8 (1953): 324–28.

Tilton, Eleanor M. "Lightning Rods and the Earthquake of 1755." *New England Quarterly* 13 (1940): 85–97.

Turner, Edward R. *The Negro in Pennsylvania.* Washington, D.C., 1911.

———. "Slavery in Colonial Pennsylvania." *Pennsylvania Magazine of History and Biography* 35 (1911): 141–51.

Twain, Mark. "The Late Benjamin Franklin." *The Galaxy* 10 (1870): 138–39.

Van Doren, Carl. *Benjamin Franklin.* Paperback ed. New York, 1964.

———. *Jane Mecom.* New York, 1950.

———, ed. *The Letters of Benjamin Franklin and Jane Mecom.* Princeton, 1950.

Vaux, Roberts. *Memoirs of the Life of Anthony Benezet.* Philadelphia, 1817.

Vigée-Lebrun, Louise Elisabeth. *Souvenirs.* Paris, n.d.

Warden, G. B. *Boston, 1689–1776.* Boston, 1970.

Wax, Darold D. "Negro Import Duties in Colonial Pennsylvania." *Pennsylvania Magazine of History and Biography* 97, no. 1 (1973): 22–44.

———. "Quaker Merchants and the Slave Trade in Colonial Pennsylvania." *Pennsylvania Magazine of History and Biography* 86 (1962): 143–59.

Wharton, Anne H. *Colonial Days and Dames.* Philadelphia, 1908.

———. *Salons: Colonial and Republican.* Philadelphia, 1900.

Wheatley, Henry B. *London Past and Present.* London, 1891.

Whitehead, William A. *Contributions to the Early History of Perth Amboy.* New York, 1856.

Wolf, Edwin. "The Reconstruction of Benjamin Franklin's Library . . ." *Bibliographical Society of America, Papers* 56 (1962): 9–10.

Woody, Thomas. *Educational Views of Benjamin Franklin.* New York, 1931.

The World, 1753–1756. New ed. London, 1767.

Wray, Lady Mary. *The Lady's Library.* Ed. Richard Steele. 3 vols. 3d ed. London, 1722.

Wright, Esmond, ed. *Benjamin Franklin: A Profile.* New York, 1970.

Wright, Louis B. *The Atlantic Frontier: Colonial American Civilization, 1607–1763.* New York, 1951.

———. "Franklin's Legacy to the Gilded Age." *Virginia Quarterly Review* 22 (1946): 268–79.

Zilversmit, Arthur. *The First Emancipation: The Abolition of Slavery in the North.* Chicago, [1967].

Index

Abbe (slave of John Jay), 305

Abercrombie, Mrs., 82

Academy of Philadelphia, 67, 90, 159; BF draws up blueprint for, 52; WTF enrolled in, 202, 205–6, 246; Ray Greene enrolled in, 207; BFB enrolled in, 288. See also Pennsylvania, University of

Adams, Abigail, 72, 284; favorably impressed with BF, 208; shocked by BF, 277

Adams, John, 232, 236, 289; disapproval of women historians, ix; disapproval of BF, 27, 239–40, 277–78; disapproval of WTF, 59, 94; in Continental Congress, 203, 213; commissioner in Paris, 239–42, 250, 270; and peace treaty, 250–51; negotiates commercial treaties, 250, 268; nostalgic for Passy, 314; Federalist leader and president, 315–17

Adams, John Quincy, 225, 277, 291

Adams, Sam, 177

Addison, Joseph, 13. See also Spectator

Advice to a Young Man on the Choice of a Mistress (1745), 36

"Advice to those who would remove to America," 282. See also *Bagatelles*

Africa, Africans, 299–300, 302

Albany, 61; Congress and Plan of Union, 63, 178, 202–3

Alexander, William (Lord Stirling), 209–10

Algiers, Divan of, 306–7

d'Alibard, Thomas-François, 47, 51

Allegheny River, 61

Allen, William, 40

Allison, Dr. Francis, 159

alphabet. See phonetic alphabet

American Philosophical Society, 223*n*, 288, 311; BF founds, 52; BF president of, 289; BF's papers collected by, 315*n*

American Revolution, 51, 151, 176, 177, 190, 237, 255, 289, 302, 310; peace negotiations, 248, 250–51; problem of slaves in, 305

American Revolution, Daughters of the, 14

Amherst, General Jeffrey, 118*n*

Anabaptists, 106

André, John, 222, 245*n*

Anglicans, 67, 122, 135, 154, 180; Society for the Propagation of the Gospel, 191, 301. See also Church of England

animal magnetism, 260–62. See also Mesmer

Annand, Alexander, 60

anti-Federalists, 316

Antigua, 111–12, 158

apprenticeship, 10, 14*n*, 15, 110

Arians, 106

Arminians, 106

armonica, glass, 98, 114, 127, 260, illus. See also music

Arnold, Benedict, 205, 216, 222, 245*n*

d'Artois, Comte (future Charles X), 260

Associates of the late Dr. Bray, 301–2, 305. See also education, slaves

atheism, 105

Auray, 219

Aurora, 315–17

Autobiography, 8, 17, 18, 20, 22, 23, 24, 37; BF writes, 1–2, 188, 293, 294; WTF postpones editing, 313

Bache, Alexander Dallas, 288*n*

Bache, Benjamin Franklin, 74, 83, 148, 205, 216, 270, 284; birth of, 144;